Trial as a Social Communication Occurrence

Ius, Lex et Res Publica
Studies in Law, Philosophy and Political Cultures

Edited by Barbara Janusz-Pohl and Anna Jaron

Volume 30

Karolina Gmerek

Trial as a Social Communication Occurrence

Interactions Between Professional and Non-professional Participants of a Trial

PETER LANG

Lausanne - Berlin - Bruxelles - Chennai - New York - Oxford

Bibliographic Information published by the Deutsche Nationalbibliothek
The Deutsche Nationalbibliothek lists this publication in the Deutsche Nationalbibliografie; detailed bibliographic data is available online at http://dnb.d-nb.de.

Library of Congress Cataloging-in-Publication Data
A CIP catalog record for this book has been applied for at the Library of Congress.

The publication was co-financed by the Faculty of Law and Administration University of Szczecin.

Cover illustration: Courtesy of Benjamin Ben Chaim.

ISSN 2191-3250
ISBN 978-3-631-90265-3 (Print)
E-ISBN 978-3-631-91162-4 (E-Book)
E-ISBN 978-3-631-91163-1 (E-PUB)
DOI 10.3726/b21373

Published by Peter Lang GmbH, Berlin, Deutschland

info@peterlang.com - www.peterlang.com

Table of Content

Foreword

The monograph is a revised (shortened, supplemented and translated) version of the book: K. Gmerek, *Rozprawa sądowa jako zdarzenie komunikacji społecznej [Trial as a social communication occurrence]*, Szczecin 2019, pp. 416. When making certain changes, I wanted to adapt the content of this book to the foreign reader as much as possible. I made the most changes in Chapter 2, in which I recreated the genre pattern of a trial viewed as a complex communication occurrence. First of all, I removed a number of detailed considerations of the legal aspects of proceedings before Polish courts in the context of a trial in its various varieties. In turn, I have highlighted the basic findings on the trial as a communication occurrence and I extended the analysis of some issues. On the other hand, I left in the least changed form Chapter 3, in which I presented the results of empirical research conducted on the basis of participant observation of court trials. However, also here I made a few significant changes. For example, I removed some of the considerations concerning the communicativeness of instructions given by the presiding judge to non-professional participants of court proceedings. This is because they concerned the use of certain grammatical structures and given linguistic means characteristic of the Polish language. Therefore, they were difficult, or even impossible, to translate into English.

Several years have passed since the research presented in this monograph was conducted. The greatest impact on the communication process at the trial in Polish courts has undoubtedly been the spread of recording trials, thereby reducing the role of the traditional written minutes, and the recognition of so-called online trial as a standard way of proceeding during the Covid-19 pandemic. I draw attention to both issues in the relevant sections of this book. Despite the changes indicated, I consider the research results presented in this monograph still current. First of all, the research presented here mainly focuses on the most constant elements of the trial (in Polish courts) and related communication phenomena. I also supplemented the book with a description of several monographs on communication process at the trial in Polish courts that have appeared since the publication of *Rozprawa sądowa...*.

The study results presented in this book are related to trials conducted in Polish courts. Therefore, they cannot be directly related to courtroom discourse in the courts of other legal systems. This raises the question: Why should the research presented in this book be of interest to a foreign reader? There may be several reasons. First, of course, it is the cognitive and comparative aspect. The results of the study described in this monograph, both analytical and empirical, make it possible to recognize the peculiarities of the communication process at the trial in Polish courts, and further to compare the described phenomena with those of other legal systems. This is facilitated by the way the results of the study are presented. The part of this book devoted to actual communication phenomena (the empirical part of the study), was preceded by a reconstruction of the model formation of a trial as a complex communication occurrence (the analytical part of the study). This allows the reader to link the actual communication phenomena with the specific pattern of the trial (in Polish courts) and see the relationships between the actual and model phenomena. Second, the foreign researcher can use the research methodology discussed in detail in the monograph. The concept of genre pattern developed in linguistics used in the analytical part of the study can be applied directly as a theoretical and methodological basis for the analysis of any communication occurrence. This is because it covers universal aspects of such an occurrence – the structural, pragmatic, stylistic and cognitive. On the other hand, the specific analytical questions and categories that I have developed for the empirical part of the study can be used either directly or after adapting them to the characteristics of the reality under consideration.

Karolina Gmerek, December 2022

Introduction

When undertaking a scientific analysis of a particular fragment of social (socio-cultural) reality, it is necessary to answer the question: To what extent the phenomenon chosen as the object of study is a momentous element of some relevant social system?

The significance of communication in the context of a trial can be characterized in terms of various aspects of the phenomenon. First, the taking of communication acts is a prerequisite for the existence of a trial – procedural acts are also communication acts, which represent a lower level of conventionalization than procedural acts. Second, taking communication acts is the primary tool for achieving non-communication goals in a trial (and in court proceedings in general). Third, any non-communication act and any behavior of the participants of the court proceedings can affect the interpretation of communication acts (and therefore procedural acts) taken at the trial. Fourth, the communication process that occurs in court proceedings is the "top layer" of the procedural activity of the participants in the proceedings. Accordingly, the communication process is that level of activity of the participants in the proceedings that is directly observable to any potential recipient of the acts undertaken at the trial; other levels already require some preparation. This, in turn, causes the very communication process at the trial to become the subject of various qualifications or assessments made both by internal observers – the participants in a given proceeding – and by external observers – everyone else. Thus, frequently the evaluation or qualification of procedural activity from the point of view of various criteria is made through the prism of the communication acts of the actors undertaking the activity in question.

The issues indicated above, of course, do not exhaust the entire scope of the relationship between the communication process and the trial in which this process is carried out, but nevertheless indicate the undoubted importance of communication in the context of the trial.

The stimulus to undertake research on the communication process occurring at the trial in Polish courts, the results of which are presented in this book, became, at least to some extent, the positions presented in Poland both in the community of lawyers[1] and outside

1 E.g., T. Gizbert-Studnicki, *Postępowanie sądowe jako złożony dyskurs – zagadnienia pragmatyki języka sali sądowej [Court proceedings as a complex discourse – issues of pragmatics of the language of the courtroom]*, paper presented on Polish Language Congress in Katowice, 4–6 of May 2011, www.rjp.pan.pl/index.php?option=com_content&view=article&id=1376&Itemid=50, access 20.12.2022, M. Strączyński, *Język prawniczy – przyczyny i charakterystyka błędów i niezrozumiałości sformułowań [Juridical language – causes and characteristics of errors and incomprehensibility of expressions]*, paper presented on Polish Language Congress in Katowice, 4–6 of May

it.[2] According to them, the communication in court proceedings (including a trial) is a formalized, complicated process, determining the emergence of communication barriers that can affect the actual access to court by people with little knowledge of the characteristics of this type of communication.[3] Not without significance was also the fact that in Poland there is an increasingly expressed belief in the need to strive for simplification of language as a means of communication, including in the administrative and legal sphere.

The studies presented in this book began in a situation where studies (especially empirical studies) on communication process at the trial in Polish courts has been the subject of only a few monographs or reports. Let's take a brief look at the characteristics of this research, including its methodological aspects.[4]

Małgorzata Rzeszutko's book[5] deals exclusively with the trial of a criminal case, and focuses on issues in textual linguistics. In contrast, Grażyna Bednarek's

---

2011, www.rjp.pan.pl/index.php?option=com_content&view=article&id=1378, access 20.12.2022.

2 Cf. e.g., research by the Helsinki Foundation for Human Rights, J. Lora, *Komunikacja sądów z obywatelami – badania empiryczne, wnioski, rekomendacje zmian [Communication of courts with citizens – empirical research, conclusions, recommendations for change]*, Warszawa 2009, cf. also the results of surveys on the comprehensibility of the language used by the judge to the hearing participants, showing, among other things, that "direct contacts with the court have little effect on the respondents' opinions on the comprehensibility of the language used by judges at trials", M. Borucka-Arctowa, *Komunikacja między sądami a społeczeństwem [Communication between the courts and society]*, in: *Sądy w opinii społeczeństwa polskiego [Courts in the opinion of the Polish society]*, eds. M. Borucka-Arctowa, K. Pałecki, Kraków 2003, pp. 80–81.

3 This, of course, is not peculiar only to trial in Polish courts. See e.g. *Handling Cases Involving Self-Represented Litigants. A Benchguide for Judicial Officers*, Judicial Council of California 2019.

4 The specific issues discussed in these publications will be referred to in appropriate places in this book.

5 M. Rzeszutko, *Rozprawa sądowa w świetle lingwistyki tekstu [Trial in the light of text linguistics]*, Lublin 2003. Rzeszutko's considerations, as the author herself points out, fall within "the research trend of contemporary linguistic textology with a pragmatic inclination" (ibidem, p. 13). The starting point of the consideration is the recognition of the trial as a text. At the same time, "the text is treated as a product of the act of communication and as a constantly co-created, by the whole complex of its parameters, process", (ibidem).The author, using the available tools of linguistic analysis, focuses her attention primarily on specific communication occurrences (the presentation of the accusation, the participants' response to the accusation, the summary of the acts, and the resolution), (ibidem, p. 90). However, she puts them in the broader perspective of the communication situation in which they occur, taking into account many extra-linguistic conditions. The author enriches the argument with examples of utterances (acting as illustrators) coming from the research material she

monograph[6] is limited in subject matter to the criminal trial and to the specific type of procedural act – the examination of a witness. At the same time, it is a comparative work, because within the scope of its interest remains the communication process in both Polish and American courts.[7] In addition, in 2014 the empirical research report by Jan Winczorek and Paweł Maranowski, which is limited in subject matter to the civil trial, was published.[8]

It is impossible at this point not to mention the publications related to the Citizens' Monitoring of Courts conducted by the volunteers of the Court Watch

---

collected – recordings (audio) of criminal trials held in two common courts (ibidem, p. 12).

6 G.A. Bednarek, *Polish vs. American Courtroom Discourse: Inquisitorial and Adversarial Procedures of Witness Examination in Criminal Trials*, Palgrave Macmillan 2014.

7 In terms of theoretical grounding, the author uses the pattern of description of the communication situation developed in the field of ethnography of communication (ethnography of speaking), conversation analysis and pragmatics (ibidem, p. 9). The author uses to describe the analyzed type of discourse (courtroom discourse) the analytical categories developed by Dell Hymes and included in the anagram Speaking (ibidem, p. 16, cf. an expanded version of this model, D. Hymes, *Foundations in Sociolinguistics: An Ethnographic Approach*, Philadelphia 1974, p. 53 et seq.). The empirical material analyzed for the purposes of this publication with regard to the judiciary in the United States of America comes from the recordings of the trial conducted as part of the criminal proceedings against O.J. Simpson. On the other hand, with regard to the Polish judiciary, the research material was collected by the author in the course of participant observation of the trial conducted as part of the criminal proceedings (ibidem, pp. 20–21). During the observation, the author took notes of the questions asked to witnesses, while the answers were obtained from the minutes in the case file. The author concludes that the way witnesses are examined in American courts corresponds to the adversarial model, while in Polish courts it corresponds to the inquisitorial model, pointing to significant differences in the organization of the examination as a communication occurrence, such as the types of questions asked (ibidem, p. 170).

8 J. Winczorek, P. Maranowski, *Komunikacja w sądach po reformie kpc. Raport z badań [Communication in the courts after the reform of the Polish Code of Civil Procedure. Research report]*, Warszawa 2014. In the publication in question, the authors address the general issues of the communication process in civil proceedings, while considering the changes in civil procedure that occurred in 2012. The research conducted is intended by the authors to make it possible to answer the question: Is it the new legal provisions or rather the found characteristics of communication that more strongly affect the exchange of information during court proceedings? (ibidem, p. 20) Two methods of empirical data collection were used in this research – individual in-depth interviews with judges and legal counsels (a total of 49 interviews) and observation of court sessions scheduled for the trial (a total of 115 sessions). Both qualitative and quantitative methods were used to analyze the data. One of the report's conclusions is that, according to the respondents, "the reform of civil proceedings has not caused far-reaching changes in the actual conduct of court proceedings." (ibidem, p. 7).

Poland Foundation. The reports, which are drawn up annually on the basis of participant observation of trials held before Polish courts, contain conclusions on, among other things, the respect of the principle of openness of the trial, the right to a fair trial, the treatment of participants of the proceedings, or various aspects related to so-called procedural justice. A significant part of the conclusions relate to the communication acts of participants (especially judges), which are formulated on the basis of the observations (sometimes feelings) of observers ("non-lawyers").[9]

The record of observations conducted by volunteers of the Court Watch Poland Foundation in 2010–2015 became part of the empirical material used by Stanisław Burdziej in his research on procedural justice as applied to the activities of the Polish judiciary.[10] Despite the fact that Burdziej's work centers around the thesis proclaiming that procedural justice is an essential condition for the perception of judicial power as legitimate,[11] it presents important research conclusions regarding communication in the courtroom.[12] It is worth citing here some of the results of surveys conducted on two groups of respondents.[13] These results draw a much more positive picture of courtroom communication than some other studies. For example, in the first survey, 81 % of respondents indicated that the judge explained procedural issues or the terms he or she used in an understandable way,[14] 80 % that

9 All reports of the Citizens' Monitoring of Courts, starting in 2010, are published on the Foundation's website: https://courtwatch.pl/?gclid=Cj0KCQiA14WdBhD8ARIsANao07iwsZKuokukvTwPLlovQPc9AiQ9aiEYxphIy0OjSb7A9jgKQjhC4I0aAizIEALw_wcB, access 20.12.2022. See also B. Pilitowski, S. Burdziej eds., *Court Monitoring Methodology*, Toruń 2013, https://courtwatch.pl/wp-content/uploads/Court_Monitoring_Methodology.pdf, access 21.06.2023.

10 S. Burdziej, *Sprawiedliwość i prawomocność. O społecznej legitymizacji władzy sądowniczej [Justice and finality. On the social legitimacy of judicial power]*, Toruń 2017, p. 108.

11 Ibidem, p. 9.

12 Interest in the communication phenomena occurring in the trial is related to the psychosocial view of procedural justice adopted by the author, which includes the following key elements: "the subjective feeling of the person subject to a given decision that (1) he or she was given the opportunity to present his or her position, (2) he or she was treated with respect, (3) he or she generally understood the process of decision-making and the significance of the decision, and finally that (4) the decision-maker was impartial", ibidem, p. 8. See also S. Burdziej, K. Guzik, B. Pilitowski, *Fairness at Trial: The Impact of Procedural Justice and Other Experiential Factors on Criminal Defendants' Perceptions of Court Legitimacy in Poland*, "Law and Social Inquiry" 2019, Vol. 44, No. 2, pp. 359–390.

13 The first sample included 321 participants in court proceedings who had received a court decision in their case, while the second sample included 228 participants for whom there was a judgment in the criminal case on the date of the study, ibidem, pp. 143 and 166.

14 Ibidem, p. 153.

the judge explained the purpose of the session or provided an agenda.[15] Specifically, the second survey found that 92 % of respondents understood the content and meaning of the judgment, 80 % indicated that the judge made sure the participant understood the judgment, 84 % of respondents understood what was happening in the courtroom, and 77 % indicated that the judge explained procedural issues or the terms he used in an understandable way.[16]

By the time the English-language version of this book was published, the several studies on the courtroom discourse in Polish courts had yet been published.[17]

In addition to the above-mentioned books, the issue of communication at the trial has been taken up in monographic works in Poland on the occasion of research generally devoted to other issues.[18] Thus, the claims about the characteristics of the communication process at the trial in Polish courts have different sources and, consequently, different relevance. Some are the result of scientific reflection on communication in the courtroom, some can be derived from findings on issues variously related to this type of communication, others, in turn, are drawn from colloquial experience and are sometimes accepted as true intuitively.[19]

---

15 Ibidem.

16 Ibidem, p. 175.

17 E.g. M. Szymków-Gac, *Przesłuchanie w polskiej rozprawie karnej. Studium pragmalingwistyczne [Examination in the Polish criminal trial. A pragmalinguistic study]*, Warszawa 2019; M. Dudek, M. Stępień, *Courtroom Power Distance Dynamics*, Cham 2021; M. Najda, A. Rutkowska, D. Rutkowski, *Psychologia sali sadowej. Jak komunikacja i emocje wpływają na postrzeganie sprawiedliwości [Courtroom Psychology. How communication and emotions affect perceptions of justice]*, Bielsko-Biała 2021. Selected research results presented in these publications will be cited at appropriate places in this book.

18 Moreover, it is possible to identify articles that directly address the issue of communication in the courtroom. Some of them will be referred to in appropriate places in this book.

19 This excerpt can be used as an example of formulating general opinions on courtroom communication based on individual experiences: "The language of lawyers – here I have some horrible experiences from courtrooms. I must say that the personal culture of lawyers, judges is at such a low level that I, at times, felt like leaving the courtroom (...)", E. Kołodziejek, A. Choduń, eds., *Mówi się, czyli o wymowie i wymowności Polaków. Materiały IX Forum Kultury Słowa. Szczecin 9–11 października 2013 [Speech, on the articulation and eloquence of Poles. Materials of the IX Forum on the Culture of Words. Szczecin 9–11 October 2013]*, Szczecin 2016, p. 175. It should be noted that this statement became the subject of polemics among the discussants. It is worth citing here an excerpt from the polemical statement, due to the fact that its author formulated the opinion on trial communication on the basis of observations made while conducting research in the courtroom: "On the other hand, I cannot agree with Professor Rocławski, who spoke about the culture of lawyers. I did not observe a disrespectful attitude of jurists towards other people in the courtroom. On the contrary, I had the impression that jurists, when they noticed that someone did not understand the question, tried to formulate their points in a simpler way.

The advantage of the research on communication process at the trial conducted in Polish courts is that its results can, in general, complement the results of the research presented in this book (given the same socio-cultural, including normative, background). However, as we have seen, studies of this type have not been realized much in Poland. The situation is quite different in the case of foreign studies, especially those on communication at the trial in the courts of the common law system. In the case of the Anglo-American system, we can even speak of a tradition of research on courtroom communication. A huge number of publications have analyzed a wide variety of issues concerning courtroom communication, using a variety of research methods.[20] However, in general the results of empirical research concerning courtroom discourse in common law system, regardless of the research method by which they were obtained, cannot be considered relevant to the communication phenomena occurring in Polish courts. At most, they can be a contribution to the analysis of a specific issue, when intuitively the particular research results seem adequate also to the communication process in Polish courts,[21] or on the contrary e.g. to show the differences. This is because of the obvious divergences between the way court proceedings (including trial) are structured in the common law system, especially jury courts, and the way court proceedings are organized in Poland. It seems that what determines to the highest degree the differences between the communication process at the trial in the common law system and communication at the trial in Polish court proceedings concerns the high degree of adversarial nature of the proceedings in the courts of the common law system[22] and the fact that certain decisions in the courts of this system can be made by a jury (composed of non-professionals).[23]

In the vast majority of trials, I also did not observe any confusion in the answers of questioned persons or off-topic statements", ibidem, p. 176.

20 In particular: participant observation, observation combined with audio or video and audio recording, analysis of official recordings and transcriptions of trials or fragments thereof, analysis of recordings obtained from other sources (e.g., university archives, radio or from other researchers), analysis of data obtained through an experiment (simulation of a trial), and analysis of interviews and questionnaires. Mixed methods were also used (e.g., observation, analysis of recordings and experiment; transcript analysis and interview).

21 In particular, some of the results of studies of lawyers' communication with jury members (non-professional participants) may be relevant to lawyers' communication with non-professional participants of court proceedings in general.

22 In the context under discussion, it manifests itself, among other things, in the limited role of the judge in shaping the interaction between the interrogator and the interrogated.

23 The difference between the jury court of the common law system and the Polish court is fundamental in the meaning that in the first case the parties have to convince the non-professionals, while in the second case the professionals. Moreover, in the Polish judiciary some of the institutions simply do not function (e.g., jury instructions or the voir-dire procedure).

Undoubtedly, on the other hand, one can draw inspiration from the research methods used, theoretical concepts, both those developed in various research fields, and those that have been developed for or as a result of the analysis of the communication process in the courtroom.[24]

All that has been written above justifies the necessity of adapting the research methods, thematic scope and theoretical basis to the subject of the study – the communication process occurring at the trial in a Polish court proceeding.

The purpose of the study is to accomplish two main research tasks expressed in the following questions:

1. **What are the characteristics of the trial (in Polish courts) as the communication occurrence considered as a model?**
2. **How non-professional participants of court proceedings cope with the involvement in the trial and what is the role performed by a presiding judge in this process?**

The distinction of the two research tasks at the very beginning of the work is intended to emphasize their equivalence and to delineate the two research fields – so that there is no doubt when one is talking about the trial in model terms, and when one is talking about the actual communication phenomena occurring within it. Nevertheless, as a consequence of these tasks, a coherent picture is to emerge showing the actual communication phenomena (the scope of which is determined by the second research task) against the background of the model formation of the trial as a communication occurrence. Each of the above-mentioned tasks will be developed and detailed accordingly in the following sections of the study.

The structure of this book, on the other hand, was designed to present as clearly as possible not only the results of the research process, but also its course. The main part of the book is formed by Chapters 2 and 3. Chapter 2 reconstructs the genre pattern of a trial (in Polish courts). Thus, the considerations contained therein focus on the model formation of the trial in terms of communication. The research material collected for the study during participant observation of 250 court sessions scheduled for the trial[25] plays a subsidiary role in these considerations.

Chapter 3 is different, as it deals with the actual communication acts (and behaviors) performed at the trial, which were revealed during the analysis of the research material. The study of the empirical material forms the basis for the

24 Some of the studies cited in the section make use of theoretical categories developed in other studies of courtroom communication, such as Yovel's study (J. Yovel, *Language and Power in a Place of Contingencies: Law and the Polyphony of Self-Representation*, "Studies in Language and Society" 2013, No. 5), using theoretical categories developed by J.M. Conley and W.M. O'Barr (e.g. J.M. Conley, W.M. O'Barr, *Rules versus Relationships: The Ethnography of Legal Discourse*, Chicago 1990).

25 The term "(court) session scheduled for the trial" was introduced for the purposes of this book and defined in Section 1.2.2.

formulation of the conclusions in this chapter. However, the considerations are closely and variously linked to the elements of the model structure of a trial – from the research procedure, which the reconstructed genre pattern of a trial was used to develop, to the description of the results obtained through the analysis of the empirical material, which draws attention to the relationship between certain actual communication phenomena and the model structure of a trial.

In the context of the considerations in Chapter 3, it is important to pay attention to what could be called the "experience" of communicating (to each other) at a trial. It is obvious that different members of society experience participation in a trial with different frequency – for some it is a permanent part of their professional role, for others it is a type of social activity that they have not yet experienced. Given the differences indicated above, the empirical research, the results of which are discussed in Chapter 3, focuses primarily on the participation of non-professional participants of court proceedings at the trial. It is recognized in this book that the study of the communication acts of people for whom the activity in question is not a permanent part of a social, including professional, role (as in the case of non-professional participants of court proceedings) is cognitively and socially particularly momentous.

Chapter 1, on the other hand, serves to theoretically ground the undertaken research process. This chapter is followed by the presentation of some basic assumptions that determine and at the same time justify further choices related to the methodological and theoretical grounding of the research process. Chapter 1 closes with basic terminological and conceptual findings.

The last part of this book is a summary of the study. Here, moreover, it returns to the issues that (in the discussion of the communication process at the trial) are considered particularly determining (even hindering) the communication process, i.e. the use of legal and juridical terminology and the formalization of the communication process. The Summary closes with comments on the importance of conducting empirical research, especially in those areas of socio-cultural reality that are co-created by the law, and the possibility of using the results of the research contained in this book in the future.

In conclusion, it should be further noted that the research activities undertaken in the study in relation to the research material collected for its purposes consist in qualifying communication phenomena from the point of view of specific criteria. These criteria are embodied in detailed research questions and analytical categories, thanks to which the research process conducted for the purposes of this publication remains, at least to some extent, intersubjectively controllable. As a result of this process, a picture of the analyzed aspect of socio-cultural reality, including the communication acts of the actors who co-create this reality, is outlined. For the reader of this book, this picture can simply be a source of cognition of the studied reality. However, it can equally well be the basis for making further qualifications and even assessments – understood as an experience of approval or disapproval of a certain state of affairs.

Chapter 1 Theoretical grounding of the study of the communication process occurring at a trial

1.1. Basic assumptions

The first methodological assumption adopted in this study is a systems approach, i.e. one in which the whole takes precedence over the parts, while the analysis of the elements of a given system is intended to understand the whole.[26] In this view, the analyzed communication process is recognized as an element of a trial. As a consequence of this assumption, the trial is treated holistically, and its characterization as a communication occurrence precedes any problematic considerations in Chapter 3.

In developing what has been stated above, it is necessary to reveal other basic assumptions that are made in this study regarding the trial as a specific structure, and to highlight those aspects that relate to the various relationships and conditions that may be associated with this structure and its elements.[27]

The trial (as well as the entire court proceedings) is treated as a structure that is the product of the rational acts of the legislator,[28] that is, the establishment of legal norms with a specific content. At the same time, it is a purposive (teleological) structure constructed for the realization of a specific goal(s). Therefore, it can be said that both the entire structure of the trial and its elements are normatively determined (conditioned). Due to the fact that it is a structure oriented towards the realization of a specific goal(s), we can also speak of the goal-determination of the structure and the instrumental determination of its individual elements by

---

26 A. Mattelart, M. Mattelart, *Theories of Communication: A Short Introduction*, London 1998, p. 47.

27 It is sometimes emphasized in the literature that it is too rare to reflect on the types of dependencies that are analyzed or are detected within the framework of specific studies, which sometimes leads to significant misunderstandings, J. Kmita, *O kulturze symbolicznej [On symbolic culture]*, Warszawa 1982, pp. 19–20. Since the characterization of the trial as a communication occurrence will require a discussion of a variety of dependencies, it was decided that already at the preliminary part of this book certain types of dependencies should be identified.

28 This refers to a certain theoretical construct developed in Polish jurisprudence, which is the rational legislator. See L. Nowak, *A Concept of Rational Legislator*, [in:] *Polish Contributions to the Theory and Philosophy of Law*, ed. Z. Ziembiński, Amsterdam 1987, pp. 137–145; T. Gizbert-Studnicki, K. Płeszka, J. Woleński, *20th-Century Legal Theory and Philosophy in Poland*, [in:] *Legal Philosophy in the Twentieth Century: The Civil Law World*, eds. E. Pattaro, C. Roversi, Springer Netherlands 2016, p. 577 et seq.

the structure (the elements of the structure serve to realize particular goals, the achievement of which leads to the realization of the goal of the structure).[29]

Particularly relevant from the point of view of this study are the types of determinants relating to the acts performed at the trial by the participants (taken as a model participants). These acts can be determined both normatively, when they are the subject of obligation or competence, and purposefully. Both of these determinants can occur together (e.g., the taking of minutes by the court clerk serves to record the proceedings, and, moreover, constitutes the implementation of the relevant procedural norms that prescribes this act), but need not (as in the case of acts that are not a manifestation of the implementation of legal norms). Equally important are the determinants of the characteristics of the participants, which can be determined normatively (when we are dealing with the construction of a conventional entity), as well as so-called "indirectly", i.e. by the characteristics of the structure itself. **A trial is not a finite and closed structure**, i.e. devoid of all those features that are not directly expressed in procedural norms. In particular, some features of the trial (or court proceedings more broadly) determine those phenomena that naturally co-occur with them (e.g., the construction of the trial on the principle of face to face communication determines the occurrence of phenomena of a kinesic and proxemic nature), or determine those features that are a concretization of a more generally understood feature of the trial (e.g., the diversity of participants of court proceedings entails a variation in the level of their communication competence). Hence, it is characteristic of determination by features of the trial that, firstly, in order to perceive the phenomena that are thus conditioned, it is necessary to go beyond procedural norms and even beyond the acts that are the realization of these norms; secondly, the relations of the type in question are objective in the sense that the participants of court proceedings do not have to be aware of them. At the same time, not all of the above-mentioned relationships are of a necessary nature. Some involve only a certain degree of correlation (e.g., the construction of the trial on the principle of contentiousness determines the occurrence of those communication phenomena that are revealed in the communication process in a conflict, while it is difficult to indicate the phenomena that accompany conflict always, without exception).

The types of conditions and relationships described above will be considered in the following discussion in three fundamentally different contexts. First, in the cognitive context – they will be the subject of description in the framework

---

29 Teological determinants, so to speak, form a "deeper layer" than normative determinants in the sense that the establishment of a legal norm with a certain meaning precedes the adoption of the purpose for the implementation of the norm in question (which is then taken into account when reconstructing the content of the norm). Due to the framework of this study, this issue will not be developed. See e.g. O. Bogucki, *The Derivational Theory of Legal Interpretation in Polish Legal Theory*, "International Journal for the Semiotics of Law" 2020, No. 33, pp. 617–636.

of reconstructing the genre pattern of a trial, that is, describing a certain model. Secondly, in the course of designing specific research questions and analytical categories for the empirical part of the study, they will serve to predict certain phenomena that may occur within the framework of actual communication in the courtroom and that are conditioned by the trial pattern. In doing so, this prediction can be of a certain, conditional or probabilistic nature,[30] depending on the nature of the relationship underlying the prediction. And thirdly, the relationships indicated in the model description will be taken into account in the exploratory context when they will "naturally" explain the communication phenomena revealed in the process of analyzing the empirical data.

In the course of planning the research process, it also became necessary to settle on a theoretical basis, that is, to adopt those specific theoretical concepts that would serve to theoretically ground of the study. As a first step, the search was focused on the science of communication.[31] At the current stage of development, communication science is a collection of many theoretical concepts and research methods. At the same time, it has not created a coherent terminological grid or developed a methodology specific to its subject.[32] Thus, this science makes use of theoretical concepts and research methods developed in linguistics, sociology, cultural studies or psychology. Consequently, it is already interdisciplinary in nature at its core. The interdisciplinary approach also seems to be characteristic to specific research on communication issues.[33] Given the above, two ways of theoretically grounding the analysis undertaken in this study were considered.

---

30 S. Nowak, *Metodologia nauk społecznych [Methodology of the social sciences]*, Warszawa 2011, p. 381 et seq.

31 In this book I use the term "communication science", although there are other names in the literature to describe the research field dealing, very generally speaking, with communication, such as "sciences (plural) of communication", "communicology", or "communication (as a practical discipline)". Some researchers also use the term "so-called communication science", in order to draw attention to important problems concerning the status of communication science as an independent discipline, its pre-paradigmatic or even non-paradigmatic nature, cf. e.g., M. Wendland, *Czy optymistyczna ocena kondycji nauki o komunikacji w Polsce jest zasadna?[Is the optimistic assessment of the condition of communication science in Poland justified?]*, "Lingua ac Communitas" 2010, Vol. 20, p. 55 et seq., idem, *Konstruktywizm komunikacyjny [Communication constructivism]*, Poznań 2011, p. 189 et seq., E. Kulczycki, *Teoretyzowanie komunikacji [Theorizing communication]*, Poznań 2012, p. 49 et seq.

32 M. Wendland, *Czy optymistyczna...*, op. cit., p. 61, B. Ollivier, *Nauki o komunikacji. Teoria i praktyka*, Warszawa 2010, s. 257 et. seq. (the original version: B. Ollivier, *Les sciences de la communication. Théories et acquis*, Armand Colin 2007); J. Fiske, *Introduction to Communication Studies*, 2nd edition, London-New York 1990, p. 1 et seq.

33 J. Bielecka-Prus, A. Horolets, *Rekonstrukcja praktyk analizy dyskursu na podstawie wybranych anglojęzycznych czasopism dyskursywnych [Reconstruction of discourse*

First, the possibility of embedding the research process in a single theoretical concept, such as the concept of genre of a text (developed in genology) or Goffman's dramaturgical vision of human interactions, was considered. However, such a solution was rejected on the grounds that adopting each of the approaches under consideration as an independent theoretical basis would lead to a limitation of the subject of analysis. Each theoretical concept considered, while focusing on certain issues, neglected others that are equally important from the point of view of the study of the communication process at the trial.

Secondly, an approach specific to communication science was considered, involving the use of different theoretical concepts considered complementary. This approach was ultimately chosen.[34] First of all, it avoids the negative consequences mentioned above, that is, the unjustified restriction of the subject of study. However, it carries a significant danger of theoretical and, consequently, terminological chaos, so it requires certain assumptions and a kind of discipline in the selection of specific approaches.

Various mechanisms were used to avoid possible chaos. First of all, the subject of study, that is, the communication process at the trial, was chosen as the starting point. The various theoretical concepts were selected so that it became possible to detect and describe the phenomena that are particularly relevant to this type of communication.[35] In addition, various mechanisms of coherence were introduced. The main one was the development of a terminological and conceptual background, and the adoption of basic assumptions that justify particular choices (cf. Section 1.2). In addition, individual theoretical concepts were selected in such a way that the assumptions that are made either *explicitly* or only *implicitly* within these concepts are (at least in those aspects that are relevant to the study) as consistent as possible. Particularly important in this regard was the assumption that the communication process is organized by various types of rules – from explicit

---

analysis practices based on selected English-language discourse journals], "Przegląd Socjologii Jakościowej" 2013, Vol. 9, No. 1, pp. 169 and 183, the authors, on the basis of the articles analyzed, even speak of a "hybridity of theoretical approaches" in communication research.

34 The interdisciplinary research process "is a process of answering a question, solving a problem, or addressing a topic that is too broad or complex to be dealt with adequately by a single discipline, and draws on the disciplines with the goal of integrating their insights to construct a more comprehensive understanding". See A.F. Repko, R. Szostak, *Interdisciplinary Research: Process and Theory*, 4th edition, Los Angeles 2021, p. 9. See also K. Huutoniemi, J.T. Klein, H. Bruunc, J. Hukkinen, *Analyzing Interdisciplinarity: Typology and Indicators*, "Research Policy" 2010, Vol. 39, No. 1, p. 83.

35 A very glaring example can be given – concepts related to speech act theory were preferred over theories of communication in private situations with gender differences.

norms of conduct to (perhaps even more importantly) less tangible conventions, patterns or schemes that operate in socio-cultural reality.

1.2. Basic terminological and conceptual choices

1.2.1. "Communication" – definition, assumptions and terms related to the communication process

The adoption or development of definitions crucial to the subject of the study is necessary because of (at least) two issues. First, the theories developed in the science of communication either do not provide precise definitions, or adopt definitions so different in scope that without first selecting and clarifying the content of these definitions, it would be difficult to speak of a specific subject of study at all. Second, the assumption that different theoretical concepts will be used to analyze the problematic issues also requires the development and presentation of a basic terminological grid. Failure to indicate what meaning is given to the basic terms could suggest an implicit transfer of such an understanding of certain terms as is adopted in the various concepts, which in turn could lead to the recognition of assumptions that contradict each other. Thus, in order for different theoretical concepts to be accepted as complementary, it is first necessary to build a basic terminological grid that allows their comparison.

Already at the very beginning of this monograph (see Section 1.1) the problem of the status of communication science (or so-called communication science) as an independent scientific discipline was signaled. Some researchers directly point to its pre-paradigmatic nature.[36] Authors formulating objections to the independence of communication science point in particular to: (1) the lack of methodological foundations (this was mentioned in Section 1.1); (2) the question of the "objective" existence of the subject of communication science;[37] (3) the problems associated

---

36 Thus, for example S.R. Olson, *Teoria komunikowania: ponowne rozpatrzenie kwestii [Communication theory: reconsidering the question]*, [in:] *Współczesne systemy komunikowania [Contemporary communication systems]*, ed. B. Dobek-Ostrowska, Wrocław 1998, pp. 42–45; T. Kuhn, *The Structure of Scientific Revolutions*, Chicago 1960, p. 13), the author, speaking of the pre-paradigmatic nature of communication science, refers to Thomas Kuhn's position that a field is pre-paradigmatic when there is no standard set of methods or phenomena that every scientist feels compelled to apply and explain.

37 See, e.g. E. Kulczycki, *Kulturowo-obiektywne istnienie procesu komunikacji [The cultural-objective existence of the communication process]*, "Kultura i Historia", http://www.kulturaihistoria.umcs.lublin.pl/archives/2997, access 20.12.2022. The author starts from the assumption that one can talk about the communication process as a research subject only when the question: What does it mean that communication (as a process) exists objectively? is answered – and seeks an answer in culturalism, recognizing that it is legitimate (and necessary for the design of an independent

with defining the term "communication",[38] in particular, with determining the relationship between the scopes of the names "communication" and "information".[39] The issues covered in (2) and (3) above make up the so-called ontology[40] of communication science, in which deficiencies are evident. The consequence of this state of affairs is the need to develop a research ontology, that is, not only to define the basic terms related to the communication process, but also to identify additional theoretical assumptions that provide grounding and justification for the definitions adopted.

The definition of "communication" proposed in this book (as well as definitions of other related terms) is a consequence of searches in various areas of communication science, and beyond. In constructing the relevant definitions, an adequate way of capturing communication was sought in concepts that conceptualized communication as transmission, understanding, interaction, community formation, interaction, exchange of meanings or a component of the social process.[41]

The definitions presented in the following sections are nominally[42] regulating definitions.[43]

---

scientific discipline) to assume that the communication process exists objectively in culture (exists culturally-objectively).

38 "[What is communication?] To ask this question is to invite controversy and raise expectations that can't be met". See E. Griffin, *A First Look at Communication Theory*, 8th edition, New York 2011, p. 6.

39 M. Wendland, *Działanie komunikacyjne a przekazywanie informacji [Communication action vs. information transfer]*, [in:] *Komunikologia. Teoria i praktyka komunikacji [Communicology. Theory and practice of communication]*, eds. E. Kulczycki, M. Wendland, Poznań 2012, p. 137 et seq. An excellent portion of publications in the field of communication science begins with a statement about the difficulty of defining the term "communication" and with information about the multiplicity of definitions of this term, see, e.g., R.B. Adler, G. Rodman, A. du Pré, *Understanding Human Communication*, 12th edition, New York 2014; p. 5; E. Griffin, *A First Look...*, op. cit., p. 6 et seq.; R.B. Adler, L.B. Rosenfeld, R.F. Proctor II, *Interplay: The Process of Interpersonal Communication*, 14th edition, New York 2018, p. 9.

40 The ontology of a given field of science is referred to in this study as a set of its key terms and the assumptions that specify its subject matter, J.F. Jacko, *Ontologie sytuacji komunikacyjnej w empirycznych naukach humanistycznych [Ontologies of the communication situation in the empirical humanities]*, [in:] *Sytuacja komunikacyjna i jej parametry [Communication situation and its parameters]*, ed. G. Sawicka, Bydgoszcz 2010, p. 125.

41 Tomasz Goban-Klas puts various definitions of communication into such definition groups, Goban-Klas, *Media i komunikowanie masowe. Teorie i analizy prasy, radia, telewizji i Internetu [Media and mass communication. Theories and analysis of press, radio, television and the Internet]*, Warszawa 2005, pp. 42–43.

42 They indicate how certain terms are understood.

43 Regulating either by specifying its content in this study, or by transferring a definition previously formulated in science.

The definitions adopted in the work are not fully and exclusively operative definitions in the sense that not all elements of the content of the defined names will be the subject (or tool) of later more detailed analysis. However, it is recognized that to assume otherwise would lead to an unjustified impoverishment of the content of the definitions adopted.

1.2.1.1. The meaning of the term "communication"

In this book, the term "communication" refers to a complex process that collectively has the following characteristics: it is interpersonal (thus occurs exclusively between people), it is a socio-cultural process, it is symbolic, it is intentional, and it performs a variety of functions (or at least has the capacity to do so).

The study talks about communication as a **process** (communication process[44]). Thus, communication is seen as a dynamic phenomenon, the essence of which is certain acts taken by the actors involved in it. This does not mean, of course, that the subject of interest is not also the effects of the acts undertaken.

On the other hand, the complexity of the communication process is evidenced by the variety of elements of the content of the adopted definition, the development and understanding of which requires the use of certain assumptions from various scientific fields, as discussed below.

It is also assumed that the communication is a **typically human process**. Such an assumption leaves outside the scope of the name "communication" the processes of transferring information between animals or machines. Even when a given communication act is attributed to a certain conventional entity, such as a court, it is still an act undertaken by a human (i.e., the material substrate of this act is always produced by a human). **Interpersonality** presupposes, at the same time, that the potential recipient in the process of communication is also a human being, so it is outside the scope of this definition to direct an utterance to some imagined being, e.g. during prayer. The above sentence, in turn, presupposes the statement that there is a recipient, at least assumed, in the process of communication. Adopting such a view of communication is in turn related to the assumption of the social dimension of the communication process. This puts the so-called intrapersonal communication[45] outside the scope of the name "communication".

Recalling the words of Bruno Ollivier, it can be said that within the definition under discussion it is recognized that " 'I' does not communicate".[46]

---

44 The terms "communication" and "communication process" will be used interchangeably.

45 Intrapersonal communication, that is, communication that takes place in the mind of one person, D. McQuail, *McQuail's Mass Communication Theory*, 6th edition, London 2010, p. 17. John L. Austin, in the context of speech acts, calls utterances made in a soliloquy "hollow" or "void", J.L. Austin, *How to Do Things with Words*, Oxford 1962, p. 22.

46 B. Ollivier, *Nauki...*, op. cit., p. 127

The literature sometimes uses the term "interpersonal communication" also as a name for a specific type of communication,[47] while this book assumes that all communication is interpersonal in the basic sense of the term.

Recognizing that communication is a peculiarly human and, moreover, interpersonal process is tantamount to adopting, as Boguslawa Dobek-Ostrowska calls it, "a humanistic or social orientation".[48] The definition in question assumes that **the communication process takes place in a specific social environment**, never outside of it.[49]

The statement that the **communication process is a cultural process**, on the other hand, boils down to the recognition that communication always occurs within a particular culture or cultures (intercultural communication[50]). The paper adopts the perspective of the socio-regulatory conception of culture developed by Jerzy Kmita,[51] that is, the culture of a given society is defined as "a set of normative and directive beliefs,[52] which: (1) are universally respected in a given community; (2) form the subjective-rational conditions of functional acts in relation to the established global state of this community treated as the structural context of these acts",[53] with the most significant being the sphere of culture called

---

47 On ways of capturing interpersonal communication, J. Stewart, *Interpersonal Communication: Contact between Persons*, [in:] *Bridges Not Walls: A Book About Interpersonal Communication*, ed. J. Stewart, 5th edition, New York 1990, p. 13 et seq.

48 B. Dobek-Ostrowska, *Podstawy komunikowania społecznego [Basics of social communication]*, Wrocław 1999, p. 12.

49 Sometimes, to emphasize the social nature of the communication process, it is used the term "social communication". In light of the accepted definition, the addition of the adjective "social" is unnecessary. However, it was used in the title of this book to eliminate those meanings that are related to movement.

50 "Intercultural communication thus is broadly defined as the communication process in which individual participants of differing cultural or subcultural backgrounds come into direct contact with one another". See Y.Y. Kim, *Intercultural Communication*, [in:] *The Handbook of Communication Science*, eds. C.R. Berger, M.E. Roloff, D.R. Roskos-Ewoldsen, 2nd edition, Sage Publications 2010, p. 454.

51 The adoption of this perspective is evident in that selected assumptions developed by Kmita (and other representatives of the Poznań school of methodology) have been used in this work and are part of the theoretical grounding of the considerations presented herein.

52 In the Polish theory of law, normative expressions (norms of conduct) are treated alongside purposive (technical, teleological) directives as a type of directive expressions, M. Zieliński, Z. Ziembiński, *Uzasadnianie twierdzeń, ocen i norm w prawoznawstwie [Justifying claims, judgments and norms in jurisprudence]*, Warszawa 1988, s. 56 et seq; see also Z. Ziembiński, *Norms of Conduct*, [in:] *Poznań School of Legal Theory*, eds. M. Smolak, P. Kwiatkowski, Leiden 2021, p. 97 et seq. In the cited definition, normative beliefs are related to the norms of conduct in force, in turn, directive beliefs are related to some statements in the nature of purposive directives.

53 G. Banaszak, J. Kmita, *Społeczno-regulacyjna koncepcja kultury [Socio-regulatory concept of culture]*, Warszawa 1991, p. 50.

"symbolic".[54]

Expanding on the assumption of the symbolic nature of communication,[55] it should be pointed out, following Zygmunt Ziembiński, that there is a difference between a sign and a symptom:

1. a "sign" is called such a state of affairs (or event) caused by someone specifically to direct someone's thoughts in a certain direction on the basis of certain rules;[56]
2. a "symptom" of a state of affairs (or event) is called anything that, co-occurring with this state of affairs (or event), causes someone's thoughts to be directed to it, although there are no rules of meaning that would dictate such a direction of thoughts.[57]

The main difference between a sign and a symptom concerns intentionality. In the case of a sign, a given state of affairs is caused in order to direct the thoughts of the potential recipient of the sign in a certain direction. In the case of a symptom, we link the existence of a certain phenomenon to another on the basis of knowledge of the co-occurrence of these phenomena. In this view, a sign would be, for example, shaking hands in greeting, while a symptom of a thunderstorm would be lightning.

The symbolic nature of the communication process, assumed in the study, refers to the acts of participants in the communication process by means of signs, understood as indicated above.[58] However, this does not mean that the problem of symptoms (e.g., symptoms of nervousness), traditionally included in the framework of so-called non-verbal communication, will not be addressed. Phenomena that are symptoms of other phenomena are considered in this book as elements of the communication situation in which the communication process takes place, and not as elements of this process (cf. the considerations on the meaning of the terms "communication context" and "situational context" in this section).

In light of the above considerations, both silently shaking someone's hand in greeting and saying the words "good morning" will be (of course, with the fulfillment of other conditions) a communication act. Thus, a communication act does not have to involve the use of linguistic signs; it can be other man-made phenomena. Thus, an assumption is made in this book about the multiplicity of codes used in the communication process.

---

54 Ibidem, p. 57.

55 No reference is made in this paper to Charles Peirce's concept of the sign, often cited in communication science.

56 Z. Ziembiński, *Logika praktyczna [Practical logic]*, 26th edition, Warszawa 2011, p. 14. The definition is given in the verbal form proposed by Zieliński.

57 Ibidem.

58 Tomasz Goban-Klas puts it similarly, stating that "cognition by means of signs is inherent only in humans, and only it can be described as communication", Goban-Klas, *Media...*, op. cit., p. 43.

Adopting the above-mentioned definition of a sign implies the intentionality of communication as a symbolic process. However, **the intentional nature of communication** is specifically related to other assumptions that are made in this study and will be presented in more detail here.

The following discussion refers to some of the findings on the essence of communication acts made by Michał Wendland, who grounded his considerations by adopting certain assumptions developed by the Poznań methodological school, mainly in terms of the social-regulatory concept of culture and the concept of humanistic interpretation.[59] The terminological grid constructed here is formed primarily by the terms developed in the Poznań methodological school,[60] but in the form (i.e., with some modifications) used by the authors of the publication *Conventional Acts in Law*.[61]

The paper adopts the term "communication act" and considers the communication act(s) as the essence of the communication process.[62] The purpose of the following discussion is to indicate the essence of these acts as communication acts, for which the starting point will be the concept of conventional act formulated in jurisprudence.

According to the definition in the publication *Conventional Acts in Law*, "conventional acts" are called cultural acts (so also rational) and at the same time aimed at someone's interpretation.[63] "Cultural act" on the other hand, is called a rational act undertaken on the basis of knowledge, which includes information about the rules of cultural interpretation pertaining to this act, i.e. knowledge that is an element of the cultural system.[64]

---

59 See also M. Wendland, *Pojęcie komunikacji w poznańskiej szkole metodologicznej [The concept of communication in the Poznan school of methodology]*, "Filo-Sofija" 2012, Vol. 12, No. 18, p. 91 et seq., idem, *Konstruktywizm...*, op. cit., Poznań 2011, p. 210 et seq. In more recent publications, Wendland presents assumptions about the essence of communication acts and communication within the framework of the so-called culturalist concept of communication, developed together with Emanuel Kulczycki, M. Wendland, *Filozoficzne i metodologiczne podstawy historii komunikacji [Philosophical and methodological foundations of communication history]*, Poznań 2014, p. 188 et seq.; E. Kulczycki, *Dwa aspekty komunikacji. Założenia komunikologii historycznej [Two aspects of communication. Assumptions of historical communicology]*, Poznań 2015, p. et seq.

60 Especially in the study J. Kmita, L. Nowak, *Studia nad teoretycznymi podstawami humanistyki [Studies on the theoretical foundations of the humanities]*, Poznań 1968.

61 L. Nowak, S. Wronkowska, M. Zieliński, Z. Ziembiński, *Czynności konwencjonalne w prawie [Conventional acts in law]*, "Studia Prawnicze" 1972, Vol. 33, pp. 73–99 (English translation: L. Nowak, S. Wronkowska, M. Zieliński, Z. Ziembiński, *Conventional Acts in Law*, [in:] *Polish Contributions...*, op. cit., p. 115 et seq.).

62 M. Wendland, *Pojęcie komunikacji...*, op. cit., p. 93 et seq.

63 L. Nowak, S. Wronkowska, M. Zieliński, Z. Ziembiński, *Czynności...*, op. cit., p. 82.

64 Ibidem, p. 81.

The concept of rational activity should be given a little more attention. The assumption of the rationality of human acts, which is accepted in the humanities, and not only,[65] is, of course, of an idealizing nature, since the actual acts of people more or less approach only a certain ideal level of rationality.[66] It is assumed in the literature that an act taken by a person under certain circumstances is rational on the basis of his knowledge and his preferences, when – according to this knowledge – it certainly leads to the realization of the state of affairs maximally preferred by this person.[67] It should be particularly emphasized that the rationality of an act is recognized on the basis of the knowledge and preferences of the person who undertakes the act, and not from the point of view of a third party. That is why one sometimes speaks of "subjective-rational" acts.[68] In doing so, the rationality of an act is combined with intentionality,[69] because according to the assumption of the rationality of the acts taken, the acting person aims at (intends) the realization of a certain goal.

It should be noticed that the entity taking a particular act may pursue different goals at different levels. This is particularly relevant when analyzing the level of rationality of the acts of the participants of court proceedings; generally the global goal of a party to the proceedings is to obtain a favorable outcome. To illustrate this issue, one can cite the authentic act of one of the participants of the proceedings recorded in the research material, which consisted of showing the another participant the sign of "cut throat" and silently uttering the words: "I will kill you!". It could be considered that such an act moves away from the ideal type of rational

65 J. Kmita, L. Nowak, *Studia...*, op. cit., p. 104 et seq.
66 L. Nowak, S. Wronkowska, M. Zieliński, Z. Ziembiński, *Czynności...*, op. cit., p. 77.
67 Ibidem, p. 76.
68 J. Kmita, *O kulturze...*, op. cit., p. 26 et seq.
69 M. Wendland, *Pojęcie komunikacji...*, op. cit., p. 94 et seq. On the other hand, within the culturalist definition of communication, it is assumed that communicative intention must be considered from the perspective of the observer as a feature of the act, and not of the participant in communication, due to the lack of access to his/her mental states (M. Wendland, *Filozoficzne...*, p. 196, E. Kulczycki, *Dwa aspekty...*, p. 69.). Recognition of communicative intention depends on the cultural knowledge of the observer (knowledge of the rules for performing certain acts) and the social context (E. Kulczycki, *Dwa aspekty...*, pp. 72 and 80). However, even when there is no "transfer" of intention from the level of characteristics of the participant in communication to the level of characteristics of the act, recognition of communicative intention is possible insofar as it is possible to infer its existence on the basis of what is available to the interpreter. Philosophy of language and pragmatics propose different approaches to intention – informative intention (see D. Sperber, D. Wilson, *Relevance: Communication and Cognition*, 2nd ed., Oxford 1995, p. 58), communication intention (see ibidem, p. 61), complex communication intention ("complex intention" – see P.F. Strawson, *Intention and Convention in Speech Acts*, "The Philosophical Review" 1964, Vol. 73, No. 4, p. 445 sqq.). This issue has been broadly discussed in the literature. Due to the scope of this book it is not presented to a broader extent.

act (due to the fact that the court may consider such an act as violating the dignity of the court, the participant may reduce his chances for a favorable settlement of the dispute, etc.). However, it should be borne in mind that the recognition of an act as rational, i.e. as an act with a certain sense, is related to the establishment of the direct purpose of the act taken.[70] In the cited example, the direct purpose of the participant's act should be considered to be the direct purpose of the threat to the participant in the proceedings, and from this point of view we should consider the degree of his rationality, which was undoubtedly significant, especially since the participant (recipient), as it seems, correctly interpreted this act.

However, failure of the person taking the act to achieve the stated goal does not mean that the act is not rational.[71] By taking linguistic acts, for example, it is possible to fail to achieve (using Austin's terminology) the goal in the illocutionary dimension – the utterance was interpreted as a question and not as a request, as well as in the perlocutionary dimension – the person to whom the request was addressed did not carry it out. Such an act is then ineffective, but this does not mean that it is irrational.

In the definition of a conventional act, it is indicated that it is an act aimed at interpretation (of someone), this means that in order to effectively carry out such an act, it is necessary that someone understands the act, that is, properly reproduces its meaning.[72] It is according to the knowledge of the one taking the act that one of the consequences of performing the act is to interpret it.[73] However, the conviction of the one taking the act may be wrong in this regard, and therefore acts aimed at interpretation may be both effective and ineffective,[74] as they are "aimed at interpretation" and not "interpreted" or, going even further, "interpreted correctly".[75]

In the proposed approach, a **communication act is a variety of conventional act**.[76] It is such a conventional act that meets the

70 L. Nowak, S. Wronkowska, M. Zieliński, Z. Ziembiński, *Czynności...*, op. cit., p. 77.

71 M. Wendland, *Pojęcie komunikacji...*, op. cit., p. 94.

72 L. Nowak, S. Wronkowska, M. Zieliński, Z. Ziembiński, *Czynności...*, op. cit., p. 78. In comparison, for the effective cleaning of an apartment, it is not necessary for someone to interpret this act, so it is not an act that is geared towards interpretation.

73 Ibidem.

74 Ibidem, M. Wendland, *Pojęcie komunikacji...*, op. cit., p. 94.

75 At the same time, it should be noted that in order for an act to be said to be "interpretation-oriented", it must somehow be accessible to the recipient. Indeed, it is difficult to grant such a characteristic to an act such as writing a letter, which the author would burn immediately after writing.

76 In the next chapter, the concept of conventional act will be further explicated in accordance with Stanisław Czepita's proposed development of the concept of conventional acts; primarily S. Czepita, *Reguły konstytutywne a zagadnienia prawoznawstwa [Constitutive rules and issues of jurisprudence]*, Szczecin 1996.

defining assumptions of the term "communication" adopted in this study.[77]

A brief further reference should be made to the term "communication act"[78] adopted after Michal Wendland, who views the act through the prism of Max Weber's grasp.[79] According to Weber, an act is a behavior with which the subject associates a certain meaning, as opposed to unreflective reflexes.[80]

Summarizing the above considerations, the following **peculiarities of a communication act** can be identified. First, assuming that the communication act is a rational and "oriented towards..." implies that it is an intentional act. On the other hand, it is not necessary for the act to be effective – it may not be interpreted at all (e.g., when the assumed recipient does not actualize) or be interpreted differently than the sender expected (a situation of communication misunderstanding will then occur).

In turn, the recognition of a communication act as a cultural act leads to the assumption of a minimum community of code between sender and (at least assumed) recipient.[81] However, some clarification should be made on this point.

77 With this understanding of a conventional act and the definition of communication proposed in this book, it seems that prayer, for example, would be a conventional act (since the authors of the concept did not explicitly indicate that the interpretation orientation does not involve some imagined being), but would not be a communication act, since it does not meet the assumption of interpersonality.

78 This is not a reference to Jürgen Habermas' theory of communicative action (communicative action is when participants coordinate plans of action not by egocentric calculation of the success, but by acts of reaching understanding), J. Habermas, *The Theory of Communicative Action*, Vol. 1: *Reason and the Rationalization of Society*, Boston 1984. This theory is not part of the research ontology adopted in the paper due to inconsistencies between some of its elements and the assumptions made in this study.

79 M. Wendland, *Pojęcie komunikacji...*, op. cit., p. 93.

80 Ibidem, after: M. Weber, *Gospodarka i społeczeństwo. Zarys socjologii rozumiejącej [Economy and Society. An outline of interpretive sociology]*, Warszawa 2002. It should be noted at this point that Weber also considered omission as an act: "Human behavior – be it external or internal activity, omission or acquiescence – will be called 'action' if and insofar as the actor attaches or subjects a subjective meaning of it" (quoted in J. Habermas, *The Theory...*, op. cit., p. 279). In the view proposed in this study, an intentional silence or, for example, a refusal to shake hands in response to a greeting is also considered a communication act, provided, of course, that the other defining conditions of a "communication act" are met, in particular, the participants in the communication are linked by a community of code, i.e. the addressee has such knowledge that allows him or her to recognize the meaning of such an act.

81 L. Nowak, S. Wronkowska, M. Zieliński, Z. Ziembiński, *Czynności...*, op. cit., p. 82. "An example, on the other hand, of an activity that is oriented toward interpretation, rather than cultural, is any activity that is defectively oriented toward interpretation", ibidem. The community of code, as it is understood in this book, is dealt with both when the participants of communication use a code understood as an ordered

This monograph assumes that such a community must exist at least at one level of conventionalization (e.g., at the level of the speech act).[82] Let us take as an example the act of promulgating a ruling to secure a claim in a case. For such an act to be considered a communication act, the linguistic community of the sender and the recipient is sufficient. What this means is that for this act to be considered communication, it is not necessary for the judge to know whether the addressee of this act is able to recognize this act at the level of a procedural act. The fact that the actual recipient of this act (including the addressee) will not recognize the meaning of this act at the level of the procedural act will also not cause this act to cease to be a communication act. In such a situation, although there will be a communication process, a communication understanding will not be reached, which is understood here as a consensual recognition by the participants in the communication process of the meaning of the communication act at the highest level of conventionalization (more on the levels of conventionalization in relation to the acts taken at the trial will be discussed in Sections from 2.3.2.14 to 2.3.2.18).

Finally, it is still necessary to refer to the assumption made in the study that the **communication process has various functions,** or at least lends itself to them. Being aware of the ambiguities associated with the meaning of such terms as "function" or "role", with reference to the linguistic tradition, this monograph speaks of the "functions" of communication process or communication act. As rightly noted in the literature, some communication scholars assume that the essence of the communication process is information (transmission of information), and sometimes even equate communication with information.[83] In turn, for example, representatives of the so-called Palo Alto school emphasized in their publications that information exchange is only a small part of communication compared to the relational dimension of this process.[84]

---

system of signs, and when they establish some single rule for the meaning of the act they take. It is even enough for the participants in communication to share knowledge of such rules of sense, which do not form an ordered system at all, but through which they are nevertheless able to give appropriate meaning to communication acts.

82 It should be pointed out that the legislator, in constructing the trial, ensured a minimum community of code, ordering procedural acts to be performed in a situation where the participant does not speak Polish, in the presence of an interpreter.

83 M. Wendland, *Działanie komunikacyjne...*, op. cit., p. 139.

84 Z. Nęcki, *Komunikacja międzyludzka [Interpersonal communication]*, Kraków 1996, p. 28. However, it should be remembered that Paul Watzlawick and other representatives of this school take communication very broadly, according to statements such as "everything communicates" or "it is impossible not to communicate", P. Watzlawick, J.B. Bavelas, D.D. Jackson, *Pragmatics of Human Communication: A Study of Interactional Patterns, Pathologies and Paradoxes*, W.W. Norton and Company 2011. In doing so, they refer to some of the assumptions of Gregory Bateson's so-called contextual theory of communication, A. Skibiński, *Gregory Bateson i kontekstowa teoria komunikacji. Różnica, która czyni różnicę i wzorzec, który łączy [Gregory Bateson and contextual communication theory. The difference that makes the*

The fact that equating communication with the transmission of information is unauthorized is pointed out by Michal Wendland[85]. In support of his position, he refers in particular to the issue of the function of speech, concluding that not every communication act has an informational function, and that the scopes of the names "communication" ("communication act") and "information" ("transmission of information") cross each other.[86]

The terms "communication function" or "communication act function" used in this book have a broader scope than the term "utterance function" in linguistics.[87] In linguistics (and not only), the functions of utterance are discussed in particular with reference to the already classic concepts of Karl Bühler, who distinguished three functions of language (understood as the use of a system, an utterance): expressive, impressive and representational, and Roman Jakobson, who, with regard to his model of communication, pointed to six such functions – representational, poetic, emotive, impressive, phatic and metalinguistic.[88] Moreover, since the formulation of the theory of speech acts by John L. Austin and its subsequent development by John R. Searle, the linguistic literature has clearly emphasized the performative function of utterance. A general distinction is also made between the intended and unintended functions of utterances.[89]

It is assumed in this monograph that communication performs a variety of functions, both intended and unintended. In addition, a given communication act can perform several functions together. Due to the fact that in the literature one can find various typologies of the functions of utterances or, more broadly, of communication acts, here we are limited only to the above statement. Individual functions will be explained in those places in this book where specific communication acts will be mentioned and it will be expedient to indicate the functions they perform.

---

difference and the pattern that connects], [in:] *Komunikologia...*, op. cit., p. 82 et seq., G. Bateson, *Mind and Nature: A Necessary Unity*, Hampton Press 2002.

85 In justifying his position, the author first refers to the definitions of information developed in science: "information is the name of the content taken from the external world as we adapt to it and as we adapt our senses to it", or: "information is a detected (registered) difference that is relevant to the act of an organism", M. Wendland, *Działanie komunikacyjne...*, op. cit., p. 141); for the sake of the framework of this study, this thread is only outlined.

86 M. Wendland, *Działanie komunikacyjne...*, op. cit., p. 141.

87 There is also a difference between the functions of language as a system of signs, and of language as the general speech activity of humans, R. Grzegorczykowa, *Wstęp do językoznawstwa [Introduction to linguistics]*, Warszawa 2007, p. 52 et seq.

88 Ibidem; R. Jakobson, *W poszukiwaniu istoty języka 2 [In search for the essence of language 2]*, Warszawa 1989, s. 81–88.

89 W. Pisarek, *Wstęp do nauki o komunikowaniu [Introduction to communication science]*, Warszawa 2008, p. 175–176.

Differently from what Michał Wendland proposed, this monograph answers the question: Do all communication acts have an informative function? In this regard, reference is made to the findings of Aleksy Awdiejew and Grażyna Habrajska made within the framework of communication grammar.[90] The informational function (representational, ideational – in Awdiejew's terminology)[91] of utterance consists in depicting the world, i.e. conveying information about the reality that is real or arises in the speaker's imagination.[92] In the speech act, the informational (representational) function is carried out by the so-called representational (ideational) content, according to the pragmalinguistic tradition usually called propositional content.[93] According to the assumptions of communication grammar, propositional content is an inherent component of the speech act; even exclamations such as "oh!" or "ah!" are not devoid of propositional content, the function of which in such a case is performed by the situation that evokes an emotive reaction.[94] When interpreting a speech act, it is necessary to first determine **what** was said (propositional content) in order to resolve **why** something was said.[95]

Thus, according to the position of the authors (also adopted in this study), every speech act, even typically emotive, has an informative function to some extent.[96]

1.2.1.2. The meaning of the terms "communication context" and "situational context"

In the linguistic and philosophical literature one can encounter the terms: "linguistic context", "situational context", "contextualization", "communication situation", "communication background" and many others. Just as the content of the above terms is undefined, the effect of context on the communication process, especially on the interpretation of communication acts, is not fully recognized by

---

90 At the core of communication grammar (the assumptions of which are repeatedly used in this book) is the concept of M.A.K. Halliday, within which he distinguished three functional levels of language: ideational (informational), interpersonal (called "interactional" in communication grammar) and textual. Cf. M.A.K. Malliday, *Explorations in the Functions of Language*, London 1973.

91 A. Awdiejew, *Gramatyka interakcji werbalnej [Grammar of verbal interaction]*, Kraków 2004, p. 9.

92 Ibidem, p. 16.

93 Ibidem, p. 44.

94 A. Awdiejew, G. Habrajska, *Wprowadzenie do gramatyki komunikacyjnej [Introduction to communication grammar]*, Vol. 2, Łask 2006, p. 48.

95 A. Awdiejew, G. Habrajska, *Komponowanie sensu w procesie odbioru komunikatów [Composing sense in the process of receiving messages]*, Łódź 2010, pp. 218–219.

96 Taking a question as an example, it can be pointed out that in addition to its basic suggestive function (inducing one to act – to give an answer), it also has an informative function in terms of the so-called assumption of the question, i.e. that knowledge which the questioner reveals by asking a specific question.

scholars.[97] Context has a special place in the study of communication in pragmatics (pragmalinguistics). Some definitions of "pragmatics" directly refer to the relationship between certain communicative phenomena and context.[98] This does not mean, however, that a fully developed concept of context has been worked out in pragmatics, or at least that some basic assumptions about what context is and how it affects the interpretation of utterances, and how utterances affect the context in which they are uttered, have been widely accepted.[99] So let's take a look at some of the proposals. One way of defining "context" is to identify those elements of reality that form, or can form, the context of a given utterance. Such a definition was proposed, for example, by John Lyons, listing: "(i) knowledge of *role* and *status* (where role covers both role in the speech event, as speaker or addressee, and social role, and status covers notions of relative social standing), (ii) knowledge of spatial and temporal *location*, (iii) knowledge of *formality level*, (iv) knowledge of the *medium* (roughly the code or style appropriate to a channel, like the distinction between spoken and written varieties of a language), (v) knowledge of appropriate *subject matter*, (vi) knowledge of appropriate *province* (or domain determining the register of a language)".[100] Methodologically useful also seem to be the proposed typologies of context, such as the one that distinguishes: (1) linguistic context; (2) utterance context; and (3) cognitive context,[101]

---

97 Cf. e.g. D. Mazzarella, A. Negro, C. Penco, *Contexts: Everything You Always Wanted to Know*
about Context (But Were Afraid to Ask), "Argumenta" 2022, Vol. 8, No. 1, pp. 9–33.

98 E.g. "[p]ragmatics is the study of those relations between language and context that are grammaticalized, or encoded in the structure of a language" (S.C. Levinson, *Pragmatics*, Cambridge 1983, p. 9) or "[p]ragmatics is the study of the ability of language users to pair sentences with the contexts in which they would be appropriate" (S.C. Levinson, *Pragmatics*, op. cit., p. 24).

99 Cf. J. Meibauer, *What Is a Context*, [in:] *What Is a Context: Linguistic Approaches and Challenges*, eds. R. Finkbeiner, J. Meibauer, P.B. Schumacher, Amsterdam-Philadelphia 2012, p. 9.

100 S.C. Levinson, *Pragmatics*, op. cit., p. 23.

101 "*Linguistic context* or co-text is mainly studied by linguists and concerns phenomena like discourse, anaphora, quotation, indirect report, and so on. *Context of utterance* is just a specific piece of what is normally called "social context" (...) or situation or nonlinguistic context; "context of utterance" is typically used to indirectly refer to the specific situation in which an utterance (a piece of a speech) is made and it is constituted by a list of the parameters necessary to interpret certain kinds of words. *Cognitive context* concerns the cognitive dimensions of beliefs, chunks of knowledge, assumptions, and is it sometimes referred to as "mental space" (...); there is both an individual and a collective view of cognitive context." See C. Penco, *Contexts in philosophy: Pragmatic competence as filter*, https://www.openscience.fr/Contexts-in-philosophy-pragmatic-competence-as-filter, accessed on: 2.06.2023.

or the one that distinguishes: (1) linguistic context;[102] and (2) extralinguistic context.[103]

In this study, the context in which the communication process takes place is particularly important. This is determined, for example, by the systemic approach adopted here, in which the communication process under study is treated as an element of a certain whole – the trial (which, in turn, is an element of court proceedings). In addition, with regard to the communication acts taken at the trial, the context plays an important role in the process of interpreting communication acts at the level of particularly momentous conventional acts. This refers to the so-called "Austinian presupposition" – "a contextual state of affairs that, first, is required by the act's felicity and, second, is determined by the conventional procedure under which the act is performed."[104]

Indeed, the importance of context (the so-called global context), as Teun van Dijk points out, increases when one considers communication as an activity that constitutes organizational or institutional proceedings.[105]

Among the various terms (including those indicated above), the terms "communication context" and "situational context" ("communication situation") were selected for the terminological and conceptual grid built in the study.

The term "communication context" means all communication acts preceding or following a specific communication act, which affect (or at least can affect) its interpretation. The definition constructed in this way is a direct reference to the so-called linguistic context (co-text), however, it was adapted to other assumptions

---

102 "*Linguistic Context*: Linguistic context refers to what precedes or follows a string of text. It is what helps understand the meaning of words in the context of a sentence or the meaning of a sentence in the context of a wider part of the text, with its anaphoric links. We speak in these cases of sentence context or discourse context." See D. Mazzarella, A. Negro, C. Penco, *Contexts...*, op. cit., p. 10.

103 "*Extralinguistic Context*: Extralinguistic context typically refers to both physical and cognitive features of a given situation. It is, first of all, what helps interpret the referents of indexicals and demonstratives. It also helps to understand the various presuppositions that underpin a speech, as well as the various moves that allow the discourse to develop and update. The two main concepts of (extralinguistic) contexts derive from Kaplan's logic of demonstratives and Stalnaker's theory of presuppositions. In the former, we speak of the context of utterance, basically defined by time, place, speaker, and possible world. In the latter, we speak of cognitive context, or common ground, which is the set of presuppositions or propositions accepted as true by participants in a conversation (the context set)". See D. Mazzarella, A. Negro, C. Penco, *Contexts...*, op. cit., pp. 10–11.

104 M. Witek, *How to Establish Authority with Words: Imperative Utterances and Presupposition Accommodation*, [in:] *Theory of Imperatives from Different Points of View (2)*, eds. A. Brożek, J. Jadacki, B. Žarnić, Warszawa 2013, pp. 145–157.

105 T. van Dijk, *The Study of Discourse*, [in:] *Discourse as Structure and Process*, ed. T. van Dijk, London 1997, p. 20.

made and the category of statements (texts, words, etc., depending on the definition) was replaced by the category of communication acts.

Defining the term "situational context" is more difficult than explaining the name "communication context" primarily because researchers, as indicated above, do not agree on the elements of the subject that could be marked by this or any other similar term. Therefore, a very general definition of "situational context" will be given first, and then some elements of situational context as an object will be indicated, along with an outlined hierarchical structure.

In this book, the term "situational context" means the conditions under which a specific communication act is undertaken. The expression "communication situation" is treated as synonymous. And the elements of the situational context can be presented within the following hierarchical structure:[106]

1. micro-context – the time and place of undertaking communication acts, participants in the communication process, including:
   (a) the number, variety or type of participants,
   (b) competence and knowledge of the participants, including the common area of knowledge of the participants (this includes both knowledge related to the topic of conversation, for example, and knowledge of the system of socio-cultural norms, to which the ability to adapt is an element of communication competence)[107],
   (c) relationships between participants, including the degree of control over other participants in the communication process, emotional attitudes (friendliness, hostility) – the so-called communication climate,
   (d) the social roles of the participants and the roles they play within the communication process (interactional roles),

---

106 Putting the elements of the situational context into a hierarchical structure is a direct reference to Joanna Bielecka-Prus' proposal, Bielecka-Prus, *Problem kontekstu w teoriach komunikacji społecznej [The problem of context in theories of social communication]*, "Studia Socjologiczne" 2012, Vol. 204, No. 1, p. 21.

107 It also includes Stalnakerian common ground – "the presumed background information shared by participants in a conversation (...)." See R. Stalnaker, *Common Ground*, "Linguistics and Philosophy" 2002, No. 25, p. 701. Dan Sperber and Deirdre Wilson point out an important issue related to the knowledge of communication participants. They indicate that [a] context is a psychological construct, a subset of the hearer's assumptions about the world. **It is these assumptions, of course, rather than the actual state of the world, that affect the interpretation of an utterance**. See D. Sperber, D. Wilson, *Relevance...*, op. cit., p. 15, emphasized – K.G. It is worth noting here that in the case of conventional acts in law (including procedural acts), the key to recognizing the meaning of these acts is those elements of the context that have been described as "Austinian presupposition," rather than the subjective assumptions of the participants in the communication about reality.

(e) so-called "communication behavior" – the term "communication behavior" is used in this monograph to refer to phenomena that are not caused intentionally, but have an impact on the way communication acts are interpreted; such behavior may include, in particular, unreflective reflexes, e.g., waving a leg, sweating, distance-related phenomena, e.g., reflexive avoidance of gaze or dress of participants in the communication process,[108]

(f) variety of contact between participants – direct contact (so-called face to face communication) or indirect;

2. meso-context – this is the broader social context, such as institutional, as well as what Zbigniew Nęcki calls "task (instrumental) context", i.e. the type of non-verbal activity that underlies contact;[109]
3. macro-context – socio-cultural reality, including a system of social norms and intersubjective patterns of communication acts (e.g., genre patterns of communication occurrences).

The above-mentioned elements of the situational context (communication situation) do not, of course, exhaust all situational factors that can affect the process of communication, including the understanding of the communication acts taken. In the literature, the problem of the elements of the situational context is approached in various ways, from the recognition that the component of the communication situation is the whole real reality, to the restriction of the communication situation to the relevant elements, which are involved in the process of interpretation of communication acts.

1.2.1.3. The meaning of the terms "feedback" and "communication barriers"

The term "feedback" is used in this study to mean any reaction of another person to a communication act that is perceptible to the sender.

This way of defining feedback requires some clarification and an indication of what place feedback has in the communication process as it is understood here.

---

108 Thus, phenomena that are traditionally defined as elements of so-called non-verbal communication were included in the study not as elements of the communication act, but as components of the situational context in which the communication process takes place. This allowed, on the one hand, for behavioral consistency within the definition of communication as an intentional process, and on the other hand, to emphasize the significant impact that such non-intentional phenomena can have on the communication process. To emphasize their importance in the context of the communication process, they have been called "**communication** behavior". It should be noted that, for example, the choice of a particular outfit can also be made intentionally from the point of view of a particular communication situation and in order to cause a particular interpretation of such an act.

109 Z. Nęcki, *Komunikacja...*, op. cit., p. 106.

First, the use of the phrase "any reaction" in the definition is intended to emphasize that both the communication act and the communication behavior can have a feedback function. Thus, the feedback in the communication process does not make it a two-way communication, involving the exchange of the roles of sender and addressee. In a situation where feedback occurs in the form of a communication act intentionally directed at the sender, such an act is called a "communication act feedback" in this study. In a situation where this act is taken by the addressee, communication becomes two-way, otherwise – it is devoid of this feature. It also does not create a two-way communication process communication act feedback intentionally directed to another entity than the sender, such an act is called "communication act quasi-feedback". Neither does the two-way effect of communication produce feedback in the form of communication behavior, which in turn is called "signal feedback". The same is called a communication act quasi-feedback interpreted by the sender.

Second, the above definition of feedback explicitly assumes that the reaction in the form of a communication act feedback or signal feedback is to be perceptible to the sender. The point is that the sender should be able to interpret such an act or behavior as a reaction to the communication act taken by him or her, since it is difficult to speak of "feedback" in a situation in which such a reaction will not be perceptible to the sender at all.

The term "communication barriers" is understood in this study to mean any factors that interfere with the communication process. Since the scope of the name so defined is vague, some types of communication barriers will be indicated below:[110]

1. physical barriers – including time constraints, so-called external noises (noise, temperature, distance between communication participants, etc.), so-called internal noises (including illness, fatigue, pain, hunger);
2. language barriers – including the use of the same terms by participants in the communication process, but with different meanings, the use of elements of jargon or terminology unfamiliar to other participants in the communication;
3. incompatibility of communication acts and communication behavior – consisting in the fact that the interpretation of communication behavior accompanying the communication act leads to the establishment of a meaning incompatible with the meaning resulting from the interpretation of the communication act;
4. perceptual and interpretive barriers – including the so-called selective perception, which involves blocking the reception of new information, especially when it is incompatible with the communication participant's existing knowledge; the phenomenon of stereotyping;

110 The distinguished types of barriers are indicated in this study after Barbara Sobkowiak, B. Sobkowiak, *Procesy komunikowania się w organizacji [Communication processes in the organization]*, [in:] *Współczesne systemy...*, op. cit., p. 37 et seq.

5. emotional barriers – emotional reactions to communication acts and behaviors;
6. lack of listening skills and taking "competing" acts to the communication process – including a situation in which communication participants "hear" but do not "listen", do not focus attention on the communication process, take acts unrelated to the process;
7. the barrier of mistrust or lack of respect for the participant in the communication process;
8. information overload barrier – related to too much detailed information;
9. cultural barriers – which can occur during the communication process of people representing different cultures.[111]

1.2.1.4. The meaning of the communication act

The purpose of the following discussion is not to formulate a definition of the term "meaning (or sense)" relativized to one or another characterized object (communication act, speech act, etc.).[112] Instead, it is to draw attention to several momentous issues related to the meaning of communication acts as conventional acts.

It should be recalled that a communication act is seen in this study as a variety of conventional act, which in turn is considered a rational act. Within the concept of conventional acts developed by the Poznań legal theorists, it is assumed that the meaning of a rational act (and, consequently, a conventional act) is the purpose of a person acting rationally, associated with the performance of this act by itself.[113] On the other hand, however, the meaning of a conventional act is considered to be the attribution, within the framework of certain rules, of the nature of a conventional act of a certain type.[114] In the first case, determining the meaning of a conventional

---

111 This monograph assumes that a minimum community of code is a prerequisite for the communication process to occur.

112 The issue of the essence or ways of determining the meaning of utterances (speech acts, communicative acts, sentences, etc.) is extremely contentious, and the literature on the subject is very extensive. In particular, two opposing positions in this regard are presented – the internalist approach and the externalist approach. Due to the thematic framework of this book, this issue will not be discussed further. See e.g. N. Riemer, *Internalist Semantics: Meaning, Conceptualization and Expression*, [in:] *The Routledge Handbook of Semantics*, ed. N. Riemer, Routledge 2015; S. Gross, *(Descriptive) Externalism in semantics*, [in:] *The Routledge Handbook...*, op. cit. In the context of legal language see I. Skoczeń, *Implicatures within Legal Language*, Cham 2019, p. 121 et seq. It is worth noting that "[s]peech act theory has its own version of the internalism–externalism debate, but it is, at least until recently, implicit rather than explicit", R.M. Harnish, *Externalism and Internalism in Speech Act Theory*, "Lodz Papers in Pragmatics" 2009, Vol. 5, No. 1, p. 28; cf. J. Navarro-Reyes, *Speech Acts, Criteria and Intentions*, "Lodz Papers in Pragmatics" 2010, Vol. 6, No. 1.

113 L. Nowak, S. Wronkowska, M. Zieliński, Z. Ziembiński, *Czynności...*, op. cit., p. 76.

114 Stanislaw Czepita also points out this ambiguity, S. Czepita, *Reguły...*, op. cit., pp. 128–130.

act would involve explanation, i.e. indicating **why (for what reason)** the entity took such an act and not another. In the second case, it would be about recognizing a particular act as a conventional act of a given type, such as waving one's hand as a greeting. From a methodological point of view, it is, of course, legitimate to distinguish between these types of mental activity, i.e., explanation and recognition,[115] but in the process of interpretation, these acts can condition and complement each other, especially when an act that is the material substrate of a given conventional act is being explained. On the one hand, the answer to the question of why someone took a certain act (e.g., why one waved once hand) makes it possible to recognize this act as a conventional act of a certain type.[116] On the other hand, the recognition of a particular conventional act makes it possible to determine at least for what purpose the act constituting the material substrate of the recognized conventional act was taken.[117]

Particularly complicated, but also quite well recognized,[118] mainly in the field of philosophy of language and linguistics, is the question of the meaning of speech acts as a certain particularly momentous type of communication acts. Traditionally[119] (in philosophy of language, pragmalinguistics), the meaning of speech acts is recognized at several levels – locutionary (propositional, ideational), illocutionary (interactional[120]) and perlocutionary.[121]

---

115 S. Czepita, *Reguły...*, op. cit., p. 129.

116 When referring this to Searle's formula of the essence of institutional facts ("X counts as Y in context C"), it could be said that variable Y represents a conventional act, whereas X represents its material substrate. See J.R. Searle, *Speech Acts. An Essay in the Philosophy of Language*, Cambridge 1969, p. 52.

117 In this regard, it should be emphasized that it is one thing to explain why an act that is the material substrate of a particular conventional act was performed (e.g., a person waved his/her hand in greeting), and another to explain why a particular person performed a particular conventional act (e.g., someone greeted another person in order to carry out a customary norm that prescribes such behavior). Explanations in the latter view require first recognizing the act in question as a conventional act of a certain type.

118 This does not mean uniformly resolved. The very essence of a speech act (primarily illocution) is the subject of numerous scholarly disputes. Maciej Witek distinguishes three basic approaches to the essence of illocution in the philosophy of language – as an intentional, institutional or interactional act, M. Witek, *Three Approaches to the Study of Speech Acts*, "Dialogue and Universalism" 2013, No. 1.

119 I.e., since the distinction of these levels by John L. Austin.

120 Interactional meaning, as it is understood in communication grammar, is close to illocution, but is not fully identical with it, A. Awdiejew, *Gramatyka interakcji...*, op. cit., p. 7.

121 However, with regard to perlocution (understood as the degree of influence on the recipient), it is emphasized that to consider it a linguistic act is a certain abuse (ibidem, p. 14), so in the following section this level will be excluded from consideration of the meaning of the speech act.

Propositional meaning is the answer to the question – **what** was said. The meaning at this level can be reconstructed independently of the situational context.[122] Interactional meaning, on the other hand, is, so to speak, superadded meaning and is primarily an answer to the question – **why** something was said.[123] At the same time, the interactional meaning cannot be recognized without understanding the propositional meaning.

What was said above about meaning, whether in the context of conventional acts or speech acts, can, it seems,[124] be applied to communication acts as they are understood in this monograph.

It is further recognized in this study that the communication context, the communication situation, and the communication barriers affect the understanding (interpretation) of specific communication acts in different ways and to different degrees, including the recognition in them of conventional acts of a certain type (this will be discussed more extensively, in different aspects, in the next chapter). In turn, feedback, in particular, allows the sender to recognize whether his communication act has been interpreted in accordance with the intention.

1.2.1.5. The communication process and the transmissive and constitutive approach

Summarizing the assumptions and definitions adopted so far, it is worth referring to the distinction presented by Emanuel Kulczycki between two approaches in the study of the phenomenon of communication[125] and determine in which approach

---

122 The issue of recognizing the meaning of an utterance at the propositional (ideational) level has been the subject of many concepts that take into account such phenomena as the systemic meaning of words and expressions of language, idiomaticity, metaphor and metonymy, explicative and imlicative meaning, implicatures, cognitive models or semantic standards (for an overview of selected concepts, see A. Awdiejew, G. Habrajska, *Komponowanie sensu...*, op. cit., p. 13 et seq. In the case of some emotive acts, the function of propositional content is performed by the situation that triggered the emotive reaction.

123 Ibidem, p. 78. Determining the interactional meaning of an speech act, at least in the view of these authors, corresponds to the mental activity of explanation. However, this involves the explanation of the utterance of specific words, which leads to the recognition of a speech act of a given type (more on the recognition of speech acts in the discussion of the impact of conventionalization and formalization on selected communication phenomena in Section 2.3.2.18).

124 The issue of propositional meaning is peculiar to speech acts. However, it should be borne in mind that for non-linguistic communication acts it is possible to formulate their equivalents in the form of utterances.

125 When the author speaks of "approaches", he means the whole perspective of reflection on communication, not a specific model, E. Kulczycki, *Teoretyzowanie...*, op. cit., p. 25.

the understanding of communication adopted in this monograph falls. Kulczycki distinguishes between two approaches in reflection on communication: transmissive and constitutive.

In the transmissive view,[126] to put it very briefly, communication is recognized as a linear process of transmitting messages, information, signals, etc.[127] The subjects of such a process are considered as abstracted from the socio-cultural context, communication begins in one subject and ends in another, and meanings are constructed in mind of the individual subject.[128] This approach also ignores the situation in which the communication process takes place, unless it is a source of noise.[129]

On the other hand, in the constitutive view, one can distinguish several aspects that seem to be common to this view: social meaning-making, interactivity (symbolism) of the communication process, being a participant in communication rather than its creator, the momentousness of the communication process not because of the transmission of information, but because of the construction of the socio-cultural reality.[130]

Applying the above remarks to the concept of communication adopted in this book, it should be pointed out that it is definitely closer to the constitutive view than to the transmissive one, from which, however, it does not abstract, drawing on some of its assumptions.[131]

---

126 The origins of the transmission approach are considered to be Wiener's information theory and the creation of the so-called transmission models of Shannon (1948) and Shannon and Weaver (1964), W. Mich, *Prolegomena do historii komunikacji [Prolegomena to the history of communication]*, Vol. 1: *O komunikacji [About communication]*, Lublin 2014, p. 38.

127 E. Kulczycki, *Teoretyzowanie...*, op. cit., p. 36.

128 Ibidem, p. 31.

129 Ibidem.

130 Ibidem, p. 36.

131 Sperber and Wilson indicate that there are two models (approaches) of communication: coded and inferential. In doing so, they point out that "[t]he code model and the inferential model are not incompatible; they can be combined in various ways. The work of pragmatists, philosophers of language and psycholinguists over the past twenty years has shown that verbal communication involves both coding and inferential processes" (D. Sperber, D. Wilson, *Relevance...*, op. cit., p. 3), and "[a] gainst these reductionist views, we maintain that communication can be achieved in ways which are as different from one another as walking is from plane flight. In particular, communication can be achieved by coding and decoding messages, and it can be achieved by providing evidence for an intended inference. The code model and the inferential model are each adequate to a different mode of communication; hence upgrading either to the status of a general theory of communication is a mistake. Both coded communication and inferential communication are subject to general constraints which apply to all forms of information processing, but these are too general to constitute a theory of communication either" (ibidem).

The fact that the proposal adopted in this monograph to understand communication and other elements related to the process falls rather within the constitutive view is indicated primarily by: (1) the recognition of communication as a socio-cultural, symbolic and intentional process; (2) the assumption that communication does not have an exclusively informational function, and therefore it is not justified to reduce the process of communication to the process of information transfer; (3) the adoption of a pragmatic understanding of the term "meaning of a word/expression" in a given language as the way in which a given word/expression is used by a group of people,[132] the social creation of meaning; (4) the recognition that the interpretation of a particular communication act is influenced by many factors related to the situation in which the communication process takes place; (5) the acceptance that the process of communication, although intentional, but not entirely predictable and controllable – can produce effects that the participants in communication did not take into account.

On the other hand, it seems that the transmission approach is to some extent related to the recognition (in this monograph) of the process nature of communication. However, it should be borne in mind that this processuality is related to the dynamism caused by the adoption of the category of communication act, which in turn is firmly rooted in the assumption of the socio-cultural nature of communication. On the other hand, an obvious reference to the transmission approach is the adoption of the categories of sender and recipient (including the addressee) in the communication process, and the directionality of communication. The aspects of the communication process indicated in the previous sentence will be further discussed in relation to the model of communication process.

1.2.1.6. Model of the communication process

Specific to the communication science is the use of models of the communication process. A considerable number of publications in this field review a greater or lesser number of exemplary models – transmission (in various variants), semiotic, orchestral and others. In linguistics, models of communication also have been formulated, including the two best-known and repeatedly reproduced models – those of Karl Bühler and Roman Jakobson.[133]

As Tomasz Goban-Klas points out, such theoretical models are a simplified (sometimes extremely simplified) picture of the reality under study, because "there is no model that faithfully represents the communication process, just as there

---

132 K. Ajdukiewicz, *Język i poznanie [Language and cognition]*, Warszawa 1960, Vol. 1, p. 149 et seq., Z. Ziembiński, *Logika...*, op. cit., p. 16.

133 R. Grzegorczykowa, *Wstęp...*, op. cit., p. 46–49; K. Bühler, *Theory of Language: The Representational Function of Language*, John Benjamins 2011, p. 35; R. Jakobson, *W poszukiwaniu...*, op. cit., p. 81

is no map that shows all the elements of the environment (...)".[134] The presented below model of communication is simplified as much as possible, however, in this study such a solution is considered justified. The proposed model is intended to be as operative as possible, as it is intended only to illustrate the various communication processes occurring at the trial and determined by the law, as well as some of their transformations made in the course of taking actual communication acts in the courtroom. Thus, it is desirable that it be as uncomplicated as possible, so it was decided to develop a model that contains only the necessary elements.[135] All other elements that either are part of the communication process or affect this process in various ways have been taken into account by formulating appropriate definitions.

The communication model proposed in the paper is shown in Figure 1.

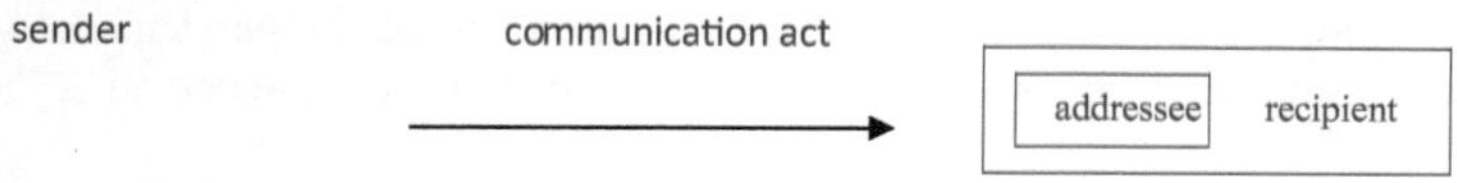

Figure 1. *Model of the communication process*
Source: Own study.

As already emphasized, the use of such a directional model of communication is a reference to the transmission approach. The clear distinction of sender and recipient, including addressee, in the communication process and direction of the communication is closely related to the type of communication that is the subject of the research conducted within the framework of this monograph. Both the trial and the communication process that occurs within it have been largely determined by the law. Thus, more than once the legislator indicates the role that an entity plays in the communication process and the direction in which the process takes place.

In view of the subject of the study, it is considered expedient to distinguish from the class of recipients the class of addressees. In this aspect, reference is made to the proposal of Marian Bugajski, who considers this distinction important for the precision of describing the various communication processes.[136] According to this proposal, the name "addressee" is used to describe that recipient (recipients) to whom the communication act is directed,[137] in other words, it can be said that

134 T. Goban-Klas, *Media...*, op. cit., p. 52–53; cf. C.R. Berger, M.E. Roloff, D.R. Roskos-Ewoldsen, *What Is Communication Science*, [in:] *The Handbook...*, op. cit., p. 10; R.B. Adler, G. Rodman, A. du Pré, *Understanding...*, op. cit., p. 5; R.B. Adler, L.B. Rosenfeld, R.F. Proctor II, *Interplay...*, op. cit., p. 10.

135 Of course, with full knowledge that the actual communication processes are more complex and less obvious than the accepted model would suggest.

136 M. Bugajski, *Język w komunikowaniu [Language in communication]*, Warszawa 2007, p. 450.

137 Ibidem.

it is an intentional recipient – the intention of the sender was that the person (addressee) should interpret the communication act. On the other hand, the term recipient is used to describe a person (group of people) who interprets the sender's communication act regardless of the sender's intention.[138]

In the context of the adopted model, reference should also be made to the placement within the model of the "communication act", i.e. in place of the traditionally occurring "message". The communication act is, of course, undertaken by the sender; its placement within the model "outside" the sender is driven solely by a desire for obtaining clarity of the model. On the other hand, the use of the term "communication act" instead of "message" is an obvious reference to the terminological choices made for the purposes of the study. The point is also not to ontologize this element of the communication process in a sense, suggesting that it exists somewhere "outside", completely independent of the participants in the communication process, as Kulczycki figuratively puts it – packed in a "box of code".[139]

1.2.2. "Trial" – definition, assumptions, and terms associated with a trial

The legislator does not consistently use the term "trial".[140] First, the term "trial" used in the legislative acts sometimes refers to a certain stage of court proceedings, and sometimes to a specific court session at which a trial is to be held. Second, the term "trial" understood as a certain stage of court proceedings differs in content depending on the legislative act in which it is used.

In this study, somewhat contrary to the legislator's choices, but for the sake of precision, the following terms are used to denote:

1. "trial" – a certain stage of court proceedings, which is carried out during court sessions scheduled for the trial;
2. "session scheduled for the trial" – court sessions at which a trial is conducted.[141]

---

138 This distinction is justified insofar as there is no example within the collected research material of a communication process that did not involve at least three actors – there was always at least a presiding judge, a court clerk and an observer present in the courtroom.

139 E. Kulczycki, *Teoretyzowanie...*, op. cit., p. 31. On metaphors capturing communication as a process of "packaging" and "unpacking" thoughts and the inadequacy of these metaphors to describe communication, D. Sperber, D. Wilson, *Relevance...*, op. cit., p. 1. This does not mean, of course, that a communication act cannot be recorded and function as such independently of the sender or addressee.

140 Even within a single legislative act.

141 The term "(court) session scheduled for the trial" was adopted solely for the purpose of the work in connection with the need to achieve precision of argument, which would not be provided by the use of legal terms in the subject matter. If the term

Defined in this way, the term "trial" is, of course, a name that is indeterminate as to content, and therefore vague in scope. Consequently, the second defined term is also not free from above indicated features. However, these obvious flaws will be remedied in the chapter on the genre pattern of a trial, when the various stages of a trial and the procedural acts that begin and end a trial will be indicated in more detail, depending on the variety of court proceedings.

Finally, it should be pointed out that for the sake of abbreviation of the text, all entities participating in the session scheduled for the trial will be referred to as "participants". In addition, in the study the term:

1. "professional participant" – refers to a participant of a court session scheduled for the trial, who plays the role of: the court, public prosecutor, defense counsel, defense counsel's deputy (trainee), professional trial attorney, professional attorney's deputy (trainee) and at the same time is a lawyer;
2. "non-professional participant" – is defined as a participant of a session scheduled for the trial, who does not play any of the roles listed in point 1 and is not a lawyer;
3. "quasi-professional participant" – is defined as a participant of a session scheduled for the trial who does not play any of the roles listed in point 1 and is at the same time a lawyer, as well as a person who plays any of the roles in point 1 and is not a lawyer.

"session" or "court session" is used, in order to achieve shorthand in the text, it will always be synonymous with the term "court session scheduled for the trial".

Chapter 2 Genre pattern of a trial

The systemic approach adopted in the study to the research carried out makes it necessary to consider the analyzed communication process as an element of a larger whole – the trial, so the consideration of the problematic issues will be preceded by a characterization of the trial. The characterization will concern the trial as a communication occurrence, which does not mean that it will be completely devoid of typically legal considerations.

No one needs to be convinced that a trial as a communication occurrence is far different from a common conversation among friends. Thus, since it is already intuitively possible to recognize a schematic nature of the trial, it seems reasonable to start considering its communication aspects precisely by reconstructing the pattern on the basis of which it is realized.

The theoretical and at the same time methodological basis for the characterization of the trial contained in this chapter will be the assumptions and methods developed in linguistic genology, supplemented in particular by knowledge drawn from other fields of linguistics or philosophy of language.

2.1. Preliminary assumptions – genre, genre pattern

The origins of linguistic genology date back to ancient Greece.[142] However, a breakthrough in genre studies came in the 20th century with Mikhail Bakhtin, who referred the concept of genre to all human verbal activity (oral and written texts).[143] The basic term for linguistic genology is "genre". As emphasized in the genological literature, the ontological status of genre is not clearly defined.[144] On the one hand, one speaks of genre as a textual actualization,[145] but more often as a certain abstract model that has its realizations,[146] or a theoretical

142 This is especially true of Aristotle, who distinguished between tragedy, epic and comedy, see Aristotle, *Poetics*, [in:] *The Complete Works of Aristotle*, ed. J. Barnes, Vol. 2, Princeton 1984.

143 M. Bakhtin, *The Problem of Speech Genres*, [in:] *Modern Genre Theory*, ed. D. Duff, New York 2014, p. 83 et seq.

144 M. Wojtak, *Genologia tekstów użytkowych [Genology of applied texts]*, [in:] *Polska genologia lingwistyczna [Polish linguistic genology]*, eds. D. Ostaszewska, R. Cudak, Warszawa 2008, p. 344.

145 On this subject M. Wojtak, *Pragmatyczne aspekty analiz stylistycznych tekstów użytkowych [Pragmatic aspects of stylistic analyses of applied texts]*, [in:] *Stylistyka a pragmatyka [Stylistics vs. pragmatics]*, ed. B. Witosz, Katowice 2001, p. 40.

146 R. Cudak, *Genologiczne pogranicza i ekwiwalencje [Genological borderlands and equivalences]*, [in:] *Gatunki mowy i ich ewolucja [Speech genres and their evolution]*,

construct.[147] As Bożena Witosz points out, genre is most often understood after Bakhtin as a type of text[148] – so it refers to a text.[149] In this chapter, "genre (of a text)" will be understood after Maria Wojtak[150] as an abstract creation, a set of conventions that prompt members of a particular communication community what verbal shape to give to specific interactions.[151]

As Małgorzata Rzeszutko has shown, a trial can be successfully captured and analyzed as a text.[152] Nowadays in text linguistics text is increasingly characterized as a dynamic process – as a communication occurrence.[153] This way of looking at the text is also adopted in this book. In accordance with the achievements of the

---

Vol. 4: *Gatunek a komunikacja społeczna [Genre and social communication]*, ed. D. Ostaszewska, Katowice 2011, p. 62.

147 B. Witosz, *Interakcyjny model relacji gatunku i dyskursu w przestrzeni komunikacyjnej [An interactive model of the relationship between genre and discourse in the communication space]*, [in:] *Gatunki mowy i ich...*, Vol. 4, op. cit., p. 28.

148 B. Witosz, *Tekst i/a gatunek. Jeden czy dwa modele? [Text and/or genre. One or two models?]*, [in:] *Gatunki mowy i ich ewolucja [Speech genres and their evolution]*, Vol. 2: *Tekst a gatunek [Text vs. genre]*, ed. D. Ostaszewska, Katowice 2004, p. 42.

149 Due to the framework of this book, the question of the discussion regarding whether every text, every utterance is a realization of a genre, i.e. whether we always "speak in genres" is omitted.

150 The author clearly indicates that in her conception of genre she refers to the thought of Bakhtin, M. Wojtak, *Wzorce gatunkowe wypowiedzi a realizacje tekstowe [Genre patterns of speech vs. textual realizations]*, [in:] *Gatunki mowy i ich...*, Vol. 2, op. cit., p. 30. "Language is realized in the form of individual concrete utterances (oral and written) by participants in the various areas of human activity. These utterances reflect the specific conditions and goals of each such area not only through their content (thematic) and linguistic style, that is, the selection of the lexical, phraseological, and grammatical resources of the language, but above all through their compositional structure. All three of these aspects – thematic content, style, and compositional structure – are inseparably linked to the whole of the utterance and are equally determined by the specific nature of the particular sphere of communication. Each separate utterance is individual, of course, but each sphere in which language is used develops its own relatively stable types of these utterances. **These we may call speech genres**", M. Bakhtin, *The Problem...*, op. cit., p. 83, emphasized – K.G.

151 M. Wojtak, *Wzorce gatunkowe wypowiedzi...*, op. cit., p. 30.

152 M. Rzeszutko, *Rozprawa...*, op. cit., p. 28.

153 B. Witosz, *Tekstowe i kontekstowe wyznaczniki stylu – próba systematyzacji(?) i problematyzacji [Textual and contextual determinants of style – an attempt at systematization(?) and problematization]*, [in:] *Współczesne analizy dyskursu. Kognitywna analiza dyskursu a inne metody badawcze [Contemporary discourse analysis. Cognitive discourse analysis vs. other research methods]*, eds. M. Krauz, S. Gajda, Rzeszów 2005, p. 32; A. Duszak, *Tekst, dyskurs, komunikacja międzykulturowa [Text, discourse, intercultural communication]*, Warszawa 1998, p. 43–44; M. Rzeszutko, *Rozprawa...*, op. cit., p. 62.

text linguistics and linguistic genology, it was assumed in this study that the text can be both written and oral.

In this monograph, a trial is characterized as a communication occurrence, which in turn is understood as an aggregate, a sequence of individual communication acts.[154] Communication by means of texts is characteristic of linguistic communication, i.e. communication by means of a linguistic code.[155] The communication act, as it is understood in this study, includes not only linguistic acts, but also communication by means of other signs. Thus, the term "communication occurrence" used in this monograph has a broader scope than the equivalent term that functions in the cited publications of linguists. However, it seems that there is no obstacle to apply the category of genre to a trial viewed as a communication occurrence in a broader sense, especially since both approaches are united by considering a communication occurrence from a dynamic, processual perspective.

The use in this study of the category of genre (or, in fact, genre pattern, as discussed below) for the purpose of characterizing a trial as a communication occurrence is not accidental. The assumptions of linguistic genology, especially those concerning genre and the purposes for which genological analyses are undertaken, correspond in an important way with the assumptions made in this study about the communication process, and in particular its location in socio-cultural reality.

Linguists situate the genre of a text somewhere between the system of language and its use, i.e. concrete utterance.[156] Genre functions on the plane of abstraction as a certain model of the text,[157] it is also placed on the level of the norm, which determines "the horizons of recipient expectations and models of creation for senders".[158] Understood in this way, the genre of a text is part of the communication competence of a person (a member of a given community), which is sometimes called genre competence.[159] In turn, considered as a cultural category, it belongs to the area of cultural conventions.[160] On the socio-cultural plane, text genre is

154 Acts are, of course, set in a specific situational context.

155 A. Duszak, *Tekst, dyskurs...*, op. cit., p. 252.

156 J. Labocha, *Odbiorca w tekście i wypowiedzi [Recipient in text and speech]*, [in:] *Styl a tekst. Materiały międzynarodowej konferencji naukowej. Opole 26–28.09.1995 [Style and text. Materials of the international scientific conference. Opole 26–28.09.1995]*, eds. S. Gajda, M. Balowski, Opole 1996, p. 58.

157 B. Witosz, *Tekst i/a gatunek...*, op. cit., p. 42.

158 I. Loewe, *Polska genologia lingwistyczna. Rekonesans [Polish linguistic genology. Reconnaissance]*, "Tekst i Dyskurs" 2008, No. 1, p. 31.

159 Cf. G. Grochowski, *Czy istnieje tekst poza gatunkiem? [Is there a text beyond genre?]*, [in:] *Gatunki mowy...*, Vol. 2, op. cit., p. 24, I. Loewe, *Polska genologia...*, op. cit., p. 31.

160 M. Wojtak, *Genologia tekstów...*, op. cit., p. 341, S. Gajda, *Gatunkowe wzorce wypowiedzi [Genre speech patterns]*, [in:] *Współczesny język polski [Contemporary Polish language]*, ed. J. Bartmiński, Lublin 2001, p. 255. The special relationship between text genres and the cultural system in which they function is emphasized by Bożena Witosz, B. Witosz, *Genologia lingwistyczna. Zarys problematyki [Linguistic Genology. Outline of the problematic]*, Katowice 2005, p. 223.

treated as a correlate of social acts – as a set of norms (genre norms) that organizes the communication activity of people.[161] In relation to the definitions adopted in the previous chapter, genres or genre patterns are part of the situational macro-context, and genre competence is part of the characteristics of the participants in a given communication process, so it is part of the situational micro-context.

From the point of view of this study, it is of particular importance that genology emphasizes the functional aspect of genre, and its connection with certain specific social situations is often considered to determine genre distinctiveness.[162] As a result, nowadays in genology attention is paid to the usefulness of genological categories not so much to create typologies of text genres, but to study and describe the relationship between communication acts and the socio-cultural reality in which they are undertaken.[163]

The last aspect that contributed to the choice of genological concepts as a basis for characterizing the trial is the possibility of using empirical material. Some linguists even postulate the necessity of conducting empirical studies involving specific communication acts and only on the basis of them making legitimate generalizations as to how certain genre norms are formed and at the same time realized.[164] Thus, adopting the category of text genre as a theoretical, and especially methodological category, makes it possible to conduct the analysis of empirical material in two ways. This is because, on the one hand, it is possible to reconstruct from this material the elements of the genre pattern, including those of an usual nature, and on the other hand, to simultaneously study the ways and level of realization of this pattern.

For the characterization of a trial, the concept of genre pattern of a text developed by Maria Wojtak was chosen. By the term "genre pattern" the author understands a certain set of rules that specify the most important levels of organization of the genre scheme, the relations between them and the ways in which each level functions.[165] The genre pattern understood in this way is formed by:

1. specific structure (compositional model) – **structural aspect**;
2. communication entanglements – **pragmatic aspect**;
3. the subject matter and the way it is presented – **cognitive aspect**;
4. stylistic determinants – **stylistic aspect**.[166]

161 G. Grochowski, *Czy istnieje tekst...*, op. cit., p. 25, M. Wojtak, *Genologia tekstów...*, p. 342.
162 M. Wojtak, *Genologia tekstów...*, op. cit., s. 342.
163 G. Grochowski, *Czy istnieje tekst...*, op. cit., p. 25.
164 On this subject I. Loewe, *Polska genologia...*, op. cit., p. 29. As Witosz, among others, emphasizes, genre is not a collection of texts, but a category abstracted from them, B. Witosz, *Interakcyjny model...*, op. cit., p. 28.
165 M. Wojtak, *Wzorce gatunkowe...*, op. cit., p. 30.
166 Ibidem.

The genre pattern with the presented structure should be considered holistically, because as a whole it exists intersubjectively in the communication competence of the members of a given community.[167] The systemic approach is also characteristic of the presented concept. Wojtak emphasizes that the genre pattern as a whole is not a simple sum of components, as the relationships between them are particularly important.[168]

In addition, depending on the fragment of socio-cultural reality in which a given text genre operates, the degree of flexibility of the pattern that defines it and the consequences of genre choices can vary.[169]

The genre pattern of a trial defined in this way forms the basis of the characterization of a trial as a communication occurrence. Before doing so, however, a few additional caveats must be made. First, as has already been made clear, the term "communication occurrence" functions in this monograph in a broad sense, encompassing more than just linguistic communication. Second, the use of the term "genre pattern of a trial" is a bit of a mental shortcut, since *de facto* there will be genre patterns of several genre varieties and sub-varieties of a trial, which co-create a particularly complex genre pattern of a trial. Third, the choice of the individual elements that will be the subject of analysis and description within the four distinguished aspects of the genre pattern and the level of detail of this description will depend on the research needs, including the problem issues.

The process of reproducing the genre pattern of a trial is intended to make it possible: (1) to characterize the trial in model terms; (2) on the basis of empirical material – to identify certain patterns of communication acts determined by the practice; (3) to identify obvious examples of transgressions of the normative pattern of a trial (if, of course, such transgressions occur); (4) to develop analytical categories for the study of problematic issues related to the participation of non-professional participants of court proceedings.

The choice of the concept of genre pattern as the theoretical and methodological basis of characterization of the trial is, of course, only one of the possible choices in this regard. It is justified by the arguments indicated above. Both the trial and the communicative acts performed within it can be successfully analyzed, for example, as speech acts.[170]

---

167 M. Wojtak, *Genologia tekstów...*, op. cit., p. 346.

168 M. Wojtak, *Wzorce gatunkowe...*, op. cit., p. 31.

169 On this subject M. Wojtak, *Genologia tekstów...*, op. cit., pp. 345–347.

170 This also applies to other communication acts, generally speaking, related to the legal realm. See e.g. R. Charnock, *Overruling as a Speech Act: Performativity and Normative Discourse*, "Journal of Pragmatics" 2009, Vol. 41, No. 3; D. Kurzon, *It is Hereby Performed...: Explorations in Legal Speech Acts*. Amsterdam-Philadelphia 1986; A. Trosborg, *Statutes and Contracts: An Analysis of Legal Speech Acts in the English Language of the Law*, "Journal of Pragmatics" 1995, Vol. 23, No. 1; I. Witczak-Plisiecka, *Legal Speech Acts in a Cognitive Linguistic Perspective: Focus on Modality*, "Comparative Legilinguistics. International Journal for Legal Communication" 2009,

2.2. The genre pattern of a trial – preliminary issues

2.2.1. Sources of the pattern and sources of the pattern cognition

The reconstruction of the genre pattern of a trial is not intended to identify a trial as a genre, for a trial is a communication occurrence so specific that its genre belonging is determined by extra-linguistic factors. It was the legislator who decided – defining the basic elements of the genre pattern – what sequence of communication acts is considered a trial and what is not. However, it should be clearly emphasized that the genre pattern of a trial is a mixed pattern – it is shaped not only by the legal norms (such a pattern can be called "normative pattern"),[171] but also, among other things, by the practice (this pattern, in turn, can be called "usual pattern").

Two terms can be distinguished – "source of the pattern" and "source of the pattern cognition". This terminological distinction is important because the issue of sources of pattern cognition and access to them is closely related to the formation through socialization of communication competence, including genre pattern of a trial competence.

The primary sources of the genre pattern of a trial in Polish courts can be considered: (1) legislative acts[172] (e.g., the Constitution of the Republic of Poland and

---

No. 1. I omit here consideration of the relationship between speech acts and speech genres. Undoubtedly, the same types of human communicative activity can be analyzed as speech acts and as speech genres, only the tools for their cognition and description will be different (at least to some extent). As Anna Wierzbicka points out "[f]ollowing Bakhtin, I regard it as essential that complex speech genres and 'speech events' (such as *lecture, letter,* or *gossip)* should be treated, on some level, in the same way as simple speech acts (such as *question, request, promise,* or *warning).* This is not to deny that terminological and conceptual distinctions such as that between 'speech genre,' 'speech event,' and 'speech act' may be useful in certain contexts. But it is also important to stress that despite the tremendous variety of speech genres (using this term in Bakhtin's sense, i.e., as a cover-all term) – in function, structure, and above all in length – they share, in an important sense, the same linguistic nature and require a unified descriptive framework". See A. Wierzbicka, *A Semantic Metalanguage for a Crosscultural Comparison of Speech Acts and Speech Genres,* "Language in Society" 1985, Vol. 14, No. 4, pp. 491–492.

171 The observation made for the study was carried out in 2014 and 2015, and thus acts that were the realization or transgression of the normative pattern were qualified as such from the point of view of the normative pattern current at the time of observation. For this reason, those elements of the normative pattern of a trial that have changed will be clearly indicated in this book.

172 Some of these legislative acts determine the normative pattern of all varieties of trial in Polish courts (such as the Constitution of the Republic of Poland or the Law on the Common Court System).

international agreements,[173] Polish Code of Civil Procedure or Polish Code of Criminal Procedure); (2) practice determining the genre pattern of a trial in those aspects in which it has not been determined by legal norms.[174]

Sources of the pattern cognition are more diverse than sources of the pattern, and, above all, they are diverse in terms of accessibility to different persons. The following sources of the pattern cognition can be distinguished: (1) normative acts (available primarily to professional participants, at least in terms of correct perception of their content[175]); (2) participation in the session scheduled for the trial (due to the openness of the trial – available in principle to all adults, but due to the nature of the legal profession – primarily available to professional and quasi-professional participants); (3) literature, case law, commentaries on normative acts, articles and monographs, texts of court decisions (available primarily to professional and quasi-professional participants); (4) media (press, information available on the Internet, television programs, films and series), information obtained from other people (available to all); (5) legal studies (completed – available only to professional participants, uncompleted – available only to non-professional and

---

173 The legal norms that make up the right to a court (*the right to a fair trial*) are expressed in the provisions of various legislative acts of different scope – Article 45(1) of the Constitution of the Republic of Poland, Article 6(1) of the Convention for the Protection of Human Rights and Fundamental Freedoms, Article 47 second sentence of the Charter of Fundamental Rights of the European Union. The norms contained in Article 6(1) of the Convention set a contemporary international standard for fair court proceedings in criminal cases and in civil cases in the broadest sense. In Polish dogmatics and case law, it is emphasized that the indispensable elements of a fair (just) court proceedings are certain warranties, which most often include the right to a hearing, the right to disclose the motives of the decision (more broadly: to inform) and to ensure the predictability of the proceedings (P. Grzegorczyk, K. Weitz, [in:] *Konstytucja RP [Constitution of the RP]*, Vol. 1: *Komentarz do art. 1–86 [Commentary on Articles 1–86]*, eds. M. Safjan, L. Bosek, 1st edition, Warszawa 2016, Legalis 2017). Of the above warranties, the right to a hearing, which combines a number of entitlements and competences (including to filing motions, making statements, being informed about the course of the proceedings or the position of the opposing party with the opportunity to respond to it), is relatively most often singled out (P. Grzegorczyk, K. Weitz, [in:] *Konstytucja RP...*, op. cit.). Issues related to the right to court and issues variously related to these right (such as procedural justice) have lived to see an extensive literature, which, due to the framework of this study, will not be discussed.

174 **Linguistic norms** should also be considered the source of the pattern, in addition to **other norms of conduct** that regulate the ways in which members of society behave in certain situations, while in this monograph the normative pattern is referred to the pattern determined by the legal norms in force.

175 It is about the ability to understand the texts of legislative acts at the normative level, that is, to reconstruct legal norms.

quasi-professional participants); (6) legal training (available to professional and quasi-professional participants).

The sources of the pattern cognition highlighted in points 1 through 5 were used in the study.

2.2.2. Complexity of the genre pattern of a trial

Even without a thorough genological analysis, it is easy to consider that the trial is a complex genre. This, of course, also applies to trials conducted in courts in non-Polish (and even Continental) legal systems. As an example, we can indicate the characterization of (criminal) jury trials conducted in courts in the UK as a complex genre. As Chris Heffer points out "[c]ontemporary jury trial remains a product of these three elements: the procedural, the adversarial and the adjudicative. From a discoursal point of view, these elements can be seen as three different perspectives that co-exist throughout the trial. Each of them, though, is foregrounded at certain points of the trial so as to form three different trial phases. The key genres associated with each of these phases are controlled discoursally by a given courtroom participant, who will tend also to have a certain type of orientation to that discourse".[176]

Using the terminology proposed by Wojtak, we can say that it is at the same time a peculiar phenomenon – the genre in the form of a collection.[177] In this

---

176 Ch. Heffer, *The Language of Jury Trial: A Corpus-Aided Analysis of Legal-Lay Discourse*, Palgrave Macmillan 2005, p. 66. "The short **procedural** phase is concerned with selecting the jury and setting their task, and it is controlled discoursally (with the judge's supervision) by the court clerks. The clerks are both severely constrained in their discourse options and severely constraining in the options they make available to their addressees, so their orientation to discourse might be described as **ritualistic**. The long **adversarial** phase is concerned with presenting the jury with the evidence in the case, and is controlled discoursally (again with the judge's supervision) by counsel for the prosecution and defence. In delivering their opening and closing speeches and conducting witness examinations, counsel are primarily engaged in argumentation. Though constrained in their discourse options, they have considerable room for manoeuvre and the choices they make might influence the outcome of the trial. This makes their dominant orientation to discourse a **strategic** one. Finally, the **adjudicative** phase is concerned with setting the jury their precise decision-making task (summing-up), the jury's decision-making (deliberation, resulting in a verdict), and (if required) sentencing the defendant. Overall, it is controlled discoursally by the judge, though the jury naturally control their deliberation and the verdict is formally taken by the court clerk. Both judge and jury have to weigh both sides of the verbal arguments and judges have to pay careful attention to achieving balance in their summings-up, so their dominant orientation to discourse will tend to be **deliberative**". See ibidem, pp. 66–67.

177 M. Wojtak, *Osobliwe byty gatunkowe i tekstowe w ich uwikłaniach komunikacyjnych [Peculiar genre and textual beings in their communication entanglements]*, [in:] *Gatunki mowy...*, Vol. 4, op. cit., p. 44 et seq.

researcher's conception, a genre in the form of collection[178] is a distinct genological phenomenon consisting of a variety of permanently co-occurring genres, which has a structural as well as functional frame.[179] Communication acts and occurrences (i.e., aggregates of communication acts) that take place at the trial can also be considered as genres. Depending on the genre variety of a trial, the presentation of charges, examination of a witness, questioning of a party or announcement of a court decision, for example, could be considered separate genres whose patterns are defined by different genre patterns. On the one hand, the genological characterization of these communication occurrences is part of the characterization of the trial, while on the other hand, it is difficult to imagine an exhaustive genological analysis of any of the aforementioned communication occurrences (e.g., examination of a witness) without a genological characterization of the trial as a whole. This is precisely because of the existence of a structural and functional frame. Within the formed structure, specific communication acts and occurrences form complex aggregates – often referred to by a common name, e.g., voices of the parties, and sequential structure – related to the sequence of acts taken, e.g., examination of a witness, which is preceded by the act of presenting charges. In addition, individual communication occurrences, while pursuing particularistic goals, serve to achieve the global goal of the trial, which in turn is expected to lead to the realization of the task posed to the entire court proceedings.

The significant level of petrification[180] of the genre pattern of a trial, which is the result of the legislator's decisions, is a factor that significantly limits another type of genre complexity, which arises as a result of contamination, i.e., mixing of genres,[181] and this is contamination through the practice of using specific genres. Despite the fact that some of the genres occurring in the trial show considerable similarity, such as the examination of a witness and the examination of a party, it is not possible for these genres to mix, since their genre distinctiveness is determined by the law. The "rigidity" of the genre pattern of a trial in this regard is a consequence of the conventionalization of the communication acts and occurrences occurring within it at a level higher than the level of the speech act (more on the levels of conventionalization in Sections from 2.3.2.14 to 2.3.2.18).

178 A genre in the form of collection should be distinguished from a collection of genres, which lacks, among other things, a structural finality and a delimiting frame. An example of a genre collection is the co-occurring resume and cover letter, ibidem, pp. 46–47.

179 Ibidem, p. 45.

180 In this regard, it should be borne in mind that the legislator can also decide on the variability of the genre pattern of a trial.

181 K. Wyrwas, *Skarga czy podanie? Kontaminacja wzorców tekstowych w strukturze adaptacyjnej gatunku mowy [Complaint or application? Contamination of textual patterns in the adaptive structure of the speech genre]*, [in:]: *Stylistyka...*, op. cit., p. 389 et seq.

Given the differences in the way the legal norms have determined the trial conducted in different court proceedings (in Polish courts), it is not possible to reproduce a uniform genre pattern of a trial for all the varieties of a trial. The genre pattern of a trial as such can only be spoken of with full awareness of the diversity outlined above. The genre pattern of the trial reproduced in this study takes this diversity into account, but with some important caveats. Due to the significant number of legislative acts determining the normative pattern of a trial, it was decided to exclude some acts or parts of them (either due to the minimal number of cases conducted under the given law, or due to the excessive complexity of the court procedure, in which the examination of the case at trial was an exception).

Taking into account the above caveats, there are two **basic genre varieties of trial**:[182]

1. trial in civil proceedings (civil trial);
2. trial (main trial – in legal terminology) in criminal proceedings (criminal trial).

The basis for distinguishing the above-mentioned varieties of trial is the fundamental source of their pattern, in the case of a civil trial – the Polish Code of Civil Procedure, while with regard to a criminal trial – the Polish Code of Criminal Procedure. However, the basic nature of the indicated genre varieties of trial is determined by the fact that the distinguished varieties of trial were not formed by references to other legislative acts.[183]

In turn, "derivative varieties" are called in this study those genre varieties of a trial, the patterns of which have been determined by the legal norms expressed in legislative acts other than the Polish Code of Civil Procedure and the Polish Code of Criminal Procedure, but these acts, to the extent that they regulate a trial, refer to the provisions of the indicated codes. Derived varieties include: (1) the trial in misdemeanor proceedings; (2) the trial in penal fiscal proceedings; and (3) the trial in the proceedings in juvenile cases.

In addition, there are sub-varieties of trial (in Polish courts) in both basic and derivative varieties, such as civil trial in contentious and non-contentious proceedings.

The issue of varieties and sub-varieties of a trial is closely as well as variously related to the so-called canonical[184] and

182 All considerations in this chapter, primarily the divisions made, apply to the trial of court proceedings in the first instance.

183 This is not to say that these acts do not contain legal provisions referring to other normative acts. However, the impact of these references on the way the normative patterns of the distinguished varieties of trial are formed is insignificant.

184 **Canonical pattern** – one that determines the identity of the genre and includes a certain range of the most enduring structural, pragmatic and stylistic determinants, M. Wojtak, *Gatunki prasowe [Press genres]*, Lublin 2004, p. 18.

alternation[185] patterns of a trial. In this study, the canonical patterns of the trial are considered:

1. the genre pattern of a civil trial in contentious proceedings;
2. the genre pattern of a criminal trial in ordinary proceedings.

The recognition of the two above-mentioned genre patterns as canonical was determined by the fact that they constitute a set of the most enduring structural, pragmatic and stylistic determinants of a trial, and that they were not formed through transformations of other genre patterns of a trial's varieties or sub-varieties.

Both the genre pattern of a civil trial in contentious proceedings and the genre pattern of a criminal trial in ordinary proceedings are the basis for the formation of alternate patterns of a trial, such as the pattern of a civil trial in non-contentious proceedings.

Finally, it is worth adding that court proceedings conducted before Polish courts have both adversarial and inquisitorial characteristics. The distribution of the various elements characteristic of the two models indicated above depends on the variety of proceedings. In civil (contentious) proceedings, it will be possible to identify more adversarial elements,[186] and in criminal proceedings more inquisitorial elements. However, already at the level of the normative pattern, the trial conducted before Polish courts deviates in many aspects from the typically adversarial pattern of the trial conducted in the courts of the common law system. This is evident, for example, in the way witnesses are examined.[187]

---

185 **Alternation pattern** – one that is formed by transforming the individual components of the canonical pattern, ibidem.

186 With the exception of civil non-contentious proceedings, which by definition are not adversarial. However, this does not mean that the cases heard within their framework are not sometimes contentious (e.g., cases on the division of property of former spouses).

187 This was shown in particular by Bednarek, see G.A. Bednarek, *Polish vs. American...*, op. cit. This also applies to other European courts – "Anglo-American observers of the [Continental] court scene are regularly struck by the rarity and the subdued nature of challenges to the witnesses' credibility. If such a challenge occurs, it [...] seldom escalates into a general attack on his character or reputation for truthfulness. With apparent insouciance, Continental courts freely rely on uninterrupted narrative accounts – the testimonial yield of relatively mild, unpenetrating interrogation (...)", M.R. Damaška, *Evidence law adrift*, Yale 1997, pp. 80–81 (quotation in S. Sønderberg Mortensen, J. Mortensen, *Epistemic Stance in Courtroom Interaction*, [in:] *Pragmatics and Law: Practical and Theoretical Perspectives*, eds. F. Poggi, A. Capone, Cham 2017, p. 404). Broadly on this topic in the context of the Danish justice system and not only, ibidem, p. 403 et seq.

2.3. Reconstructing the genre pattern of a trial

As previously announced, the genre pattern of a trial in Polish courts will be reconstructed taking into account the proposal of Maria Wojtak, who distinguishes four aspects of the genre pattern. Before the presentation of the various aspects, however, it is necessary to point out several important issues:

1. the reproduced genre pattern of a trial applies only to a court proceedings conducted in the first-instance proceedings;
2. the collected empirical material will be used to reconstruct the pattern, which will make it possible to distinguish those elements of the pattern that have been determined by the law from those that are determined by the practice, and furthermore to illustrate the issues under discussion with examples of communication acts;
3. according to the definition of genre pattern adopted in this study, attention will be focused on the most important levels and elements of the genre pattern of a trial;
4. individual elements of the pattern will be discussed in relation to the particular variety or sub-variety of trial in which they occur, but phenomena that can be considered characteristic of all the varieties or sub-varieties of trial (or at least some of them) will be discussed without appropriate relativization.

2.3.1. Structural aspect

The reconstruction of the compositional structure of the trial in Polish courts, and for each of its varieties or sub-varieties, in principle, does not pose many difficulties. The legislator has clearly defined in the legislative acts both the delimitation framework of varieties or sub-varieties of trial, as well as its main stages, the diagrams of which will be presented below. At the same time, this determines the content of the term "trial" defined in the previous chapter.

Based on the legislative acts listed in Section 2.2.1, four compositional schemes can be reconstructed. Figure 2 illustrates the structure of a civil trial (primarily in contentious proceedings).

statements of the parties	evidentiary proceedings	voices of the parties	*decision ending the proceedings*[*]
calling the case			closing the trial

Figure 2. *Compositional structure of the trial, part I*

[*] In civil and other court proceedings conducted in accordance with the norms expressed in the Polish Code of Civil Procedure, the announcement of the decision ending the proceedings, the statement of the essential reasons for the decision or the announcement of the justification of the decision and the possible instructions take place after the closing of a trial. This fact is emphasized in the figure using italics. Despite the fact that these acts take place after the closing of a trial, they are a necessary consequence of the acts taken at the trial, so it is considered necessary and fully justified in this study to include these acts within the presented compositional structure of the trial.

Source: Own study.

Figure 3 shows a diagram of a civil trial in non-contentious proceedings.

statements of the applicant or participant(s)	evidentiary proceedings	voice of the applicant or participant(s)	*decision ending the proceedings*
calling the case			closing the trial

Figure 3. *Compositional structure of the trial, part II*

Source: Own study.

Figure 4 illustrates the structure of a criminal trial.

preliminary acts	brief presentation of the charges	explanations	further evidentiary acts	voices of the parties	decision ending the proceedings
calling the case				closing the judicial process	

Figure 4. *Compositional structure of the trial, part III*

Source: Own study.

In the presented diagrams of the compositional structure of the trial, and in fact the various compositional structures of the varieties and sub-varieties of the trial, the **maximum structure** is presented, that is, a structure that includes all the main stages of the trial and does not take into account the exceptions provided for in the procedural norms. The maximum compositional structure of the trial is subject to certain modifications not only by possible infringement of the norms that form the normative pattern, but also the normative pattern provides for certain possibilities to modify the compositional structure of the trial. The modification may be in particular a consequence of:

1. the non-attendance of participants in court proceedings at the court session scheduled for the trial in situations where the court has authorization to conduct the trial in their absence;
2. the performance by authorized participants of the proceedings of procedural acts specified in the norms, which can lead to:
   (a) limitations of the trial in such a way that a certain stage of the trial or a specific part of it is omitted,
   (b) the termination of court proceedings by issuing a decision ending the proceeding.

Each of the distinguished compositional structures of the varieties and sub-varieties of trial may be reduced due to the various factors indicated above. The **minimum compositional structures** of the two basic varieties of trial: criminal in ordinary criminal proceedings[188] and civil in contentious proceedings[189], are presented below.

preliminary acts	decision ending the proceedings
calling the case	

Figure 5. *The minimum compositional structure of a trial in ordinary criminal proceedings*
Source: Own study.

statements of the parties	*decision ending the proceedings*
calling the case	closing the trial

Figure 6. *The minimum compositional structure of a trial in in contentious civil proceedings*
Source: Own study.

Presented in Figures 5 and 6, the minimal structures of the two basic varieties of trial take into account the necessary compositional elements of both these two varieties, as well as any other variety and sub-variety of trial highlighted in this study.

188 In particular, such a maximally reduced structure will have a trial in criminal proceedings in which the public prosecutor withdraws the indictment at the main trial before the opening of the judicial proceedings, and the result will be discontinuance of the proceedings.

189 The maximum reduction in the compositional structure of a civil trial in contentious proceedings will be led, for example, by the effective withdrawal of the claim before the opening of evidentiary proceedings.

First, for the existence of a trial, of course, an initiating moment is necessary. Second, regardless of whether the participants in the court proceedings appear at the court session scheduled for the trial, acts will be taken by the court as part of the first stage (which is appropriately referred to here as "preliminary acts", "statements of the parties", "statements of the applicant or participants"), even if these are only so-called technical acts. Thirdly, each court proceedings ends with a decision – either on the merits of the case or on the discontinuance of the proceedings without a substantive consideration of the case.

According to the pattern determined by the procedural legislative acts, the existence of these three elements determines the existence of a trial. The clear distinction within the structure of the trial of its main stages makes it possible to equally clearly indicate the boundaries between them, the outer limits of the first and last stages being, of course, the boundaries of the trial.

The delimitation of the trial and within the trial has different functions at different levels of conventionalization. Firstly, the functions of these boundaries can be relativized to that level of conventionalization at which the trial is considered as a complex communication occurrence. In this context, the possibility of delimiting the boundaries of the trial by indicating clear initial and final signals is particularly important, first of all, from the point of view of text linguistics, since in some linguistic concepts the comprehensiveness of the text is a defining element of the term "text".[190] The clear delimitation of compositional segments is also variously associated with the coherence of the text, especially with semantic, thematic coherence.

Secondly, the boundaries of the various stages of the trial perform a particularly important function at this level of conventionalization, at which certain procedural acts are performed. The systemic view of the trial, which is adopted in this study, makes it necessary to consider the stages of the trial as elements of a coherent whole. In this view, both the main stages of the trial distinguished in this monograph, as well as their compact fragments, and, moreover, the individual procedural acts form a mereological structure, that is, a certain collection in collective terms (aggregate).[191]

---

190 E.g. R. de Beaugrande, W. Dressler, *Introduction to Text Linguistics*, Longman 1981; M.R. Mayenowa, *Poetyka teoretyczna. Zagadnienia języka [Theoretical poetics. Issues of language]*, Wrocław 2000, p. 246 et seq.

191 Mereology, speaking in very general terms, is understood as a theory of collections in the collective meaning, possibly as a theory of the relation of parts to the whole. The term "mereology" or "mereological structure" is used in legal theory in the context of conventional acts, which is why it appears in this monograph. The term "mereology" was introduced by the Polish logician Stanisław Leśniewski to describe his theory of collective sets. However, the term has become so much more widespread in the literature that it is now also used to describe other theories of collective collections, cf. A. Pietruszczak, *Podstawy teorii części [Fundamentals of parts theory]*, Toruń 2013, pp. 13–15 and 17–30. The use of the term, it seems, therefore requires at least an indication of whether its adoption entails recognition of all axioms of Leśniewski's mereology, or whether it is used as a name for collective set theory in general. In this book, the term is used in the second of the meanings indicated above.

There are various relationships between the elements of this collection. Particularly important is the relationship between the various stages of the trial and the procedural acts undertaken by the participants of court proceedings. Many times, the rules set forth in the procedural legislative acts for the performance of given procedural acts (and thus conventional acts) indicate at what stage or by which moment of the trial a given act should be taken.[192]

Another issue that will be briefly discussed in the context of the structural aspect of the genre pattern of a trial is the issue of explicit information (or only indirect signaling[193]) by the presiding judge about the moments of transition between the different stages of a trial. Such information can take the following form, e.g. **Presiding judge [hereinafter "P"]:** *I open the judicial process.*[194]; **P:** *Before closing a trial, I give the floor to Mr. Counsel*; **P:** *Please listen to the reason for our meeting* [signaling that a motion for punishment will be read]; **P:** *I order evidentiary proceedings*; **P:** *I open the judicial process, I give the floor to the Prosecutor*; **P:** *I open the trial of XY against YX for payment.*

In Poland procedural norms do not assign to either the court or the presiding judge the duty to inform the participants of the beginning or end of the various stages of the trial. The only duty assigned to the presiding judge by the procedural norms in connection with the delimitation of the compositional segments of the trial is, respectively – the duty to close a trial or to close a judicial process. Undoubtedly, a fairly uniform procedural practice has been formed in this regard, according to which the presiding judge formulates, in the presence of the participants in the session scheduled for the trial, a performative statement, which

---

192 This refers to such situations in which the taking of a certain procedural act at a certain time or up to a certain point in the trial is a structural rule for its performance, but one that formalizes rather than conventionalizes (on the rules of conventionalizing and formalizing more extensively in Section 2.3.2.15). On the temporal aspect of procedural acts in criminal proceedings, B. Janusz-Pohl, *Formalizacja i konwencjonalizacja jako instrumenty analizy czynności karnoprocesowych w prawie polskim [Formalization and conventionalization as instruments of analysis of acts in criminal proceedings in Polish law]*, Poznań 2017, p. 315 et seq.; eadem, *Definitions and Typologies of Acts in Criminal Proceedings. Perspective of Conventionalisation and Formalisation*, Poznań 2017, p. 122 et seq.

193 The signal to proceed to the next stage of the trial will be, for example, to give the floor to the public prosecutor to present the accusations of the defendant (in penal case), which is the signal to begin the judicial process. Such a statement by the presiding judge insofar as it has an informative function in terms of proceeding to the next stage of the trial, provided that the recipient is particularly competent to know the compositional structure of the trial and the procedural acts involved.

194 In translating oral speech acts into written form, punctuation marks were added, paralinguistic sounds were omitted, some data were replaced with variables, while addressable phrases were distinguished by the use of a capital first letter. In addition, the written transcript corresponds to the oral speech act.

at the same time has an informative function, e.g. **P:** *The presiding judge, deeming the case sufficiently clarified, closes the trial*; **P:** *In that case, I close the trial*; **P:** *And that's it, I close the judicial process*; **P:** *I close the judicial process and give the floor to the prosecution.*

In addition, the analysis of the collected research material made it possible to identify the practice related to informing the parties (quasi-parties) present in the courtroom of the intention to close a trial or a judicial process, e.g. **P:** *The court is going to close a trial. Before closing the trial, would any of you like to request something or speak?*; **P:** *The presiding judge would like to close a trial, does any party still want to speak?*

Closing a trial or judicial process is the conclusion of the substantive examination of the case, its purpose is to learn the main fact, which in turn is to provide the factual basis for the final decision.

A special signal of the closing of the judicial process is the question that the presiding judge is obliged to ask the parties according to the Polish Code of Criminal Procedure – Do the parties request that the evidentiary proceedings be supplemented? Only after receiving a negative answer the presiding judge closes the judicial process. However, although the norm precisely defining this act, in principle, determines the wording of this question, its actual verbal shape sometimes varies, such as **P:** *Are there any more motions to adduce evidence?*; **P:** *Do the parties want to supplement the evidence?*

The final issue addressed in the section dealing with the structural aspect of the genre pattern of a trial is the relationship of the various stages of a trial to the individual court sessions scheduled for the trial.

The appropriate model for this relationship is set by the law. According to the procedural legal norms, either the court or the presiding judge, respectively, should strive for a decision at the first court session scheduled for the trial. However, the normative pattern provides for significant exceptions in this regard.

In the collected research material, both such court sessions where a full trial was conducted with the announcement of the decision ending the proceedings,[195] and those where a fragment of a stage (e.g., examination of the parties), one stage (e.g., preliminary acts), one stage and a fragment of another stage (e.g., statements of the parties and a fragment of the evidentiary proceedings) were identified.

All of the ways of conducting the trial at the various court sessions scheduled for the trial highlighted above are consistent with the normative pattern.

---

195 In the collected research material, there are **31 court sessions** in which a full trial was realized (11 – in family cases; 8 – in social security cases; 6 – in civil cases in non-contentious proceedings, only in inheritance acquisition proceedings; 3 – in misdemeanor cases; 2 – in criminal cases; 1 – in juvenile cases).

2.3.2. Pragmatic aspect

According to the genre pattern conception proposed by Maria Wojtak, within the framework of the pragmatic aspect, the so-called communication entanglements, that is, in particular, the image of the sender and the recipient, the illocutionary potential (the purpose of the communication act) and the so-called life context of the genre should be discussed, to use the terminology of the researcher.[196]

The description of the pragmatic aspect of the genre pattern of a trial will be done in two stages. The first stage will cover those issues that can be framed as a situational micro-context, which is primarily issues related to the time and place of the communication acts, the participants in the communication process (including the social and interactional roles of the participants, the relationships between them, their knowledge and communication competence), and the directness or contentious nature of the communication. Since the elements of the situational context will be described as elements of the genre pattern of a trial, it will be about the type of communication situation, rather than the specific situation in which an individual communication act is undertaken.

In the second stage, attention will be paid to the specific communication acts (and their aggregates) undertaken by the participants of court proceedings. Particular attention will be paid to their conventionalization and formalization.

The distinction of the two stages discussed above is purely technical – organizing the flow of the argument. They, of course, interpenetrate each other, creating specific relationships between the various elements of the situational micro-context and the communication acts undertaken within it – some of these relationships will also be displayed.

2.3.2.1. Elements of situational micro-context – time

The issue of time in the context of a trial can be considered using various references. First, in the context of the court's obligation to examine of the case without unjustified delay (or within a reasonable time).[197] In this aspect, in Poland, the court is obliged to counteract the lengthiness of the entire proceedings, and therefore also the lengthiness that may arise during the consideration of the case at the trial. A special duty in this regard is set by legal norms, instructing either the court or the presiding judge to strive for resolution at the first court session scheduled for the trial, but this is not a non-exclusive duty (thanks to the institution of pause in the trial and adjournment of the trial). The time limitation relating to the entire court proceedings, including the trial as part of it, is not explicitly specified. The limiting moment can be considered that moment when it will be justified to qualify the proceedings as protracted.[198]

196 M. Wojtak, *Wzorce gatunkowe...*, op. cit., p. 30.

197 Cf. for example, Article 6(1) of the Convention for the Protection of Human Rights and Fundamental Freedoms.

198 It is worth adding that the term "protraction of proceedings" – defined by the Polish legislator as a situation where the proceedings in a case last longer than necessary

Secondly, the issue of time, or in principle time limits, is best seen in the context of sessions scheduled of the trial. Just as the need for examination of the case without unjustified delay sets a more or less vague boundary for the conduct of proceedings, including a trial, the time limits of a session scheduled for the trial are, in principle, strictly defined and related to the case list in a given court session day. In addition, the scheduling of certain procedural acts (such as the examination of witnesses) within a specific session results in internal time limits. The way of scheduling procedural acts within the session scheduled for the trial is shaped by the practice of individual judges. However, it is not always possible to carry out all the planned procedural acts precisely because the time limit provided for carrying out a particular act is exceeded. Then, in particular, it becomes necessary for the so-called release of witnesses, e.g. **P:** *Today the court will certainly not examine all of you, so I will release some of you in a moment and you will receive summons for the next date* (...). *I apologize to you very much, unfortunately, it happened so.*

Both of the above-discussed aspects related to time create time pressures that the judge preparing the trial must face. In this aspect, (limited) time is a strong functional determinant of the acts undertaken at the trial, as judges themselves admit.[199]

Thirdly, the issue of time is related to the mereological structure, which is a trial recognized as a sequence of procedural acts that are always distributed in time.

Furthermore, it is noted that "[courtroom] interaction is a temporally dense achievement. Past, present, and future realities are socially organized in several unique ways. In order to disclose and examine obvious as well as more ambiguous features of the *past* involving an alleged criminal activity, lawyers interrogate and witnesses testify to produce the bulk of *present* communication. The rendering of *future* jury verdicts and sentencing decisions by the court, each occurring in its present allotted time within the sequence of trial proceedings, nevertheless reflect how visions were constructed and conclusions were drawn from observed courtroom interactional attempts to reconstruct the reality of past, typically unobserved, settings and circumstances"[200]. The issue of "time travel" at the trial is closely related to the cognition of facts in court proceedings, so it will still be discussed in the context of the cognitive aspect of the genre pattern of a trial.

---

for the explanations of those factual and legal circumstances that are important for the resolution of the case, or longer than necessary for the settlement of an enforcement proceedings or any other case concerning the execution of a court case – is clearly vague.

199 J. Winczorek, P. Maranowski, *Komunikacja w sądach...*, op. cit., pp. 5 and 9. For this reason, some activities are considered by judges to be too time-consuming, such as soliciting settlements or giving instructions, ibidem, Appendix 1, Figure 7.

200 W.A. Beach, *Temporal Density in Courtroom Interaction: Constraints on the Recovery of Past Events at Past Events in Legal Discourse*, "Communication Monographs" 1985, Vol. 52, No. 1, p. 1.

2.3.2.2. *Elements of situational micro-context – place*

The trial is held before the court, which, as the subject matter and local jurisdiction, conducts the proceedings. In Poland the principles are that the court session scheduled for the trial is held in the court building, in the courtroom, and all participants in this session are present in the same place (unity of place). However, the legal provisions stipulate certain exceptions in this regard.[201]

Procedural legal norms further stipulate that, under certain circumstances, procedural acts are performed outside the courtroom. This applies in particular to the examination of victims of certain crimes who are under the age of 15 or the hearing of minors in cases involving them. It should also be borne in mind that an unspecified number of recipients may participate in a court session scheduled for the trial in a mediated manner whenever its proceedings are broadcast by the mass media.

In elaborating on the issue of the courtroom as an essential venue for conducting the trial, three issues will be addressed:

1. the normative pattern that determines the organization of the courtroom;
2. the usual pattern;
3. the symbolism of the courtroom.

Addressing the first issue, it should be pointed out that the normative standard for the organization of the courtroom in Polish courts is quite modest. The equipment of the courtroom is determined by legal norms, which prescribe that (as far as possible) the room in which the court session is to be held should be equipped with a judge's table and a national emblem.[202] Another norm, which relates to the organization of the space in the courtroom, prescribes that, as far as possible, the public should be separated from the part where the judge's table is located, as well as places for those participating at the trial.[203] The places in the courtroom occupied by individual participants are also normatively specified.

Other elements of the courtroom organization pattern are usual by nature. This applies in particular to the elements of equipment (court furniture), as well as the location of those participants of the session scheduled for the trial who are not mentioned in the legal provisions.

---

201 During the Covid-19 pandemic (starting in 2020), however, conducting an online trial has become the rule.

202 Legal norms also mandate that the courtroom be equipped with the technical equipment needed, especially for the so-called electronic minutes or online trial.

203 In no courtroom where observations were made for study purposes was the audience separated from the rest of the participants. Nor was there a special criminal dock (open, partly o completely surrounded by glass or metal bars) in any of the courtrooms. It is worth adding that preliminary experimental studies (on jury trials) suggest that such a location of the defendant may favor being found guilty, see M. Rossner, D. Tait, B. McKimmie, R. Sarre, *The Dock on Trial: Courtroom Design and the Presumption of Innocence*, "Journal of Law and Society" 2017, Vol. 44, No. 3.

The location of the benches of the parties to the proceedings perpendicular to the judge's table should be considered a rule, although there are exceptions to this rule as well.[204] The courtroom is usually equipped with a gavel.[205]

In contrast, it is difficult to identify any regularity in the size of the rooms in which court sessions are held. In the course of conducting this study, sessions were observed to be held in large courtrooms (several rows of benches for the audience), but much more often in medium-sized courtrooms (several benches for the audience) and in small and very small[206] (one bench for the audience). A certain regularity, although not without exception, applies to the bench allocated for the defendant and his/her defense counsel. In courtrooms adapted for criminal, penal fiscal or misdemeanor proceedings, the defendant's bench is often located behind the defense counsel's bench, resulting in a characteristic positioning of the defense counsel and the defendant in relation to each other.

Figure 7 shows a diagram of the standard layout of the courtroom, along with the location of the participants of the session scheduled for the trial. The diagram has been limited to the normative pattern.[207]

204 The three courtrooms in which the observation was conducted deviated from the indicated regularity, in particular, in two of them the parties' benches were arranged parallel to the judge's table. In all cases, such a different distribution of courtroom equipment from the model was forced by architectural constraints.

205 In the course of conducting observations, not a single situation of gavel use was recorded (which is not to say that there was no disruption of the session). In many courtrooms, the gavel was out of the presiding judge's reach, such as on the edge of the table or on the windowsill.

206 In very small courtrooms, court furniture sometimes almost touched each other. During the course of the study, there were several occasions when the observer had to sit in the bench for a party. In addition, due to the insufficient number of seats, in one case two persons appearing as a party were forced to stand during the session. It is worth noting in this context that the size of the courtroom may limit the audience's access, and consequently may affect the actual implementation of the principles of open trials, R. Koper, *Jawność rozprawy głównej a ochrona prawa do prywatności w procesie karnym [Publicity of the main trial and the protection of the right to privacy in the criminal process]*, Warszawa 2010, p. 247.

207 Cf. the organizational chart of the courtroom in courts in the UK (Crown Court), Ch. Heffer, *The Language of Jury Trial...*, op. cit., p. 37.

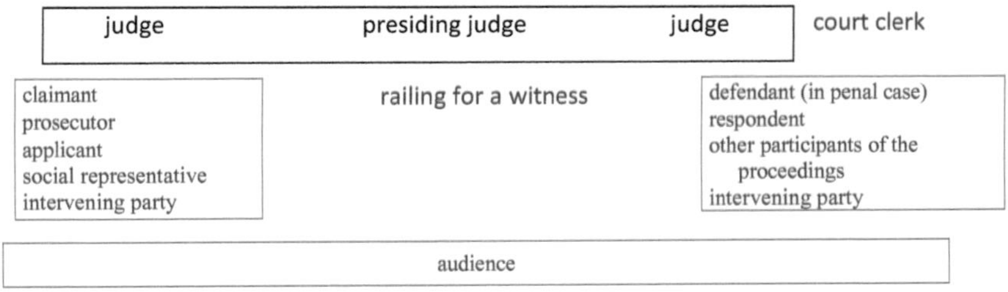

Figure 7. *Organization of the courtroom*
Source: Own study.

The location of the other participants is determined by practice – participants acting as an active party or variously associated with that party will be seated on the right side of the judge's table, while those acting as or associated with a passive party will be seated on the left side of the judge's table. Witnesses who have given a testimony and the victim sit in the bench for the audience.

The symbolic dimension of the organization of the courtroom, on the other hand, seems to be strongly rooted in culture.[208] Numerous publications in both legal studies and humanities repeatedly emphasize the symbolic nature of certain elements of the organization and equipment of the courtroom, as well as the historical conditions that accompany this aspect of the shaping of justice system. Given that some elements of courtroom symbolism are present in various areas of culture (including literature or film), it can be assumed that a certain awareness of this symbolism in society exists. The elements of the courtroom equipment, together with the appropriate official attire of the professional participants, serve, to use Erving Goffman's terminology, to dramatize the acts being performed, and consequently lead to the creation of a characteristic facade that becomes part of social consciousness.[209] In view of the above, it seems fully justified to consider this symbolic dimension as part of the genre pattern of a trial.

208 The semiotic status of courtroom symbolism is not clear, as it may have formed both as a sign and as a symptom. However, it seems that due to their strong (and sometimes centuries-old) cultural roots, those elements of the courtroom equipment that are considered symbolic in this study are now used with awareness of their meaning (they are sign-like in nature).

209 E. Goffman, *The Presentation of Self in Everyday Life*, New York 1986. See also K. Zeidler, *Aesthetics of Law*, Gdańsk-Warszawa 2020, p. 140 et seq.

In order to highlight the symbolic dimension of the courtroom,[210] the metaphor of a stage is sometimes used,[211] on which the various "actors" are arranged. On this "stage" particularly symbolic are: (1) the location of the court and the presiding judge in relation to the other participants of the court session; (2) the location of the parties to the proceedings in relation to each other and the court; (3) the presence of the national emblem in the courtroom.

With regard to the first issue, the organization of the courtroom should and does serve to emphasize the importance of the court.[212] The location of the court in the central place of the courtroom and on an elevated platform is considered to be symbolic in emphasizing the importance of the court and, consequently, the decisions it makes.[213] The location of the court behind a large table (judge's table)[214] can be considered equally symbolic – highlighting the momentous position of

---

210 See about courtroom (high-level, middle-level and low-level) "meanings" from the Rapaport's conception point of view M. Stępień, M. Dudek, *The courtroom as a built environment: On the usefulness of Amos Rapoport's theoretical framework*, "Oñati Socio-Legal Series" 2021, Vol. 11, No. 6(S), p. 18 et. seq. The problem of symbolism also applies to court buildings (or court architecture more broadly).The issue of architecture related to the justice system is discussed in many publications, see e.g., L. Mulcahy, *Legal Architecture: Justice, Due Process and the Place of Law*, London 2010; N. Temple, J. Simon eds., *Architecture and Justice: Judicial Meanings in the Public Realm*, London 2013. Due to the thematic framework of this book, it will not be analyzed.

211 G. Skąpska, *Dramaturgia procesu sądowego [Dramaturgy of the judicial process]*, [in:] G. Skąpska, J. Czapska, M. Kozłowska, *Społeczne role prawników (sędziów, prokuratorów, adwokatów) [Social roles of lawyers (judges, prosecutors, advocates)]*, Wrocław 1989, pp. 55–58.

212 W. Domachowski, *Funkcjonowanie sali sądowej [Functioning of the courtroom]*, [in:] *Psychologia i prawo. Między teorią a praktyką [Psychology and the Law. Between theory and practice]*, eds. E. Habzda-Siwek, J. Kabzińska, Sopot 2014, p. 195.

213 Ibidem, pp. 196–197. In each courtroom where observation was conducted for the purposes of this study, the court was located on an elevated platform. As Roman Tokarczyk points out, the vertical layout of courtroom space appeared in Roman culture and became widespread in medieval state law culture, including in Polish culture, R. Tokarczyk, *Proksemika ogólna jako podstawa proksemiki sądowej i proksemiki prawniczej [General proxemics as the basis of forensic proxemics and legal proxemics]*, "Annales Universitas Mariae Curie-Skłodowska. Sectio G, Ius" 2009/2010, Vol. 56–57, pp. 195–197.

214 Indeed, the symbolic significance of the table once overshadowed the question of the usefulness of this piece of furniture. In the former (Polish) Crown Tribunal, deputies were obliged to give evidence at the table confirming their election for the position, answer any accusations and take an oath. Therefore, the party, which did not want the Tribunal to be constituted, tried to "control" the table, which hindered the proceedings, W. Maisel, *Archeologia prawna Polski [Legal archaeology of Poland]*, Warszawa–Poznań 1982, p. 155.

the court, but more importantly the distance between the court and the other participants present in the courtroom.[215] There is also a clearly symbolic dimension to the placement of the presiding judge in the most prominent place, i.e. in the middle of the court, and on a chair larger and more ornate than the chairs of the other members of the court. It is meant to emphasize the presiding judge's special position, including, first and foremost, the leadership function he/she performs at the trial.[216] In addition, the image of the presiding judge using a gavel is strongly ingrained in the culture, which also emphasizes his/her leading function at the trial, primarily in terms of maintaining order in the courtroom. However, it seems that this piece of equipment functions mainly in a symbolic dimension, rather than a real one.

In turn, the positioning of the parties to the proceedings (in the vertical dimension) lower than the court can be interpreted as an expression of the desire to emphasize their inferior position in relation to that of the court.[217] In particular, it is an expression of the fact that the parties have entrusted the court with the settlement of the dispute, so to speak, transferring to it their competence in this regard (as in civil proceedings) or fulfilling a legal obligation (as in criminal proceedings). On the other hand, the way in which the parties (quasi-parties) to the proceedings are positioned in relation to each other is, of course, to emphasize their equal status in the proceedings – this currently applies to all court proceedings.[218] Of all the elements of the organization and equipment of the courtroom that are attributed a symbolic character, the symbolism associated with the national emblem hanging in the courtroom (which is part of the normative pattern) seems to be particularly important. The presence of this emblem is the presence of the state and its interests.[219] Acts that are taken in the courtroom are done on behalf of the state or towards the state, and are regulated by the state (legal system).

---

215 This positioning of the participants of the court proceedings vis-à-vis the court can be interpreted as part of the court's organizational culture, which increases the power distance between participants. Cf M. Dudek, M. Stępień, *Power Distance...*, op. cit.

216 W. Domachowski, *Funkcjonowanie...*, op. cit., p. 198.

217 G. Skąpska, *Dramaturgia procesu...*, op. cit., p. 61.

218 Before 1990 in Poland, the prosecutor had a seat at the judges' table.

219 In the old Polish judiciary, God was also "present" in the courtroom through the presence of the crucifix or reliquary, W. Maisel, *Archeologia prawna...*, op. cit., p. 167, M. Borucki, *Temida staropolska. Szkice z dziejów sądownictwa Polski szlacheckiej [Old Polish Temida. Sketches from the history of judiciary of the Polish nobility]*, Warszawa 1979, p. 131. Moreover, in the medieval Polish process, divine intervention was also "possible" – during the so-called ordalia, or trial of iron or water, M. Tkaczuk, *Średniowieczny proces w zwyczajowym prawie polskim [Medieval trial in customary Polish law]*, "In Gremio" 2005, No. 12, p. 32; A. Lis, *Studies on the Legal Culture of 13th and 14th Century – the Book of Elbląg and the Book of Henryków*, "Przegląd Prawno-Ekonomiczny" 2013, No. 23, p. 5 et seq.

Concluding the discussion of issues related to the symbolism of the courtroom and the courtroom in general, it is possible to point to the historical context of the formation of the pattern of the trial (in Polish courts) in this regard. Indeed, it should be noted that in the historical development the pattern of courtroom equipment, and therefore its symbolic dimension, has become decidedly impoverished.[220]

2.3.2.3. Elements of situational micro-context – participants of court proceedings and participants of court sessions scheduled for the trial

Since the considerations undertaken in the study focus primarily on the communication acts of those present in the courtroom, primary importance is given to the participants of court session scheduled for the trial. However, this does not mean that the category of participants of court proceedings in general will be overlooked. On the contrary, most of the participants of court sessions are participants of court proceedings.

Both the one and the other category of participants are spoken of here as a certain theoretical construct that is part of another construct – the trial that is part of court proceedings, rather than specific participants taking specific communication acts (these will be discussed in the next chapter).

As the genre pattern of a trial takes into account the different varieties of a trial, the participants are also significantly different. This is not simplified by the fact that some types[221] of participants are found in several varieties of court proceedings, or even in all of them, while others are peculiar to only one variety. This rather diverse element of the normative pattern is also compounded by doctrinal disputes regarding certain types of participants, in particular the parties to court proceedings.[222]

---

220 The old courtrooms (during the First Republic of Poland) were furnished with numerous paintings or frescoes – presenting, among other things, the trial of Solomon, the trial of Cambyses over Sisamnes, the trial of the Arians or the Last Judgment, which was intended to remind the judge of the duty to decide justly. The walls of the courtroom were also decorated with Latin sentences from the Holy Bible concerning just judging. The court benches were also decorated with paintings, such as allegorical representations of virtues, especially justice. In addition, portraits or statues of rulers and their wives, city founders (real and legendary), private city owners, state, royal and city coats emblems were placed in the courtrooms. There are known examples of placing a statue of the goddess of justice in the courtroom, and even a picture of Emperor Charles V, W. Maisel, *Archeologia prawna...*, op. cit., pp. 155–156 and 168.

221 It is possible to combine some procedural roles, such as private prosecutor and witness.

222 S. Waltoś, P. Hofmański, *Proces karny. Zarys systemu [The criminal process. Outline of the system]*, 11th edition, Warszawa 2013, pp. 178–180.

Therefore, only examples of participants of proceedings in Polish courts are indicated here, taking into account their procedural roles:

1. main procedural authorities – the court and the presiding judge;
2. parties[223]:
   (a) active party – e.g., claimant, prosecutor, insured,
   (b) passive party – e.g., respondent, defendant (in criminal or misdemeanor case);
3. other participants – e.g., attorney, intervening party, representative of a social organization, Ombudsman, expert, witness.

The minimum personal structure in a trial consists of the court and the parties to the proceedings. Generally, a necessary element for the existence and duration of court proceedings is the presence of two parties. The exception is non-contentious civil proceedings; the term "party" is not used in the Polish Code of Civil Procedure for these proceedings.[224] The withdrawal from the proceedings of one of the parties or the so-called accumulation of parties (in civil proceedings) leads to the termination of the proceedings.

However, exceptionless is the principle that there are a maximum of two parties to court proceedings. This, of course, does not exclude the phenomenon of the so-called multiplicity of entities of court proceedings, the essence of which boils down to the fact that there are at least two entities as a specific party. The multiplicity of entities in the proceedings applies to various varieties of court proceedings and can be, in particular, a consequence of: (1) co-participation in a dispute in civil proceedings; (2) multiplicity of defendants or (3) participation in criminal proceedings of an auxiliary prosecutor alongside the public prosecutor.

The participants of court session scheduled for the trial are primarily the participants of court proceedings, but other participants also take part in the session. This category includes the victim (for example, in criminal proceedings), the court's auxiliary authorities (interpreter, court clerk or police officers – escorts) and the audience.

In addition, the two categories of participants differ in their minimum personal structure, since sometimes a sufficient condition for a court session scheduled for the trial to take place is the presence of a judge acting both as court and presiding judge, as well as a court clerk.[225]

However, the fundamental difference between the two categories of participants relates to the nature (essence) of these entities and boils down to the obvious

---

223 There are also quasi-parties, especially in non-contentious proceedings, such as applicants and participants.

224 For the existence of non-contentious civil proceedings, sometimes either the applicant alone or only the participant (when the proceedings were initiated by the court ex officio) is sufficient.

225 In fact, this is not an uncommon situation.

statement that only a person can participate in a court session, while a participant in the proceedings can be an entity of a conventional nature.

It is possible to point to two dimensions of the diversity that characterizes the participants of court session scheduled for the trial. The first dimension could be called the conventional dimension, the second – the real dimension. These dimensions are not independent of each other and intermingle on some planes, making it difficult to draw a precise line between them.

The basis for the separation of the two dimensions is the activity of the legislator. On the diversity of the participants in the **conventional dimension**, the legislator decides directly. On the other hand, the legislator decided on their diversity in the **real dimension** indirectly, allowing entities with diverse characteristics to participate in court proceedings. In addition, there are planes of diversity that are located on the borderline between the two dimensions (see Table 1).

As has been signaled several times before, the legislator has specified in which procedural roles both in the proceedings themselves and at the court session, certain entities are involved. First, the procedural norms specify what characteristics a given entity must have and what acts it must take to be able to act in a certain procedural role.[226] Second, they delineate numerous competencies and obligations for the entities that are already in a particular procedural role.

Table 1. *Dimensions and planes of diversity of participants of court session scheduled for the trial*

Dimensions of the diversity of participants	**Planes of diversity of participants**
conventional dimension	procedural roles
	interactional roles
conventional dimension / real dimension	social roles
real dimension	communication competence
	knowledge
	other features

Source: Own study.

The roles of the procedural authority or party can be called primary or basic roles. On the other hand, the distinguished names of the participants of court proceedings (claimant, respondent, defendant, etc.) are at the same time the names of

226 It is a matter of having certain characteristics in accordance with the rules of construction of a given conventional entity, in other words, the "possibility of being", for example, a party to civil proceedings.

procedural roles, which can be called detailed roles. According to this distinction, the main (basic) procedural role will be that of a party, the detailed role – that of the claimant or defendant. The essence of procedural roles are the basic functions.[227]

Due to the adversarial nature of court proceedings, its main axis is formed by the parties. It is the party that initiates court proceedings, during which it presents interests that diverge from those of the opposing party (at least initially).[228]

Based on the above assumption, it is possible to organize the various categories of participants (and thus the corresponding procedural roles) by indicating their position in the proceedings relative to the parties of the proceedings. Subsequently, the basic functions associated with a given procedural role can be organized in a similar manner, focusing them around the basic functions performed by the parties of the proceedings.

The question of the basic procedural functions performed by participants in criminal proceedings is relatively clear (see Table 2).

Table 2. *Basic procedural functions performed by participants of criminal proceedings*

Basic procedural functions performed by participants in criminal proceedings				
Function of the prosecution – demand that the criminal liability of the defendant be established	Function of liability settlement of the defendant	Function of defense against accusations of the prosecution	Additional functions consisting of	
			to protect the public interest or one's own	providing evidences
Active party: – public prosecutor, – auxiliary prosecutor, – private prosecutor Participants acting "for" the active party: auxiliary prosecutor's attorney, private prosecutor's attorney	Participant acting independently of the parties to the proceedings: court	Passive party: defendant Participants acting "for" the passive party: defense counsel	Participants acting independently of the parties, such as: advocate of public interest	Participants acting independently of the parties: witnesses, experts

Source: Own study.

227 **Procedural functions** are the essential lines of activity in the proceedings determined by the purpose of this activity, S. Waltoś, P. Hofmański, *Proces karny...*, op. cit., pp. 201–202.

228 The exception to this is a non-contentious civil proceeding, which in certain cases can be initiated by the court ex officio and, as a rule, it is not adversarial.

In a similar way, it is possible to reconstruct the basic procedural functions of participants in civil proceedings, which focused around the parties to the proceedings – the claimant, i.e., the entity that on behalf of itself demands the court to grant legal protection, and the respondent, i.e., the entity against whom this demand is directed.

Interactional roles are also situated in the conventional dimension of participant diversity. In this study, by "interactional role" is meant the role of a particular participant in which he or she appears in a specific interaction, taking a specific communication act (for example, in the role of questioner or answerer).[229] The conventional nature of the interactional roles is determined by the fact that it was the legislator who decided in which interactional roles the various participants appear at the trial.[230] The distribution of interactional roles will be presented when discussing the structural aspect of the various acts and communication occurrences that take place at the trial.

The term "social role" is understood in this study as "a set of normative expectations in relation to a person occupying a certain position, occurring in his or her frame of reference".[231] According to Janina Czapska, a social role consists of two elements: expectations external to the subject performing a given social role, and the concept of a role, i.e. a set of ideas of a given subject about what acts he or she should undertake, what goals to pursue or what values to prefer.[232] The cited definition of a role is part of the normative perspective in the perception of social roles. Such a perspective is also adopted in this book.

---

229 The concept of interactional role was transferred to the study from communication grammar, A. Awdiejew, *Gramatyka interakcji...*, op. cit., p. 65. In terms of another typology, interactional roles are the equivalent of "linguistic impermanent roles in official contacts in one-to-one interactions", S. Grabias, *Język w zachowaniach społecznych [Language in social behavior]*, Lublin 1994, pp. 270–271.

230 To some extent, these roles are also determined by the practice.

231 J. Czapska, *Konflikty związane z pełnieniem roli prawnika-uczestnika wymiaru sprawiedliwości [Conflicts related to the role of a lawyer-participant in the justice system]*, [in:] G. Skąpska, J. Czapska, M. Kozłowska, *Społeczne role prawników...*, op. cit., p. 32.

232 Ibidem. The content of the names "social role", "procedural role" and "interactional role" adopted in the study varies. The relations between the scopes of these names are also different. Due to the adopted understanding of social role, procedural roles can be seen as varieties of social roles. In addition, the characteristics of certain procedural roles co-create the characteristics of certain social roles (such as attorney). In contrast, interactional roles are not seen as a variety of social roles. Without developing the full argument here, it is only stated that the intentional adoption of a given interactional role does not determine the establishment of a certain social position (in a given frame of reference), but the opposite is true – social position (related to the social role played, even a procedural role) affects the recognition of the essence of the interactional role.

Each of the participants of court session plays various social roles, including occupational roles.[233] The huge number of court actors makes it impossible (at least in this study) to make an in-depth consideration of the diversity of social roles of participants and their possible relationship to the communication acts undertaken at the trial.

In order to simplify the issue as much as possible, the issue of the social roles of the professional participants of court proceedings and the other participants will be discussed separately.

Starting – differently than usual – with the second issue, it should be pointed out that the occupational role of a specific participant is the content of the question,[234] which the presiding judge asks the participant before the examination. Determining the occupational role of the examined person makes it possible, at least to some extent, to get an idea of what general knowledge and communication competence he or she may have. It also makes it possible to determine whether there are circumstances that actualize the prohibition of examination due to professional secrecy.

The presiding judge's question about the occupational role of the examined person made it possible, on the basis of the empirical material collected, to make some observations about the professional structure and level of education of the participants.[235] However, a fully accurate reconstruction of this structure is hindered by the inconsistent manner in which the said question was asked, so the summary is fragmentary in the meaning that it was not possible to obtain the necessary data in all cases.

Of the 298 examinations in which the presiding judge asked about the occupational role, 148 could be determined by the level of education, and 120 could be determined by professional (occupational) activity or lack thereof. The results are shown in Table 3.

---

233 Occupational roles can be recognized as varieties of social roles.

234 This question is sometimes quite problematic for participants. This is a consequence of the different practice of individual judges, who, in formulating the question, use a variety of terms: "occupation", "profession", "learned occupation", "learned profession", "learned and practiced profession". Procedural acts insufficiently specify what the content of the question is to be – the norm in the Polish Code of Civil Procedure orders the presiding judge to begin the examination by asking the witness questions about his/her person and relationship to the parties, while the Polish Code of Criminal Procedure, designating a similar obligation, uses the term "occupation".

235 The cited data extracted from the research material is only illustrative, the characteristics of the actual participants in the proceedings are obviously not part of the trial pattern.

Table 3. *Education and professional activity of examined persons at the trial*

<table>
<tr><th>Education</th><th>Professional activity</th></tr>
<tr><td>primary – less than 1 % (1 person)</td><td>active people – about 58 % (70 persons).</td></tr>
<tr><td>vocational – about 45 % (66 persons)</td><td rowspan="3">economically inactive persons – about 42 % (50 persons):
– retirees – 66 % (33 persons),
– students and pupils – 20 % (10 persons),
– inactive for another reason – 14 % (7 persons)</td></tr>
<tr><td>secondary (general and technical) – about 11 % (16 persons)</td></tr>
<tr><td>higher – about 44 % (65 persons)</td></tr>
</table>

Source: Own study.

As a comment on the content of Table 3, it should be noted that although the data cited do not fully illustrate the professional structure of the participants, they do indicate a particularly significant regularity – a large variation in both education and professional activity. In addition, it can be noted that only three people among those with higher education were lawyers. However, with regard to the structure of professional activity, it is noteworthy that among economically inactive persons, retirees have the highest percentage.

Consideration of the social roles of professional participants will instead be limited to the occupational roles of judges, prosecutors, advocates and legal counsels.

The occupational roles of the indicated entities are special in that they also include procedural roles, and to be more precise, the occupational roles of the distinguished lawyers are co-created by the same legal norms that define the duties and competences associated with acting in a specific procedural role. Of course, not only these norms, but also many other legal norms externally determine the roles of judges, prosecutors, advocates and legal counsels, since the "main creator" in this regard is the legislator. In addition to the norms contained in legislative acts, the roles in question are also determined by normative acts issued by professional self-governments, and in addition, as Czapska points out, the system of informal connections and dependencies and the personality of the implementer of the role.[236] Given the different sources of the formation of occupational roles of lawyers (as well as some other participants of court session), this plane of diversity of participants is placed in the study on the borderline between the conventional and real dimensions.

The juxtaposition of selected elements of lawyers' occupational roles makes up the so-called ethos image of the social role.[237]

---

236 J. Czapska, *Konflikty...*, op. cit., p. 36.

237 E. Łojko, *Działalność zawodowa prawników a wykluczenie prawne [Professional activities of lawyers and legal exclusion]*, [in:] *Prawo i wykluczenie. Studium empiryczne [Law and exclusion. An empirical study]*, ed. A. Turska, Warszawa 2010, p. 149. The

In the context of the communication acts carried out at the court session (in Polish courts), the following issues related to the occupational roles of the lawyers-participants of the court session come to the fore: (1) the relationship between these categories of lawyers is formed primarily on the principles of interaction, distance, and mutual respect and understanding of the roles played, including the dominant role of the judge; (2) the presiding judge's concern for order during the court session and adherence to procedures; (3) the impartiality of the judge; (4) the clarification of procedural issues, the judge's explanation of the reasons for the decision, and the provision of instructions.

Re 1. The pattern of relations between lawyers-participants can be called professional. However, it is not only an external element of the professional roles of lawyers, since lawyers themselves consider such a pattern to be the most appropriate and desirable when acting in the courtroom.[238]

Re 2. The judge, acting in the presiding judge's procedural role, serves as the host of the session, with this function comes a number of competences and duties to maintain order in the courtroom and the proper conduct of procedural acts. Acting, in turn, in the role of the court, he/she has the authority to apply disciplinary sanctions.

Re 3. The impartiality of the judge in the justice system, in addition to his/her independence, seems to be the essence of the judge's occupational role. The norms of conduct not only obligate a judge to remain impartial,[239] but also to avoid any behavior that could undermine confidence in judge's impartiality. At the same time, a judge's impartiality is clearly desired by the public, and its absence is extremely negatively evaluated,[240] and it is the judge's communication acts in the

---

image of individual lawyers-participants of the court session is co-created by the appropriate official dress, which makes it possible to recognize both the procedural role and appurtenance to a particular professional group. Against this background, of course, the outfit of the presiding judge stands out, who also wears the symbol of the state – a chain with an eagle. Official dress depersonalizes the person who plays a given procedural role, and is an outward expression of the competencies associated with this role, A. Choduń, M. Zieliński, *Jak sądy i trybunały komunikują się z obywatelami [How courts and tribunals communicate with citizens]*, [in:] *Kultura zachowań językowych Polaków. Materiały z VIII Forum Kultury Słowa. Rzeszów 20–22 października 2011 [The culture of linguistic behavior of Poles. Materials from the VIII Forum on the Culture of Words. Rzeszów 20–22 October 2011]*, ed. M. Krauz, K. Ożóg, 2013, pp. 121–122.

238 "[O]ne may think that the paradigmatic, standard model of communication in Polish courts, expected by attorneys and courts, is the model of cooperating partners, each of whom recognizes the limitations of the role (...). However, this does not contradict the definitely dominant position of the court (...)", J. Winczorek, P. Maranowski, *Komunikacja w sądach...*, op. cit., p. 5.

239 This is reflected in the rote of the oath taken by the judge.

240 E. Łojko, *Działalność zawodowa prawników...*, op. cit., pp. 140–141.

courtroom that are particularly sensitive to evaluation by participants from the perspective of impartiality.[241]

Ad 4. The last aspect concerning the occupational roles of lawyer-participants is extremely important from the point of view of the subject of interest of this study. In this aspect, lawyers, as professional participants of court session, act as a link between the legal system and the non-professional participants. In Poland the legislator has assigned special competences and duties in this regard to the judge, acting either as a court or presiding judge. Ethical norms, moreover, specify how certain communication acts should be carried out. In this context, attention should be paid to § 11 of the Collection of Principles of Professional Ethics for Judges and Judicial Assessors, which states in paragraph 1 that "a judge, when explaining procedural issues to the parties and giving reasons for a decision, should do so in a way that is **understandable** to them [emphasis – K.G.]".

Legal or ethical norms do not specify analogous competences or duties with respect to other lawyers participating in a court sessions. However, it seems that in relation to advocates and legal counsels, the duty to explain procedural issues to non-professional participants can be deduced from the general duty to protect the interests of their clients. The ability to anticipate certain difficulties that may be associated with the participation of a client in a court session, especially when a person is taking part in court proceedings for the first time, and the ability to prepare him or her for this participation should be considered a manifestation of the diligent performance of the role of an advocate or legal counsel.[242] In contrast, in the case of a prosecutor acting in a specific procedural role, this element of the occupational role is significantly limited. At most, an auxiliary prosecutor who is not represented by an attorney, and a party for whom the prosecutor acts in the proceedings when not acting as a public prosecutor, could be considered a subject to whom the prosecutor could provide some procedural guidance.

On the basis of the presented description of the professional roles of judges, prosecutors, advocates and legal counsels participating in the court sessions, it is possible to point to a certain mutual relationship, which seems to have a direct impact on the communication acts undertaken at the trial. Given that the norms of conduct regarding participation in the court sessions co-create the occupational roles of the lawyers-participants in the session, the reliable and correct implementation of the elements of these roles contributes to the correct implementation of the normative pattern of the trial itself.

241 It is emphasized in dogmatics and case law the importance of the external symptoms of impartiality, i.e. such behavior of the judge that corresponds to the standards of impartiality as assessed by external observers, including the parties to the proceedings, e.g., A. Łazarska, *Rzetelny proces cywilny [A fair civil trial]*, Warszawa 2002, pp. 225–226.

242 Such an act can prevent some communication barriers.

To conclude the consideration of the diversity of participants, it is necessary to briefly refer to the three plans of the real dimension.

First, the participants are – sometimes very clearly – differentiated by their level of communication competence. Secondly, the level of participants' knowledge is also different, both that which is part of communication competence and factual knowledge unrelated to the subject of cognition in a given proceeding (e.g., expert knowledge). In addition, the level of participants' knowledge of the facts that are the subject of judicial cognition is also different.

Third, in addition to communication competence and knowledge, there are many factors that differentiate the participants. Not all of these factors determine the process of communication in the courtroom. Instead, the influence of some characteristics of the participants is significant – especially when it leads to communication barriers,[243] including cultural barriers.[244]

---

243 This includes, in particular, hearing disorders that can cause so-called internal noise, emotional attitudes toward the subject matter of the case, or stereotypical perceptions of the justice system, which can in turn create perceptual barriers; all of the exemplary characteristics of the participants were noted in the research material. It has been shown in scientific studies that people suffering from such disorders as autism spectrum disorder, intellectual disability, schizophrenia, attention deficit hyperactivity disorder, traumatic brain injury or conduct disorder, among others, have poorer pragmatic language skills in some aspects then people without such disorders. In particular, they may have trouble recognizing types of speech acts or adhering to Grice's conversational maxims (more on Grice's maxims in Section 2.3.2.13). The research report in this regard can be found in L. Cummings, *Pragmatic Disorders in Forensic Settings*, [in:] *Pragmatics and Law...*, p. 349 et seq.

244 No clear cultural barriers were noted in the research material. However, as studies for other countries show, cultural differences between trial participants can be a significant communication barrier. As an illustration of this issue, it is worth citing two articles on the participation of indigenous inhabitants of Australia in court proceedings due to the fact that, first, they show how powerful the influence of the mode of communication (communication tradition) can be in shaping a participant's position in court proceedings; second, the importance that empirical research can have on the communication process occurring in court proceedings. The first and chronologically earlier article (D. Eades, *"Evidence Given in Unequivocal Terms": Gaining Consent of Aboriginal Young People in Court*, [in:] *Language in the Legal Process*, ed. J. Cotterill, Palgrave Macmillan 2002, p. 162 et seq.) discusses certain communication phenomena characteristic of Aborigines, i.e. long pauses (silence), which are interpreted differently than in Western societies, and the tendency to give affirmative answers to closed questions requiring either confirmation or denial, regardless of the conviction of the content of the answer given (!). On the basis of empirical material, the article addresses the question of the possible (or rather, undoubted) impact of such culturally shaped communication phenomena on the participation, and thus the procedural situation of Aboriginal people in court proceedings in Australian courts. The second article (N. Stroud, *Non-Adversarial Justice: The Changing Role of Courtroom Participants in an Indigenous Sentencing Court*, [in:]

2.3.2.4. *Other elements of the situational micro-context*

Among the elements of situational micro-context, the directness (indirectness) of the contact and the relationship between the participants in the communication stand out in this study.

Referring to the first issue, it should be pointed out that the legislator, creating the trial on the principle of orality, indirectly decided to supplement the normative pattern with certain phenomena naturally accompanying face to face communication,[245] some of which the procedural norms significantly modify.

There are characteristic features of face to face communication between participants in the communication process and texts understood as products of this process. Thus, among the peculiarities of face to face communication, copresence, visibility, audibility, (4) instantaneity, evanescence, recordlessness, simultaneity, extemporaneity, self-determination and self-expression are mentioned.[246] In addition, linguists point to the specific linguistic means associated with dialogicity that perform the phatic function of establishing, maintaining and terminating contact, as well as the use of kinesic and proxemic phenomena.[247] In contrast, the spontaneity of communication acts in direct contact contrasts with the unspontaneity of producing written texts, which can be carefully prepared.[248] Therefore, during the course of communication acts, especially linguistic ones, repetitions, corrections of one's own statements or syntactic irregularities occur.[249] Moreover, communication

---

Proceedings of the International Association of Forensic Linguists' Tenth Biennial Conference, Centre for Forensic Linguistics, Birmingham 2012, pp. 115–125) deals with the special judiciary that operates in Australia, dealing exclusively with the cases of its indigenous people. The author presents the judiciary for one of the indigenous ethnic groups (the so-called Koori Courts). The main reason for the creation of a special court was the very high percentage of indigenous Australians among the convicted and the recognition that the reason for this lies, among other things, in cultural differences, including the failure to adapt the course of the proceedings in its communicative layer to the tradition of communication formed among indigenous Australians. Proceedings before the Koori Courts (as well as other courts of this type) meet these needs – they are non-contradictory, participants sit around an oval table, the participation of elders and the most respected members of the group is ensured, more casual (than in common courts) conversation is aimed at reaching agreement, legal and juridical terminology is not used, the typical structure of an examination is also absent, and the principles of linguistic politeness, including linguistic taboos, are respected.

245 This is an example of the determination of certain communication phenomena by the characteristics of the trial.

246 H.H. Clark, *Using Language*, Cambridge 1996, pp. 9–10.

247 K. Ożóg, *Ustna odmiana języka ogólnego [Oral variety of the common language]*, [in:] *Współczesny język...*, op. cit., pp. 91–92.

248 Ibidem, p. 92, S. Grabias, *Język...*, op. cit., p. 286.

249 K. Ożóg, *Ustna odmiana...*, op. cit., pp. 92–93.

acts in direct contact are irreversible – they cannot be undone, due to the direct interaction with the recipient.

The way in which the normative pattern of the trial in Polish courts is formed limits the occurrence of some of the above-mentioned features. First, certain aspects of spontaneity are limited, for example, in the case of the presentation of charges, the announcement of the judgment, the repetition of the rote of the oath, since these are derivatively oral linguistic acts. Secondly, the possibility to act of a proxemic nature is definitely limited,[250] i.e. to freely shape the spatial distance between the participants, due to their specific distribution in the courtroom, and, moreover, in connection with the obligation set by legal norms to keep a standing position, applicable in various circumstances. Thirdly, the issue of the irreversibility of communication acts carried out at the trial deserves special attention. On the one hand, the irreversibility of some communication acts has a particularly momentous social dimension – among these acts, the announcement of the judgment is the most momentous. On the other hand, some communication acts can be revoked by the same entity that carried them out, canceled by another entity, declared non-existent. The first refers to authorization to revoke complaints and motions, such as an indictment, a lawsuit, a motion to adduce evidence, the second refers to the situation when an entity revokes a statement that was made on its behalf by another entity, while the third refers to an order to omit certain acts, that is, to assume the fiction that they were not taken.

At this point, the issue of the contentiousness of court proceedings (including trial) in the context of the relationship between the participants of court proceedings should still be discussed. However, this is a problematic task, as it could be the subject of a separate monograph.[251] From the point of view of the communication characteristics of the trial, at least three issues deserve interest: (1) contentiousness

---

250 In turn, the kinesic code played an important role in the past judiciary in Poland, often providing a rule for the performance of a certain procedural act, such as the proper placement of fingers on the cross when taking an oath. "5.8 (…) If he puts his finger elsewhere, then he falls in the oath", *Najstarszy Zwód Prawa Polskiego [The Oldest Law of Poland]*, compiled by J. Matuszewski, J. Matuszewski, Łódź 1995, p. 64. The rules for performing procedural acts also included raising the hands, lifting the fingers, lowering the fingers, grabbing the collar or lifting the sleeve-wrapped thumb of the right hand, W. Maisel, *Archeologia prawna…*, op. cit., pp. 318–319. Nowadays, such acts do not play such a momentous role; at most, they can update the court's authority to impose a sanction (for example, if the gesture is offensive).

251 The issue of communication in a conflict situation is also one of the more widely discussed aspects of communication in general, cf. on this topic and on works addressing the issue in question A.L. Silars, *Interpersonal Conflict*, [in:] *The Handbook of Communication Science*, eds. C.R. Berger, M.E. Roloff, D.R. Roskos-Ewoldsen, 2nd edition, Sage Publications 2010, p. 273 et seq.

(adversarialism) of court proceedings, understood as a principle-pattern[252] of the formation of court proceedings; (2) conflict underlying court proceedings; (3) characteristics of the communication process in a conflict situation. Below will be discussed issues of all three aspects of contentiousness distinguished above.

The principle of adversarialism determines the model of the process, in which the disposers of the process are the parties, while the court is an impartial observer, which is supposed to resolve the conflict in a neutral manner,[253] while in the context of the subject of interest of the present considerations the most relevant is the issue of disputes between the parties to the process. The manifestations of contentiousness in the normative pattern of Polish court proceedings (and further trial) are many. The contentiousness (incompatibility) of the aspirations of the parties to the proceedings is noticeable already at the level of basic procedural functions. The level of contentiousness in the normative pattern is, of course, not the same in all varieties and sub-varieties of court proceedings.[254] Most prominently, the legislator determines contentiousness in the framework of contentious civil proceedings – as procedural norms order the respondent to enter into a dispute on the merits. In the framework of criminal proceedings (and other varieties of court proceedings in which a party has the right of defense), contentiousness in the dimension under discussion is limited insofar as the party with the right of defense is authorized to refuse explanations. The contentious nature of court proceedings is also indicated by legal or juridical terms that define the elements of court proceedings, directly referring to the conflict situation (the situation of dispute), such as "subject of dispute", "party",[255] "defense" or "prosecution". The least contentious character (and even non-contentious) is at the level of the normative pattern of the trial in non-contentious civil proceedings. The non-contentious nature of this variety of civil proceedings is particularly emphasized by the use of the legal terms "participant" and "applicant" instead of the term "party". However, in the case

252 This refers to a principle of law in the basic descriptive sense, i.e. a model for the formation of some legal institution, O. Bogucki, M. Zieliński, *Rozdział 1. Zasady prawa z perspektywy ogólnej teorii prawa [Chapter 1. Principles of law from the perspective of general legal theory]*, [in:] *System prawa karnego procesowego [System of criminal procedural law]*, Vol. 3: *Zasady procesu karnego [Principles of the criminal process]*, ed. P. Wiliński, Warszawa 2014, p. 51 et seq.; M. Peno, O. Bogucki, *Principles of Criminal Liability from the Semiotic Point of View*, "International Journal for the Semiotics of Law" 2021, Vol. 34, p. 563.

253 E.g., A. Łazarska, *Rzetelny proces…*, op. cit., p. 224; H. Dolecki, *Postępowanie cywilne. Zarys wykładu [Civil procedure. Outline of a lecture]*, 6th edition, Warszawa 2015, p. 54 et seq.

254 As already indicated, in general, proceedings before Polish courts have elements characteristic of both adversarial and inquisitorial proceedings.

255 The literature emphasizes that there are always "parties" in a conflict, C. Sikorski, *Język konfliktu. Kultura komunikacji społecznej w organizacji [The language of conflict. The culture of social communication in an organization]*, Warszawa 2005, p. 36.

of non-contentious proceedings, a strong functional determinant of the contentiousness of a given proceeding is its subject matter (often a clearly contentious character can be attributed to proceedings for the division of property, the repeal of co-ownership or inheritance proceedings due to the fact that the basis for their initiation is sometimes a deep conflict).

Taking into account conflict studies, litigation might be treated as one of the levels on the conflict escalation spiral.[256] In doing so, a dispute (including litigation) is an open conflict.[257] Within the framework of the court proceedings, the disclosure of disputed elements is particularly served by the so-called informational examination in civil proceedings, which will be discussed more extensively in the considerations on structural aspect of communication occurrences.

Between the situation of the dispute (or, more broadly, conflict) in which the parties to the proceedings are embroiled and the proceedings themselves, there are various relationships involving mutual functional determination. First, the initiation of court proceedings, as described above, makes the conflict public, and entering into litigation makes it impossible to avoid it.[258] Second, submitting a dispute to a court (whether in the realization of competence or in the performance of a legal duty) establishes a structure of dominance (power) between the parties to the dispute – the parties become equal in relation to each other. Third, due to the fundamental contentiousness of court proceedings already at the level of the pattern, it should be taken into account that the parties may present different approaches to resolving the conflict. In this aspect, the literature speaks of the so-called cooperative context, in which the parties are oriented towards finding an agreement, and the so-called competitive context, in which the parties seek to defeat the opponent.[259] Court proceedings, including trial, are primarily accompanied by a competitive atmosphere, but the normative pattern also provides for certain acts of consensus (e.g., authorization of the parties to reach a settlement before a judge or mediator). Fourth, the situation of a dispute may determine certain communication acts that are characteristic of conflict communication, especially those

256 On conflict spirals see W.W. Wilmot, J.L. Hocker, *Interpersonal Conflict*, 10th edition, New York 2018, p. 30 et seq.

257 A dispute is sometimes defined in the literature as "a conflict in which the contradiction between the parties is clearly defined", C. Sikorski, *Język konfliktu…*, op. cit., p. 52. Court proceedings focus primarily on the substantive dispute rather than the relational dispute. Sometimes, in addition to the disclosed conflict centered around the subject matter of the dispute, the parties are embroiled in other conflicts not disclosed during the proceedings.

258 The inability to avoid conflict after entering into litigation does not mean that the parties cannot, in fact, take steps to avoid or reduce as much as possible their contact with each other (for example, acting through an attorney).

259 C. Sikorski, *Język konfliktu…*, op. cit., p. 51.

that are undertaken in a competitive context, including in a situation of destructive fight.[260]

2.3.2.5. The communication process at the trial – communication acts and occurrences

The individual communication acts and occurrences that take place at the trial can also be considered as genres. However, the genological characterization of individual communication acts or occurrences requires consideration, and thus a repetition of the findings regarding the genre pattern of a trial itself. Undertaking such a detailed genological analysis is considered unjustified from the point of view of the purpose and scope of the study. It will therefore be limited to a model representation of selected communication acts and occurrences in structural and functional terms (taking into account the elements of normative and usual pattern) and a discussion of issues related to their conventionalization and formalization.

In the course of a court session scheduled for the trial communication acts are constantly taking place. Some of these acts are clearly defined by the normative pattern, while some are an element of usus, and others fall outside the genre pattern of a trial, with the boundary between the last two categories sometimes being blurred.[261]

The following discussion will focus on communication acts and occurrences that can be characterized on the basis of a normative pattern of a trial in Polish courts. In addition, this characterization will be enriched with usual elements, while issues of possible transgression of the pattern will be addressed exceptionally.

2.3.2.6. Directionality of the communication process at the trial

To a large extent, it was the legislator who determined the direction of taking certain communication acts, the interactional roles of the various participants, and, moreover, the existence of feedback within the framework of a specific communication process. For the rest, the elements highlighted in the previous sentence are determined by the practice.

---

260 This primarily involves communication acts aimed at degrading the other party to the conflict, expressing resentment, criticism, dislike, demands, etc.

261 The practice shaping the genre pattern of a trial is referred to in this study when the communication act taken is indifferent from the point of view of legal norms, primarily procedural norms, legal norms determine the obligation to take a particular act, without specifying how to do it, or when the communication acts in question are determined by the features of the trial, such as the directness of the contact. Thus, to say that an element of the pattern is shaped by the practice is not equivalent to saying that it is a uniform practice. The absence of an element of a normative pattern regarding a particular communication act determines that the act in question cannot be considered a realization (or transgression) of that pattern.

Recognizing, on the basis of a normative pattern, which entity performs the function of sender in a given communication process is unlikely to be a problem. On the other hand, the precise identification of the addressee, that is, the recipient to whom the communication act is intentionally directed, is sometimes problematic. In this study, it is assumed that the addressee is that entity on whose interpretation the communication act of the sender is primarily aimed. In this view, for example, the addressee of the decision announced by the court will be the entity that requested the decision, since it is these entities (the court and the requested entity) that should care most about the correct interpretation of the communication act taken.

Below will be presented models that synthesize the reproduced on the basis of the normative pattern of communication acts and simpler communication occurrences taking place at the trial in Polish courts (during face to face contact). Communication occurrences that are more complex, and at the same time constitute a functionally distinct whole, will be characterized separately.

2.3.2.7. One-way communication acts of either the court or the presiding judge

On-way communication acts are considered in this study to be those for which the normative pattern does not provide for communication act feedback, in other words – it does not form with another communication act the so-called adjacency pair[262] within the framework of direct contact. Such acts[263] are, in particular, one-way communication acts of either the court or the presiding judge (Tables 4 and 5).

---

262 The concept of adjacency pairs is a pragmatic analytical category adopted especially in conversational analysis, cf. S.C. Levinson, *Pragmatics*, op. cit., p. 303 et seq., A. Awdiejew, *Gramatyka interakcji...*, op. cit., p. 68.

263 This refers to communication acts that are initiated by either the court or the presiding judge as part of a given interaction, and therefore are not a direct response to the act of another participant, such as an orally filed motion that was immediately resolved, because such an act is then a communication act feedback, that is, an element of a two-way communication occurrence.

Table 4. *One-way communication acts of the court or of the presiding judge, part I*

Announcement of decisions by the court
court ——→ addressee of the decision, e.g. party (addressee[264])
Examples *The court decided to admit and take evidence from X's case file on (...).* *The court decided to accept inheritance assurances from participant XY to establish the basis of inheritance from the deceased (...)*
Giving instructions by either the court or the presiding judge
court/presiding judge ——→ addressee of the instruction, e.g. witness (addressee)
Examples *I order evidentiary proceedings, instruct that you have the right to ask witnesses questions.* *You are obligated to tell the truth, because if you don't, there is a penalty.* *I instruct you to tell the truth, there is criminal liability for giving false testimony.* *You may refuse to answer the question if (...).*
Giving reasons for decisions/justifying decisions by the court
court ——→ addressee of the decision, e.g. party (addressee)
Examples *(...) this crime is punishable by up to eight years of deprivation of liberty, but taking into account the fact (...) the court found that the court will not impose such a harsh punishment on you.* *In the present case, without evidentiary proceedings, the court issued of the judgment by default, due to the fact that the respondent did not defend his rights, did not respond to the content of the lawsuit, nor did he appear on today's session (...)*

Source: own study

264 Other participants of court session scheduled for the trial are always recipients.

Table 5. *One-way communication acts of either the court or the presiding judge, part II*

Announcement of orders by the presiding judge
presiding judge ⟶ addressee of the order, e.g. party (addressee)
Examples *I am opening the judicial process.* *I consider the case sufficiently clarified and order the closing of a trial.* *I order evidentiary proceedings. I strongly request witnesses to leave the courtroom* (...).
Reading reports of testimony or explanations
presiding judge ⟶ entity whose testimony or explanations are read out (addressee)
Example *Then sit back, the court will still read your explanations, at the police you said so* (...).
Opening and announcing a will by the court
court ⟶ applicant or participant of inheritance proceedings (addressee)
Example *The court shall open and announce the will drawn up on XX by XY. The will was drawn up in handwriting on A4 size checkered paper, it begins* (...).

Source: Own study.

Some of the communication acts of either the court or the presiding judge indicated in Tables 4 and 5 are a condensation of two conventionally different acts. This applies to those decisions and orders that are issued at the session scheduled for the trial – one communication act is then both the issuance and announcement of a given act. In addition, the presence of the addressee of the act in question at the session is not necessary for the effectiveness of the specified acts (except for the giving of instructions, which is related to the nature of this communication act). Accordingly, it can happen (and many times does happen) that either the court or the presiding judge takes the given communication act only to the recipients (not to the addressees).

Moreover, it was made clear in the introduction to this discussion that the analysis undertaken of the directionality of the communication process is limited to the face to face communication taking place at the trial. This is an extremely important caveat, since the relativization of the same communication acts to the entire court proceedings (situational meso-context) significantly change the perception of directionality. This issue relates to decisions promulgated by the court, which are appealable. However, a possible action in the form of an appeal of a decision made by an authorized entity does not constitute a communication act feedback, but at most a communication act quasi-feedback, since it is directed to another entity – the court of second instance. In this context, the court's act will still remain one-way communication act, but will be the first of a sequence of communication acts of different entities.

However, there are also some exceptions. In some cases, the party is authorized to submit an objection to the minutes regarding procedural defects. Such a request may be a direct response to the performance of a specific act, such as the announcement of an evidentiary ruling, which consequently makes the communication process two-sided. However, this exception does not fundamentally change the nature of the communication acts included in Tables 4 and 5.

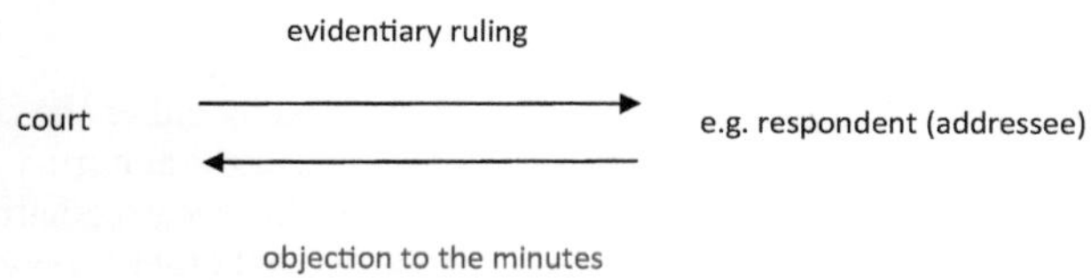

Figure 8. *Example of a two-way communication occurrence*

Example

P: *The court ruled to admit evidence from the examination in the character of witnesses XY and YX on the health, well-being and effects of the minor (...).*
Attorney: *Your Honor, I submit an objection to the minutes under Article 162 of the Polish Code of Civil Procedure, due to the fact that the Court admitted evidence late. This is a violation of Article 207 § 6 of the Polish Code of Civil Procedure, as well as Article 217 § 2 of the Code.*
Source: own study.

2.3.2.8. Two-way communication occurrences involving either the court or the presiding judge

The communication acts of either the court or the presiding judge, for which the normative pattern explicitly provides for communication act feedback, are primarily a variety of questions that either the court or the presiding judge is obliged to ask certain which primarily constituting components of more complex communication occurrences. In this way, we can distinguish, in particular, questions posed in the framework of an examination (of the defendant, witness, party, expert, etc.), so-called informational examination (in civil proceedings) and hearing (e.g., of a juvenile, executor of a will or spouse). A model diagram of such the simplest communication occurrence, in which an adjacency pair is formed by a question and an answer, is shown in Figure 9.

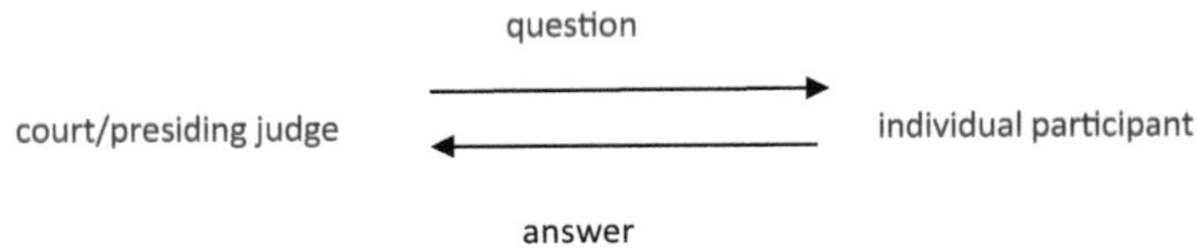

Figure 9. *Two-way communication occurrence with a question-answer structure initiated by either the court or the presiding judge*
Source: Own study.

The fundamental obligation to answer questions posed by either the court or the presiding judge is modified in various ways by Polish procedural norms. First of all, the defendant may refuse to answer a question posed during the explanation without giving a reason. The legal provisions also modify the general order for witnesses and certain other participants of the court proceedings to answer. However, the refusal to answer a question does not deprive this communication occurrence of its bilateral character, nor does it necessarily lead to the termination of the interaction. In this case, the answer is replaced by a statement of refusal to answer the question.

In addition to the communication acts of either the court or the presiding judge indicated here, which are clearly defined at the level of the normative pattern, one can distinguish a number of communication acts of either the court or the presiding judge created by the practice. The communication practice in this regard is shaped on two intertwining planes. The first is related to the presiding judge's leading function specified in the normative pattern. The realization of this function consists, in particular, in shaping the interaction during the performance of complex procedural acts, such as examination (giving the floor, authorizing asking questions, taking the floor). The second plane is related to the way face to face communication is shaped in general. The communication acts taken in this regard, in particular, have a phatic function – to initiate, sustain and terminate contact.

Examples of this type of communication act can be found in the consideration of complex communication occurrences.

2.3.2.9. One-way communication acts of other participants of court session scheduled for the trial

One-way communication acts of other participants are those for which the normative pattern generally does not provide for communication act feedback in the form of direct contact. Exemplary communication acts are shown in Table 6.[265]

265 Responses to questions were not considered one-way communication acts, because these acts as either feedback or quasi-feedback communication acts are part of communication occurrences, including two-way communication occurrences.

Table 6. *One-way communication acts of other participants of court session scheduled for a trial*

Procedural acts of participants	
Examples: – withdrawal of the claim, – withdrawal of indictment, – withdrawal of private prosecution, – cancellation of attorney's statements.	participant ——→ court
Examples *I agree, I want to accept everything* (...) [acceptance of the claim]. *I want to withdraw the appeal* [withdrawal of the appeal in social security proceedings].	
Presentation of charges or reading of motion for punishment	
prosecutor ——→ defendant/court	
Examples *Chief of Police Station XY accuses defendant YX of the following on* (...). *I request the punishment of Mr. XY residing in X, accused (in misdemeanor case) of* (...). *I accuse XY that: act one* (...) *and for act two* (...).	
Questions of the party (quasi-party) addressed to the examined person	
party/quasi-party ——→ examined person	

Source: Own study.

With regard to the content of Table 6, several issues should be noted. It seems somewhat problematic to clearly define the addressee of the presentation of charges or motion for punishment. It would seem that the subject who is primarily to interpret such an act is the defendant (in criminal or misdemeanor case) as the subject (at least in assumption) most interested in the content of the act. However, it seems that the court should also be considered an addressee (this is clearer when using the form of the request, cf. the second example cited). The distinguished one-way communication processes, as has been signaled several times, occur in the setting of many other communication acts and occurrences. Some of the communication acts indicated in Table 6, although not necessarily coupled with a communication act feedback at the level of the normative pattern, in certain circumstances initiate a quasi-feedback, or even a sequence of several communication acts. An example would be the withdrawal of the claim without waiving the claim performed at the trial. Given that one of the rules for carrying out this act is the respondent's consent to the withdrawal of the claim, the communication process under such circumstances can proceed as shown in Figure 10.

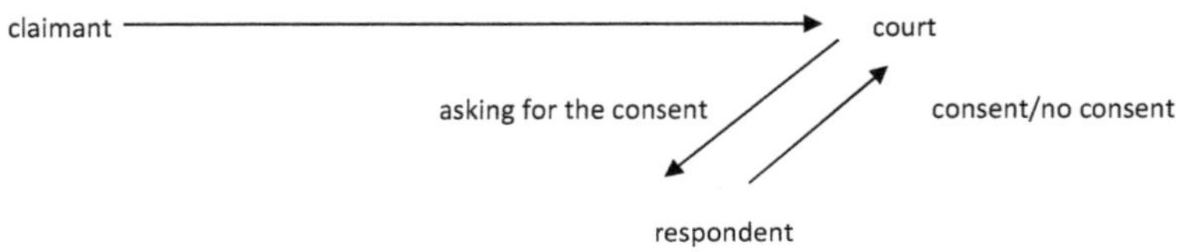

Figure 10. *Withdrawal of the claim without waiving the claim*
Source: own study.

A similar communication occurrence can be initiated by the withdrawal of an indictment or the private prosecution, and, somewhat more complicated, by the defendant's request for so-called voluntary submission to punishment performed at the trial, since consent in this case must be given by two entities: the public prosecutor and the victim. In addition, the attempt to obtain consent on the part of the indicated entities may in practice turn into a series of communication acts similar to the negotiating acts characteristic of settlement in, for example, civil proceedings:

P: [after defense counsel requests the so-called voluntary submission to punishment] *Okay, we are listening in that case to what the defendant has to say. Do you request as defense counsel does?*
Defendant: *Yes.*
P: ***And what does the Victim say about this?*** *Please stand up, I will explain what is going on. The defense counsel with the defendant have made a request under Article 387 of the Polish Code of Criminal Procedure. consisting in this (...).*
Auxiliary prosecutor (victim): *But will that involve, for example, a restraining order, no contact?*
P: *Well, that is what we can work out right away, some... indication you propose, we will see what the other side says.*
P: *Under what conditions would you give your consent?*
Auxiliary prosecutor: *I have already filed a statement for compensation of X thousand zlotys.*
P: *Mr. Defense Counsel...*
Defense counsel: *No, no, we do not recognize this claim, because we believe that it has no reasons here (...), it is here, in my opinion, unjustified, at least as to the amount.*
P: *As to what amount, if any, would you agree?*
Defendant: *Y zlotys.*
(...)
P: *You heard, the lady requests compensation, the amount is X thousand zlotys, of course you can determine this amount less or more. When you determine something together, then we will consider what to request.*

In this extended example of a communication occurrence, the element of the normative pattern is basically only the bolded fragment of the presiding judge's utterance. The rest of the communication acts do not constitute the implementation of the normative pattern, nor do they exceed it, but complement it.

In the framework of an examination (during the trial in Polish courts), the asking of a question by a participant other than the court (or the presiding judge) does not create a two-way communication occurrence, since the answer is not the communication act feedback, but the communication act quasi-feedback directed to the court.[266] The pattern of such a communication occurrence differs significantly from the standard interaction in other communication situations (Figure 11).

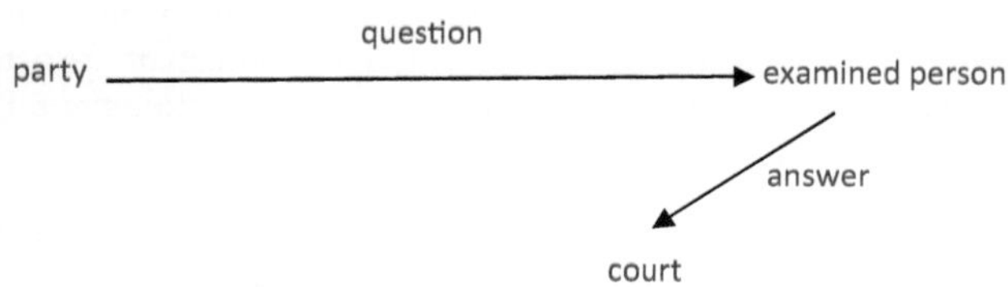

Figure 11. *Communication occurrence with question-answer structure during the examination*[267]

Source: Own study.

2.3.2.10. Two-way communication occurrences involving other participants of court session scheduled for the trial

Two-way communication occurrences initiated by the communication acts of participants other than the court and the presiding judge should be considered primarily motions filed at the trial, which are immediately considered. Among such motions, so-called formal motions are particularly common in practice, including, first of all, a request for either a pause in the trial or an adjournment of the trial. A diagram of such a simple two-way communication occurrence is shown in Figure 12.

266 The procedural act of examination is attributed to the court, O. Bogucki, *Przeprowadzanie dowodów w postępowaniu cywilnym z perspektywy koncepcji czynności konwencjonalnych [Taking evidence in civil proceedings from the perspective of the concept of conventional acts]*, [in:] *Konwencjonalne i formalne aspekty prawa [Conventional and formal aspects of law]*, ed. S. Czepita, Szczecin 2006, p. 117. Directing the answer to the court, regardless of who formulated the question, is furthermore justified practically, especially when it is necessary to create a written minutes.

267 Cf. "[s]imple schema of a Question-Answer sequence in witness examination" at jury trial, Ch. Heffer, *The Language of Jury Trial…*, p. 48.

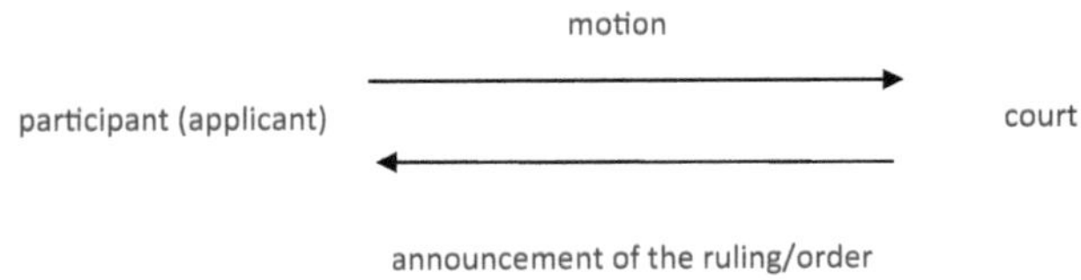

Figure 12. *Two-way communication occurrence initiated by a participant (applicant)*
Source: Own study.

Communication practice, moreover, shapes other communication acts taken by the participants at the trial. Among others especially important are acts that communicate the desire to make a motion or other procedural statement. Examples of such communication acts can be found in the next chapter.

* * *

Analysis of the directionality of the communication process at the trial, formed at the level of the normative pattern, allows to make some important observations.

The first and particularly important observation concerns the significant limitation of communication occurrences without the court or presiding judge as either sender or addressee. The normative pattern of a trial in Polish courts provides, in principle, for one type of one-way communication act, in which neither the court nor the presiding judge is an addressee – it is the questions of the party (quasi-party) addressed to the examined person. On the other hand, it is impossible to identify in the normative pattern two-way communication occurrences to be carried out without the court (presiding judge) as either sender or addressee. The above leads to the observation that just as court proceedings are organized around the two parties to the proceedings, so **the communication process at the trial in Polish courts is centered around the court, and especially the presiding judge**. This is a consequence of assigning the function of leading the session to the presiding judge and reducing direct communication between the parties as much as possible.[268]

The second observation, on the other hand, boils down to the claim that the normative pattern of a trial in Polish courts is not sufficient to form a coherent interaction between the participants of court session. First of all, the implementation of only the communication acts specified in the normative pattern would require very good knowledge – by all participants – of the nature of procedural acts and the order in which they are undertaken, which, given the diversity of participants, is not possible. Besides, even with the participation of only professional participants,

268 Such shaping of interactions is extremely important in the context of the contentiousness of the proceedings, especially certain features of conflict communication, the occurrence of which contentiousness can determine functionally.

the formation of a coherent communication process at the trial is not possible without the communication acts accompanying common interaction. Therefore, the communication acts that are part of the normative pattern are supplemented by the acts shaped through the practice, which fill the space between the acts determined by the law.

The communication process at the trial and its directionality becomes significantly complicated when an interpreter (both foreign language and sign language) is involved. Between communication acts of certain participants, an additional communication act of the interpreter appears when direct communication between them is not possible. A detailed discussion of this issue is beyond the capacity and scope of this book.[269]

2.3.2.11. Characteristics of complex communication occurrences

Both a trial and court proceedings in general can be viewed as an aggregate of communication acts that form a mereological structure with different properties. One of these properties is the way in which the individual communication acts are organized as successive steps towards recognition certain facts and, as a result, resolving the case. Another property is the grouping of specific communication acts into structurally and functionally separate communication occurrences, which, while pursuing specific goals, aim at the main purpose of the proceedings.

The structure of these occurrences is mainly shaped at the level of the normative pattern, the structural and functional separation is evidenced, among other things, by the legislator, possibly by dogmatics, giving these occurrences separate names. The first to be discussed will be those communication occurrences whose pattern is determined primarily by procedural norms, and these are examination – of witnesses, defendants, parties, experts, etc., the so-called informational examination and the making of inheritance assurances. In the second place, attention will be paid to selected communication occurrences, the structure of which is determined primarily by the practice, and of such occurrences, the following communication occurrences will be briefly discussed on the basis of the research material: hearing, inducing the parties to conciliate the case, and drafting minutes. The last two occurrences, due to their functional dissimilarity compared to the other distinguished communication occurrences, will be discussed when analyzing the functional aspect.

---

269 It is worth adding that in the old Polish judiciary, direct communication between the parties and the court was significantly limited, as the parties contacted each other in court through the court usher, Z. Rymaszewski, *Z badań nad funkcjonowaniem sądów prawa polskiego w średniowieczu. Czynności woźnego sądowego [From research on the functioning of Polish law courts in the Middle Ages. Activities of a court usher]*, Warszawa 2010, pp. 292–293.

2.3.2.12. Communication occurrences – structural aspect

The examination of a witness will be characterized as a communication occurrence clearly shaped by the legislator and occurring in all the varieties and sub-varieties of trial highlighted in this monograph.

The structure of the communication acts carried out in the examination of a witness is mainly determined by the norms contained in the Polish Code of Criminal Procedure and the Polish Code of Civil Procedure. On this basis, two different patterns can be reconstructed (see Tables 7 and 8), which are slightly modified by norms contained in other legislative acts.

Table 7. *Examination of the witness (Polish Code of Criminal Procedure) – structural aspect*

The normative pattern	
Communication acts	Commentary
1. Pre-examination activities: - warning of criminal liability for telling untruths or concealing the truth	In practice, the acts of points 1 and 2 are sometimes taken against all witnesses together before the presiding judge orders them to leave the courtroom.
2. Preliminary acts: a) - introductory questions: – name, – age, occupation, – criminal record for false testimony or accusation, – relationship to the parties, b) instruction of right to refuse to testify or answer a question, (c) receipt of the oath or reminder of the oath.	There is no obligation to receipt of the oath when the parties present at the court session do not object*; other exceptions.
3. Testimony: a) - free speech b) - questions from other participants, in order: public prosecutor, auxiliary prosecutor, his/her attorney, private prosecutor, his/her attorney, expert, defense counsel, defendant, members of the court. In addition to the questions, the presiding judge may read excerpts from the minutes of testimony.	– In fact, the examination does not always begin with a free speech, sometimes the presiding judge begins by asking specific questions, which in this regard exceeds the normative pattern. – The legislator modifies this order, specifying that the first to ask questions is the party whose motion to adduce evidence was accepted, or the court if it admitted the evidence ex officio; members of the court also have the authority to ask questions out of turn.

* *As emphasized in dogmatics, the possibility of waiving the taking of the oath should be used rather rarely by the presiding judge, due to the fact that "the taking of the oath has a psychological significance, as (at least in assumption) it is supposed to build a barrier against lying, which would lead to perjury", P. Hofmański, S. Zabłocki, Elementy metodyki pracy sędziego w sprawach karnych [Elements of the methodology of the judge's work in criminal cases], 2nd edition, Warszawa 2011, p. 191.*

Source: own study.

Table 8. *Examination of the witness (Polish Code of Civil Procedure) – structural aspect*

The normative pattern	
Communication acts	Commentary
1. Pre-examination activities: - instruction of right to refuse to testify and criminal liability for giving false testimony	In practice, the actions of points 1 and 2 are sometimes taken against all witnesses together before the presiding judge orders them to leave the courtroom.
2. Preliminary acts: - introductory questions: concerning the person of the witness, relation to the parties; - receipt of the oath or reminder of the oath.	The court is authorized to release of the obligation to take the oath, with the prior consent of the parties; other exceptions to this order are defined by legal provisions.
3. Testimony: a) - presiding judge's question: What and from what source is known to the witness in the case?, b) - questions from judges and parties.	In practice, the examination does not always begin with a normatively designated question, but also with other general questions, such as: – *Do you know what the summons was for?* – *Do you know what the case is about?* – *Are you familiar with the parties?* and even specific questions, thus exceeding the normative pattern.

Source: own study.

As a commentary on the contents of Tables 7 and 8, several points should be noted. First, the examination of a witness may be fully blocked as a consequence of refusal to testify by the authorized person. Second, the witness's testimony is accompanied by a laborious process of producing minutes, unless the course of the trial is recorded. The need to produce minutes significantly affects the course of the communication occurrence in question, as well as all others (more on minutes in the discussion of functional aspects of communication occurrences). Third, the normative pattern of conducting the examination, reconstructed on the basis of procedural norms, is supplemented in the course of its implementation by communication acts shaped by the practice. Fourth, a comparison of the two basic normative patterns of the examination of a witness clearly shows that the pattern formed by the norms expressed in the Polish Code of Criminal Procedure is more detailed than that defined by the norms contained in the Polish Code of Civil Procedure, consequently, the level of supplementation of the actual conduct of the examination of a witness with usual elements differs.

The discussion of other varieties of examination is possible by pointing out those elements that structurally differentiate the examination of other participants in the proceedings from the examination of a witness.

Special features can be identified with regard to the normative pattern of the examination of the defendant (in criminal case), within the framework of which the defendant provides explanations. First of all, the beginning of the examination of the defendant and the end of the examination are of a different nature (see Table 9).

Table 9. *Examination of the defendant (in criminal case) – structural aspect*

Normative pattern without modifications (canonical pattern)	Modifications
1. Preliminary acts (prior to examination): - instruction on the right to make explanations and refuse to explain or answer a question, a) - other instructions, b) - introductory questions: – - Whether he/she confession to the alleged act?, - Whether he/she wants to make explanations and what explanations?	There are no modifications for preliminary acts.
2. Explanations: - taking into account the general legal provisions on examination (see Table 7).	- refusal to provide explanations, - refusal to answer questions, - refusal to provide explanations and answer questions, - so-called voluntary submission to punishment.
3. Post-examination activities: - instruction on authorization to ask questions of examined persons and to give explanations for each piece of evidence.	- so-called voluntary submission to punishment – no evidentiary proceedings

Source: Own study.

Referring to the content of Table 9, it should be noted that the court does not instruct the defendant about criminal liability for giving false testimony, nor does it take an oath from the defendant, as the defendant is giving explanations, and the act of giving false explanations is not within the scope of the norm expressed in the Polish Penal Code. Consequently, the defendant cannot bear criminal liability for making false explanations. In addition, within the normative pattern of examination of the defendant, a significant activity of the court is evident in the provision of instructions to the defendant, which relate not only to the examination itself, but also to further actions that the defendant is authorized to take. The canonical pattern of the examination of the defendant is in this aspect, against the background of the patterns of other communication occurrences under discussion, particularly extensive. The strongest modification of the canonical pattern is the defendant's so-called voluntary submission to punishment, which can transform the examination into a series of communication acts related to the submission.

Finally, it is worth noting that the normative pattern of explanations does not provide for questions about personal information, as the pattern of testimony does. Analogous questions about the name, age, occupation, as well as other questions about the personal and professional situation of the defendant are asked in practice most often before the presentation of charges (or the reading of the motion for punishment in misdemeanor proceedings).

Examination of the parties, on the other hand, is a complex procedural act peculiar to civil proceedings. The legal provisions concerning witnesses apply to the examination of parties accordingly, but with some significant modifications in the structure of the examination (see Table 10).

Table 10. *Examination of the parties (in civil proceedings) – structural aspect*

First examination	Re-examination
- warning the parties of their obligation to testify the truth and the possibility of re-examination after taking the oath, - no oath, - further course of examination (appropriate application of the legal provisions concerning witnesses)	- the first examination did not sufficiently display the facts, - warning the parties of criminal liability for giving false testimony, - the oath (appropriate application of the provisions concerning witnesses), - further course of examination (appropriate application of the provisions concerning witnesses)

Source: Own study.

In the case of examination of the parties, changes in the structure of the examination significantly affect the legal position of the parties to the proceedings. During the first examination, the court warns the parties of their obligation to tell the truth, but does not warn of criminal liability for giving false testimony, thus the party is not subject to criminal liability (according to Polish Penal Code) for such an act. However, if the court finds that the examination did not sufficiently display the facts, it is authorized to re-examine the party, after warning of criminal liability for giving false testimony and after taking the oath. This time the party's testimony may expose him or her to criminal liability for giving false testimony.

Finally, it is important to note a certain practice in the civil trial, which is to begin the examination of a party by reading out what the party said during the so-called informational examination,[270] e.g.,

P: [after reading a portion of the minutes] *Do you confirm what you said during the informational examination?*
Claimant: *Yes.*
P: *Is there anything you would like to add?*
Claimant: *Of course.*

This practice sometimes evidently alludes to the reading of testimony or explanations in criminal proceedings (as suggested, among other things, by the use of phrases specific to these proceedings), such as:

P: *I will now read to you the testimony that you gave*[271] *on (...). Please listen and tell me whether you testified like this, whether you stand by this testimony and whether it is true* [reading the minutes].
P: Is that how you testified, do you stand by that testimony, is it true?
Claimant: Yes.
P: *Is there anything you want to add?*
Claimant: *No.*

In turn, the structure of the examination of an expert is not fundamentally different from that of a witness. However, it should be noted that the legal provisions of the Polish Code of Civil Procedure explicitly refer to the appropriate application of the provisions concerning the witness to the expert being examined. In criminal proceedings, on the other hand, the examination of an expert is largely shaped by the practice (taking into account, of course, the general provisions on examination). The structure of the examination of the expert is determined by the special function of such an examination, related in particular to the need to comment objections to the expert's opinion, such as:

P: *Do you maintain the opinion issued in its entirety?*
Expert: *Yes, I maintain.*
P: *If you would like to comment on the letter of objections, please do.*
Expert: *Regarding objections to the opinion given, I state that* (...).

---

270 An informational examination is not part of the evidentiary proceedings, even if it was conducted after this stage of the trial had already begun, E. Rutkowska-Ząbczyk, [in:] *Kodeks postępowania cywilnego. Komentarz [Polish Code of Civil Procedure. Commentary]*, ed. A. Marszałkowska-Krześ, Legalis 2017. Due to this fact, confirmation during the examination of the parties of what a party said during the informational examination results in the inclusion of the information obtained outside the evidentiary proceedings in the evidence gathered during it.

271 The Polish Code of Civil Procedure does not use the term "testimony" in relation to the so-called informational examination.

At the end of these considerations, the structure of the so-called informational examination (this is a juridical term), submission of inheritance assurances and hearing will be characterized. The above-mentioned types of procedural acts have two features in common – they are peculiar primarily to civil proceedings, and the procedural norms do not prescribe the appropriate application of the provisions on the examination of a witness to these acts.

According to the Polish Code of Civil Procedure: "The court at the trial, by asking questions of the parties, shall strive to have the parties cite or supplement the assertions or evidence in support thereof, and provide explanations necessary to truthfully establish the factual basis for the rights or claims they assert. In the same way, the court seeks explanations of the relevant circumstances of the case that are in dispute".[272] The informational examination remains, as far as structure is concerned, a simple sequence of communication acts in the form of adjacency pairs – a question formulated by the court and a response from the party being heard, which usually begins with informing the parties that they will be "listened to for information", e.g.

P: *Today I would like to informatively examine at least one person from each side to get a rough idea of what it looks like from your point of view.*

P: [for the minutes] *The presiding judge ordered an informational hearing of the parties.*

Considering the text of the Polish Code of Civil Procedure and the practice, one can easily see that not only the name of this complex procedural act is a creation of dogmatics or juridical practice, but also the clear structural distinction itself.

In turn, the act of making so-called inheritance assurances (a juridical term) is clearly structurally distinguished in the normative pattern. The inheritance assurances are part of the evidentiary proceedings in the inheritance proceedings (it is the sub-variety of non-contentious civil proceedings). According to the Polish Code of Civil Procedure, the submission of inheritance assurances by an heir is to concern everything known to him/her about the existence or non-existence of persons who would exclude known heirs from inheritance or inherit with them, and about the heir's wills. Before making the statement, the judge is obligated to instruct the heir that "in terms of criminal consequences, the assertion is equivalent to making an oath". The communication occurrence in question is structurally interesting in that the analysis of the empirical material revealed a clear practice

272 The rules for conducting an informational examination contained in the Polish Code of Civil Procedure do not specify the location of this activity in the structure of the trial. In practice, it precedes evidentiary proceedings, which praxeologically seems fully justified.

of the procedure[273] of extending the normative pattern with numerous specific questions and preceding the hearing of the proper statement with questions about the personal data of the heir, along the lines of the examination of a witness or a party, for example [for the sake of brevity, only the statements of the presiding judge will be cited, statements in bold are elements of the normative pattern]:

P: *We will accept inheritance assurances from you as to who is included in the circle of heirs from Mrs. X.*
P: *Ms. XY, I am instructing you on the obligation to tell the truth, this is equivalent to giving testimony after taking the oath, in short, we only tell the truth.*
P: *How old are you?*
P: *Do you have a profession, education or what is your current occupation?*
P: *Do you live in X?*
P: *You have not been punished for giving false testimony?*
P: *Mrs. X* [the testator] *is your mother?*
P: *She died on September X, XXXX in X, yes?*
P: ***As a married woman, yes?***
P: *Before her death, she lived in X, on Y Street, right?*
P: **Mrs. X had children?**
P: ***Other children out of wedlock, adopted children, nothing?***
P: *The inheritance does not include the farm?*
P: *Is this your mother's first inheritance case?*
P: *No statements were made to the notary by you?*
P: *No certificates of inheritance were there?*
P: **Do you know anything about wills?**

Another undoubted practice, which takes shape in connection with the act of making inheritance assurances, concerns the confirmation by the participants of the inheritance proceedings the assurances made by the applicant,[274] e.g.:

P: *Now we will do a short version so as not to tire you.*
P: *Mr. X at the end, you also have an obligation to tell the truth.*
P: *How old are you?*
P: *Your profession, education?*
P: *Do you live in X?*
P: *Were you not punished for giving false testimony?*
P: **Did you hear what the sister said?**
P: **Do you confirm everything?**
P: *Okay, you can sit down.*

---

273 This practice was followed in all the proceedings analyzed in this regard. In one case, however, the presiding judge indicated the point at which the receipt of inheritance assurances was completed and the examination of the participant began.

274 In the empirical material collected, this is a practice without exception.

2.3.2.13. Communication occurrences – functional aspect

With regard to individual communication occurrences, it is possible to indicate which basic interactional strategy an occurrence is supposed to implement. The concept of interactional strategies is taken, for the purposes of this study, from communication grammar. Within the framework of communication grammar, the so-called interactional strategies are: informational-verification, axiological-emotional, behavioral, and metadiscursive strategies.[275] Determining what type of interactional strategy a given communication occurrence implements makes it possible to indicate a certain expectations for the participants of such an occurrence, and, moreover, to delineate the range of undesirable acts within a certain type of strategy.

The communication occurrences, the structural aspect of which was discussed above (i.e., the examination, the so-called informational examination and the making of inheritance assurances), from a functional point of view, are elements of the cognitive strategy carried out during the trial. **Their primary purpose is to gather assertions of facts**. These facts[276] in the decision phase of the proceedings will be used as the so-called factual basis for the decision. Therefore, the interaction strategies carried out during these occurrences are informational-verification strategies, which, however, in the normative pattern of the trial undergo certain modifications in relation to the determinants of this type of strategy in common conversation.

Using informational-verification strategies, the sender seeks to obtain information that is part of the addressee's knowledge or to propose information that he or she has.[277] Therefore, the basic micro-strategy implemented within the framework of this main strategy is the process of communication with a question-answer structure, and the basic function of speech acts – the descriptive-informational function.[278]

For the basis of analysis of informational-verification strategies implemented within the framework of this study will be used Paul Grice's conversational maxims (see Table 11), taking into account the extensions of certain assumptions proposed in communication grammar. The four maxims (postulates) distinguished by Grice express the general principle of cooperation, that is, the cooperation of participants

---

275 A. Awdiejew, *Gramatyka interakcji...*, op. cit., p. 71. Actual communication occurrences, in addition to elements that implement the basic interaction strategy, usually contain elements that implement other types of strategies.

276 It is the facts, and not the set of statements of fact or the arguments cited in support of them, that constitute the subject of judicial cognition, M. Zieliński, *Poznanie sądowe a poznanie naukowe [Judicial cognition vs. scientific cognition]*, Poznań 1979, pp. 69–71.

277 A. Awdiejew, *Gramatyka interakcji...*, op. cit., p. 72.

278 In the context of the communication occurrents in question, statements reporting on the source of knowledge of the facts are also important.

in communication. In the context of informational-verification strategies, Aleksy Awdiejew sees the cooperation of communication participants as an effort to adopt a jointly worked-out configuration of reality[279] or to establish through so-called modal negotiation[280] a generally acceptable degree of its probability.

Since the possibility of applying the Grice's conception to, generally speaking, legal realm, is widely discussed in jurisprudence, it is necessary to address this issue a little more extensively. On the question of the possibility of using the Grice's conception to analyze the processes of communication within legal realm, various solutions are adopted. The point of reference of these considerations, however, is primarily communication through the texts of legislative acts. In particular, it is assumed that the Grice's conception (in its original form) is inapplicable to this type of communication,[281] or that it can be applied but with appropriate modifications.[282] These considerations, given the different object of reference, cannot, of course, be directly transferred to the communication process at the trial. When considering the possibility of using Grice's conception to analyze the communication in the courtroom, several issues should be noted. In particular: Do we have in mind a model way of shaping the trial as a communication occurrence (including the normative pattern of a trial), or the actual communication activity undertaken by the participants at the trial?; What is the purpose of referring to the Grice's conception, i.e. what is the purpose of analysis using this conception?

With regard to the first question, it is important to start with the principle of cooperation as the basic assumption made in Grice's conception and consider whether communication in the courtroom can be considered cooperative. The answer is, it depends. It depends, among other things, on what type of communication occurrence we are considering: whether, for example, we are analyzing the communication between the parties to the proceedings (e.g., through procedural

279 A. Awdiejew, *Gramatyka interakcji...*, op. cit., p. 76.

280 Ibidem, p. 74. The modalities in question are epistemic modalities, i.e. those that relate to knowledge and the degree of conviction about something.

281 E.g.: "The theory of conversational implicatures is not applicable to statutory interpretation or interpretation of other authoritative legal acts; it is applicable, instead, to the interpretation of contracts and other acts of private autonomy", F. Poggi, *Law and Conversational Implicatures*, "International Journal for the Semiotics of Law" 2011, Vol. 24, p. 39; see also M. Matczak, *Does Legal Interpretation Need Paul Grice? Reflections on Lepore and Stone's Imagination and Convention*, "Polish Journal of Philosophy" 2016, Vol. 10, No. 1; I. Skoczeń, *Implicatures...*, op. cit., p. 27 et seq.; F. Poggi, *Against the Conversational Model of Legal Interpretation: On the Difference between Legislative Intent and Speaker's Intention*, "Revus" 2020, Vol. 40.

282 See I. Skoczeń, *Implicatures...*, op. cit.; cf. A. Marmor, *The Language of Law*, Oxford 2014. See also the model developed on the basis of Grice's conception which is applicable to the normative discourse, F. Poggi, *P Discourse*, [in:] *Further Advances in Pragmatics and Philosophy: Part 2 Theories and Applications*, eds. A. Capone, M. Carapezza, F. Lo Piparo, Cham 2019, p. 251 et seq.

documents) or the examination of a witness, and whether we are interested in the model formation of these communication occurrences (including a specific normative pattern) or their actual implementation. Let's analyze this issue in relation to the examination of a witness. Among other things, science points out that the interaction in the examination of a witness is far from cooperative interaction. However, it should be added that such characterization refers primarily to the so-called cross-examination peculiar to the Anglo-American judiciary. The following excerpt illustrates well the difference between direct and cross-examination: "[w]hen this "friendly" [direct/in chief] examination ends, the cross-examiner begins and turns the interaction on its head. While examiners in chief are, for the most part, not allowed to lead the witness and will be piecing together a (generally chronological) story through the witness's answers to their own "open" or gently guiding questions, cross-examiners are advised in advocacy manuals to ask only leading questions. This is achieved through a preponderance of declarative ("You lied to me.") and tag ("You lied to me, didn't you?") questions. If the legal function of cross-examination is to "test" the evidence presented by the witness, its rhetorical function is to discredit the witness in the eyes of the jury, often by suggesting that he has lied. Cross-examiners, in legal control of the interaction, make use of various rhetorical devices that can intimidate and trap the witness – for example strategic silence, repeated questions, presuppositions, relexicalization, reformulation"[283] And it is also stressed that "participants will often assume (a level of) goal-specific non-cooperation on the part of their interlocutor, during the cross-examining phase of a trial (...); lawyers tend to construct a witness or defendant as someone who is seeking to give a misleading impression, for example, and witnesses and defendants, in turn, tend to expect (some of the) lawyer's utterances during cross-examination to be pragmatically misleading (...)".[284] In this context, two points should be noted. First, this characterization of the witness cross-examination is not adequate for the witness examination in Polish courts. The normative pattern of this communication occurrence is the same, regardless of whether the questions are asked of the witness by the court, the party that requested the examination, or the opposing party. It is also unacceptable to ask witnesses questions that are tricky and suggest an answer,[285] as well as assessing

283 Ch. Heffer, *Jury Trial Discourse*, [in:] *The International Encyclopedia of Language and Social Interaction*, K. Tracy, general ed., C. Ilie, T. Sandel, associate eds., John Wiley and Sons 2015, pp. 4–5.

284 D. Archer, *Cross-Examining Lawyers, Facework and the Adversarial Courtroom*, "Journal of Pragmatics" 2011, Vol. 43, p. 3222.

285 Asking so-called leading questions (questions with an explicit assumption) is a common way of conducting an examination of a witness (especially within the framework of the cross-examination). Such questions can affect witnesses' memory by causing them to consider certain non-existent events as facts (cf. N. Schwarz, *Cognition and Communication: Judgmental Biases, Research Methods and the Logic*

the credibility of the witness (this is up to the court). Secondly, the works analyzed in terms of the characteristics of the witness examination did not make a clear distinction between the model formation of this communication occurrence (especially its normative pattern) and its implementation, that is, the actual communication acts in the courtroom. This seems to be a characterization that combines the two indicated dimensions. On the other hand, the analyses conducted in this chapter are concerned with the model formation of the trial and the communication acts and occurrences within it. The important thing is how the legislator has shaped the pattern of such a communication occurrence, possibly how this pattern is supplemented by the practice, not how this pattern is implemented in reality. Applying this to the witness examination, at the level of the normative pattern it is a cooperative communication occurrence (about this issue more in a moment), and in reality the attitude of the witness can be both cooperative and non-cooperative.

Referring to the second question (What is the purpose of analysis using the Grice's concept?), the following explanations should be pointed out. Grice's maxims will be in this subsection a starting point for the description of the **communication process at the trial in Polish courts considered as a model**, and not a contribution to inferences of the nature of conversational implicatures, for which in Grice's conception these maxims mainly serve,[286] or for the characteristics of actual communication activity at the trial (such acts will be considered in the next chapter). These maxims determine a certain pattern of behavior of the participants in the communication process and the relations between them, and are treated as such in this study.[287] This pattern will serve as a reference point for characterizing those communication occurrences that (at the pattern level) implement an information-verification strategy.[288]

As already indicated above, in the context of informational-verification strategies the cooperation of communication participants is seen as an effort to adopt a jointly worked-out configuration of reality or to establish through modal negotiation a generally acceptable degree of its probability. It is already possible to detect in the normative pattern of the trial significant dissimilarities in terms of the

---

of Conversation, Hillsdale 1996, p. 36 et seq.). For this reason, such questions could be considered suggestive in a Polish court, and consequently unacceptable.

286 It is noted in jurisprudence that "it is possible to view Paul Grice's implicature theory as a purely epistemological theory", I. Skoczeń, *Implicatures...*, op. cit., p. 22. It answers the question "how hearers infer implicatures", ibidem.

287 Grice's maxims, as a pattern of behavior, are sometimes a reference point in the analysis of communication activity during cross-examination, which, however, is characterized as a non-cooperative occurrence. In particular, it is shown how participants in the examination violate specific maxims. Such analysis seems to be justified. See e.g. L. Cummings, *Pragmatic Disorders...*, op. cit., p. 364 et seq.

288 It is considered fully justified in this study that Grice's concept (in its original form) is adequate for the analysis of communication occurrences implementing (to use the language of communicative grammar) an information-verification strategy.

principle of cooperation so understood, and these dissimilarities apply to all the communication occurrences previously distinguished. First, the only entity authorized to make a binding decision on the facts considered, that is, to put it in the language of communication grammar – an authoritative determination of the configuration of reality, is the court. Secondly, modal negotiation, which presupposes the expression of modal judgments by all participants in this type of strategy, is excluded. The use of modal negotiation is blocked, first of all, by norms of conduct concerning the impartiality of the judge. This refers to the obligation to avoid behavior that could undermine confidence in his or her impartiality. From this obligation, one could derive a prohibition on the judge expressing modal judgments at the trial as to the facts cited by the participants of the proceedings. The expression of such judgments could also be blocked by the principle of judicial impartiality[289] in a situation where such a modal judgment would involve an act that would not meet the so-called impartiality test.[290] In addition, an important restriction is the prohibition of asking examined persons questions that suggest the content of their answers, which could thus suggest a particular modal judgment.[291]

It is also characteristic of the implementation of informational-verification strategies at the trial that achieving the goal of this strategy of obtaining certain information does not block (does not make unnecessary) undertaking the same strategy again and for the same object of cognition. This is determined by procedural norms and not by general principles of conversation. The court, despite obtaining information from one participant, re-examines subsequent participants about the same facts, as long as it has admitted examination evidence in this regard.

Grice's four maxims (postulates),[292] are particularly useful for describing the desirable way of taking communication acts by examined persons in the framework

289 This refers to the principle of impartiality in directive terms, as a binding legal norm, S. Wronkowska, M. Zieliński, Z. Ziembiński, *Zasady prawa. Zagadnienia podstawowe [Principles of law. Basic issues]*, Warszawa 1974, p. 180.

290 In this case, it is about the methodological understanding of impartiality "according to which about every behavior of the court it is possible to judge whether it is or is not impartial", O. Bogucki, M. Zieliński, *Zasada bezstronności – art. 4 k.p.k. a podstawy środka odwoławczego [The principle of impartiality – Article 4 of the Polish Code of Criminal Procedure and the grounds of appeal]*, "Palestra" 2009, No. 11–12, p. 93. In a situation where the modal judge's expression of the circumstances presented by one of the parties to the proceedings would lead to a failure (at least to some extent) to examine the another party's version, such an act could be qualified in terms of the impartiality test. In such a case, it is not enough that the judge's expression of a modal judgment undermines confidence in the judge's impartiality, but that it is linked to an act that does not meet the impartiality requirement in the methodological sense.

291 An explicit prohibition on asking questions that suggest the content of the answer is formulated in the Polish Penal Code of Criminal Procedure and the Polish Code of Procedure for Misdemeanor Cases.

292 P. Grice, *Studies in the Way of Words*, Cambridge 1989, pp. 26–27.

of the communication occurrences previously distinguished. These maxims are presented in Table 11.

Table 11. *Grice's maxims*

1. Quantity	"Make your contribution as informative as is required (for the current purposes of the exchange)" "Do not make your contribution more informative then is required"
2. Quality	"Do not say what you believe is false" "Do not say that for which you lack adequate evidence"
3. Relation	"Be relevant" (Make your speech relevant to the topic).
4. Manner	"Avoid obscurity of expression" "Avoid ambiguity" "Be brief (avoid unnecessary prolixity)" "Be orderly"

Source: Own compilation based on P. Grice, *Studies...*, op. cit., pp. 26–27.

In terms of the postulate of quality, the normative pattern of the trial in Polish courts formulates requirements for participants that are stricter than Grice's postulates – this applies to criminal liability for giving false testimony[293] and the legal obligation to tell the truth uncoupled from the criminal sanction.[294]

The postulates of quantity and relevance are associated in the normative pattern of the trial with a specific thematic line – relating to the entire evidentiary proceedings of the case and specified in the evidentiary ruling (more on this in Section 2.3.3 on the cognitive aspect). In addition, the legislator reinforces the first part of the quantitative postulate by prohibiting the concealing of information on the same principles as giving false testimony.

Referring, in turn, to the postulate of the manner of speaking, it should be pointed out that the procedural norms do not explicitly regulate this issue (this will be further discussed in Section 2.3.4 on the stylistic aspect). Since the testimonies (explanations) of participants are the premises of the court's inference in the process of cognition, as well as may be subject to legal qualification in connection with the prohibition of giving false testimony, it can be assumed that they should

293 The legislator extremely strengthens the postulate of quality with regard to witnesses of oral wills, who are not entitled to refuse to testify and answer questions, in addition, they cannot be released from the oath. It seems that such a decision is related to granting a higher standard of protection to the subject of inheritance proceedings and the importance of examination as a means of evidence in proceedings concerning oral wills.

294 E.g., the first examination of the parties in civil proceedings.

be suitable for deciding their logical value (true or false). Thus, they should meet the defining assumptions of sentences in the logical sense, i.e., statements that have the character of indicative sentences in the grammatical sense and that are sufficiently unambiguous.[295]

It is worth adding that the above-described pattern of communication activity within the framework of communication occurrences implementing the information-verification strategy makes it possible to formulate certain normative expectations (of telling the truth, reporting the facts, etc.) with respect to the participants of communication. However, this does not mean that it is equally justified to formulate predictive expectations to the same extent.[296] For example, it is entirely rational for a judge to formulate a normative expectation of truth-telling with respect to a witness under examination, and at the same time not to formulate a predictive expectation that this will actually happen.

Given that the communication occurrences previously highlighted (especially those carried out in the context of evidentiary proceedings) consume a lot of the time intended for conducting the trial, **informational-verification strategies are the dominant strategies at the trial**.

In order to briefly address the other strategies, it is necessary, in particular, to go beyond the scope of the communication occurrences highlighted in the previous section, i.e. the examination, the so-called informational examination and the inheritance assurances.

Within the framework of axiological-emotional strategies, the sender seeks to introduce and agree with the addressee on value judgments toward a particular object.[297] These strategies realize the subjective, including emotional, attitude of the participants of communication toward a given object.[298] The primary means of expression are speech acts that perform an expressive function, including evaluative utterances.[299]

In the normative pattern, it is difficult to point to such a part of the trial, in which the legislator explicitly provided for the use of axiological-emotional strategies. Undoubtedly, blocked within the normative pattern is that aspect of the strategy in

295 In this context, communication acts that serve to clarify the statements of participants, which sometimes function as incomplete statements within the process of communication, should be considered a fully legitimate element of the communication occurrents in question.

296 "I may expect of a person that he be polite toward people around him [normative expectation] and yet, taught by prior experience, expect that he will not [predictive expectation]". See K. Paprzycka, *Normative Expectations, Intentions and Beliefs*, "The Southern Journal of Philosophy" 1999, Vol. 37, p. 631.

297 A. Awdiejew, *Gramatyka interakcji...*, op. cit., p. 72.

298 Ibidem.

299 By "evaluative utterance" in this monograph is meant an utterance expressing an assessment, that is, approval or disapproval of some state of affairs.

question, which concerns the joint agreement of the participants in the process of communication on value judgments concerning a particular subject. On the other hand, it is possible to identify some communication occurrences at the trial in which the use of axiological-emotional strategies is not explicitly blocked by the legislator. This applies primarily to the explanations of the defendant, when the use of the strategy in question can be seen as an element of the right to defense.[300] Also, the final voices of the parties (the so-called "closing speeches") can be seen as this stage of the trial, within the framework of which the participants can allow themselves to formulate evaluative and other utterances expressing their subjective attitude to the proceedings, including their subject matter.

Behavioral strategies, on the other hand, are used to persuade the addressee to take a particular act or take a definite position on the acts proposed by the sender.[301] The primary means of expression of these strategies are utterances that perform a suggestive function, including directive expressions. The main and most important in the entire court proceedings behavioral strategies are used during the initiation of the proceedings. The initiator of the court proceedings (unless, exceptionally, it was initiated ex officio) requests the resolution of a particular case, proposing a way to end it. Consequently, the entire court proceedings can be seen as the implementation of that entity's behavioral strategy. However, the focus of this study is on the communication acts undertaken at the trial, not the entire proceedings, especially since the acts initiating the proceedings are a manifestation of written communication.[302] At the trial, the use of behavioral strategies is manifested, among other things, during the announcement of the court decision, especially when the decision takes the form of an individual and specific norm, and in the participants' motions to the court. An example of the participant's suggestive communication acts, which were explicitly singled out by the legislator in the Polish Code of Civil Procedure, are the statements of the parties that begin the trial, but the normative pattern is quite sparse in this regard. On the other hand, in practice, due to the use of intertextual references, these acts are sometimes significantly limited.[303] Undertaking a behavioral strategy in the course of the statements of the parties does not, at least at the level of the normative pattern, give rise to a complex communication occurrence, in which there would be

300 Samborski E., *Zarys metodyki pracy sędziego w sprawach karnych [Outline of the methodology of the judge's work in criminal cases]*, 6th edition, Warszawa 2013, p. 324. Suggestive or optative utterances (expressing wishes) can also appear in explanations.

301 A. Awdiejew, *Gramatyka interakcji...*, op. cit., p. 72.

302 In communication grammar, interaction strategies are referred to face to face communication.

303 Sometimes the statements of the parties are reduced to the following statements, e.g. "I request as in the lawsuit..., I request as in the response to the lawsuit..., As in the response to the appeal..., As before...".

a sequence of communication acts aimed at inducing a given person to perform a certain act (negotiation sequence). However, this can happen if the court induces the parties to conciliate at the preliminary part of the trial.[304] Due to the fact that the procedural norms only set the court an obligation in this regard, without specifying how it should be carried out, the communication acts related to inducing the parties to settle the case are basically shaped only by the practice. However, the research material collected for the purpose of this study does not allow to formulate conclusions generalizing a certain uniform practice in this regard. Rather, the observed ways of the court's pursuit to settle the case revealed idiolectal features of individual judges and individually thought-out behavioral strategies – sometimes less, at other times more complex.

Finally, it is still necessary to refer to metadiscursive strategies, which, as auxiliary strategies, accompany the basic strategies, refer to their course, and are often introduced when the proper strategy has been interrupted for some reason.[305]

A particularly important metastrategy that accompanies the communication acts at the trial, and even significantly conditions the communication process, is the strategy of producing written minutes. When the research was being conducted, the course of the observed trials was mostly recorded by means of written minutes. The minutes were drawn up by the clerk[306] under the direction of the presiding judge. Nowadays, in Poland, it has become standard to record court trials by electronic minutes.[307] However, the written minutes have a subsidiary role, so it is still the element of the trial in Polish courts. The act of taking

---

304 According to the norm expressed in the Polish Code of Civil Procedure, the court is obliged in every state of the proceedings to seek a settlement, and the presiding judge should at the right time induce the parties to reconcile.

305 A. Awdiejew, *Gramatyka interakcji...*, op. cit., pp. 72 and 85.

306 It is worth noting that "Polish clerks are not the equivalent of, for instance, US law clerks – broadly understood as assistants to judges (...)", M. Dudek, M. Stępień, *On the Need to Study Processes of Taking Minutes from Case Hearings: Contribution to and Call for Future Research*, "International Journal for the Semiotics of Law" 2021, Vol. 34.

307 The prepatation of electronic minutes is related to the recording of sound and video during the trial. Interestingly, in the courtrooms of Polish courts, screens are mounted facing the parties to the proceedings and the examined persons. During the trial, they can watch themselves live on the screen. This is an unusual practice and has been critically analyzed in jurisprudence, see M. Dudek, M. Stępień, *"I (can) see myself... But what for?" On Live Camera Feeds in Courtrooms (from the Perspective of Witnesses)*, "International Journal for the Semiotics of Law" 2019, Vol. 32. The authors consider the following explanations, among others: "[c]ameras with their live feeds on television screens can enhance this security by a certain extent or enhance the subjective sense of security (...)" (ibidem), or "[t]his could be an incentive for the witnesses to control their behavior and exercise self-discipline" (ibidem), etc.

minutes is considered in this study to be a metastrategy[308] due to the fact that it is not an independent activity, but dependent on other communication activities undertaken. Taking minutes, however, exhibits peculiarities that significantly distinguish this type of act from other acts that implement metadiscursive strategies. The strategies in question are primarily supportive in nature, e.g. they make it possible to determine the reason for the interruption of communication and return to the proper strategy. In contrast, the need for minutes is precisely the circumstance that causes the interruption of communication, and only the correct implementation of this strategy allows the return to the proper strategy, e.g. the continuation of the examination.

The method of producing court minutes, given the rather laconic regulation of this issue in the procedural legislative acts in Poland, is determined primarily by the practice, with the prevailing practice being the dictation of the content of the minutes by the presiding judge.[309] Accordingly, it is possible to create a scheme for the production of minutes that corresponds to the dominant practice, which significantly determines the actual course of other communication occurrences. An example of a communication occurrence, within the framework of which minutes are produced, can realize the scheme (for simplicity, the category of recipients other than the addressee is omitted) shown in Figure 13.

308 The change in the point of reference from face to face interaction at the trial to the entire court proceedings also changes the perception of the essential function of the minutes, which carry out an informational-verification strategy within the proceedings. The addressee of the minutes is first and foremost the court of second instance, which, through the minutes, is supposed to learn about the procedural acts carried out at the trial, and, especially importantly, the content of the testimonies, explanations or other procedural statements made.

309 On the basis of the research material, only three court sessions scheduled for the trial were identified, during which the participants' statements were recorded without the mediation of the presiding judge (these sessions were presided over by the same judge, but this was not an uncommon practice for this judge, as during other sessions he dictated the participants' statements into the minutes). In other cases, either the contents of the minutes were dictated in full by the presiding judge, or partially and in the remaining parts were completed independently by the court clerk. Cf. on this topic, based on other empirical studies in Polish courts, M. Dudek, M. Stępień, *On the Need to Study Processes of Taking Minutes...*, op. cit.

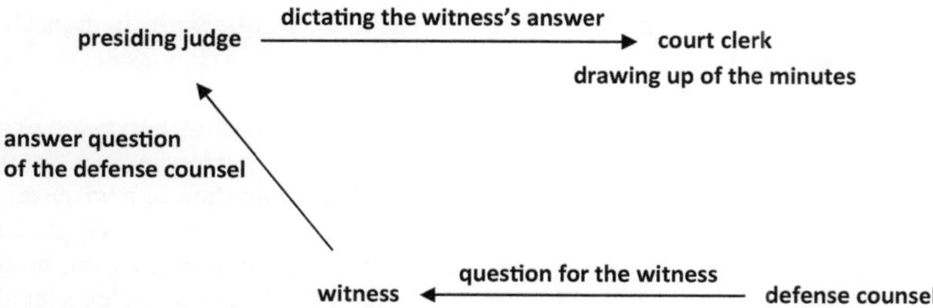

Figure 13. *Diagram for producing written minutes (during the witness examination)*
Source: Own study.

Against the background of the practice in question, it is still necessary to draw attention to the problem of writing the statements of a participant in the minutes. Given that the primary function of the court proceedings minutes is a reporting function related primarily to the control proceedings, it is not without significance not only whether it adequately reflects the content of the participant's statements (which is obvious), but also whether the statement recorded in the minutes reflects the participant's way of formulating it (e.g., choice of lexis). After all, the style of expression and, above all, the choice of vocabulary can indicate both the communication competence of the participant and the level of his or her knowledge or way of perceiving reality. Thus, the participants' statements contained in the minutes always presents (reveals) some images of them. How adequate this image is to what the participant presents in the proceedings depends, in particular, on how the participant's statements are transposed into the minutes. However, already at the level of the pattern of the trial, it can be noted that it is possible that the participant's statement included in the minutes will not be *de facto* formulated by him or her. Such a situation can occur when a participant gives answers to closed questions, such as:

P: *Sir, the deceased testator XY was your spouse, yes?*
Participant: *Yes.*
P: [for the minutes] *The deceased testator was my spouse.*

Thus, it should be borne in mind that the image of the participant, which can be reconstructed on the basis of his or her statements contained in the minutes, can be distorted not only by inaccurate reproduction of these statements in the minutes, but also by posing closed questions (which is in line with the normative pattern of the trial).[310]

* * *

In order to illustrate the issues raised in the summary of considerations of the structural and the functional aspect of communication occurrences that are part of the genre pattern of the trial, an excerpt from the examination of a witness will be cited. With regard to the structural aspect, will be marked those excerpts from the examination that are elements: (1) of the normative pattern of the examination of the witness; (2) of the normative pattern related to the presiding judge's leading function; (3) of the practice, in particular, relating to the drafting minutes; (4) unrelated to the communication occurrence in question; (5) constituting a transgression of the pattern. On the other hand, with reference to the functional aspect, those parts of the examination that implement strategies other than informational-verification will be indicated.

P: *I invite you to the railing* (3, behavioral strategy). *I instruct you that you will be examined in the character of a witness, therefore you are obliged to testify the truth, there is criminal liability for giving false testimony* (1). *Do you understand?* (3, metadiscursive strategy).
Witness: *I understand* (3, metadiscursive strategy).
P: *Your name* (1).
Witness: *XY* (1).
P: *How old are you?* (1).
Witness: *Twenty-eight. No, sorry, thirty-three, my wife had her twenty-eighth birthday* (1).
P: *Usually it is women who are wrong. Right* (4).
P: [for the minutes] *Thirty-three years* (3, metadiscursive strategy).
P: *Do you live in X?* (1).
Witness: *In X, yes* (1).
P: *Have you been punished for giving false testimony?* (1).
Witness: *It did not happen to me* (1).
P: *In relation to the parties to these proceedings, are you a stranger or a relative?* (1).
Witness: *Stranger* (1).
P: [for the minutes] *Stranger to the parties* (3, metadiscursive strategy).
P: *What do you do for a living?* (1).
Witness: *I am a construction engineer* (1).

---

310 At the same time, it should be noted that the analysis of the research material in terms of transposing participants' statements into the minutes revealed the prevailing practice of not noting in the minutes the questions posed to the participants and the uniform practice of including in the minutes testimonies and explanations in the first person, which suggests that the statement contained in the minutes comes directly from the person who, through the use of the first-person form, is revealed as its author. This, as we know, in light of the above observations, is not always true.

P: *Ladies and gentlemen, what about the oath?* (2, behavioral strategy, metadiscursive strategy).

Attorney 1: *Thank you very much* (1, behavioral strategy, metadiscursive strategy).

Attorney 2: *I do not request, thank you* (1, behavioral strategy, metadiscursive strategy).

P: [for the minutes] *By consent of the parties, witness heard without oath* (3, metadiscursive strategy).

P: *Mr. X, do you know what the proceedings are about?* (1).

Witness: *I know* (1).

P: *What is the subject matter of these proceedings?* (1).

Witness: *Generally speaking, an error in the delineation of* (...) (1).

P: [for the minutes] *It concerns a delineation error* (...) (3, metadiscursive strategy).

P: *Please say something more about it, what building, on what plot of land, when did it take place?* (1).

Witness: *I will not give the plot number, because it is like the event took place* (...) (1).

P: [for the minutes] *The event took place* (...). (3, metadiscursive strategy).

P: *Please tell the court what the error was?* (1) (...).

P: [for *the minutes*] *We will record here – the respondent's attorney left the courtroom. We will record – the witness continues to testify* (3, metadiscursive strategy).

P: *Ms. Attorney, you are very welcome* (2, behavioral strategy).

Attorney 1: *Please tell us what are the responsibilities of a surveyor in the construction process* (1).

Witness: *Generally speaking, a surveyor has a duty* (...) (1).

P: [for the minutes] *In the construction process, the surveyor has an obligation* (...) (3, metadiscursive strategy).

P: *You are very welcome* (2, behavioral strategy).

Attorney 1: *Who bears the consequences when a building is misplaced?* (5).

Attorney 2: *Your Honor, but these are questions for the expert, here the witness is not an expert, these are general questions about the nature of things* (3, metadiscursive strategy).

P: *Ms. Attorney, when it comes to the guilt the court will not allow questions concerning guilt, this is a legal assessment* (2, metadiscursive, behavioral strategy) (...).

P: *You are very welcome. Mr. Attorney, do you have any questions?* (2, behavioral strategy, metadiscursive strategy).

Attorney 2: *Not anymore* (3).

P: *Therefore, thank you very much* (3), *you are free to leave the room, you can stay in the room* (1, behavioral strategy).

Witness: *Goodbye* (3).

P: *Goodbye* (3).

The course of communication occurrences implemented at the trial is determined not only by procedural norms that define the structure of specific complex procedural acts. In addition to the acts explicitly defined as elements of the normative pattern of a given procedural act (e.g., examination of a witness), there are also communication acts that constitute the implementation of the presiding judge's leading function. These acts are aimed at organizing a given communication occurrence, while being a manifestation of the implementation of communication strategies other than the descriptive-informational strategy.

In addition to the acts described above, the communication occurrences carried out in the trial are co-created by acts shaped by the practice (relating to the way the minutes are taken, having a phatic function, related to the reaction to the transgression of the pattern, etc.), as well as those that have an accidental character (such as asking for the opening the window or indicating where the witness can put his or her coat away). Of the acts indicated in this paragraph, the creation of written minutes has a particular impact on the communication process due to the fact that it requires the interruption of the main communication strategy.

During the execution of a specific communication occurrence within a trial, there may also be such communication acts or behaviors that will constitute a clear transgression of the normative pattern. The structure of the relevant elements of a specific communication occurrence depends primarily on the degree of detail of the normative pattern delineating the communication occurrence in question, the activity of the presiding judge in carrying out his or her duties, and the level of adaptation of the pattern of the trial by other participants.

2.3.2.14. Conventionalization and formalization of the communication acts at the trial

According to the theoretical assumptions made in the study, communication acts are conventional acts. The source of conventionalization of these acts is the sociocultural system. The communication acts undertaken at the trial in the context under discussion are characterized by both conventionalization and formalization.

The distinction between these two phenomena characterizing conventional acts was made by Maciej Zieliński.[311] The above-mentioned terminological and,

---

311 A. Choduń, S. Czepita, *Profesor Maciej Zieliński. Uczony, Nauczyciel, Wychowawca [Professor Maciej Zieliński. Scientist, Teacher, Educator]*, [in:] *W poszukiwaniu dobra wspólnego. Księga jubileuszowa Profesora Macieja Zielińskiego [In search of the common good. A jubilee book by Professor Maciej Zieliński]*, eds. A. Choduń, S. Czepita, Szczecin 2010, pp. 32–33; S. Czepita, *Polish Legislative Procedure and the Role of the Polish Constitutional Tribunal from the Perspective of the Theory of Conventional Acts and Formal Acts in Law*, [in:] *Poznań School...*, op. cit., p. 234. The idea of distinguishing between conventionalization and formalization became the inspiration and theoretical basis for considering conventional acts in law. It was theoretically developed primarily by Czepita, S. Czepita, *Formalizacja a konwencjonalizacja działań w prawie [Formalization vs. conventionalization of actions in law]*, [in:] *Konwencjonalne i formalne...*, p. 9 et seq.

consequently, conceptual distinction is currently used as one of the theoretical foundations of studies in dogmatics.[312]

2.3.2.15. Conventionalization and formalization in the concept of conventional acts

The discussion of the issue of conventionalization and formalization of conventional acts should be preceded by at least a sketchy presentation of the way in which the concept of conventional acts is developed, taking into account the characteristics of constitutive rules, by Czepita.[313] Within the framework of the development in question, the author, in particular, made an explication of the meaning of the term "conventional act" by indicating the definitional postulates of the term, but by characterizing its designators. These postulates are as follows:[314] (1) a given conventional act must be legitimized by a material substrate in the form of the conduct of a specific human being (although its performance may be attributed to an entity other than a human being);[315] (2) for any conventional act, it is possible to indicate a term in a given language that is its name; (3) for any conventional act, it is possible to indicate the rules that determine the consequences of its performance,[316] since an act is conventional only if its performance affects the normative situation of the entity performing the conventional act or other entities.[317] As the author himself emphasizes, this definition, while clarifying selected elements of the content of the name "conventional act", nevertheless preserves the vagueness

---

312 E.g., T. Kiełkowski, *Nabycie prawa na mocy decyzji administracyjnej [Acquisition of a right by administrative decision]*, Warszawa 2012, p. 134 et seq., K. Markiewicz, *Zasady orzekania w postępowaniu nieprocesowym [Rules of adjudication in non-adversarial proceedings]*, Warszawa 2013, p. 21 et seq., B. Janusz-Pohl, *Formalizacja i konwencjonalizacja...*, op. cit., eadem, *Definitions and Typologies...*, op. cit.

313 S. Czepita, *Reguły...*, op. cit.

314 S. Czepita, *Reguły...*, pp. 145–148.

315 In the case of particularly complex conventional acts such as court proceedings – even several entities, S. Czepita, *O koncepcji czynności konwencjonalnych w prawie [On the concept of conventional acts in law]*, [in:] *Wykładnia Konstytucji. Aktualne problemy i tendencje [Interpreting the Constitution. Current problems and trends]*, ed. M. Smolak, Warszawa 2016, p. 127.

316 Such an assumption is also made in this study, despite the fact that the author has made some exceptions in this regard in his recent publication, S. Czepita, *On the Concept of Conventional Act in Law and its Types*, "Ruch Prawniczy, Ekonomiczny i Socjologiczny" 2017, No. 1, p. 85 et seq. Among the philosophical concepts that place special emphasis on normatively determined consequences is, among others, the concept of John R. Searle (M. Witek, *Three Approaches...*, op. cit., p. 136 et seq.), to which, in terms of constitutive rules, Czepita refers.

317 S. Czepita, *Reguły...*, pp. 146–147.

of its scope.[318] What is particularly important from the point of view of the theoretical grounding of the present study, Czepita also indicates in what relation the definition formulated by him remains to the definition formulated by the authors of *Conventional Acts in Law*.[319] This is because the author reveals that the conception of conventional acts adopted by him leads to limiting the scope of such acts to those that have at least minimal social significance. Therefore, the concept of the Poznan legal theorists seems, in the author's opinion, broader. The difference indicated does not negatively affect the possibility of using further theoretical solutions proposed by Czepita, since it is assumed in the study that all communication acts are more or less socially important.

The characterization of conventional acts must take into account both the rules for performing a given act (rules of construction) and the rules that determine the consequences of performing a given act (rules of consequence).[320] Those of them, the violation of which causes that a given act is not recognized as a conventional act of a given type, and this due to the linguistic content (connotation) of its name,[321] are called constitutive rules.[322]

Performing a certain act contrary to the rules of **conventionalization** (constitutive rules) means that it is not recognized as a conventional act of a given type.[323] On the other hand, the **formalization** of a given act consists in the determination by the relevant norms of conduct of how to perform a given act, while an act performed against the rules of formalization remains an act of a given type.[324]

---

318 Ibidem, p. 146.

319 L. Nowak, S. Wronkowska, M. Zieliński, Z. Ziembiński, *Conventional Acts...*, op. cit.

320 S. Czepita, *Reguły...*, op. cit., p. 148, idem, *Formalizacja a konwencjonalizacja działań...*, p. 13.

321 The term "connotation" in the concept of conventional acts is understood, following Kazimierz Ajdukiewicz, as a peculiar set of characteristics of the designators of a given name, one that makes it possible to identify a certain object as the designator of a given name, S. Czepita, *Reguły...*, op. cit., p. 155. A clear indication of the meaning of this term is important, since this term is (it seems even more commonly) used in another sense – as certain properties commonly (sometimes stereotypically) associated with objects of a certain type, I. Szczepankowska, *Semantyka i pragmatyka językowa. Słownik podstawowych pojęć z zadaniami i literaturą przedmiotu [Linguistic semantics and pragmatics. Dictionary of basic concepts with tasks and literature on the subject]*, Białystok 2011, p. 82; "a feeling or idea that is suggested by a word in addition to its basic meaning, or something suggested by an object or situation", Cambridge Dictionary, https://dictionary.cambridge.org/dictionary/english/connotation, access 3.07.2023.

322 S. Czepita, *Reguły...*, op. cit., p. 151, idem, *Formalizacja a konwencjonalizacja działań...*, p. 13.

323 Cf. S. Czepita, *Formalizacja i konwencjonalizacja w systemie prawnym [Formalization and conventionalization in the legal system]*, [in:] *System prawny a porządek prawny [Legal system vs. legal order]*, eds. O. Bogucki, S. Czepita, Szczecin 2008, p. 109.

324 S. Czepita, *Formalizacja a konwencjonalizacja działań...*, p. 11.

Formalization of a particular act can occur in two forms: (1) formalization by designating an obligation – norms order (prohibit) the performance of an act in a certain way; (2) formalization by designating consequences – performance of an act in a designated manner will result in positive consequences, which will not occur if the act is performed against the rules of formalization, alternatively, performance of an act differently from the rules of formalization will result in certain negative consequences.[325] The two forms of formalization are not mutually exclusive.

2.3.2.16. Levels of conventionalization of communication acts undertaken at the trial

In the discussion of communication acts (see Section 1.2.1.4), only some aspects of the particularly complicated issue of the meaning of communication act were discussed. With reference to the concept of conventional acts developed in jurisprudence, it was pointed out that the meaning of a conventional act is grasped as either the recognition of a given act as a conventional act of a certain type or the explanation of a given act, i.e. the indication of why (for what) it was undertaken. On the other hand, with reference to the theory of speech acts, the distinction between propositional (locutionary) meaning as an answer to the question of what was said and interactional (illocutionary) meaning as an answer to the question of why something was said was indicated.

The meaning of a communication act can also be recognized in relation to different levels of conventionalization, which has particularly momentous consequences in the case of communication acts undertaken at the trial.

Since the most momentous communication acts undertaken at the trial are part of the linguistic communication process, the following discussion will be limited to linguistic acts (speech acts).[326]

The starting point for discussing the issue of the level of conventionalization of communication acts taken at the trial is this way of understanding of meaning, which concerns the recognition of a given act as a conventional act of a certain type. With regard to communication acts that are particularly important from the point of view of the trial, two levels of conventionalization can be intuitively distinguished: **the level of the speech act** and **the level of the procedural act**. Recognizing in a given communication act a specific speech act, such as a statement, request or demand, requires not only reference to a specific linguistic system, but also to a system of obligations forming in the sphere of communication as part of socio-cultural reality. On the other hand, the recognition of a given speech act as a procedural act further requires reference to the system of legal norms.

---

325 S. Czepita, *Formalizacja i konwencjonalizacja w systemie...*, pp. 109–110.

326 Although it is, of course, possible to imagine performing at least part of a complex procedural act, for example, by nodding in place of a speech act (analysis of empirical material reveals few examples of this type).

In the context of the first level of conventionalization, one should wonder whether it is not reasonable to distinguish an even lower level of conventionalization at the level of locution, i.e. what is also called ideational meaning or propositional content. This is because it is assumed that ideational meaning (objectified propositional content) can exist without interactional meaning (illocution).[327] However, it seems that in the definitional postulates of a conventional act, cited after Czepita, it is the speech act that should be considered as the first level of conventionalization, for the reason that the determination of the rules of consequence of a given linguistic act becomes possible when this act is recognized as a speech act that, at the level of illocution, affects the normative situation of the subject taking the given linguistic act or other subjects.[328] Such a perspective is taken in this study.[329]

The term "procedural act" is not uniformly understood in dogmatics. Here, in direct reference to the accepted concept of conventional acts, it is recognized that in order to speak of a procedural act, a conventional act must at least be conventionalized at the level of procedural norms.[330]

---

327 A. Awdiejew, *Gramatyka interakcji...*, op. cit., pp. 18 and 44. The classic formula of illocution F(p) can be transformed into p (i.e. distinguish an objectified propositional content) instead of transforming it into the formula F(?) has no sense regardless of whether on how many levels the act is conventionalized – F′(F(?)). See the formula in J.R. Searle, *Speech Acts...*, op. cit., p. 31.

328 See about consequences in the form of creating a possibility for a proper reaction analyzed by Austin when characterizing the effects of successful and binding illocutions in J.L. Austin, *How to do...*, op. cit., p. 116.

329 John R. Searle considers the speech act to be the basic and smallest unit of linguistic communication, J.R. Searle, *Speech Acts...*, op. cit., p. 16. On the other hand, within the framework of communication grammar, the speech act is the basic unit at the interactional level of linguistic communication, A. Awdiejew, *Gramatyka interakcji...*, op. cit., p. 18.

330 Accepting the assumption that the level of a procedural act is the level of conventionalization of a given action means that it is not enough to formalize (even at the level of procedural norms) a given speech act in order to speak of a procedural act. In addition, a communication act (as defined in this monograph) should be viewed not as the substantive substrate of a procedural act, but as a lower level of conventionalization of that substrate. In constructing an elaborate definition of the term "procedural act", it is worth referring to the definition of the term "act in criminal proceedings" proposed by Barbara Janusz-Pohl due to the fact that it was developed taking into account the concept of conventional acts (developed by the author in some of its aspects) –"An act in criminal proceedings is a formalised legally relevant conventional act (formalised cA), consisting in a conscious and free execution of its material substrate for the purpose of performing this act (direct goal = illocutionary effect), pursuant to constitutive rules proper to it, with the execution of the trial effects (so-called final goal) of a formalised cA being covered by its formalization", Janusz-Pohl, *Definitions and Typologies...*, op. cit., p. 71. Given the general theoretical foundation of the formulated definition applied by the author,

The level of procedural acts is the most important level of meaning of the communication acts taken at the trial. For this reason, it is the starting and reference point of the following considerations.

2.3.2.17. Rules of conventionalization and rules of formalization of procedural acts

Highlighting the level of the procedural act as the level of conventionalization of the communication acts taken at the trial makes it possible to notice the special role of situational context and communication context in the communication in question. Indeed, some elements of the situational context, as well as of the communication context, may constitute either rules of construction or rules of consequence of particular procedural acts, which may be both conventionalizing and formalizing in nature. These relationships are illustrated in Tables 12 and 13.

Table 12. *Situational context and the rules of conventionalization and formalization of procedural acts*

Situational context	Rules of conventionalization and formalization of procedural acts
Micro-context	– Characteristics of participants (procedural roles, interactional roles), location, time
Meso-context	– The existence of court proceedings, the existence of a trial as a stage of court proceedings
Macro-context	Rules formed outside the legal system

Source: own study.

it seems that it could at least serve as a starting point in defining procedural acts in general. However, the literature points out that it is possible to identify procedural acts that are not formalized. An example of such an action is considered to be the approval of an attorney's act in civil proceedings, G. Szacoń, *Proces cywilny na tle koncepcji czynności konwencjonalnych – formalizacja czynności faktycznych i konwencjonalnych [Civil process against the background of the concept of conventional acts – formalization of factual and conventional acts]*, [in:] *Konwencjonalne i formalne aspekty...*, op. cit., p. 95. At the same time, it should be noted that the solution adopted by the author certainly does not assume that the legal effects of a procedural act are covered by formalization (as Janusz-Pohl does), otherwise this act also would have to be considered formalized.

Table 13. *Communication context and the rules of conventionalization and formalization of procedural acts*

Communication context	Rules of conventionalization and formalization of procedural acts
	Relationship to other procedural acts, sequentiality of acts*

* *It should be recalled that the sequentiality of procedural acts (or communication acts in general) undertaken at the trial is also captured as an element of time characteristics, which is in turn an element of situational context.*

Source: Own study.

Constitutive rules are rules of construction or rules of consequence, the violation of which causes that a given act is not recognized as a conventional act of a certain type, and this is due to the linguistic content (connotation) of the name of this act. At the same time, the linguistic content of the names of conventional acts of legal significance (including procedural acts) is formed not only in juridical language, but also in common language.[331] In this context, the role of situational macro-context is revealed, because in order to formulate an exhaustive catalog of constitutive rules of a given type of conventional act in law, it is also necessary to refer to cultural systems other than the legal system, such as rules of custom.[332]

In the theory of law, the rules of conventionalization of procedural acts primarily include the existence of court proceedings as a certain sequence of acts,[333] and for some procedural acts the existence of a trial as a stage of court proceedings. The sequentiality of a proceeding or trial considered in mereological terms as the location of certain acts in the aggregate of other acts, or the location of acts in relation to each other that make up a more complex procedural act, is also sometimes recognized as a rule of conventionalization of certain procedural acts.[334] The

331 S. Czepita, *Reguły...*, op. cit., pp. 178–179.

332 S. Czepita, *Reguły...*, op. cit., pp. 178–179. This applies not only to conventional acts in law, but also to conventional acts in general, including speech acts, cf. F. Recanati, *Meaning and Force. The Pragmatics of Performative Utterances*, Cambridge 1987, p. 79.

333 S. Czepita, *Formalizacja i konwencjonalizacja w systemie...*, p. 114.

334 Both aspects of the mereological structure of the court proceedings are considered in the literature as constitutive rules of judgment – a given act will be recognized as a judgment if it is undertaken at a specific moment of the trial and if it is an aggregate of the acts indicated in the Polish Code of Criminal Procedure, J. Wieczorkiewicz-Kita, *Zagadnienie wyrokowania w procesie karnym w świetle koncepcji czynności konwencjonalnych [The issue of sentencing in the criminal process in the light of the concept of conventional acts]*, [in:] *Konwencjonalne i formalne...*, op. cit., pp. 57–59. Barbara Janusz-Pohl even formulates a thesis of a general nature, referring to procedural acts in criminal proceedings, according to which "the conventionalization of procedural acts is based primarily on the thesis of their sequentiality, and is not

most important aspects of the characteristics of the subjects performing a certain procedural act also seem to be conventionalizing in nature.[335] From the point of view of the communication characterization of the trial, it is important to highlight the connection between the rules of construction or consequence regardless of whether they are of a conventionalizing or formalizing nature, and the interactional roles of the participants of court proceedings scheduled for the trial. The specification of the participants' interactional roles characteristic for the communication taking place at the trial is determined precisely by the fact that the characteristics of the entity undertaking a given communication act or being the addressee of such an act is the rule of conventionalization or formalization of this act at the level of the procedural act. In turn, with regard to procedural roles, it should be pointed out that the performance of a certain procedural act is attributed to a certain conventional entity as a participant in court proceedings, but the communication act itself (primarily a linguistic act) is taken by a human being, with one that exhausts the characteristics of a certain conventional entity.[336]

A significant part of the rules of construction or rules of consequence of procedural acts is of a formalizing nature.[337] It should be emphasized in this context that in dogmatics formalism is associated with the form, place or time of procedural acts. Thus, from this point of view, it includes both rules of formalization and rules of conventionalization of a particular procedural act, as they are understood in the concept of conventional acts.[338]

2.3.2.18. Impact of conventionalization and formalization of procedural acts on some communication phenomena

It is not the purpose of this discussion to present a typology of speech acts[339] or procedural acts. Instead, it is to consider some problems related to the delimitation of the levels of conventionalization of communication acts performed at the trial,

---

the result of a particular exposition of the constitutive rules for acts of particular types", B. Janusz-Pohl, *Formalizacja i konwencjonalizacja...*, op. cit., p. 616.

335 S. Czepita, *Formalizacja i konwencjonalizacja w systemie...*, pp. 113–114. E.g., a decision issued by a non-judicial entity will not be a decision at all, and court proceedings conducted by such an entity will not be court proceedings at all.

336 An entity authorized to perform a certain procedural act either on its own behalf or on behalf of another conventional entity.

337 S. Czepita, *Formalizacja i konwencjonalizacja w systemie...*, p. 113.

338 S. Cieślak, *Formalizm postępowania cywilnego [Formalism of civil proceedings]*, Warszawa 2008, p. 64.

339 Typologies of speech acts or their criticism can be found, for example, in J.L. Austin, *How to do...*, op. cit.; J.R. Searle, *Speech Acts...*, op. cit.; S. Levinson, *Pragmatics*, op. cit.; A. Awdiejew, *Gramatyka interakcji...*, op. cit.

presented in this study, and to discuss selected aspects of the modification of certain communication phenomena by a higher level of conventionalization.[340]

Distinguishing the levels of conventionalization of communication acts performed at the trial is not problematic when the two levels can easily be labeled by different names. At the same time, it should be borne in mind that the legislator is unlikely to specify what speech act should be used for a particular procedural act,[341] this issue is determined by the practice. Thus, for example, within the motion to adduce evidence, two levels of conventionalization could be distinguished (Table 14).

Table 14. *Motion to adduce evidence as an example – levels of conventionalization*

Speech act – first level of conventionalization	**Procedural act – second level of conventionalization**
Examples of standard speech acts that can be used in order to file a motion to adduce evidence: request, request expressed indirectly (form of question), wish, demand	motion to adduce evidence

Source: Own study.

The submission of a motion to adduce evidence, depending on the speech act chosen, could take the form with the use of the explicit performative verb, e.g. *Your Honor, I **request** the taking of evidence…, Your Honor, I **demand** the taking of evidence…* or without the performative verb, e.g. *Would Your Honor please take evidence…, I would like Your Honor to take evidence…* When complying with other rules for performing the procedural act in question, each of the distinguished speech acts could lead to an effective submission of the motion to adduce evidence. In this case it is easy to distinguish two levels of conventionalization. Firstly, because of the specific name of the procedural act, and secondly, to the fact that the

340 More extensively on this topic in the context of achievements in pragmatics and philosophy of language, K. Gmerek, *Procedural Acts as Double-Conventionalized Acts: Considerations on Conventional Acts Performed in a Courtroom Discourse*, "International Journal for the Semiotics of Law" 2021, Vol. 34, No. 1, pp. 473–495.

341 An important exception is, of course, questions as an element of complex procedural acts, such as examination. In this case, the normative pattern of the trial in Polish courts places special requirements on the manner in which questions are used, which consequently causes numerous problems with the implementation of this element of the pattern (cf. the results of empirical research in this regard, Section 3.7.2.2).

recognition of the procedural act in question is related to its content[342] (the propositional content of this act is the future act of taking evidence).

It is also possible to recognize with some ease the distinguished levels of conventionalization in more complex procedural acts, such as the giving of testimony or explanations, which are otherwise part of an even more complex act such as examination. The basic type of speech act used in testifying or explaining is, of course, statements as acts of a descriptive and informative nature. However, it should be borne in mind that within the framework of the examination there may be, for example, emotive acts (expressive in nature). Recognition of the acts taken as procedural acts of testifying or explaining will be primarily related to the entity performing the act and its location within the examination, rather than to the speech act of a particular type used.

Sometimes, however, the attempt to recognize (distinguish) the levels of conventionalization in question encounters significant difficulties. Let us take as an example the decision on discontinuance of the proceedings issued as a consequence of the effective withdrawal of the claim.[343] The standard statement of the court might be as follows: *The court decides (decided) to discontinue of the proceedings...* – using the word "decides" as a performative verb, or *The court discontinues the proceedings...* – using the performative verb "discontinues". In that case, it is difficult to identify such a level of conventionalization that could be distinguished by naming it with a name other than "decision" or "discontinuance" – the name of a particular speech act.

Equally problematic are situations in which the legislator, in order to designate the acts of participants of court proceedings, uses in the text of the legislative act names peculiar to speech acts, i.e. instruct, inform or warn (e.g. *The court instructs (informs, warns) about...*), that is, it does not construct a separate name for a procedural act. The importance of the lack of terminological distinction is most apparent when reconstructing the constitutive rules of such an acts from the text of legislative act.

The purpose of the following considerations is to present the relationship between the two levels of conventionalization, including the role of speech act level identification in the recognition of a given procedural act and the impact of conventionalization at the level of the procedural act on certain communication phenomena.

As emphasized above (cf. the example in Table 14), some procedural acts can be effectively performed by different speech acts. This is because the use of a specific

342 In this context, it is worth citing one of the provisions of the Polish Code of Criminal Procedure, which states that "the meaning of a procedural act shall be judged according to the content of the statement made".

343 In this case, a single act taken by the court can condense both the act of issuing and announcing the ruling.

(strictly characterized) speech act is not a constitutive rule for performing a particular procedural act. However, the catalog of speech acts that can be used to perform a specific procedural act is not unlimited. It is related to the so-called **standard interpretation of speech acts**,[344] the mechanism which will be characterized, using the already cited example of motion to adduce evidence. The recognition in a participant's request, demand, or even an optative speech act (wish), the propositional content of which is the future act of taking evidence, is the result of the standard interpretation. Making a standard interpretation is a prerequisite for recognizing in this act the procedural act of submitting a motion to adduce evidence. If the participant's act was to deny, for example: *Your Honor, the claimant does not file motions to adduce evidence...* – then, of course, identification of this act as an act of denial would block further interpretation leading to recognition this act as a motion to adduce evidence. In this sense, the recognition of the level of the speech act is primary, especially when the procedural act in question can be done through different types of speech acts. The important role played by speech act level recognition in the identification of procedural acts (at least some of them) indicates the importance of the delineation of levels of conventionalization made in this study.

However, the essential features of the relationship between the two levels of conventionalization are related to the determinant nature of conventionalization at the level of the procedural act. First, regardless of what type of speech act is recognized on the basis of a standard interpretation, if a specific procedural act is also recognized, only the interpretation at the level of the procedural act counts. Secondly, conventionalization (as well as formalization) at the level of the procedural act determines the sphere of obligations and the so-called sphere of domination between the entities who, generally speaking, are connected with the act in question.

The structure of dominance in a specific communication process is determined by social roles and interactional roles.[345] The former refers to social status (higher, lower, equal), while the latter refers to roles assumed in connection with a specific communication occurrence, including the speech act used.

With regard to the trial (or court proceedings in general) in Polish courts, it seems reasonable to assume a dominance structure related to social status, as shown in Table 15.

---

344 The standard form of a given speech act becomes linked to the standard situation of its use, A. Awdiejew, *Gramatyka interakcji...*, op. cit., pp. 44–45.
345 Ibidem, pp. 66 and 80.

Table 15. *Social status of selected participants of court proceedings*

Court	dominant position	higher social status of the court – acting on behalf of the state, higher status highlighted in a symbolic way
Other participants	subordinate position to the court equal position of the parties (quasi-parties) in relation to each other	lower social status before the court equal social status of the parties (quasi-parties) with respect to each other

Source: Own study.

In turn, with regard to interactional roles and the associated structure of dominance, the linguists adopts some basic resolutions,[346] in particular: (1) demand implies a dominant role of the sender and a subordinate role of the addressee; (2) request – a dominant role of the addressee and a subordinate role of the sender; (3) proposal – equality of participants.

In a particular communication process, different structures of domination can be formed, depending on how strong a determinant a certain social role turns out to be.[347] In the case of the trial, the phenomenon under discussion seems particularly complicated. In order to illustrate it, two examples of the hypothetical use of the act of requesting to perform two different procedural acts will be cited. The first is the court's asking of questions during the examination of a witness (Table 16), and the second is the witness's motion for reimbursement of expenses for appearing in court (Table 17).

346 Ibidem, p. 65.

347 For example, it is noted that act of proposal in an unequal structure (e.g., a speech act standardly interpreted as a proposal expressed by a superior) will be treated as a demand, ibidem, p. 80. It should be noted that such a rule cannot be transferred to communication at the trial (cf. examples in Tables 16 and 17).

Table 16. *Exemplary structure of dominance, part I*

Asking questions by the court during the examination of a witness *Would you be willing to tell the Court...*	
standard interpretation: request*	non-standard interpretation taking into account the situational context: a question from the court that is part of an examination of a witness
dominance structure determined by standard interpretation: addressee (witness) dominant position and sender (court) subordinate position	dominance structure determined by legal norms (normative structure): the dominant position of the sender (court) and the subordinate position of the addressee (witness)
inconsistent with the dominance structure determined by social status	consistent with the dominance structure set by the social status

* *In this example, the features of a request are intentionally emphasized, although questions in general can be seen as a variety of request, cf. F. Poggi, Conversational Implicatures..., op. cit., p. 256, footnote 8 and the works cited therein; cf. A. Awdiejew, Gramatyka interakcji..., p. 109.*

Source: Own study.

In the example presented in Table 16, the structure of dominance is determined by the normative structure formed by the procedural norms – norms of competence.[348] In this case, the court is authorized to ask the witness a question. This competence is connected with the witness's obligation to answer, which is only modified under certain circumstances. The reconstructed structure of domination is consistent with the assumed structure of domination determined by social status.

348 According to Zygmunt Ziembiński's concept of the norm of competence, the norm is structured as follows: "Addressee A is obligated to do B if subject S performs conventional act C", cf. Z. Ziembiński, *Competences and Competence Norms,* [in:] *Poznań School...*, op. cit., p. 91 et seq.

Table 17. *Exemplary structure of dominance, part II*

Witness's motion for reimbursement of expenses for appearing in court *Your Honor, I would like to ask for reimbursement of travel expenses….*	
standard interpretation: request	non-standard interpretation taking into account the situational context: witness's motion for reimbursement of expenses for appearing in court
dominance structure determined by the standard interpretation: the dominant position of the addressee (court) and the subordinate position of the sender (witness)	dominance structure determined by legal norms (normative structure): the dominant position of the sender (witness) and the subordinate position of the addressee (court)
consistent with the dominance structure determined by social status	inconsistent with the dominance structure set by the social status

Source: Own study.

In the second example presented in Table 17, the dominance structure is also determined by the normative structure formed by the legislator, but in this case even more complicated. This is because the witness is an authorized entity to file a motion for reimbursement of expenses for appearing in court, and this authorization is matched by the court's obligation to examine such a motion. In addition, if the witness demonstrates the incurred costs, the court is obliged to accept the motion, since the witness is an entity entitled to reimbursement for the costs of appearing in court to give a testimony.[349] Characteristic of the example in question is the incompatibility of the dominance structure determined by legal norms with the assumed dominance structure determined by the social status of the participants in the proceedings.

A similar structure of dominance (including the inconsistency in the structure of dominance indicated within the second example) can be recognized with requests made by parties (or quasi-parties) using the act of requesting.[350]

349 The situation of entitlement as a complex legal situation is that some entity is entitlement (in this case, the witness), because another entity is obliged to provide a benefit to him or her. In the considered case, in fact, it is the state acting through the relevant authority (the court) that is obliged to provide benefits to a witness who has incurred the expense of appearing in court to give a testimony.

350 The obligation to recognize a given motion is, of course, not equivalent to the obligation to resolve it in an certain manner. This issue is determined by other norms, and sometimes the whole set of them.

The relations in the dominance structure described above would change significantly if the participant's motion had a form of a demand (Table 18).

Table 18. *Exemplary structure of dominance, part III*

The participant's motion performed in the form of a demand *Your Honor, I demand reimbursement of travel expenses....*	
standard interpretation: demand	non-standard interpretation that takes into account the situational context: a motion for reimbursement of expenses for appearing in court
dominance structure determined by the standard interpretation: dominant position of the sender (e.g. witness) and subordinate position of the addressee (court)	dominance structure determined by legal norms (normative structure): the dominant position of the sender (e.g. witness) and the subordinate position of the addressee (court)
inconsistent with the structure of domination determined by social status	inconsistent with the structure of domination determined by social status

Source: own study.

It seems that against the background of these peculiar relations in the dominance structure, a specific speech act is being formed, which can be called "motion" or "application" and which could be typologically placed between request and demand. The use of this speech act (e.g., by means of the expletive formulas "I apply for"), on the one hand, provides an opportunity to avoid the act of demanding, which emphasizes the dominant position of the sender and can thus be considered to violate the rules of linguistic politeness. On the other hand, it avoids signaling the addressee's freedom of response while maintaining certain standards of politeness.

* * *

The issue of conventionalization and formalization is of particular importance within the reconstructed genre pattern of the trial. Indeed, the performance of procedural acts is the main purpose of the communication process undertaken at the trial, which directly leads to the realization of the purpose of the entire proceedings. This does not mean, of course, that communication acts that are not procedural acts are not undertaken at the trial, but they are auxiliary, supplementary or typical for the ordinary course of communication. In this sense, a trial is an aggregate of procedural acts and other communication acts.

The analysis of conventionalization (including its levels) and formalization reveals the special importance of both communication and situational context, the elements of which constitute the rules of conventionalization or formalization of specific procedural acts. In this context, it should be noted that the recognition that the exhaustive characterization of the constitutive rules of conventional acts of legal significance (in this case, procedural acts) should also take into account extra-legal rules. It opens the normative pattern to elements outside the legal system.

2.3.3. Cognitive aspect

In the theoretical model for describing a genre pattern proposed by Maria Wojtak, the cognitive aspect of a pattern includes the subject matter and the way it is presented.

The legislator decided on the subject matter of the trial in two ways – directly and indirectly. The direct way of determining the subject matter is to select from the entire universe of issues those that can be the subject of court proceedings (as a court case), then within the varieties of court proceedings (as a civil case, criminal case, etc.) and still within the sub-varieties (as a divorce case, for acquisition of inheritance, for payment, etc.). The thematic limitation within the varieties and sub-varieties of court proceedings is, of course, of practical value, exceptionally only for some sub-varieties procedural norms authorize the consolidation of selected cases.

Further determination of the thematic scope of the court proceedings is indirect in the sense that it is part of the rules for performing acts initiating court proceedings to indicate the circumstances of the case. Thus, the circumstances described in the act initiating the proceedings (indictment, lawsuit, etc.) determine the main thematic scope of the proceedings in question. However, the subject matter so determined may sometimes be modified in the course of the proceedings.[351] This aspect of the thematic scope of the proceedings (determined by indicating the circumstances of the case) is directly connected with the subject of court cognition. As previously signaled, the subject of court cognition is certain facts.[352] In this study it is assumed that within the scope of the main subject matter is the so-called main fact. In this sense, the main thematic scope coincides with the main cognitive task in court proceedings relating to the so-called factual basis, which can be reduced to the question: How was it? (How is a certain fragment of reality represented?).[353]

The main thematic scope proposed above makes it possible to clearly see the cohesive role of the main theme, which, like the main cognitive task, accompanies all stages of the trial (and, more broadly, the entire proceedings). Of course, the main thematic scope is accompanied by side topics – they concern auxiliary facts, as well as issues unrelated to the subject of court cognition.

From the point of view of the communication process at the trial, the formation of the subject scope, which could be called partial, and which consists in the thematic limitation of the examination, is of particular importance. In proceedings

351 The degree of permissible modification depends on the variety of the proceedings.
352 M. Zieliński, *Poznanie sądowe...*, op. cit., pp. 69–71.
353 Ibidem, p. 65.

before Polish courts the proposal of the thematic scope of examination is contained in the motion to adduce evidence (unless, exceptionally, the court conducts evidence ex officio). Indeed, according to procedural norms, the motion to adduce evidence should specify the circumstances to be proved, whereby the subject of the examination may concern both the main fact (or selected aspects of it) and only side facts. The binding specification of the theme of the examination takes place primarily in the evidentiary ruling and, as part of the content of this ruling, may take the following form,[354] e.g. **P:** *The court decided to admit evidence of witness testimony* (...) *on the conditions of work, the claimant's health and medical treatment.*

The thematic scope of the examination can be modified only by amendment of the motion to adduce evidence made by an authorized entity (e.g., a party) and included in the evidentiary ruling, possibly by the court. Whether the determination of the thematic framework of the examination actually determines the course of the communication process in this procedural act will be discussed in the next chapter.

In turn, the issue of the presentation of the main subject matter was determined by the legislator on the principle of variability.[355] Most strongly this variability is accentuated in the normative pattern of the civil trial in contentious proceedings (in Polish courts). The procedural norms order the respondent to enter into a dispute on the merits of the case. In addition, it should be borne in mind that before the start of the trial, the court always has at least one version of a certain fragment of reality,[356] (revealed in the letter initiating the proceedings, exceptionally in another way, when the court initiates the proceedings ex officio). The last version of the main fact of the case presented at the trial is the version of the court – that is, the one that, in its opinion, on the basis of certain rules, has been proved.[357]

It is not difficult to notice that the cognition of facts in a trial is connected with narrative. It is about a specific way of presenting a given fragment of reality, which the narrator intends the court to find most relevant. However, narration in the courtroom differs from narration in other situational contexts (especially within non-institutional discourses). Finally, let us recall a brief characterization of the "forensic

354 On the basis of the empirical evidence gathered, one can observe a certain emerging practice, otherwise utilitarian, of accurately repeating in the ruling the circumstances indicated in the motion to adduce evidence.

355 Małgorzata Rzeszutko writes in this context about the polyphonic technique of text creation, M. Rzeszutko, *Rozprawa...*, op. cit., p. 89. However, the level of variability depends on the characteristics of a specific trial – from full agreement (e.g., the dispute is only about the legal consequences of a fact that occurred) to complete contradiction (e.g., the respondent denies the claimant's statement about the existence of a certain fact).

356 M. Zieliński, *Poznanie sądowe...*, op. cit., p. 86.

357 Ibidem, p. 87.

narrative", which (with minor modifications[358]) is also applicable to the trial in Polish courts: "[f]irstly, forensic narrative is highly evidential in contrast to conversational narrative. Hearsay is not permitted and any unsubstantiated claims will be challenged by the opposing party. Secondly, forensic narrative is subject to legal constraints, both in terms of what can be talked about (it must be relevant to the charges) and how it can be talked about (the rules of evidence). Thirdly, and certainly within adversarial systems, lawyers are engaged in an overall rhetorical practice of persuading the legal decision-maker (judge, jury, magistrate) of the guilt or otherwise of the defendant. As in all rhetorical situations, the persuasive goal is paramount. While research has often focused on the way legal constraints shape trial discourse, the persuasive goal is arguably far more important in terms of narrative practices. Thus, the lawyer will control the witness not so much to ensure that the rules of evidence are followed as to ensure that the story develops in the most rhetorically efficacious fashion. Furthermore, each genre within the trial comes with its own narrative forms, rules and expectations."[359]

2.3.4. Stylistic aspect

In Wojtak's conception, the stylistic aspect of the genre pattern includes the following "a set of: (a) extralinguistic features having linguistic exponents; (b) rules that define both the relations between features and the conditions of features. In addition, the stylistic component of the genre pattern contains rules for the choice of linguistic means, correlated with the choices of the structural and communicational model of the scenario, as well as a model-defined set of possible linguistic means".[360]

It should be made clear at this point that no discussion of style or stylistics of a general nature will be conducted in this section.[361] Only issues situated in the genre pattern fragment outlined above will be discussed.

Before doing so, however, it is worth looking at Rzeszutko's findings on the style of the trial in Polish courts. The author's consideration of style is carried out within the framework of the analysis of the trial (criminal trial) as a genre

358 This characterization applies to the courts of the common law system, and therefore takes into account the participation of the jury or the key role of lawyers in questioning witnesses. As a reminder, in Polish courts, the court has the authorization to question the participants in the proceedings, and in fact uses this very often.

359 Ch. Heffer, *Narrative practices and voice in court*, [in:] *Handbook of Communication in the Legal Sphere*, ed. Jacqueline Visconti, Berlin-Boston 2018, p. 264.

360 M. Wojtak, *Pragmatyczne aspekty...*, s. 39.

361 The basis for such a decision is, first of all, the huge scope of studies (stylistic studies has a long tradition), which would have to be thoroughly explored and then its results presented. The purpose and subject of this monograph do not justify such a solution. In addition, the problem is the variety of terms and concepts adopted in stylistic studies.

variety of the text.[362] At the same time, it should be noted that Rzeszutko does not introduce the category of normative pattern (as it is understood in this study) and thus does not indicate which of the discussed linguistic features are part of this pattern and which exceed it. The findings made by the author are the result of the recognition of the specific features of the trial (including extra-linguistic features) and the insights made during the observation of actual communication acts in the courtroom. On this basis, Rzeszutko recognizes that the trial (in Polish courts) is characterized by a peculiar style syncretism[363] consisting in the co-occurrence of official and colloquial variety of language.[364] Moreover, she adds, the style syncretism understood in this way is complemented by linguistic elements belonging to the "neutral, emotional and careful register of the colloquial variety of Polish language".[365]

The consideration of the stylistic aspect of the genre pattern of the trial undertaken in this study will further focus on the use of lexical means. In doing so, they will take into account the results of observations in this regard. However, it is not forgotten that the analysis is carried out from the model point of view. Three issues will be discussed below, respectively, related to: (1) the category of officialness/unofficialness of contact; (2) the linguistic norm; and (3) lexical means.

Re 1. In Polish linguistic works, the category of the officialness and unofficialness of a contact (or communication situation) is associated in particular with the study of the varieties of Polish language (often forming the basis of the classifications made),[366] as well as with the issues of linguistic correctness undertaken in normative

---

362 In doing so, the author captures the text genre in terms of cultural convention, M. Rzeszutko, *Rozprawa...*, op. cit., p. 181.

363 Ibidem, p. 190.

364 Ibidem. The author, speaking of the indicated registers, refers primarily to Jerzy Bartmiński, ibidem, p. 193, footnote 39. It is worth noting here that Bartmiński considers the neutral register of colloquial style to be basic, both for this style itself and for ethnic language in general, J. Bartmiński, *Styl potoczny jako centrum systemu stylowego [The colloquial style as the center of the style system]*, [in:] *Synteza w stylistyce słowiańskiej [Synthesis in Slavic style]*, ed. S. Gajda, Opole 1991, p. 42. As Agnieszka Choduń notes, it is described by the author as "joint vocabulary", that is, using the same term used to refer to lexical means that can be used in all lexical varieties of Polish language, A. Choduń, *Słownictwo tekstów aktów prawnych w zasobie leksykalnym współczesnej polszczyzny [Vocabulary of texts of legal acts in the lexical resource of modern Polish language]*, Warszawa 2007, p. 68. Choduń also notes, based on the linguistic studies analyzed, that "only in the works of J. Bartmiński is colloquial language captured so broadly that it is suitable for use in both official and unofficial situations", A. Choduń, *Słownictwo tekstów...*, op. cit., p. 162.

365 M. Rzeszutko, *Rozprawa...*, op. cit., p. 193.

366 B. Dunaj, *Kategoria oficjalności [Category of officiality]*, [in:] *Współczesna polszczyzna mówiona w odmianie opracowanej (oficjalnej) [Modern spoken Polish in the elaborated (official) variety]*, eds. Z. Kurzowa, W. Śliwiński, Kraków 1994, p. 23 et seq.

linguistics or the culture of language.[367] In particular, some researchers assume that the formality of a communication situation is determined by an institutional relationship, as well as a non-institutional one combined with the lack of ties between the participants in the communication process, while the informality of a situation is determined by a non-institutional relationship, as well as strong ties between members of a given group.[368] Linguists emphasize the institutional and public nature of official contacts[369] and the private nature of unofficial contacts.[370]

In the model (basic) view of,[371] which can be reconstructed from selected linguistic studies, it is assumed that the official situation corresponds to the official variety of general Polish language,[372] for which the so-called linguistic model norm is appropriate.[373]

There is no doubt that courtroom contact is contact in an official situation – both public and institutional.[374] However, it should be noted that this is a specific situation for at least two reasons. First, the fact that the type of communication situation in question exists at all in socio-cultural reality was decided by the legislator. In addition, the legislator decided **who** can participate in this situation and **how**, and even **where** this situation is to occur. A strong normative determination thus differentiates contact at the trial from contact in other official situations, and determines the place of the type of communication situation in question in the broader legal sphere. In particular, this has consequences in terms of the vocabulary used at the trial, as will be discussed further in this section. Secondly, despite its public nature, the subject matter of the trial (or more broadly, of the proceedings) is sometimes the subject matter characteristic of private and even intimate

---

367 M. Bugajski, *Język...*, op. cit., p. 168 et seq.

368 B. Dunaj, *Kategoria...*, op. cit., p. 24.

369 K. Zabierowska, *O „wielogłosowości" tekstów oficjalnych [On the "polyphony" of official texts]*, [in:] *Współczesna polszczyzna...*, op. cit., p. 81 et seq.

370 A. Markowski, *Kultura języka polskiego. Teoria. Zagadnienia leksykalne [Culture of the Polish language. Theory. Lexical issues]*, Warszawa 2005, p. 109.

371 Linguists, of course, point out the model character of such an approach and that the situation itself does not always condition the use of a particular variety of language, K. Zabierowska, *O „wielogłosowości"...*, op. cit., p. 81 et seq.

372 A. Markowski, [in:] H. Jadacka, A. Markowski, D. Zdunkiewicz-Jedynak, *Poprawna polszczyzna. Hasła problemowe [Correct Polish. Problem entries]*, Warszawa 2008, p. 49.

373 Ibidem, p. 88.

374 Cf. M. Rzeszutko, *Rozprawa...*, op. cit., p. 193. "[D]istinct from face-to-face conversation, jury trial discourse is similar in some ways to other forms of institutional discourse. Notably it conforms to Drew and Heritage's (...) three distinctive features of institutional interaction: It has a set of institutionally defined 'goal orientations'; it has 'special constraints' on allowable contributions; and it has 'inferential frameworks' specific to the legal context that 'may reconfigure the interpretive «valence» that may be attached to particular actions.' ", see Ch. Heffer, *Jury Trial...*, op. cit., p. 5.

contacts (e.g., in some family or criminal cases). In turn, despite the undoubtedly institutional dimension of the contact, some participants are linked by certain ties, sometimes very close ones. There are, moreover, other peculiarities revealed in the course of reconstructing the genre pattern of the trial, about which in a moment. In this context, the question undoubtedly arises: How much the manner in which the trial is shaped affects the above-mentioned model view of the relationship between the officialness of the situation, the official variety of Polish language and the linguistic model norm?

Re 2. As Andrzej Markowski points out, the **linguistic model norm** consists of the following elements of language that are used consciously (and with a sense of their value), remain in accordance with grammatical and semantic rules, linguistic tradition, but also with developmental trends.[375] At the same time, it should be borne in mind that this is a "high norm", so it can introduce significant restrictions (for the sender), especially with regard to the variability of linguistic means.[376] The so-called **linguistic utilitarian norm**, on the other hand, includes linguistic elements characteristic of contacts in which language is treated instrumentally, i.e. as a tool to achieve specific goals, used primarily in casual, informal contacts.[377]

This naturally raises the question of whether the solutions adopted in legal studies in terms of the linguistic norm, which apply to the language of the texts of legislative acts,[378] could be considered equally adequate to the communication process at the trial. With regard to the requirement of linguistic correctness directed to the editors of the texts of legislative acts, it is assumed that this is a requirement of correctness at the level of the linguistic model norm and the use of common language in the official variety, and this is already determined by the communication situation accompanying the legislator's communication act.[379] However, it seems that the above rule cannot be transferred to the trial (taken as a model) i Polish courts, at least without taking into account certain modifications.

Procedural norms do not explicitly regulate the issue in question, but given the type of contact (official), the linguistic model norm must be taken as a starting

---

375 A. Markowski, [in:] H. Jadacka, A. Markowski, D. Zdunkiewicz-Jedynak, *Poprawna polszczyzna...*, op. cit., p. 88

376 Ibidem.

377 Ibidem.

378 A. Choduń, *Norma językowa a dyrektywy redagowania tekstów aktów prawnych [Linguistic norm and directives for drafting legal texts]*, [in:] *Konwencjonalne i formalne aspekty...*, op. cit., p. 47 et seq.; eadem, *Założenia dotyczące zasad techniki prawodawczej i wprowadzania ich zmian (język, teksty i konteksty) [Assumptions about the principles of legislative technique and their amendments (language, texts and contexts)]*, [in:] *Zasady techniki prawodawczej – perspektywa zmian. Materiały pokonferencyjne [Principles of legislative technique – a perspective of change. Post-conference materials]*, Warszawa 2014, p. 99.

379 Ibidem.

point. Further, it is necessary to identify those elements of the trial as a communication occurrence that possibly justify moving to the level of the linguistic utilitarian norm.

In this context, it seems most relevant that the purpose of the trial (or court proceedings more broadly) is an extra-linguistic, extra-communication purpose, since the acts carried out at the trial are primarily aimed at resolution of the case at hand. **In relation to the purpose of the trial language plays an instrumental role** – a means (a necessary one) to achieve the goal set by the legislator. Two aspects of this issue should be noted. First, linguistic elements that do not conform to the linguistic model norm, or even the utilitarian norm, may appear at the trial as a consequence of the implementation of certain procedural norms (i.e., fully in accordance with the normative pattern), when, for example, the court reads out testimony or explanations, a witness or a party recalls in the course of examination words spoken in a different communication situation.[380] The examples indicated above, which are manifestations of intertextual references, have the character of meta-linguistic acts, so it can be said that a given participant, while implementing a certain procedural norm (e.g., the obligation to tell the truth during an examination), does not affect the quality of the recalled statements. In this sense, the presence of linguistic elements inconsistent with the linguistic model norm is determined by the way the trial is designed.

Secondly, going beyond the scope of the linguistic model norm can be justified by the need to reach a communication agreement between participants with different levels of communication competence, as well as when the act in question is undertaken by a non-professional participant. In both cases, communication effectiveness is particularly important, as it determines the course of procedural acts. Therefore, in this context, **what is** said and **for what purpose** is more important than **how** it was said.

The method proposed above for resolving the issue at hand does not, of course, imply arbitrariness. There should be indicated the limiting moments, which are determined by the legislator. The first of these is related to the obligation of public authorities to protect the Polish language.[381] This protection consists, among other things, in taking care of the correct use of language and preventing its vulgarization. Just as certain pragmatic considerations, mentioned above, may justify going beyond the area of model correctness, it is difficult to imagine a justification for the use of vulgarisms. So it seems that an impassable limit can be identified – it is the use of vulgar words and phrases. In relation to the other participants, the limit of the use of vulgarisms is also valid, since counteracting the vulgarization of language is the subject of an order addressed to the court, then at least at the

---

380 Such statements were also noted in the research material, some of them can even be considered as full of vulgarities.

381 In accordance with the Polish Language Act of October 7, 1999 (Journal of Laws of 2018, item 931).

level of the pattern such linguistic acts of the participants are blocked. Violation of the solemnity of the court can also be considered an impassable limit (although very vague).

Re 3. Returning to the model relationship cited above (official situation – official variety of language – linguistic model norm), in discussing issues related to the lexis used at the trial, it is also necessary to start from the official variety of language and the corresponding vocabulary. Keeping in mind that the considerations carried out in this part of the study concern the model approach to the trial (in Polish courts),[382] it is necessary to consider whether, in addition to the use of joint vocabulary and official lexis, the genre pattern allows the use of vocabulary characteristic of unofficial varieties of language. It seems that the resolution and justification for this should be the same as in the case of the linguistic model norm (see Re 2). However, emotionalisms should be considered separately. This is because the linguists emphasize that "the fundamental linguistic difference between official and unofficial varieties of language lies in the extent of use of expressive words, especially emotionalisms",[383] the use of which in official varieties is much less frequent than in unofficial varieties.[384] With regard to the genre pattern of the trial, the solution adopted in this regard should be consistent with the way individual communication occurrences are shaped in their functional aspect. Thus, the use of expressive and, above all, emotional lexis is justified in relation to the pattern of the trial to the extent that the use of evaluative-emotional strategies is not explicitly blocked (e.g., within the explanations of the defendant).[385]

382 Thus, it is not possible to simply generalize the empirical data on the use of the lexis of each variety, since specific linguistic acts may well constitute a transgression of the genre pattern of the trial – that approach that will be entitlement in Chapter 3.

383 A. Markowski, [in:] H. Jadacka, A. Markowski, D. Zdunkiewicz-Jedynak, *Poprawna polszczyzna...*, op. cit., p. 49

384 Ibidem.

385 The level of expressive, including emotional, of the actual communication acts taken at the trial can be significant. However, it is a matter of performance, not a pattern. The actual communication acts, including emotional in nature, will be discussed in Chapter 3.

Chapter 3 Non-professional participant of court proceedings in a normatively determined communication situation

3.1. Preliminary assumptions

In the previous chapter, the genre pattern of a trial in Polish courts was reconstructed, taking into account the most important aspects of designing a trial as a complex communication occurrence. This made it possible to carry out the first of the two main research tasks posed in this study.

In this chapter, the focus has shifted to the actual communication acts performed by the participants of court session scheduled for the trial, so the subject of any analysis is the empirical material collected. However, this does not mean that the issue of the model design of the trial will no longer be addressed – on the contrary. This is because, in accordance with the assumptions about the goals for which the genre pattern of the trial was reconstructed in this study, the individual elements of the pattern served to develop detailed research questions and analytical categories, which will be discussed in the following sections.

Knowledge of the genre patterns of various communication occurrences – as already emphasized in this book – co-creates the communication competence of members of a given society. The issue of communication competence, often taken up in modern linguistics,[386] has not been discussed more extensively in this book so far, although the location of communication competence in relation to the other phenomena discussed has been pointed out several times. Here the concept of communication competence will be considered, but only to the extent that it is necessary from the point of view of the research task carried out in this part of the study.

The term "communication competence" is understood in linguistics in particular as conscious or unconscious knowledge of the system of speech acts that is validity in a given community, that is, the rules of language use in various situations created by this community.[387] Such an understanding of the term in question is also

386 Linguists also use the terms "proficiency (linguistic, communication, etc.)" or "awareness (linguistic, communication, etc.)", the scopes of which remain in different relations to the scope of the name "communication competence".

387 S. Grabias, *Język*..., op. cit., pp. 36–37. This view of communication competence relates directly to Dell Hymes' concept of communication competence, the formulation of which was the result of a critique of linguistic competence in terms of Chomsky's generative-transformational grammar, cf. D. Hymes, *Vers la compétence*

adopted in this study, however, that it is not just about speech acts and language use, but about communication acts and the use of various semiotic systems. Some authors, within the framework of communication competence understood in this way, distinguish genre competence,[388] that is, knowledge of genre conventions.[389] When the previous considerations are taken into account, it should not be surprising to conclude that it is this element of communication competence, and the part in which it concerns the genre pattern of a trial, that is most relevant in this context.

Communication competence, or the part of it called "genre competence", is a natural bridge between the model view of a trial, i.e. in the form of a genre pattern, and the real actors taking communication acts within the framework of real communication situations in the courtroom. Thus, it seems that the concept under discussion would also provide a good methodological basis in this part of the study. However, the attempt to use the concept of communication competence – as a methodological basis – faces significant difficulties in the context under discussion.

First, competence itself (as it is understood in this study[390]) is unobservable, since only communication acts can be perceived and

---

de communication, Paris 1991, p. 130 et seq.; N. Chomsky, *Aspects of the Theory of Syntax*, Cambridge 1964, p. 4.

388 Some of linguists distinguish a number of different competences that make up communication competence, such as: (1) **linguistic** competence (after Chomsky); (2) **sociolinguistic** competence (S. Grabias, *Interakcja językowa i jej uwarunkowania. Perspektywa lingwistyczna [Linguistic interaction and its determinants. A linguistic perspective]*, [in:] *Bariery i pomosty w komunikacji językowej Polaków [Barriers and bridges in language communication of Poles]*, eds. J. Bartmiński, U. Majer-Baranowska, Lublin 2005, p. 33); (3) competence **in the field of discourse** (A. Duszak, *Tekst, dyskurs...*, op. cit., p. 253); (4) **pragmatic** competence (B. Grochala, *Kompetencja komunikacyjna a gatunek – o relacji internetowej na żywo [Communication competence and genre – about live internet reporting]*, "Acta Universitatis Lodziensis. Kształcenie Polonistyczne Cudzoziemców" 2013, Vol. 20, p. 303); (5) **stylistic** competence (M. Wojtak, A. Siwiec, *Świadomość stylistyczna na tle wybranych składników jej kontekstu pojęciowego [Stylistic awareness against the background of selected components of its conceptual context]*, [in:] *Mowa rozświetlona myślą. Świadomość normatywno-stylistyczna współczesnych Polaków [Speech enlightened by thought. The normative-stylistic awareness of contemporary Poles]*, ed. J. Miodek, Wrocław 1999, pp. 49–50, G. Habrajska, *Kompetencja stylistyczna w interakcji [Stylistic competence in interaction]*, [in:] *Stylistyka...*, p. 50); (6) **genre** competence (M. Wojtak, *Genologia tekstów...*, op. cit., p. 345); (7) **cultural** competence (W. Pisarek, *Wstęp...*, op. cit., p. 71).

389 M. Wojtak, *Genologia tekstów...*, op. cit., p. 345.

390 In communication science, communication competence is also framed not so much as knowledge or skill, but as an act; communication competence in this view is the use of a verbal or nonverbal act to achieve preferred goals in a way that is appropriate to the context, cf. S. Morreale, B. Spitzberg, J. Barge, *Human*

described,[391] on the basis of which it is more or less reasonable to infer the level of a person's communication competence.[392] Second, an attempt to estimate the level of communication competence (or just genre competence) of participants of court proceedings would require the creation of a scale built on the basis of certain indicators, which should be the same for each person subjected to the study. This procedure would either be impossible to carry out reliably or would yield only fragmentary data, which in turn would not allow the use of the created scale. This is because the participants of court proceedings engage in different communication acts at the trial – which does not allow for the collection of uniform data. Moreover, the researcher does not have any influence on the communication acts taken by the participants, which in turn does not allow for the profiling of the study to obtain uniform data.

Due to the problems described above (and others that have been omitted), the concept of communication competence will not serve in this study as a methodological basis for the analysis presented in this chapter. However, it should be borne in mind that each of the actual communication acts that will be cited as an example in the following discussion will be a manifestation of either higher or lower communication competence. In addition, it is assumed in this study that there are two extremely different levels of genre competence that can characterize the participants of proceedings in Polish courts. The highest level of genre competence is attributed to the judge (either acting as a court or presiding judge), while the lowest level is attributed to the non-professional participant. (Of course, this is a simplification and applies to the participants considered as a model. The level of genre competence may even vary considerably within a single category of subjects, but at this stage of the design of the research procedure it is of little significance.) Therefore, the non-professional participants of court proceedings may encounter difficulties during their activities at the trial, whereas the presiding judge is able to, at least to some extent, counter these difficulties. In further consideration, the communication acts of the presiding judge[393] and the non-professional

---

Communication: Motivation, Knowledge and Skills, 2nd edition, Thomson Wadsworth 2007, p. 29.

391 I. Kurcz, *Psychologia języka i komunikacji [Psychology of language and communication]*, Warszawa 2005, p. 33; G. Sawicka, *Konwencja a kompetencja komunikacyjna [Convention and communication competence]*, [in:] *Język w komunikacji [Language in communication]*, ed. G. Habrajska, Łódź 2001, Vol. 1, pp. 123–124.

392 This raises the question of motivation – whether a person really lacks sufficient competence or is not motivated to communicate competently.

393 Both those that are conventionally (in the normative pattern) attributed to the presiding judge, and those that are undertaken by the judge, acting as a court.

participants[394] will be of interest. The above assumption sets two complementary scopes of analysis:

1. the scope of the presiding judge's communication acts addressed to the non-professional participants of court proceedings;
2. the scope of communication acts of the non-professional participants of court proceedings.

3.2. Methodology of empirical research: The method of selecting the research sample

The primary research method adopted to obtain empirical data for the purpose of this study is participant observation (active and direct) conducted in natural settings. The observation was made during court sessions scheduled for the trial in person by the author of this book. The course of the sessions subjected to observation (though not all, as discussed below) was also recorded using a dictaphone.[395]

Adoption of the research method in question required the observer to take certain steps related to obtaining permission to conduct research in the manner indicated above – from the presidents of the courts where the research was conducted,[396] to the presiding judges and other participants in specific court sessions scheduled for the trial.

The presiding judges did not always agree to audio recording. On five occasions, permission to record trials in criminal proceedings was denied,[397] on four occasions in family court proceedings[398] (primarily due to the subject matter of the proceedings) and once in commercial proceedings. In these situations, of course, the observer was limited to observation.

Other participants were informed by the presiding judge of the observer's intention to record the session for research purposes. On two occasions, one of the parties refused to allow audio recording; in one case, consent was refused by the defendant's defense counsel (in criminal case). In these situations, the observer

394 Of all the communication acts of non-professional participants of court session scheduled for the trial, the acts of non-professional participants of court proceedings will be analyzed.

395 In the case of one regional court department, audio recordings of observed sessions were obtained from case files.

396 In each case, such approval was obtained on the basis of a written motion indicating the methods and purpose of the research.

397 The legal provision of the Polish Code of Criminal Procedure regarding the recording of the trial by representatives of the mass media was cited as justification for the refusal.

398 With regard to criminal and family proceedings, the disagreement concerned the entire case list.

was limited to observation. In two cases, the party's attorney requested hearing the case on closed court session – in one case the request was granted.[399]

The presence of an observer conducting participant observation may has a greater or lesser impact on the phenomena under study. This, of course, does not lead to the rejection of this method as ineffective or unjustified.[400] However, it should be made clear what roles the observer played in the research conducted for this study, and what impact her presence may have had on the acts taken at the trial.

During the participant observation conducted as part of this study, the observer played three fundamentally different roles. First, in the context of the research being conducted, the role of the observer-researcher; second, with regard to the communication process, the role of the recipient; and third, based on the court session being conducted, the role of the audience.

On the other hand, with regard to the possible influence of the observer on the conduct of the court session, the obvious manifestations of such influence can be pointed out first. This applies to all situations related to consent to observation and audio recording, which were described above. This is because it is clear that the research activities would not have been undertaken at all if it were not for the presence of the observer in the courtroom. However, the impact may be less evident.

The literature points to certain types of researcher interactions that cause difficulties within the framework of the observation being conducted. Among these difficulties are the possibility of unconscious influence on events, lack of trust in the observer, various levels of acceptance of the researcher's participation, or the desire to hide certain issues from the observer.[401]

That the presence of an observer can, in this regard, exert a certain influence on the course of the court session can only be more or less reasonably inferred from the acts or behaviors of its participants. As has already been pointed out, the parties have on several occasions refused to allow the recording or have submitted requests for hearing the case on closed session. In justification of the motions for hearing the case on closed session, the attorneys indicated an intention to hide sensitive issues, in their view, from outsiders. Sometimes the parties formulated

---

399 The manner in which the research process was conducted did not violate the provisions of the then-current Act of August 29, 1997 on the Protection of Personal Data (Journal of Laws of 2016, item 922, as amended).

400 A. Trzeciakowska, *Obserwacja jako metoda stosowana w badaniach nad procesem komunikacji [Observation as a method used in the study of the communication process]*, [in:] *Komunikowanie się w sytuacjach społecznych. Analizy psychologiczne [Communicating in social situations. Psychological analysis]*, ed. T. Rzepa, Szczecin 2002, p. 56. In particular, observation allows one to see the complexity of the communication process, including at the trial, cf. M. Dudek, M. Stępień, *Courtroom Power....*, op. cit., p. 90 and the works cited therein.

401 K. Rubacha, *Metodologia badań nad edukacją [Methodology of education research]*, Warszawa 2008, pp. 156–157.

objections to the presence of the observer as an audience.[402] This was the case when a party was unaware that the trial was being held in public. Once the presiding judge was informed of this, the level of acceptance of the observer changed.

On the other hand, it is difficult to determine whether the observation conducted had an impact, and if so, what impact, on the way (e.g., greater diligence) the participants communicate at the trial, as there is a lack of adequate comparative material.

In the process of selecting the research sample, three common courts were of interest: (1) the Regional Court of Szczecin (acting as a court of first instance); (2) the District Court Szczecin-Centrum in Szczecin; (3) the District Court Szczecin-Prawobrzeże and Zachód in Szczecin. Thus, all other courts have been omitted, including administrative courts, special courts, and among common courts, courts of appeal and regional courts acting as courts of second instance. In Poland proceedings before the court of first instance are characterized by the greatest number and diversity of both cases and participants. Proceedings before the court of second instance as appeal proceedings are poorer in terms of procedural acts taken at the trial. Moreover, as is obvious, not all cases heard by the court of first instance are heard in appeal proceedings. Similarly, the omission of administrative courts, whose task (in Poland) is primarily to formally control the acts of administrative authorities in terms of the legal compliance of administrative decisions and rulings, should be justified – it also impoverishes court proceedings, by limiting them to formal issues. The elimination of special courts (military courts in Poland) from the scope of interest is justified, in turn, by limiting the class of entities involved in proceedings before these courts.

The choice of Szczecin courts was dictated by pragmatic issues – all research activities were undertaken in Szczecin, but substantive considerations also justify the territorial limitation of the research. First of all, the manner in which court proceedings, including the trial, are conducted is in Poland largely determined by the law. Thus, the pattern of the communication process at the trial in essential elements is the same regardless of the court conducting the proceedings. In addition, the procedure of analysis of the research material designed for the purpose of this study is focused around those communication phenomena that are related to the way the trial is shaped in model terms. In this sense it deals with issues that are as universal as possible for the communication process at the trial in Polish courts.

It should also be noted that due to historical conditions, the language of the inhabitants of northwestern Poland, including Szczecin, is devoid of elements characteristic of regional varieties of Polish language.[403] Conducting research on the communication process at the trial in courts located in some other parts of Poland would require including in the research procedure the issue of the use of

---

402 This refers to two court sessions that were not recorded.

403 A. Wilkoń, *Typologia odmian językowych współczesnej polszczyzny [Typology of linguistic varieties of contemporary Polish language]*, Katowice 2000, p. 29.

linguistic means peculiar to a particular regional variety, due to the fact that this is a factor that can affect understanding of the communication act. If such linguistic means were indeed detected in the course of the research, conclusions on this subject could, by their very nature, only be applied to a specific area. In the case of the Szczecin courts, the probability of the use of linguistic means of a regional nature by the participants is low, and thus the communication process under study in the aspect in question can be considered as universal as possible.

In addition, the selection of research material was guided by the principle of maximum diversity, i.e. such a way of selecting material that will allow to observe and analyze the greatest possible number of factors that can affect the communication process occurring at the trial.[404] The selection of research material in this regard was done in **two stages**.

The first stage consisted of separating the relevant part of judicial reality. There is no doubt that the natural division made by the courts is the division of court cases based on their subject matter. The selection of cases made on the basis of this division will be called **vertical selection**. The selection of the various varieties of court cases was guided (as courts do) by the division of cases adopted in the ordinance of the Minister of Justice of December 12, 2003 on the organization and scope of operation of court secretariats and other departments of judicial administration.[405] Based on the aforementioned criteria[406] and the division adopted in the cited order, the following varieties of cases were selected: (1) civil cases (in contentious and non-contentious proceedings); (2) commercial cases; (3) labor law and social security cases; (4) cases proceeded by family courts; (5) criminal cases and penal fiscal cases; (6) misdemeanor cases.

To ensure that the research material reflects reality as much as possible, the most objective data – from court reports[407] – were taken into account. The percentage distribution of the observed court cases of certain types (e.g. civil, criminal

404 In doing so, the scope of the analysis was limited to oral communications occurring at the trial, so written communication acts were left out of interest (either due to lack of access or difficult access to the case files).

405 Official Journal of the Ministry of Justice No. 5, item 22, as amended.

406 Since the subject of interest is the communication process at the trial, those proceedings that do not involve the trial, such as registries, were not included in the research material.

407 According to § 449 of the order cited in this section, "the record-keeping and information systems maintained at the ministry are the source of data for collecting, gathering and processing information for the purposes of public statistics under the legal provisions of Article 2 of the Law of June 29, 1995 on Public Statistics (...)". Thus, court statistics (reports) are conducted on the basis of the division of cases adopted in the cited order and reflected in this study.

or commercial) is the same as those disclosed in court reports[408] from the year preceding the beginning of observation:

1. civil cases:
   (a) in contentious proceedings – 25 %,
   (b) in non-contentious proceedings – 17 %;
2. commercial cases – 6.5 %;
3. labor law and social security cases – 13 %;
4. cases proceeded by family courts – 16.5 %;
5. criminal cases and penal fiscal cases – 12 %;
6. misdemeanor cases – 10 %.

Stage two, on the other hand, concerned the selection of individual court sessions scheduled for the trial (**horizontal selection**). The criterion for selection were factors that could shape the communication process at the trial, which are not taken into account by vertical selection. Such factors are considered to be:

1. participants of court proceedings (i.e., diverse procedural roles, participation of professional and non-professional participants, including those not represented by professional attorneys, composition of the court, including participation of lay judges);
2. the course of the trial (i.e., the stage of the trial carried out at a given session);
3. the place where the court session is conducted (size of the room, elements of equipment);
4. recording the session (by means of audio or video and audio recording devices; by means of traditional written minutes).

In summary, based on the variety of cases examined before the courts, a part of court reality was first identified (vertical selection), and then within this reality a detailed selection of individual court sessions was made (horizontal selection).

It should be further pointed out that the court in which the observation was conducted on a given day was selected randomly. In turn, the specific case list was selected to meet the assumption of maximum diversity as much as possible, primarily in terms of the diversity of participants and planned procedural acts.[409] Finally, it should be added that the court sessions scheduled for the trial closed to the public (by the law or by the court's decision) were not observed.

In accordance with the principles of research sample selection discussed in this section, 250 court sessions scheduled for the trial were observed, the quantitative

408 The data came from the courts where the observation was conducted, provided by administrative staff under access to public information.

409 This way of selecting a case list had an impact on the total number of observed sessions, since the primary issue was the number of scheduled procedural acts within a session, not the number of sessions within the entire case list. As a result, sessions of several hours or even an entire day were often selected.

structure of which fully corresponds to that revealed by the statistical data. The audio recording, on the other hand, includes almost 160 hours of recordings. The observation was conducted between June 2014 and June 2015.

3.3. Methodology of empirical research: Additional notes and the limitations of the research method

In reconstructing the genre pattern of the trial in Polish courts the collected research material (both audio and written records of the observations carried out) has been used to identify communication acts that are manifestations of practice or to illustrate certain communication phenomena. In this part of the study, the research material is the starting point of any analysis conducted.

As indicated above, not all observed court sessions scheduled for the trial were recorded in the form of an audio recording (primarily some criminal cases and cases proceeding by family courts). Court sessions, the proceedings of which were recorded using a dictaphone (or the audio recording was obtained from the case file), were selected for analysis, with some exceptions, however.[410] As a result, the research material suitable for analysis in this part of the study includes 200 of the 250 observed sessions. It should be noted, however, that not only court sessions with non-professional participants were recorded. Twenty three of the recorded sessions involved only professional or quasi-professional participants, and these sessions were obviously not suitable for analysis from the standpoint of communication acts by or addressed to non-professional participants of the proceedings.

The written records of the sessions that were not included in the collection described above will play a supplementary role in this part of the study, in particular, during the description of the results of the analysis of the research material will provide additional examples.

Based on the developed research questions and analytical categories, the table in Excel[411] was created to code the data obtained during the analysis of the empirical material.

---

410 Three sessions were excluded from the analysis, which, were recorded in this way, but due to interference (related, among other things, to the noise caused by the construction work) the audio material collected was inaudible in many places. In addition, a transcript of selected sessions that took place before the family court, and permission to record them was not obtained, was added to the collection thus compiled. Due to their peculiarities (the sessions were quite short, uncomplicated in terms of the communication acts taken), it was possible (omitting the statements dictated by the presiding judge for the minutes, which are not relevant from the point of view of the designed analysis) to record *in extenso* the statements of individual participants (but only those sessions selected for which there was certainty in this regard).

411 All research questions and categories were entered into the table. Obtained through the analysis of the empirical material, the answers to the individual questions were

The analysis of empirical data, the results of which will be presented in the following sections, is qualitative data analysis. There will, however, be references to quantitative data (where this proves possible), primarily to show the scale of the phenomenon in question. The primary role, however, is assigned in this study to the characterization of specific communication phenomena, their peculiarity due to the situational meso-context, and the detection of relationships between the trial in model terms and the phenomena revealed by the analysis of the research material.[412]

The choice of a basic research method, i.e. participant observation of trials combined with audio recording, has numerous advantages, but also numerous limitations. The former include, in particular, the possibility of obtaining empirical data that can be returned to after the observation is completed. With audio recording, the research questions and analytical categories developed can be attributed to the actual statements of the participants. This allows not only to enrich the content of this book with examples of statements, but also to supplement the qualitative analysis with quantitative data. It also significantly reduces the risk of making assertions based solely on impression or memory (unreliable after all) of the interaction observed in the courtroom. At the same time, due to the nature of the empirical material (audio recording), only linguistic acts were analyzed. Other (non-linguistic) communication acts and the communication behavior of the participants in the proceedings will be mentioned in the following sections only occasionally. This is because an optimal study of so-called non-verbal communication at the trial requires analysis of both voice, facial expressions, gestures, body posture or spatial interaction.[413] The research material in the form of audio

---

included in the table in an appropriate relativization to, among others, the individual court sessions analyzed, categories of participants, stages of the proceedings and procedural acts. The same was done with regard to the analytical categories. Each statement corresponding to a specific research question or analytical category was also entered into the table, but excluding any data identifying the individual participants of the proceedings.

412 Such an approach is in line with general assumptions about qualitative data analysis, cf. M.B. Miles, A.M. Huberman, *Qualitative Data Analysis*, 2nd edition, Thousand Oaks 1994, p. 9 et seq.

413 The well-known and often-cited empirical research on the non-verbal communication of judges and its impact on the jury was conducted by the team of Peter David Blanck and others (cf. e.g., P.D. Blanck, *Off the Record: Nonverbal Communication in the Courtroom*, "Stanford Lawyer" 1987, Vol. 21, No. 2, p. 18 et seq. (Trial judges have a responsibility in a jury trial to avoid any word, action, or behavior that could indicate or "transmit" his or her beliefs, attitudes, or expectations for the defendant's guilt or innocence.); P.D. Blanck, R. Rosenthal, A.J. Hart, F. Bernieri, *The Measure of the Judge: On Empirically-Based Framework for Exploring Trial Judges' Behavior*, "Iowa Law Review" 1990, Vol. 75, No. 3, p. 653 et seq.). See also A. Burnett, D.M. Badzinski, *Judge Nonverbal Communication on Trial: Do Mock Trial Jurors Notice?*, "Journal of Communication" 2005, Vol. 55, No. 2, p. 209 et seq.; J. Bloom,

recording does not allow for this.[414] In addition, the restriction of the research material to verbal communication, for example, prevented the optimal analysis of the research material from the point of view of the trial narrative (in the context of the cognitive aspect). This is because the core of the narrative is presented in procedural documents, i.e. as part of written communication. Within the trial itself, the narrative is sometimes very fragmented, including with the use of intertextual references to procedural documents. At the stage of designing and conducting the research, it was impossible for the researcher to access the files of pending cases.[415]

It was also decided not to obtain research material in the form of questionnaires or interviews with trial participants. The main reason for this decision was that the research was conducted by a single researcher, and it was not possible for her to be in the courtroom and talk to participants (whether in or out of the courtroom) at the same time.[416]

Evidently, the scope of the study is limited by the research questions and analytical categories developed for it. The complexity of the phenomenon of communication, even when limited only to the trial, and the multiplicity of research approaches and methods[417] is so great that a clear definition of the scope of analysis

---

K. Powdermaker, *The Jury Likes Me, the Jury Likes Me Not: Building Rapport in the Courtroom*, "Texas Bar Journal" 2006, Vol. 69, No. 6, p. 540 et seq.; J. Lee Hoffman, A. Weiner, *The Juror as Audience: The Impact of Non-Verbal Communication at Trial*, "Litigation Journal" 2013, Vol. 32, No. 3, p. 1 et seq.

414 It is rightly pointed out that the overall perception of the participant of the trial or the persuasiveness of the message is influenced not only by the linguistic means used, but also by elements of the so-called non-verbal communication (this, of course, also applies to communication in other situational contexts), cf. M. Szczyrbak, *Closing Argument as Multimodal Oratory: Insights from the Chauvin Trial*, "International Journal for the Semiotics of Law" 2023, Vol. 36, pp. 1109–1145.

415 It was theoretically possible to combine observation of the hearings with analysis of the procedural documents contained in the case file. However, it was necessary to wait until the case was completed. However, taking into account the significant number of observed trials (250) and the risk that a case may last even several years, such a solution was not decided. It is worth noting that after the spread of online trials in Polish courts (in some sense forced by the Covid-19 pandemic), it is already possible to design the trial communication study in a different way. In particular, because the observer (researcher) can observe the faces of all participants in the online trial. In contrast, this is not possible in the courtroom in Polish courts (primarily due to the location of examined persons with their backs to the audience).

416 See on interviewing participants in Polish court proceedings and the problems that come with it, M. Dudek, M. Stępień, *Courtroom Power...*, op. cit., p. 91.

417 See e.g., J.N. Levi, *The study of language in judicial process*, [in:] *Language in the Judicial...*, op. cit., p. 3 et seq. The author mainly points to psycholinguistics, sociolinguistics, semantics, pragmatics and discourse analysis, including speech act theory, conversation analysis and the concept of communication competence, as the theoretical basis for the study of communication in the courtroom.

was necessary. Focusing on specific aspects of the interaction between the presiding judge (a professional participant of court proceedings) and non-professional participants of court proceedings, leaves out of scope many issues that are or could be the subject of separate research.

3.4. Presiding judge's communication acts addressed to the non-professional participants – a research procedure

Given the numerous duties and competences of the presiding judge related to the presiding of the court session in Polish courts, it is assumed in this study that the presiding judge can perform the following functions in relation to non-professional participants (and also others): (1) a **leading-intermediary function**; (2) a **leading-coordinating function**; (3) a **leading-order enforcing function**. In the performance of the first, the presiding judge is an intermediary between the legal system and the non-professional participants. Under the second, he or she coordinates the acts of the participants during direct interaction. And under the third, the presiding judge ensures the proper implementation of the pattern (primarily normative) of the trial.

In designing the research questions for the first two categories, attention was paid to communication acts that can (at least in the assumption) facilitate non-professional participants participation in the court session scheduled for the trial (or in the court proceedings in general). In turn, the questions formulated under the third category serve to show the acts of non-professional participants, which, from the point of view of the presiding judge, are unacceptable due to the way the pattern of the trial was formed.

The following research questions were formulated with regard to the presiding judge's leading-intermediary function:

Question 1. How does the presiding judge perform communication acts related to the leading-intermediary function?

1a. What instructions does the presiding judge give to non-professional participants: explicitly specified in the normative pattern, developed through the practice, or perhaps formulated *ad hoc*?

1aa. What do these instructions refer to?

1b. How does the presiding judge give instructions to non-professional participants?

1ba. Does the presiding judge give instructions by reading (or quoting) the legal provision?

1bb. Does the presiding judge give instructions by indicating the legal situation of the participant determined by a specific legal norm(s)?

1bc. Does the presiding judge give instructions in another way?

1c. After giving an instruction, does the presiding judge ask the non-professional participant if he or she understood the instruction?

1ca. Does the presiding judge continue to give instructions if the answer is negative?

1d. After giving the instruction, does the presiding judge ask the non-professional participant to paraphrase the instruction? (Repetition in his/her own words)

1da. Does the presiding judge continue to give instruction when a communication misunderstanding is found?

With reference to the presiding judge's leading-coordinating function, the following research questions were formulated:

Question 2. How does the presiding judge perform communication acts related to the leading-coordinating function?

2a. How the presiding judge shapes the interaction between him or her and a non-professional participant at the trial?

2aa. Does the presiding judge refer to the vocabulary used by the non-professional participant? If so, is the reference made to addressable phrases used by the non-professional participant, other words and expressions, or both?

2ab. Does the presiding judge use legal terms and juridical terms when interacting directly with a non-professional participant?

2ac. If the presiding judge uses legal and juridical terms, does he or she explain their meaning or the essence of their designators?[418]

2ad. Does the presiding judge inform non-professional participants of procedural acts taken or the stage of the case investigation?

2ae. Does the presiding judge ask the non-professional participant whether he or she understood the meaning of the procedural act performed (e.g., the procedural decision made), or does he or she explain its meaning? If the answer is negative, does the presiding judge explain its meaning?

2af. Does the presiding judge inform non-professional participants on the essence of the proceedings?

2ag. Does the presiding judge inform non-professional participants about the procedural functions associated with a given procedural role, or about the nature of a given interactional role? If so, which roles are involved?

2ah. Does the presiding judge inform non-professional participants about the thematic framework of various communication occurrences? If so, which communication occurrences does this apply to?

---

418 The names of participants corresponding to their procedural roles are excluded from the scope of this question. Within the scope of this question remains not only the question of explaining the meaning of a given term by giving a nominal definition, but also the various characteristics of the object to which the term refers, for example, by indicating the function performed by a legal institution with a particular name.

2ai. Does the presiding judge ask non-professional participants if they want to perform a certain procedural act?[419]

2b. Does the presiding judge interfere with how the interaction between a non-professional and professional participant is shaped? (e.g., between a witness and a professional attorney)

2c. Can any other acts taken by the presiding judge facilitate non-professional participants to communicate in the courtroom, including the performance of procedural acts?

The following research questions were formulated with regard to the presiding judge's leading-order enforcing function:

Question 3. How does the presiding judge perform communication acts related to the leading-order enforcing function?

3a. What kind of communication acts (or behaviors) of non-professional participants does the presiding judge respond to? (this includes both admonition and blocking the act)

3aa. Does the presiding judge respond to direct communications between participants (i.e. omitting the presiding judge) in situations where the normative pattern does not provide such an omission?

3ab. Does the presiding judge respond to non-professional participants taking communication acts at the moments when the normative pattern does not provide for it? If there is no reaction (admonition, blocking), does the presiding judge treat such a statement as a procedural statement?

3ac. Does the presiding judge respond to a non-professional participant going outside of a specific thematic frame?

3ad. Does the presiding judge respond to non-professional participants' substitution of legal and juridical terms, including addressable phrases?

3ae. Does the presiding judge respond to other words and expressions used by non-professional participants? (especially colloquial or vulgar)

3af. Does the presiding judge react to the communication acts of non-professional participants related to the creating of the participant's "face" in the proceedings? (With reference to the analytical categories developed for this question, cf. Section 3.5)

3ag. Does the presiding judge respond to other communication acts or behaviors not included in the content of questions 3aa through 3af?

---

419 Questions formulated by the presiding judge (usually either at the beginning of the trial or before the closing of a judicial process or trial), addressed to all participants and regarding possible motions, as well as the questions addressed to participants regarding their willingness to ask questions of examined persons, are excluded from the scope of this question.

3.5. Communication acts of non-professional participants – a research procedure

As emphasized at the beginning of the previous chapter, the genre pattern determines "the horizons of receiver expectations and creation models for senders".[420] Thus, it can be assumed that the lower the level of communication competence (including genre) of a person, the higher the sense of uncertainty in a specific communication situation, and vice versa. On this basis, it can be concluded that from the point of view of a non-professional participant of court proceedings, a trial as a communication occurrence manifests a high degree of difficulty.[421] As it seems, two parameters of this difficulty – unknown and important – play an important role in the case of the trial. The first is obvious – learning the genre pattern of a trial requires adequate socialization training, which is hard to demand from a non-professional participant. The second, on the other hand, is related to the individual case decided in court proceedings, to which the participants have a certain relationship.

Taking into account the above two parameters, the reconstructed genre pattern of a trial was searched for such aspects of its design that, with the participation of a non-professional participant, may (due to the high level of difficulty) cause various communication barriers.

The first research scope is related to the language of the trial, which concerns the use of legal and juridical terminology. Within its framework, the following questions are posed:

Question 4. How do non-professional participants deal with the use of legal and juridical terms?

4a. Do non-professional participants use legal and juridical terms, including appropriate addressable phrases? If so, what terms do they use on their own initiative?

4b. Do non-professional participants substitute legal and juridical terms for words and expressions outside of this terminology?

4ba. Do they perform procedural acts in a "non-juridical" manner, i.e. without using typical (for lawyers) forms, including the relevant legal and juridical terms? If so, are such acts communicatively effective?[422]

---

420 I. Loewe, *Polska genologia...*, op. cit., p. 31.

421 The level of difficulty of a particular communication occurrence depends on how complicated, unfamiliar, unexpected and important it is to a person, A. Duszak, *Tekst, dyskurs...*, op. cit., p. 47.

422 This refers to such situations in which a given participant performs a simple (in terms of structure) procedural act, such as withdrawal of the claim. Question 4ba is whether non-professional participants use standard, canonical formulas from the point of view of professional participants, e.g., *Your Honor, I withdraw the lawsuit* (...), *Your Honor, I request that evidence be taken from* (...), or otherwise express their

4c. Do non-professional participants engage in metalinguistic acts related to the use of legal and juridical terms?

4ca. Do they inform the presiding judge (or another participant) that they do not understand a term or phrase, or ask for clarification?

4cb. Do they report that they do not know how to express a given thought using legal or juridical terms?

As a result of the answers to the questions posed, a picture of the non-professional participants related to the use of legal and juridical terminology was outlined. On this basis, and taking into account the results of the analysis of the use of terminology by the presiding judge, an attempt was made to answer an additional question: To what extent can the use of legal and juridical terminology (in such a way and on such a scale as occurs within the framework of actual communication in the courtroom) actually constitute a significant communication barrier when dealing with non-professionals?

The communication acts of the participants are closely linked to the performance of various procedural functions related to the procedural role played in the proceedings. However, with regard to the parties or quasi-parties, a certain regularity can be indicated, at least in model terms – striving for a favorable decision for oneself. Against this background, several issues arise with regard to the formation of one's own position in the proceedings, and these include the need to take a number of procedural acts, control the course of the proceedings, and shape the perception of certain states of affairs and persons.

In this context, special problems may be posed by the way certain elements of the pattern are shaped. As mentioned earlier, the acts of a party (quasi-party) in the proceedings can be seen as the implementation of a global **behavioral strategy** – this strategy is therefore related to the procedural role played. In turn, as was demonstrated in the discussion of communication occurrences from a functional aspect, the main complex communication occurrences undertaken at the trial (e.g., examination) serve to implement **informational-verification strategies**. Thus, already the way in which the normative pattern of the trial is shaped is conducive to the emergence of conflict in terms of the roles played and interaction strategies pursued, as illustrated in Figure 14.

---

will. The question of effectiveness, on the other hand, is whether, in such a situation, the communication act of a non-professional participant is recognized as having performed (or at least attempted to perform) a certain procedural act. This does not raise the question of legal effectiveness, which is related to the fulfillment of all the rules for performing such an act and to the production of an effect determined by legal norms. Hence, the question refers to communication effectiveness.

procedural role (e.g., claimant) and functions associated with it ↓ behavioral strategy	The area of conflict of interactional strategies against the background of conflict of roles (procedural and interactional)	interactional role (e.g., claimant making a statement during the examination of a party) ↓ informational-verification strategy

Figure 14. *Conflict of interactional strategies and conflict of roles (procedural and interactional)*
Source: own study.

The difficulties described above also apply to the witness. The procedural function associated with this role is to be a personal source of evidence, that is, to provide during examination information relevant to the proceedings. The procedural role (and its related function) can sometimes conflict with the social role played by the witness (e.g., as a friend of a party),[423] who cares about the favorable resolution of the case in favor of a particular participant. The described conflict can be represented by a diagram (Figure 15).

procedural role (witness) and functions associated with it ↓ Informational-verification strategy	The area of conflict of interactional strategies against the background of conflict of roles (procedural and social)	social role (e.g., friend of the defendant) ↓ behavioral strategy

Figure 15. *Conflict of interactional strategies and conflict of roles (procedural and social)*
Source: own study.

The specific questions that will be posed with reference to the roles played by the participants (procedural, interactional) will address selected elements related to the extent of the difficulties that the normative pattern creates in this aspect. The interpretation and description of the results, on the other hand, will take into account and highlight those difficulties that relate to the role conflict described above. These questions are as follows:

423 The legislator sometimes gives priority to the social role and authorizes refusal to testify, which avoids possible conflict over different roles.

Question 5. How do non-professional participants handle the implementation of certain procedural and interactional roles?

5a. Do non-professional participants initiate procedural acts?

5b. How do non-professional participants cope with the complex procedural acts that require special self-reliance?[424]

5ba. Does asking questions of examined persons pose a difficulty for non-professional participants? How do non-professional participants deal with the difficulties?

5bb. Does the realization of free speech during examination pose a difficulty for non-professional participants? How do non-professional participants deal with this difficulties?

5c. Do non-professional participants control the content of the minutes being prepared?

5ca. Do they ask the presiding judge to put certain statements on the record?

5cb. Do they request the presiding judge to read the portions of the minutes?

5cc. Do they call the presiding judge's attention to the improper transposition of the participant's statements into the minutes?

5cd. Do they supplement or correct their statements when dictating them into the minutes?

5d. Do non-professional participants ask the presiding judge to provide information on legal issues, including duties, entitlements and powers related to participation in court proceedings? If so, what is the presiding judge's response?

5e. Do non-professional participants ask the presiding judge to provide information on the procedural acts undertaken during the proceedings? If so, what is the presiding judge's response?

5 f. Do non-professional participants use so-called "linguistic means of security" in connection with their duty to report facts and tell the truth?

5fa. Do they use modal acts? (epistemic modalities).[425] If so, which ones?

5fb. Do they use other linguistic means of security? (pointing to a source of knowledge, telling that a given claim is the result of an inference, etc.) If so, what are they?

Further analytical categories are related to the formation a perception of states of affairs and persons by non-professional participants and require a brief theoretical introduction.

---

424 On the basis of the genre pattern of the trial in Polish courts, as well as observations of its actual course, the activities that require special self-reliance are considered in this book to be the act of asking questions to the examined person and the free speech that begins the examination.

425 The question is whether non-professional participants provide certain information with an indication of the degree of conviction that a given fact exists (or does not exist), using acts of supposition or doubt.

Participation in court sessions at the stage of collecting empirical material allowed the observation that the formation (creation) of the position of a given participant in the proceedings is an extremely complex phenomenon, and at the communication level it far exceeds the framework set by the procedural functions associated with a given procedural role. This observation was taken into account when designing the analytical categories.

In doing so, the analytical categories distinguished below have one thing in common – whether they refer to states of affairs or persons, they serve to create the image of a given participant in the proceedings. In order to emphasize this feature, reference will be made in this context to the shaping of the "face" (by) of the participant of court proceedings.[426]

The analysis of ways of shaping the "face" of the participant in the proceedings will include three issues: (1) formation of perception of events and states of affairs;[427] (2) formation of perception of persons; (3) use of persuasive means of blocking verification (truthfulness or accuracy) of statements and strengthening acts of certainty and exclusion.

Re 1. Creating the "face" of the participants in the proceedings can be done by shaping the perception of certain states of affairs,[428] which, generally speaking,

---

426 The use of the term "face" in this book is not accidental – it is a reference to the way the term is used in sociology, and later in other humanities, popularized by Erving Goffman. "Face" is the image of one's own person (one's "self") "delineated in terms of approved social attributes" (E. Goffman, *Interaction Ritual: Essays in Face-to-Face Behavior*, New Jersey 2005, p. 5), generally flattering, which a person seeks to successfully evoke in others (E. Goffman, *The Presentation…*, op. cit.). "Face" of the participant of court proceedings is a peculiar phenomenon against this background, which will be further discussed in the section devoted to the results of the analysis of the research material in this aspect. To emphasize the peculiar meaning of the term "face" it will be used in quotation marks.

427 The two terms ("event" and "state of affairs") are sometimes given distinctly different meanings (e.g., Z. Ziembiński, *Logika…*, op. cit., p. 64). However, taking into account the fact that a certain event can be seen as the cause of a given state of affairs and, as such, can be included in its description, the term "state of affairs" is used in this book.

428 The formation of "face" in this aspect is primarily related to the presentation of a particular version of the main fact. However, as it was mentioned, the collected empirical material does not allow an in-depth analysis of the ways in which the main fact is presented at the representational level – that is, at the level of factual description. This is not possible for at least two claimants. First, a full description of the facts is usually part of written communication; second, there is insufficient material to compare the different versions of the facts, such as those presented by the parties, due to the fact that single court sessions were recorded, which covered different stages of the trial.

have some connection with a particular participant in the proceedings. The procedure for analyzing this aspect of non-professional participants' communication acts was constructed on the basis of analytical categories developed in attribution theory.[429]

Within the framework of the designed analytical procedure, the central point of reference is the state of affairs, which from some point of view (primarily from the point of view of the subject matter of the proceedings) is either favorable or unfavorable for a given participant. In doing so, it is assumed in this study that a state of affairs that is unfavorable from the point of view of the subject of the proceedings for one party is favorable for another party to the proceedings. Taking this assumption (which is, of course, a simplification) into account, the various analytical categories are presented below (Figure 16).

429 Attribution theory explains how people perceive the acts of others or their own, how they determine the motives for acts and the reasons for the occurrence of certain events and states of affairs. According to this theory (or, in fact, one version of it), perception in the field in question are made on the basis of four main principles: (**1**) **the rule of stability** – which relates to perception on the basis of similarity of traits or acts regardless of time and place (a person consistently exhibits a certain trait or consistently acts in the same way); (**2**) **the rule of selectivity** – which relates to perception on the basis of specific traits or unique acts associated with a particular situation (a person does not usually exhibit certain traits or does not usually act in certain ways); (**3**) **the rule of location** – which refers to the perception of the causes of a particular act or event as either internal or external to a particular person; (**4**) **the rule of controllability** – which refers to the perception of the degree of controllability of a particular event or state of affairs by a particular person, cf. S. Morreale, B. Spitzberg, J. Barge, *Human Communication...*, op. cit.. This is primarily the reference to the approach proposed by Bernard Weiner, (see V.M. McDermott, *Attribution Theory*, [in:] *Encyclopedia of Communication Theory*, eds. S.W. Littlejohn, K.A. Foss, Sage Publications, 2009, pp. 60–63). As some authors point out, although there are many variants of this theory, they all make a similar set of basic assumptions (see e.g., D.G. Myers, *Social Psychology*, 10th edition, New York 2010, p. 103; on attribution theories and attributional theories see F. Försterling, *Attribution: An Introduction to Theories, Research and Applications*, Hove 2001). The purpose of referring to attribution theory is not to analyze the actual ways in which given events or states of affairs are perceived as the thought processes of individual participants in the proceedings, since the empirical material collected does not allow for this. The categories that have been developed in attribution theory are only intended to provide a convenient framework for analyzing the communication acts (as argumentative acts) undertaken by specific participants in the proceedings, which, at least in assumption, can influence the way other participants in the proceedings perceive specific states of affairs.

Elements of the theory of attribution – analytical categories	
STATE OF AFFAIRS:	
favorable to I **favorable** to HE/SHE/THEY	**unfavorable** to I **unfavorable** to HE/SHE/THEY
SHAPING THE PERCEPTION OF THE STATE OF AFFAIRS AS:	
STABLE I always/never... HE/SHE/THEY always/never...	**UNSTABLE** I exceptionally... HE/SHE/THEY exceptionally...
LOCATED externally internally (relative to the person)	**CONTROLLABLE/ NON-CONTROLABLE** (by the person concerned)

Figure 16. *Shaping the perception of the states of affairs – analytical categories*
Source: own study.

The analytical categories highlighted in the figure above were not included this time in the form of detailed research questions, but were directly placed in the table in Excel.

Re 2. The analytical categories indicated above make it possible to study those communication acts that serve to shape the image of the participant in the proceedings, but by reference to certain states of affairs, more or less relevant to the subject matter of the proceedings. However, the shaping of the "face" of a participant in the proceeding can take place without the described subject reference and concern only what is directly related to the person in question – in particular, traits, feelings or value system.[430]

The communication acts taken by the participants of the proceedings may be directed at shaping either their own "face" in the proceedings or the "face" of others. The analytical categories highlighted below take this assumption into account.

430 The reason for distinguishing two separate scopes of analysis (see Re 1 and Re 2) was the observation that the participants' statements in the context in question have different references, e.g. **Respondent**: *I was not able to read the contract* (...) – the respondent's statement refers to a specific state of affairs and points to the external factors that shaped this state of affairs and the lack of controllability; **Claimant**: *I am trampled, I just feel trampled,* **Witness:** *They are very diligent, dutiful* (...) – in turn, in these statements, the participants directly refer to the person (feelings and qualities, respectively).

Table 19. *Shaping the perception of people – analytical categories*

Shaping the perception of people	
Regarding I: traits, feelings, value system, etc.	Regarding HE/SHE/THEY: traits, feelings, value system, etc.

Source: Own study.

The analytical categories adopted within the two research scopes discussed above are not disconnected in the sense that it is not possible to exclude the communication act of the participant, which at the same time will be suitable for shaping the perception of states of affairs, as well as persons. Such cases during the analysis of the research material will also be taken into account.

Re 3. The last research scope related to the way of shaping the "face" of the participants in the proceedings concerns acts of a metacommunicative nature. The research material will be analyzed in terms of the use of selected linguistic means of persuasion.[431] The analysis procedure includes the identification of linguistic acts that lend themselves to blocking the verification of the truthfulness of descriptive statements or the accuracy of expressed assessments[432] or to reinforcing acts of certainty or exclusion – and, moreover, have a systemic character (i.e., can be subject to grammatical description).[433] The indicators of persuasiveness highlighted below include:[434]

1. use of such **persuasive operators** as "after all", "however" and (as assumed in this study) "of course";[435]
2. use of operators referring to **the general knowledge** or **the knowledge of the recipient** (e.g., *Everyone knows that…, You well know that…*);
3. use of operators that **suggest verifying a given piece of information** (e.g., *As it turned out…*);

431 Such means that serve to strengthen the effectiveness of communication acts.

432 Blocking is when the sender, through the use of an appropriate linguistic means of persuasion in an utterance, signals that he/she considers it unnecessary for the recipient to verify either its truthfulness or accuracy, A. Awdiejew, *Gramatyka interakcji…*, op. cit., p. 143).

433 A. Awdiejew, *Systemowe środki perswazji [Systemic means of persuasion]*, [in:] *Manipulacja w języku [Manipulation in language]*, eds. P. Krzyżanowski, P. Nowak, Lublin 2004, pp. 71–72.

434 The analytical categories are based on: A. Awdiejew, *Gramatyka interakcji…*, op. cit., pp. 143–148, idem, *Systemowe środki…*, op. cit., pp. 71–79.

435 The use of such operators suggests that a certain fact is known to both the sender and the recipient and cannot be doubted, A. Awdiejew, *Gramatyka interakcji…*, op. cit., p. 143.

4. use of operators that **introduce a given piece of information as routine, recurring** (e.g., *As always..., As usual...*);
5. use of operators that **introduce the information in question as unique** (e.g. *It seems strange, but..., You will not believe that...*);
6. use of operators that directly **refer to the sender's sincerity** (e.g., *To tell the truth..., To be honest...*);
7. **thematization of specific information**, that is, transferring it to the level of assumed information;
8. introducing so-called **observer effects** (e.g., *And here suddenly..., Imagine..., And then she screams...*);[436]
9. use of **operators that reinforce acts of certainty or exclusion** (e.g., *I am* [absolutely, totally, completely] *sure that...*).

The distinguished means of persuasion represent a certain communicative surplus and can accompany various linguistic acts.

3.6. Presiding judge's communication acts addressed to non-professional participants

3.6.1. Implementation of the leading-intermediary function

3.6.1.1. Presiding judge's instructions – addresses and the subject matter

According to the assumption made at the stage of designing the research procedure, the leading-intermediary function of the presiding judge is carried out, in particular, by giving appropriate instructions (information, warning) to the participants of the proceedings.[437] In this sense, the **presiding judge is an intermediary between the legal system and the participant of the proceedings**. Instructions concern the obligations, competences or entitlements of individual participants.[438]

The research material recorded 398 instructions given by the presiding judge (also acting as a court) to non-professional participants. The largest number of instructions, 202, were given to witnesses. As for the parties and quasi-parties to the proceedings, the most instructions were given to participants in non-contentious civil proceedings (46), applicants in non-contentious civil proceedings (42), claimants (34), respondents (27), insureds, defendants in misdemeanor cases

436 Quoting statements (either one's own or another person's) is also considered in this book to be a manifestation of the so-called observer effect.

437 The legislator is not consistent in the use of the distinguished terms, which sometimes describe similar or even identical acts. Instead, in this book the term "instruction" is used.

438 Thus, the content of the instruction may relate to the obligations of non-professional participants, as well as to the obligations of the court or presiding judge.

and defendants in criminal cases (18 each). While the least were given to entities representing an organizational unit in the proceedings (5), interested parties in proceedings concerning social security matters (4), juvenile, parents, legal representatives and non-professional attorneys (2 each), auxiliary prosecutor and another entity in proceedings concerning social security matters (1 each).[439]

To non-professional participants, presiding judges gave instructions of all three types highlighted in research question 1a, i.e., those explicitly specified in the normative pattern, those developed through practice and those formulated *ad hoc*, in addition instructions of a mixed nature. The quantitative differences in giving instructions of a given type are shown in Graph 1.

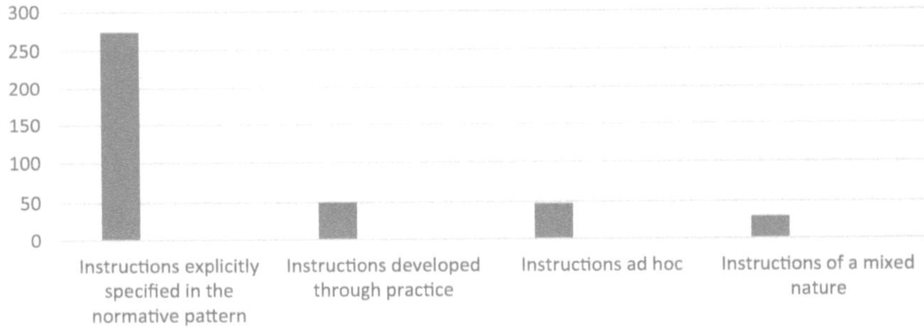

Graph 1. *Types of instructions given to non-professional participants*
Source: Own study.

Before the detailed figures, summarized in the graph above, are presented, a brief reference should be made to the way in which the different types of instructions are distinguished. The category of instructions explicitly specified in the normative pattern includes those instructions whose subject matter is specified by the relevant procedural norms. The second and fourth categories include those instructions that procedural norms do not oblige to give. In reference to instructions developed through the practice a certain repetition could be observed.[440] *Ad hoc* instructions,

439 It should be clearly noted that the number of instructions addressed to participants in each category (424 in total) is higher than the number of instructions formulated by the presiding judge in general. This is due to the fact that some instructions were addressed simultaneously to participants of different categories (e.g., simultaneously to the claimant and the respondent, or the applicant and the participant in non-contentious civil proceedings).

440 Repetitiveness was recognized primarily directly, i.e., by observing repeated communication acts, but sometimes also indirectly, when the formulas for particular instructions were prepared in the court minutes.

on the other hand, are those instructions that are closely related to the course of the court session or the subject matter of a particular case. Mixed instructions include those communication acts that combine the distinguished types of instructions. In the research material, combinations of categories one and two and one and four were noted.

The most numerous class among the instructions given to non-professional is made up of those explicitly specified in the normative pattern (273), among which we can distinguish instructions concerning: liability for giving false testimony (103), liability for giving false testimony and authorization to avoid answering the question (40), obligation to tell the truth (53), authorization to refuse to testify (34), way of appealing the decision (13), authorization to refuse to give explanations by the defendant (in penal case and misdemeanor case) (10), the so-called procedural rights of the defendant (in penal case and misdemeanor case)[441] (8), liability for making false inheritance assurances (6), evidence preclusion (5), and juvenile's right to defense (1).

The least numerous class of instructions, however, is made up of mixed instructions (29). They are created by supplementing the content of instructions from the first category with additional information. Thus, instructions on liability for giving false testimony were supplemented with information on the essence of testifying without an oath (2). Instruction relating to how to appeal a decision, in turn, included additional information: on finality, enforceability of the decision, how to obtain copies of final decisions, the possibility of changing the decision to the detriment of a party, and others (24). Instructions related to the so-called procedural rights of defendants, on the other hand, were combined with information on the consequences of absence during the conduct of the trial[442] (3).

Forty-nine instructions were, in the course of analyzing the empirical data, classified into a class of instructions developed through the practice. This class included instructions regarding: the absence of a written summons or notice of the date of the court session (12, including 8 expanded to information on the consequences of failure to appear), the entitlement of a witness to remain in the courtroom after the examination (16), the lack of an obligation to be present at the announcement of the decision (8), the lack of an obligation to be present during the conduct of the trial (5), the principles of inheritance and the consequences of (not) submitting

---

441 This refers to the competence to ask questions of the examined person and provide explanations for any evidence that is taken.

442 It should be noted here that since the observation for the study, the wording of one of the legal provisions of the Polish Penal Code has been significantly changed by adding explicit instructions that the presiding judge is obliged to give. At present, the obligation to instruct on the consequences of failure to appear at the trial, including at the announcement of the judgment, is clearly stated in the legal provisions.

inheritance declarations on time (4), the finality of the decision (2), and the obligation to excuse absence from the court session scheduled for the trial (2).

Slightly fewer (47) instructions were *ad hoc* instructions. Instructions of this type varied considerably in subject matter. The *ad hoc* instructions revealed in the research material concerned, in particular, issues related to participation at the trial,[443] the so-called dispositive acts of the parties to the proceedings,[444] the consequences of the settlement of the case,[445] the rules for making and the consequences of making procedural acts,[446] the substantive law,[447] other issues related to participation in court proceedings.[448]

Analysis of the research material in terms of the types of instructions described above revealed that the core of the instructions given by the presiding judge are those explicitly specified in the normative pattern. Not only do they form a class of their own, but they also co-create all the distinguished instructions of a mixed nature. The largest number of instructions of this type are related to main complex communication occurrences, primarily examination. There is also a clear correlation between the number of instructions given to participants of a specific category and the number of instructions with a specific content. The largest number of instructions collected in the research material was given to witnesses and also the largest number related to liability for giving false testimony. Instructions given to non-professional participants and classified in the first type are mostly universal in nature.[449] First, as a rule, instructions of this type are given to participants regardless of whether they are represented by professional legal representatives. Second, they are not related to the subject matter of the case under consideration. The

443 E.g., entitlement to reimbursement of court appearance expenses, not being required to stand during the announcement of the ruling, liability for violating the solemnity of the court, the presence of the victim at the court session scheduled for the trial, the consequences of failing to appear, the order in which evidence is taken in the trial.

444 E.g., withdrawal of the motion, appeal or lawsuit; the court's duties related to settlement.

445 E.g., the effect of an order for payment of outstanding remuneration for work, the effect of the settlement of the case in the context of the labor certificate, suspension of execution of the punishment, default judgment and objection to the default judgment.

446 In particular, the elements of a motion to adduce evidence, the consequences of missing a court deadline, the initiative of proof and the burden of proof, rules for filing procedural documents, inheritance declarations, court fees.

447 In particular, parental authority, child contact, pension entitlements.

448 E.g. entitlement to ex officio legal assistance, suspension of the proceedings, proceedings on division of the inheritance.

449 Except that the legal provisions of the Polish Code of Civil Procedure limit the obligation to provide instructions on evidentiary preclusion and how to contest the court decision to participants not represented by professional attorneys.

instructions distinguished under the first type are instructions of particular importance, as they concern the basic obligations, competencies and entitlements of the participants – the duty of truthfulness, the authorization to appeal the decision or the many competencies and entitlements that co-create the right to defense.

It is worth noting further that the revealed examples of instructions of the first type do not exhaust all the instructions explicitly stated in the normative pattern. Among other things, the research material did not record the instructions on the submission of objections to the minutes or on the so-called undisputed facts, to which the court was obliged by norms expressed in the Polish Code of Civil Procedure.[450]

It should be emphasized that the instructions revealed in the research material are characterized by varying degrees of detail, from significantly extensive – as in the first example below, to those that contain a minimum of content – as in the second example: **P:** *You will be examined in the character of a witness, you are obliged to testify the truth, for giving false testimony you face up to three years imprisonment. A witness may repeal of the question put to him when the answer to the question would involve criminal liability for the witness, severe property damage, disgrace, or would be related to the violation of professional secrecy, otherwise the witness is obliged to answer the questions put to him*; **P:** *I would like to instruct you before testifying about your obligation to tell the truth before the court, the penalty of the deprivation of liberty for giving false testimony is up to three years in prison.*

Just as the analysis of instructions of the first type allows one to look at the manner of implementation of a well-defined fragment of the normative pattern of the trial, the separation of instructions of the other types allows one to see and describe the scope of communication acts related to the initiative of individual presiding judges.[451] Consequently, this makes it possible to reveal those situations involving non-professional participants in which the presiding judge decided to take a particularly active attitude in giving instructions. And in view of the research objectives adopted in the study, it is worth examining this issue in more depth.

It is first necessary to indicate what information the presiding judges supplemented the instructions specified in the normative pattern with. Taking into account all the examples of instructions included in the category of mixed instructions, of particular importance are those given after the announcement of

450 It is possible that the court gave the relevant instructions in the case in writing, for example, by serving a copy of the lawsuit or motion.

451 It should be borne in mind that the presiding judge's act in this regard also implements norms for the provision of instructions, but norms of a more general nature, e.g. "The authority conducting the proceedings should, moreover, as necessary, provide information to the participants of the proceedings about their obligations and entitlements, also in cases where the law does not expressly provide for such an obligation" (Polish Code of Criminal Procedure).

the decision ending the proceedings in the case, which contained a lot of additional information in addition to information on how to contest them.

The instructions referred to in the previous sentence were supplemented with information on the validity of the decision and other issues related to finality, including how to obtain a copy of final decision, e.g. **P:** (...) *If none of you complain about it and it becomes final, we do not send it home. To get a copy of the ruling, you need to fill out a form, there is a stamp for six zlotys, you know, yes?* **P:** (...) *in the event that none of the parties submit either a motion for justification or an appeal, the ruling will be final in twenty-one days from today.*

In other instructions of this type, the emphasis has been clearly shifted to issues related to the finality of the decision,[452] e.g. **P:** *The ruling that the court issued is not final, it will become final at the earliest after three weeks from today. This is the statutory term for any appeal of the ruling. To challenge the ruling, you can file a motion for justification and delivery of a copy of the ruling with a justification within seven days from today, and then within fourteen days of receiving the ruling with a justification, you can file an appeal to the Regional Court in X, through our court. If you fail to do so, then after twenty-one days the ruling will already have legal effect, then you will be able to apply here at the registry office for a copy of the final ruling, and using this ruling, you will be able to complete possible inheritance formalities. Then you will also need to remember to report the acquisition of inherited property to the competent tax office. For this you have six months from the time of validation of the ruling. You only have to keep this deadline in order to take advantage of the tax exemption to which you are entitled as the closest person to the deceased.*

In the context of the above example, it is worth noting other information that the instructions have been supplemented with, e.g. **P:** (...) *Using this ruling, you will be able to handle possible further formalities involving this consensual division of the inheritance* (...); **P:** *Agreeing* [to reject the inheritance on behalf of the child] *is not the same as rejecting the inheritance, yes. After the validation of this decision, you will have to perform this action before a notary, unless there are proceedings initiated still before the court* (...); **P:** (...) *As the judgment is issued at your request, the court may change the judgment, including to your disadvantage.*

Instructions given after the announcement of the decision ending the proceedings were further supplemented with information on enforceability, e.g. **P:** (...) *the decision on the establishment of legal guardianship is enforceable as soon as it is announced* (...); and even with information on the content of any appeal, e.g. **P:** (...) *this complaint can only relate to this ruling on discontinuance, yes, the form of termination of the proceedings, because I emphasize that at the moment you withdraw the appeal* [against the administrative decision], *the court does not consider the case on the merits, yes, it only ends the process with the discontinuance of the proceedings.*

Among the instructions considered in this study to have been developed through the practice, the most numerous (43 in total) were those that concerned

452 This was the case when the instruction was given to those participants whose demand was fully considered.

participation of the court session, and were universal in the meaning that they did not refer to the subject of the case. At the same time, instructions of this type accompanied other procedural acts carried out at the trial,[453] e.g. **P:** *I am closing the trial and postponing the announcement of the judgment to the day* (...) *I am notifying you of this date, there is no obligation to appear, you can find out by phone the next day* (...) *about the resolution of the case* (...); **P:** *Okay, I release you from your position as a witness, you can leave the court, you can stay as you wish.*

In contrast, a significant proportion (29) of the *ad hoc* instructions were closely related with the subject of the case and addressed to the parties or quasi-parties. Therefore, such instructions should be considered particularly momentous for the above-mentioned categories of participants, as well as particularly important from the point of view of the equality of the parties to the proceedings and the impartiality of the court. In the research material analyzed, instructions of this type were given in the framework of proceedings: (1) in civil non-contentious cases (primarily in inheritance cases);[454] (2) conducted before the family courts; (3) in labor law cases; (4) in social security cases; (5) in criminal cases; (6) in misdemeanor cases.[455] In addition, it should be noted that most of them were addressed to participants not represented by professional attorneys,[456] and therefore to participants with a weaker, at least assumed, position in the proceedings.

In some of the cases revealed in the research material, the instructions of the type in question was closely related to the situational or communication context and involved, among other things, an attempt to perform certain acts that do not comply with procedural norms or such procedural acts that cannot be performed in a given proceeding, such as the following: **P:** *Mr. X, the court may give you a deadline today to submit the documents, but this will already be the deadline, and we are not delaying it anymore, because the applicant also has the right to review these documents and only then answer your questions, if any* (...);[457] **P:** (...) *because it is the*

453 E.g., instructions about the absence of a written summons or notice and the consequences of failing to appear always accompanied the oral summons or notice formulated by the presiding judge at the trial, as did instructions about the absence of an obligation to be present at the trial, including the announcement of the judgment. In turn, instruction on the entitlement of a witness to remain in the courtroom after examination accompanied the act of releasing the witness.

454 Some instructions given in inheritance proceedings and related to their subject matter, due to their repetitive nature, have been included in the class of instructions developed through the practice.

455 In the proceedings referred to in points 3 through 6, instructions of the type in question were given to employees, insureds, defendants (in misdemeanor cases) and defendants (in penal cases), respectively.

456 Four instructions are excepted here – two given in labor law proceedings and two in inheritance proceedings.

457 This instruction was the presiding judge's response to the participant's attempt to change the order of evidentiary acts carried out at the trial, which was determined on the basis of the normative pattern.

case that in the proceedings for the acquisition of inheritance, the inheritance can be accepted or also rejected (...), *so in our proceedings, you cannot transfer your share to your mother, but it can be done by such a consensual division, if there is such an agreement between you* (...).

The presiding judge's decision to give instructions of the type in question can also be linked to doubts about the sense of taking certain procedural acts or the participant's proposed way of resolving the case, for example: **P:** (...) *there is a difference between damages and remuneration, because damages are sort of... you do not pay off the benefits associated with it, whereas it is different with remuneration, it is taxed and if we were to award remuneration* (...), *it has to be with tax* (...); **P:** (...) *If you are able to come to an agreement on your own, I am not obligating you to anything, I am just informing you that there is a possibility that you can withdraw your application in the present proceedings and generally the case will be discontinued, and there will be no further continuation, the status quo will remain as it is* (...).

In addition, with the revealed awkwardness of the participant, such as **P:** *You can also in this application possibly ask for the appointment of ex officio attorney for Mr. X, then you need to attach, there such forms are about assets and family status with us in the registry office, and if such an application is filed, then perhaps the court will appoint this attorney (...) since Mr. X is indeed such an awkward person who has a very low income, then after the assessment of the court, such a preliminary one, he could benefit from such assistance* (...).

Others were in response to problems related to the performance of a procedural act, such as **P:** *The penalty that can be suspended is up to two years, the suspension can be from two to five years* (...), or active participation in the proceedings, such as **P:** (...) *a guardian for a person unknown from the place of residence* (...) *can be appointed.*

Finally, mention should be made of those instructions that pertained to substantive law, and such in the analyzed material were given in inheritance proceedings, proceedings before the family court and in social security proceedings, for example, **P:** (...) *after Mr. XY, your daughter comes to inherit. And now from today the time limit for your child's possible inheritance begins to run, here you will no longer be able to plead ignorance, lack of awareness of the existence of the debt* (...); **P:** (...) *parental authority is independent of contact, even a parent who is deprivation of parental authority has the right to contact the child, unless there is a court decision that would prohibit such contact, yes* (...); **P:** *Sir, this is an early retirement pension, or as the name says, privileged, so to speak. These conditions must be met* (...).

Giving instructions is among such activities of the presiding judge, the purpose of which is to make participants aware of their obligations, as well as their competences and entitlements. The analysis of instructions in their subject matter aspect, carried out for the purposes of this section, revealed, in particular, that not all of them relate to the participation of non-professional participants at the trial. Some of them are much broader in nature, as they concern procedural norms related to participation in court proceedings in general, and even norms of substantive law related to the subject matter of a particular case. As a result, the impact of the instructions given on the conduct of the trial varies. Those that relate to the activity of the participants in the trial undoubtedly facilitate participation in the session where it is carried out. Other instructions, of course, facilitate the non-professional participants' orientation of their legal situation, but do not have a direct impact on their activity at the trial itself.

3.6.1.2. Ways of giving instructions – basic types

Presiding judge's instructions are communication acts with a significant degree of difficulty – they convey information that is important to the addressee, not necessarily known to him or her, and, moreover, at least to some extent, specialized. Given the high risk of communication barriers during the implementation of the acts in question, it is necessary to take a closer look at the ways in which instructions are given to non-professional participants.

Answering the research questions about the ways of giving instructions, it can be said that the research material did not record examples of instructions providing by reading the relevant legal provision or recalling its wording from memory.[458] The form of information about the legal situation of a given participant took of 126 instructions. The remaining 272 instructions had a verbal form different from the types of instructions distinguished above, and formed an internally differentiated class.

In the course of the analysis of empirical data, the distinctive feature of instructions on the legal situation of the participant was considered to be this way of informing about obligations, entitlements or competences, which was combined with the corresponding addressee phrase directly indicating the individually specified addressee of the instruction.[459] The research material revealed the following ways of giving this type of instruction: (1) with the use of the word "obligation" or similar words, e.g. (...) ***you*** *all* ***have the obligation*** *to testify to the truth* (...); (...) *as a party,* ***you have the obligation*** *to tell the truth* (...); (...) ***you have the obligation*** *to prove* (...); (...) ***you are obligated*** *to tell the truth* (...); (...) ***you are obligated to*** *testify to the truth* (...); (2) with the use of modal terms such as "may" or "must", e.g. (...) ***you may*** *give explanations, or you may refuse to give explanations* (...); (...) ***you may*** *apply for appointment of ex officio attorney* (...); *Mr. X,* ***you cannot*** *refuse to answer the court's question,* ***you must*** *answer those questions* (...); (...) ***you do not have to*** *be,* ***you can*** (...); (...) ***you must*** *tell the truth and* ***you cannot*** *conceal the*

458 An instruction of this type was given at the trial conducted in a commercial proceeding, for which no permission to record was obtained.

459 We are talking about the so-called basic and derivative (e.g., competence, entitlement) legal situations, that is, those that arose for a given subject due to the validity of a particular legal norm, Z. Ziembiński, S. Wronkowska, *Zarys teorii prawa [Outline of legal theory]*, Poznań 2001, p. 100 et seq. There are various ways of expressing this type of situation, in particular by means of modal terms ("may", "must", etc.).

truth (...); (3) with the word "right", e.g. *As a relative, **you have the right** to refuse to testify* (...); ***You have the right** to make explanations* (...); ***You have the right** to apply to the court for reimbursement of travel expenses* (...); (4) with the use of the word "should", e.g. (...) ***you should testify** truthfully to the best of your knowledge* (...); (5) combining some of the ways highlighted above, e.g. ***You can come** to the reading of the judgment, there is **no obligation*** (...); ***You are not obligated** to come, but as a victim **you can*** (...); ***Your presence is not mandatory**, you have defense counsel, **you do not have to** come* (...).

The instructions, which were included in the last and most numerous class (272 instructions), convey information of different content and in a variety of ways. They, in particular, conveyed information: (1) about sanctions, e.g. *I am instructing you about the responsibility for giving false testimony, the penalty of the deprivation of liberty for telling untruths or concealing the truth is up to three years*; (2) that something will or may happen, e.g. (...) *according to the circumstances you will be able to be re-examined after taking the oath*; (3) about the fact that something will not happen, e.g. (...) *please save yourself* [the note], *because separate summonses will not come* (...); (4) about obligations – concerning certain participants in general or related to certain circumstances, e.g. *A person who requests the examination of a witness should give the details of the witness*; (...) *before the court, the truth must be told* (...); (5) about the entitlements or competencies of generally specified subjects, e.g. *Even a parent who is deprived of authority has the right to contact*; (...) *a witness has the right to evade answering* (...); (6) about the participant's acts that exceed the legal norms, e.g. (...) *it can't be that you submit some additional documents at every court session* (...); (7) about the absence of an obligation of a certain type, e.g. (...) *this is a ruling, not a judgment, you do not have to stand up*; (8) about the consequences of doing certain things: (a) specified positively (what will happen), e.g. (...) *if Mr. Applicant makes such a statement, then we will be able to terminate the case* (...); (b) specified negatively (what will not happen), e.g. (...) *a potential heir who has made a declaration of rejection of the inheritance within the statutory term of six months, does not come into the inheritance, does not inherit from the deceased person* (...); (9) about the consequences of not doing certain things: (a) specified positively, e.g. (...) *if you do not appear, the court will disregard the evidence of your examination* (...); (b) specified negatively, e.g. (...) *failure to appear will not result in no announcement of the judgment* (...); (10) concerning the manner in which certain acts are performed, e.g. (...) *then you will be able to report to the registry office of our court, apply for a copy of the already final judgment* (...); (11) concerning the nature of an act of a certain type or basis, e.g. (...) *this judgment is a court of first instance, that is, it is a non-final judgment* (...); (...) *the claims that the employee may assert against the employer* (...) *are supplementary in nature* (...); (12) about the obligations of the court, e.g. *the labor court has an obligation to keep an eye on whether the settlement does not harm the legitimate interest of the employee* (...); (13) about the court's competence or lack thereof, e.g. (...) *these are the instruments that the court has to issue such an obligation* (...); (...) *the court can never force you to submit documents* (...); (14) in the form of a request, e.g. (...) *in a moment both of you will be examined, please tell the truth* (...); (15) combining the instruction with handing out the appropriate form, e.g. (...) *please fill it out to the end, submit it and we will send you a ruling*; (16) combining the above ways.[460]

3.6.1.3. Ways of giving instructions – further analysis

In view of the special importance of instructions to the participants of court proceedings and their significant level of difficulty as communication acts, it is worth looking at certain elements of instructions, which in the literature (especially linguistic literature) are considered to facilitate contact, that is, to promote communicative understanding, or, on the contrary, to hinder understanding. A deeper analysis of this issue is also important in the context of ethical norms, which, in particular, set the judge's duty to explain procedural issues in a communicative manner.[461]

In view of the significant number of instructions recorded in the research material and, above all, their varying importance and subject matter, the instructions that are as similar as possible in these two distinguished aspects were selected for in-depth analysis. Instructions given after the announcement of the decision ending the proceedings in the case are considered as such in this study, with special attention paid to that part of the instruction which concerns the performance of certain procedural acts. Thirty-six instructions of this type were recorded in the research material.

In turn, the research procedure used is to reveal, within the framework of the instructions analyzed, the linguistic elements that are recognized in the literature as either facilitating or hindering communicative understanding and that remain relevant to face to face communication.[462] For example, in the context of

---

460 It should be noted here that some instructions of the type in question also contained passages describing the legal situation of the participant.

461 And, in addition, because of the clear modern trend related to the simplification of language, especially with regard to texts produced by various types of organizational units, both of a public and private nature. With regard to written instructions formulated in court proceedings, proposals are being put forward to simplify them, as well as templates of such instructions, e.g., "You may request reimbursement of the necessary travel expenses, accommodation costs and lost earnings or income associated with your arrival at the Court. (...) For each unexcused absence, the Court may order you to pay a fine. In the case of repeated absences without proper justification, the Court may order detention and forced bringing to trial", J. Lora, *Komunikacja...*, op. cit., p. 53 et seq. Cf. one of the jury instruction formula proposed in American courts: "[*Name of party*] is representing [himself] [herself] in this trial. This fact must not affect your consideration of the case. Self-represented parties and parties represented by an attorney are entitled to the same fair consideration", https://www.ce9.uscourts.gov/jury-instructions/node/758, access 7.07.2023.

462 Not all categories of this type developed in the linguistic literature or communication science can be transferred to face to face communication. This applies in particular to certain elements of composition (visual distinction of a text fragment)

jury instructions (in jury trials), it is pointed out that many factors can affect the intelligibility of instructions, not only legal jargon: "[s]everal decades of empirical research tell us that legal jargon is neither the sole nor a major source of incomprehensibility in jury instructions, long known to present problems to jurors, though it can present special problems (proximate cause, stipulate, mens rea, beyond a reasonable doubt, etc.). The textual problems are sentence structure and grammatical constructions such as nominalizations, vague or unusual prepositional phrases, doublets, especially of legal terms, and passive constructions, particularly in subordinate clauses. Other problems include presuppositions underlying jury instructions in opposition to the presuppositions underlying attorney strategies, the nature of the task, the highly abstract nature of the instructions, and the mode of delivery of the instructions".[463]

First of all, attention was paid to whether the instructions given to participants inform only what the participant is authorized to do, or additionally how to perform a certain procedural act.

The analysis revealed three examples of instructions that informed only of authorization, two of which were for authorization to file an appeal[464] and one for requesting a copy of the final decision.

In addition, the remaining 33 instructions contained information on the rules for performing certain procedural acts or information relating to the consequences of their performance. However, it should be clearly emphasized that not all instructions were equally comprehensive and detailed in this aspect. The poorest in terms of content was the instruction, which indicated only the time limit for performing an act, e.g. **P:** ***The*** *party who disagrees with the judgment has seven days to file a request for delivery of a copy of the judgment with justification, and after delivery – seven days to file an appeal.* Subsequent instructions were enriched with information on: (1) where to make the act, e.g. (...) *to the regional court through the local court* (...); (2) the obligation and method of payment of the fee, e.g. (...) *you have to buy court fee stamps for six zlotys at the office* (...); (3) when the act made will begin to have effect, e.g. (...) *the decision, however, will be sent, a copy of the decision, only after it is certainly validation*; (4) the possibility of using a form, e.g. (...) *such forms are available at the secretary's office of the Department* (...);[465] (5) the content

---

or sentence length, since within the oral linguistic act the function of punctuation marks can also be performed by appropriate intonation and speaking dynamics.

463 B.K. Dumas, *Language of Jury Instructions*, [in:] *The Encyclopedia of Applied Linguistics*, ed. C.A. Chapelle, Blackwell Publishing 2013, p. 5.

464 The addressee of both of these instructions was only a non-professional attorney (employee) of Social Insurance Institution, thus the situational context fully justified this limitation of the instruction.

465 In one case, the instructions for a copy of the final decision were combined with the handing of the form: (...) *please fill it out to the end, submit it and we will send a ruling.*

of the act, e.g. (...) *you can* (...) *make a note that you will receive it in person* (...); (...) *it is important that you write in this application "with a statement of finality"* (...); (...) *request for a justification of a judgment – this is an ordinary letter, where you give the case number and write that you are asking for a justification of a judgment* (...); (...) *in the appeal you should already state more, because you should state why you disagree possibly with the judgment, what the court did wrong, in your opinion, and what you request* (...); (6) the consequences of (not) doing a certain action, e.g. (...) *if you do not do it, the judgment will be validated, the case will be closed. On the other hand, if you appeal, the case will be handled by the court of appeal* (...); (...) *then the court must schedule a trial, summons you again* (...); (...) this *document* [a copy of the final ruling] *can be used anywhere and show that you are the heir of Mrs. XY.*

Of all the instructions analyzed, the most exhaustive in content were the instructions given to the insured in social security proceedings, secondarily the instructions given in civil non-contentious inheritance proceedings and some in family proceedings. Two aspects are worth noting in the context of this issue.

The comprehensiveness of the instruction in terms of content is, of course, a primary concern,[466] but it is worth asking whether the information is conveyed in the instruction in a way that facilitates its applicability, or not. Among the linguistic procedures that facilitate the use of the information that has been learned and revealed in the instructions analyzed in this study are, in particular: (1) the use of singular names instead of general names, e.g. (...) *to the District Court in X* (...) instead of (...) *to the district court* (...) or (...) *through our court* (...) instead of (...) *through the district court* (...); (2) providing information in a casuistic manner, e.g. by indicating precisely where the action is performed within the organizational structure of the court, e.g. (...) *at the registry office of our court* (...); (...) *at the cashier's office of the court* (...); (...) *in that building next door* (...), or indicating the amount of the fee, e.g. (...) *pay it with court fee stamps in the amount of six zlotys* (...), or indicating when exactly the deadline for performing a certain act expires, e.g. (...) *you should within seven days from today, that is, by next Wednesday, file a motion to justify the judgment* (...).

Providing information as specific as possible reduces the need for the addressee of the instruction to engage additional knowledge and carry out additional inference in order to obtain information that is fully applicable, i.e. to actually perform a specific act. The linguistic means in question were used in the 22 instructions analyzed, with the most frequent use of those included in point 1, i.e., single names referring to the court as the place where the action was performed.

The instructions subjected to in-depth analysis were also examined structurally. During the analysis, attention was paid to two issues: (1) whether the instruction

466 At the same time, it should be borne in mind that a linguistic act containing too much detailed information can lead to information overload, and it is very difficult, if at all possible, to determine the "moment of overload", as it depends on many factors, including the individual perceptual abilities of the recipient.

includes an introduction; (2) whether the sequence of information conveyed was kept.

The introduction to an oral instruction has the same function as the heading in a written instruction (or any other written text). Since the instruction given at the trial always occurs in the setting of other communication acts, it also has a delimiting function. In addition, the introduction to the instruction can promote the orientation of the addressee towards the perception of the particular type of information conveyed in the instruction. Because of all these properties, the introduction to an instruction is considered in this study to be an act that promotes communicative understanding. Among the instructions analyzed, only eight contained an introduction, such as **P:** *And now regarding obtaining a copy of this ruling, possibly further steps you can take* (...); **P:** *Now the court instructs you on how to file an appeal* (...); **P:** *And now briefly the court will instruct* (...).

However, referring to the order of the information provided, no uniform pattern can be identified in this regard in the instructions analyzed. This is not only a consequence of differences in the content of these instructions, but also of the shift of emphasis in some instructions to issues related to the finality of the court decision. Despite these differences, it can be noted that the order of the information provided is, in principle, quite natural in the sense that it reflects the order in which the various events occurred and certain acts were performed. This natural order is somewhat modified especially in instructions where the emphasis is shifted to issues related to finality.

The basic pattern (8 cases) that can be reconstructed from an analysis of instructions focusing attention on issues relating to contesting the court decision is as follows:

the non-finality of the decision – the possibility of appeal – the method of appeal.

Other schemes (12 in total) were more elaborate and took the following form in particular:

1. **the non-finality of the decision – the possibility of appeal – the method of appeal – finality (as a result of the lack of appeal);**
2. **non-finality of decision – possibility of appeal – method of appeal – finality (as a result of lack of appeal) – method of obtaining a copy of the decision/effects of finality.**

In contrast, the structure of the subsequent instructions (5 in total) was poorer relative to the basic scheme and took the following form, among others:

the non-finality of the decision – the possibility of an appeal; the possibility of an appeal – the manner of an appeal; and even **the manner of an appeal.**

Analysis of the instructions also revealed such a scheme, which, with respect to the basic scheme, can be considered both poorer and more elaborate:

the possibility of an appeal – the method of an appeal – additional information on the effects of appeal.

The natural order in which information was conveyed was somewhat disrupted in instructions that emphasized the finality of the decision (10 in total). The following scheme was used most often (6 cases):

non-finality of the decision – finality (moment of being final) – the manner of an appeal [brief] – finality as a result of lack of an appeal – method of obtaining a copy of the decision – other additional information.[467]

Such a way of modifying the natural structure, as presented by the example previously cited, can be considered justified. Indeed, it represents a kind of compromise between the presiding judge's duty to instruct on appealing [the court decision] and adapting the content of the instruction to the situational context (e.g., when the decision was in line with the party's or quasi-party request).

To conclude the discussion of issues related to the structure of the instructions under review, it is worth noting that, in principle, they do not contain those linguistic elements that are sometimes referred to as "talking about talking".[468] This seems to be caused by the fact that the instructions are given in a face to face communication situation, and the limited time available to the presiding judge during the court session.[469]

The last issue related to the in-depth analysis of instructions concerns the use of legal and juridical terminology. It should be pointed out that each of the 36

---

467 E.g., **P:** *The ruling that the court has issued is not final, for it to become final, twenty-one days must elapse. This is the statutory term for appealing the ruling. If it is not appealed, it will begin to have legal effects after these twenty-one days. Then you will be able to report to the office of the registry of our court, apply for a copy of the already final ruling, and using this ruling, you will be able to handle any formalities* (...).

468 These are linguistic acts that make it difficult for the recipient of a text to reach information that is relevant, T. Piekot, E. Moroń, G. Zarzeczny, *Prosto po polsku – przyjazne upomnienia [Simple in Polish – friendly admonitions]*, pp. 10–12, https://biznes.newseria.pl/files/1097841585/raport_prosto_po_polsku_-_przyjazne_upomnienia.pdf, access 22.12.2022. In the course of analyzing the instructions, only two examples of linguistic means that could be considered "talking about talking" were noted – (...) *the court decided in accordance with your position, however, I am obliged to inform you that* (...) and the second with a similar verbal form. However, the use of both phrases should be considered justified, since in this way the presiding judge was simultaneously explaining why he was instructing participants, despite the fact that the court's decision was in line with the request.

469 Indeed, it can be assumed that in a time-constrained situation, the presiding judge will want to get straight to the point. This is a positive aspect of the time constraints involved in conducting the trial, but it should be remembered that there are negative aspects as well (this has been written about, discussing time as an element of micro-context).

instructions analyzed contained legal or juridical terms. The terms appearing in the instructions were primarily related to procedural issues – the settlement of a case, an appeal or the validity of a decision, e.g. *appeal, (non-)finality, court fee, decision, ruling, statutory term, validation, judgment, complaint.* Others referred to the subject matter of a particular case, e.g., *early retirement pension, inherited property, rejection of inheritance, legal guardian, tax, tax credit.*

It is worth noting that none of the instructions reviewed included information on the legal basis.

As a rule, the presiding judge did not explain in the instructions under review the meaning of the legal or juridical terms used.[470] However, it is worth recalling at this point that the rules of construction (performance) and rules of consequence of a particular conventional act, including procedural acts, are elements of the content of the name of the act.[471] Thus, information on how to perform a certain act and what will be the consequences of making such a choice and not another, at least partially explains the meaning of the name of the procedural act in question.

3.6.1.4. Instructions – problem of one-way communication acts

The final issue that will be discussed in the context of the presiding judge's communication acts related to the leading-intermediary role will be the directionality of instruction as a communication act.

According to the normative pattern, the giving of instructions at the trial is an one-way communication act. Undoubtedly, taking one-way communication acts increases the risk of communication misunderstanding,[472] while in a face to face communication situation any one-way communication act can easily be transformed into a communication occurrence. The same may be true of giving instructions at the trial.

This issue was addressed by research questions 1c through 1da. The answers to these questions were intended to provide a picture of the extent to which presiding judges, when giving instructions to non-professional participants, take advantage of the opportunity to transform an one-way communication act into a communication occurrence. The results of the analysis of the research material in this regard are as follows.

Regarding research question 1c (Does the presiding judge, after giving an instruction, ask the non-professional participant whether he or she understood

---

470 With the exception of the following: *appeal, non-final judgment, copy of the ruling with a statement of finality, statement of finality, motion for justification of judgment, court of first instance judgment.*

471 See on constitutive rules as forming definitions of the names of certain acts, J.R. Searle, *Speech Acts...*, op. cit., p. 34.

472 With feedback, the sender has a better chance of figuring out if there is a communication misunderstanding, such as when the addressee gives the wrong answer to a question.

the instruction?) and 1ca (Does the presiding judge continue to give an instruction if the answer is negative?), it should be pointed out that among all the cases of instruction recorded in the research material (and there were 398 of them), in 75 cases the presiding judge, after giving an instruction, directly asked the participant whether he or she understood the instruction. Moreover, in not a single case did the presiding judge receive a negative response from the participant.

In addition to the above-described way of transforming an one-way instruction into a communication occurrence, which could be called direct, acts of an indirect nature were also noticeable in the research material. The first of this type of act was the question directed to the participant after the instruction on the right to refuse either testimony or explanations regarding whether he or she wanted to exercise this right. The content of the given answer made it possible to find out whether the participant understood the instruction correctly.[473]

Another indirect form used by presiding judges was the use of a linguistic mean, which in this study was called "questioning yes". This refers to instructions that the presiding judge ended with the word "yes" in the intonation of the question, e.g. **P:** *I am instructing you on your obligation to tell the truth, yes(?)*; *You are obligated to tell the truth, yes(?).*

The above way of formulating the statement in a certain sense forces a reaction from the addressee, so it is the beginning of a communication occurrence. However, it is problematic in the sense that it forces not so much any reaction as a convergent reaction, consisting of confirmation (nodding),[474] and it is difficult to decide whether it is a confirmation of the understanding of the utterance or only of its reception.

Sometimes, of course, the presiding judge was able to figure out whether the participant understood the instruction correctly without initiating a feedback act, such as when, as a consequence of the instruction, the participant had to choose between taking one procedural act or another. This is also true of communication acts and behaviors that are extra-linguistic in nature, such as nodding one's head, which occur as feedback due to the fact that the instruction is given in a face-to-face situation.

---

473 Or misunderstanding, as it was in this case: **P:** *You are the closest person to the defendant, therefore you have the right to refuse to testify. It is up to you whether you testify or not. Do you want to testify or not?*, **Witness:** *Well,* ***if I am sued****, I will testify, I have nothing to hide.*

474 On the so-called convergent and divergent communication acts in the context of a trial, see A. Di Conza, L. Abbamonte, L. Scognamiglio, A. Gnisci, *Accommodation Strategies in Italian Courtroom Examinations: A Cross-Disciplinary Analysis of the Reciprocal Effects of Question-Answering*, "US-China Law Review" 2012, Vol. 9, p. 330 et seq.

On the other hand, with regard to research questions 1d (After giving an instruction, does the presiding judge ask the non-professional participant to paraphrase[475] the instruction?) and 1da (Does the presiding judge continue to give the instruction if a communication misunderstanding is found?), it should be pointed out that not a single case was recorded in the research material in which the presiding judge asked to paraphrase the instruction given in order to figure out whether the participant understood it correctly. Besides, within the whole research material[476] only one situation was revealed in which the presiding judge asked to paraphrase his statement.[477]

3.6.2. Implementation of leading-coordinating function

The leading-coordinating function of the presiding judge is related to the face-to-face communication between the participants in a given session scheduled for the trial, while its implementation involves various acts related to coordinating the communication process that occurs between them. The manner (and not the duty itself) of coordinating the course of communication acts undertaken at the trial is, in principle, outside the normative pattern of the trial, so the presiding judge has considerable freedom in shaping the process. In designing the research questions related to the leading-coordinating function, possible communication acts of the presiding judge addressed to non-professional participants were taken into account, which, at least in principle, can facilitate the non-professional participant's participation at the trial. The answers to the research questions posed are intended to give a picture of the presiding judge's activity in taking such communication acts. In turn, research question 2ab (Does the presiding judge use legal and juridical terms when interacting directly with a non-professional participant?) addresses the presiding judge's linguistic acts that may impede communicative understanding. However, this issue will be discussed below in a broader context of communication acts that may facilitate communicative understanding.

3.6.2.1. The problem of presiding judges adapting to the level of communication competence of non-professional participants

Both linguistics and communication science formulate a general technical directive stating that if the sender wants to communicate in a way that promotes communicative understanding, he or she should adapt the form of expression to the

475 Paraphrasing the statements is one of the linguistic tools to facilitate communication with non-professional participants of the trial, see *Handling Cases...*, op. cit., pp. 10-10-10-11.
476 This is including all 250 court sessions scheduled for the trial.
477 Such an example has been noted in juvenile proceedings: **P:** *Do you understand, do you understand what I expect from you? Then what do I expect?*, **Juvenile:** *To break contact with companions, to take up studies....*

level of communication competence of the addressee.[478] The general nature of this directive is, of course, related to the fact that the manner of adaptation in each case depends on the specific communication situation. This causes, by the way, that the category of "adaptation to the addressee" is difficult to operationalize in the process of designing a research procedure for analyzing actual communication processes. This problem also had to be faced in the present study. Within the framework of the research procedure proposed therein, first of all, it was searched in the research material for such cases in which the presiding judge particularly visibly (to the observer) referred to the peculiar features of the speech of a non-professional participant (a specific way of naming certain events or people) and in this sense adapted to him or her.[479] In the second place, in a sort of reverse research procedure, selected lexical means that can impede communicative understanding were searched for in the empirical material. The legal and juridical terms are considered as such in the study.

3.6.2.2. Presiding judge's explicit reference to vocabulary used by non-professional participants

During the analysis of the research material, the class of particularly clear cases of presiding judges referring to the vocabulary used by a non-professional participant included only 18 communication occurrences. In seven cases, the act consisted of referring to the way the non-professional participant called other participants,[480] e.g. **P:** ***The colleague*** *realized the repayments of these loans, there were no problems?*; **P:** *How was* ***the driver*** *dressed?*; **P:** ***The brother-in-law*** *did not take unpaid leave?* Other examples involved referring to the way events are named, for example:

Witness: *Or they got pissed off and left* [the tools] *at the construction site.*
P: *And was there a situation where they were pissed off?*
Witness: *It was.*
P: *What was the claimant's reason for being pissed off?*
Witness: *The payout wasn't there because there was something....*

They concerned both events and states of affairs, for example:

---

478 E.g., in the context of plain language, see Ch. Stephens, J. Pringle, *Identify Your Audience*, [in:], *Plain Language in Plain English*, ed. Ch. Stephens, Vancouver 2010, p. 27. Sociolinguists also speak in this context of code-switching, that is, the ability to switch from one sociolect to another, S. Grabias, *Interakcja językowa...*, op. cit., p. 33.

479 This is the most literal understanding of the phrase "adaptation to the addressee".

480 This refers to such cases in which a non-professional participant speaks of another participant using a term that is not the name of his or her procedural role, and the presiding judge continues such naming.

Insured: (...) *it was as manager X was talking here, first there was this "Belarusian", once I had my license, I drove this "Belarusian", then there was a "pelican"* (...) *well then I sat on the "Belarusian", then the other "pelican" and so on until the end of the ride.*

P: *And it was often the case that you had to dismount from this "Belarusian" or from this "pelican" and do something else?*

They concerned other issues, for example:

Insured: *Well as a physical* [worker].

P: *As a physical ... and what did you do?* (...) *Then how long did you work as a physical* [worker]*?*

Although in all the analyzed cases of the type in question the reference to the manner of speech of the non-professional participant was evident, it is difficult to see any particular significance of these (specific) linguistic means for the communication process between the presiding judge and the non-professional participant. The effect of simplifying the process of communication could only have been caused by the reference to the names "Belarusian" and "pelican" as sociolectal means, which are part of the sociolect familiar to the participant, and moreover because these terms are much shorter than the full names of these devices (devices used in melioration). However, it should be clearly noted that the process of adaptation of the sender to the addressee (way of speaking, level of communication competence, etc.) tends to be more subtle in nature and of considerable significance – this is also evidenced by the examples of presiding judges' statements cited in this book.

3.6.2.3. Presiding judge's use of legal and juridical terms in communication with non-professional participants

3.6.2.3.1. Legal and juridical terms – conceptual framework

Issues of legal and jurisprudential terminology both appear in this study in theoretical considerations and are an important part of some research procedures, but have not been discussed more extensively so far.

It is assumed in this book that a "legal term" is a term that occurs in the text of a legislative act[481] and all its applicability criteria are determined by the legal

481 Such a term is therefore part of the legal language. It is worth adding at this point that "[a]s has been remarked by many authors, such an expression ['legal language'] is ambiguous in that it could refer to both the language that law is, the language of the sources of law, and to the (meta) language used to speak about law", F. Poggi, *Law...*, op. cit., p. 32. It is assumed in this book that **the legal language** is the language in which the texts of legislative acts are formulated, **the language related to the law** (or rather languages) is the one in which various subjects formulate statements about the law or about issues related to them. Languages related to the

definition, as well a term that has additional non-statutory applicability criteria that legal dogmatics has developed before its use in the text of a legislative act or has already agreed upon after its use in the text of a legislative act.[482] In turn, the name "juridical term" is used here to describe those terms that do not appear in legal texts, but have been developed by lawyers, for example, as the names of legal institutions, types of crimes or situations designated by legal norms. The scopes of the two above-mentioned names, moreover, fall within the scope of the name "term", which denotes a word or expression of a professional, scientific and technical meaning, which, in particular, is characterized by its accuracy, systematicity and limitation.[483] In this sense, the name "term" functions in linguistics.[484] The fact that legal and juridical terms fall within the scope of the name "term" in the linguistic sense is determined by the specific meaning of these lexis – either defined in the legal text or developed in legal studies or legal practice.

Just as making conceptual arrangements for the issue at hand did not cause much difficulty,[485] operationalizing these concepts was problematic.

The difficulties in this regard are primarily related to the need to relate the category of legal terms, a category specific to legal language, to a communication occurrence such as a trial. First, the scope of the legal definition contained in a legislative act is specified. In Poland, as a matter of principle, the definition establishes the meaning of a given word or expression within that particular legislative act. Legal terms are thus terms (in the linguistic sense) within the law. Doubts may arise as to the meaning in which a given term, which is a legal term, is used at the trial. The situation is further complicated by the fact that some words and expressions are defined differently in different legislative acts, and there are some that are defined in some legislative acts and no longer in others (e.g., "document", "property"). This is especially problematic when we are dealing with a term that functions in common language, but is defined in some legislative act (e.g., "building", "street" or "renovation"). In the cases discussed above, a particularly

---

law "surround" the legal language, M. Zieliński, *Języki prawne i prawnicze [Legal and juridical languages]*, [in:] *Polszczyzna 2000. Orędzie o stanie języka na przełomie tysiącleci [Polish language 2000: An announcement on the state of language at the turn of the millennium]*, ed. W. Pisarek, Kraków 1999, p. 64. This concept is a development of Bronisław Wróblewski's proposal for a conceptual distinction between legal language and juridical language, B. Wróblewski, *Język prawny i prawniczy [Legal and juridical language]*, Kraków 1948, p. 54.

482 M. Zieliński, *Wykładnia prawa. Zasady, reguły, wskazówki [Legal interpretation. Principles, rules, hints]*, 7th edition, Warszawa 2017, pp. 248–249.

483 S. Gajda, *Styl naukowy*, [in:] *Współczesny język...*, op. cit., pp. 185–186.

484 Or at least in meanings close to it, since there is no complete consensus among linguists on all the criteria for the applicability of this name.

485 This does not mean that the recognition of a given word or expression as a legal term is not problematic, especially since there is a lack of dictionaries devoted legal and juridical terms, M. Zieliński, *Wykładnia prawa...*, op. cit., pp. 247–248.

well-founded doubt arises as to whether or not the participant is using the given phrase as a legal term.

The basis for deciding which words and expressions will not be taken into account when analyzing the empirical material for the use of legal and juridical terminology was the purpose for which this issue is discussed in this study at all. The use of legal and juridical terminology in the communication process with a non-professional participant, at least by assumption, can be a factor that impedes communicative understanding. Therefore, from the point of view of the research procedure designed for the study, those features of terms that are emphasized in linguistics – clearly defined meaning and limited use – are important. Therefore, in the course of analyzing the research material, as a matter of principle, those words and expressions that occur in common language and are defined in some legislative acts only by means of regulating definitions were left out of the scope of interest. In the process of analyzing the research material, terms that are the names of conventional acts (including procedural acts), the names of parties to legal relations and conventional entities defined in the legal text, the names of normative acts, terms of juridical language referring to various issues related to the law (its validity, interpretation or application) were primarily considered.[486]

3.6.2.3.2. Legal and juridical terms – findings of empirical studies and contextual analysis

Since the issue of the presiding judge's use of legal and juridical terms in communicating with a non-professional participant is considered particularly momentous in the study, it was decided, in accordance with the above assumptions, to extract all legal and juridical terms in the research material[487] and include them in Appendix 1. The terms were arranged according to the variety of proceedings,[488] in which they occurred. Some terms were referred to in their typical word combinations, while some required supplementation based on the linguistic context.[489]

486 A legal basis, that is, an indication of a particular editorial unit of a legislative act, the citation of which is preceded, for example, by the term "on the basis of", is considered a term of a special type in the study.

487 In this regard, it should be emphasized that the extracted terms are derived both from statements made by the presiding judge directly to a non-professional participant, and from statements made to all participants of the court session, as long as there was a non-professional participant among them.

488 Terms related to insurance and labor law proceedings have been included separately due to the diversity of the subject matter of these proceedings.

489 If a term was included in the list of terms based on linguistic context, it was placed in square brackets. Those legal and juridical terms that were used by participants other than the presiding judge in direct interaction with the non-professional participant were also included. Such terms were few and, with few exceptions (i.e. *renter, legal status, legal situation, [marital] property contract, disinheritance, according to the provision*) overlapped with those used by presiding judges.

All the legal and juridical terms revealed in the research material that appear in the presiding judge's statements to non-professional participants can be divided into three classes: (1) terms related to court proceedings; (2) terms related to substantive law and non-court proceedings; (3) other terms, particularly juridical terms.

The largest class (see Appendix 1) is formed by terms related to court proceedings. Within this class, it is possible to identify those considered universal:[490] *case file, appeal, delivery, evidence, penalty of the deprivation of liberty* [in instruction], *punished for giving false testimony, costs of proceedings, dismissal, criminal liability* [in instruction], *adjournment of the trial, deciding, ruling, proceedings, evidentiary proceedings, instruction, right to refuse to testify, examination, oath, examination of the case, trial, giving false testimony, case, summons, motion to adduce evidence, order, notice, complaint, testimony, testifying.*

The least numerous (cf. Appendix 1), on the other hand, is the third of the distinguished classes. As a result of the analysis of the research material, the following terms were included in the third class: *legislative act, dogmatics, legal fiction, interpretation of legal provisions, juridical language, norm, (valid) legal provisions, case law, normative basis, legal assistance, legal advice, law, sanction, legal effects, legal status, application of the provisions, content of the provisions, law, legislator, elimination of the provision from the legal system, by force of law,* ministerial *order, legality, compliance with the provision.*

In contrast, the number of terms included in the second class varies quite a bit depending on the variety of court proceedings. The least number of terms relating to substantive law and non-court proceedings was recorded in commercial, criminal and misdemeanor proceedings (see Appendix 1).

It should be noted that in addition to procedural acts in which the citation of the legal basis is mandatory,[491] there were relatively few (35 cases) statements in which the presiding judges indicated the legal basis, e.g. **P:** *I am instructing you about the obligation to tell the truth and criminal liability for giving false testimony. According to Article 233 § 1 of the Polish Penal Code* (...). Most often, presiding judges cited the legal basis within the framework of instructions (19 cases), less often giving reasons for the decision (7 cases), within the framework of informative acts (6 cases) and in other individual cases (3 in total).

The issue of the use of phrases and names of participants corresponding to the names of procedural roles has been analyzed separately.[492] Referring to the

---

490 These terms in the research material occurred in most (i.e., at least 5) varieties of proceedings. As a result, there is a high probability that these are the terms that a non-professional participant will encounter, regardless of which proceedings he or she will be involved in.

491 E.g., in a judgment in criminal proceedings.

492 For the purpose of analyzing the research material, with regard to both addressable phrases and participant names, three situations were distinguished, i.e. those in which the presiding judge, within a given session, used: (1) only procedural role

addressable phrases used by the presiding judge in relation to non-professional participants, it should be noted that in cases where the use of addressable phrases was recorded, the form without the names of procedural roles was used most often, e.g. *Ladies and Gentlemen, Mr. X, Mrs. Y* (105 sessions). This was followed by presiding judges using mixed forms – within a phrase, e.g., *Ms. Claimant*, or within a session (60 sessions in total). On the other hand, completely exceptional were such sessions, when the presiding judge used only addressable phrases containing the names of procedural roles (2 such sessions were recorded).

On the other hand, as for the names of participants of the proceedings that do not appear in addressable phrases, in this case the proportions are slightly different. Of all the cases of presiding judges' use of participant names, the most numerous are examples of the use of mixed forms (126 sessions). There are far fewer examples of such meetings sessions, when presiding judges did not use names of procedural roles at all to designate participants (16 meetings). In contrast, there are the fewest where presiding judges used only the names of the participants' procedural roles (only 5 sessions).

The results of the analysis of the research material presented in the two paragraphs above indicate that presiding judges are abandoning forms of addressing non-professional participants, as well as talking about them exclusively using procedural role names. This occurs in favor of either mixed forms or forms completely devoid of procedural role names.

It is worth adding that the way the presiding judge addresses non-professional participants of the trial can either increase or decrease the power distance in the courtroom.[493] As the authors of studies on the subject point out: "the mere way in which a judge addresses the questioned witness can make a difference in the sense of PD [power distance]. Namely, one can suppose that a judge referring to a witness in a very formal way (e.g., constantly stressing the status of the questioned person with the word "witness" and avoiding honorific forms, such as "Ma'am" or "Sir") can be ultimately increasing PD, whereas deviations from such an official tone can be regarded as decreasing PD. However, such a guess is very basic (...)".[494] The results of the analysis of the research material presented above, that presiding judges chose forms of addressing non-professional participants of the proceedings that reduced the power distance rather than increasing it.

As a starting point for the **contextual analysis** of the legal and juridical terms, the assumption was made that the presiding judge's use of such terms in communication acts addressed to non-professional participants at the trial impedes communication understanding. Instead, the purpose of this analysis is to detect communication phenomena occurring in the research material and aspects

---

names; (2) only names other than procedural role names; (3) both procedural role names and other names.

493 See M. Dudek, M. Stępień, *Courtroom Power...*, op. cit., p. 11.

494 Ibidem. Cf. results of the analysis in this regard, ibidem, p. 111 et seq.

of the trial pattern, the disclosure of which will not allow the above assumption to be taken as a general assertion. The influence of: (1) the situational context, and (2) the communication context on the communication understanding between the presiding judge and the non-professional participants will be discussed.

Re 1. The discussion of the first issue should begin with a description of the relationship between selected elements of the situational meso-context and the terms used at the trial. First of all, it should be noted that the lexis of a given trial is co-created by the vocabulary associated with the subject of cognition and, consequently, the thematic scope of the given trial. In some cases, this can determine the occurrence of legal or juridical terms. This is especially the case when the subject of cognition are issues related to the performance of legal acts or the functioning of some entity of conventional nature. Among the legal terms directly related to the subject matter of the proceedings, which were revealed in the research material, the following can be distinguished in particular: *contractual penalty, countersignature, liquidation of the cooperative, declaration of bankruptcy of the company, cooperative, will, lease contract, matrimonial property contract, fixed-term employment contract, contract of mandate, housing community.*

The relationship described above, in turn, is closely related to certain aspects of the situational micro-context, as it is obvious that a court case is always "someone else's case". Thus, if certain legal terms are closely related to the subject of cognition in a given case, it is highly likely that at least a party (quasi-party) to the proceedings has come into contact with these terms (e.g., a claimant who is pursuing a claim for wrongful termination of employment). The same applies to the name of the subject matter of the claim asserted before the court, as it is difficult to demand payment on account of reserved portion without knowing both the term itself ("reserved portion") and its meaning. Such terms noted in the research material include *alimony, railroad retirement pension, protection of personal rights, damages, disability pension for incapacity for work, declaration of acquisition of inheritance, pre-retirement benefit, reserved portion, consent to reject inheritance on behalf of a child,* among others.

Knowledge of certain legal terms or even juridical terms may be related to the social, including occupational, roles in which the various participants of court proceedings perform on a daily basis. Such cases were very evident in the research material. For example, it can be pointed out that all the terms related to the functioning of the housing community, which were included in Appendix 1 (the list on civil proceedings), came from proceedings for the repeal of the resolution of the community, and all the participants (including witnesses) were either involved in the management of the community or, as owners, were actively involved in its functioning. The same applies to other terms included in this appendix, such as *discount, discipline of public finance, leaseholder, person authorized to represent the municipality, cooperative board member, lease rent, announcement of liquidation of the cooperative, employee-owned company.*[495] A similar set of terms is included in

495 All these terms related to the cooperative appeared in the presiding judge's communication with the non-professional participant of the proceedings, who was a cooperative board member.

Appendix 1 (in the list for social security proceedings), and is formed by the following terms: *member of the supervisory board, member of the board, declaration of bankruptcy (of the company), chairman of the supervisory board, resignation from the board of a bankrupt company, receiver.*[496] It is difficult to assume that in this type of case, the participants are unfamiliar with terms closely related to the social and, in particular, occupational role in which they perform on a daily basis.

In connection with the characteristics of the participants (as an element of the situational micro-context), it is important to note the particular dimension of the participant's experience related to either the participation in the court proceedings themselves or the proceedings preceding them. As for the first aspect, participation in the session scheduled for the trial is always preceded by some procedural act – the filing of an initiating motion, notice of the initiation of proceedings ex officio, exchange of procedural documents, delivery of an indictment or motion for punishment. In this way, non-professional participants of court proceedings at least have the opportunity to familiarize themselves with certain terms, primarily related to court proceedings. The second aspect of this issue, on the other hand, concerns those court proceedings that always precede some other proceedings, but with the same subject of cognition. These are, first of all, investigations preceding criminal proceedings and proceedings before the public administration authority preceding social security proceedings. In these cases, non-professional participants have the opportunity to familiarize themselves with certain terms (relating to both procedural and substantive law) that may later be used in court proceedings.

It is worth noting at the end of this discussion that knowledge of legal or juridical terms related to the social, including occupational, roles of non-professional participants of court proceedings and to life experience, including the experience of participating in court proceedings, involves those classes of knowledge of legal norms that was called in jurisprudence "ad hoc knowledge".[497]

---

496 These terms occurred in face to face communication with the participants in the proceedings, who were either members of the board of directors or members of the supervisory board of the bankrupt company, as directly indicated by the presiding judge's questions, e.g. **P:** (...) *from what the court is aware of ex officio, you were chairman of the supervisory board. Please tell us how long you have been on the supervisory board?*

497 Franciszek Studnicki distinguished three classes of knowledge about legal norms available to members of society: (1) basic knowledge – among other things, essential knowledge about the norms that determine the state system or about basic procedures; (2) minimum-role knowledge – related to the necessity of knowing those legal norms that are necessary for the fulfillment of certain social roles; (3) ad hoc knowledge – which is neither basic knowledge, nor necessary for the fulfillment of certain social roles, but their knowledge depends on the situation in which a certain subject finds himself or herself, F. Studnicki, *Znajomość i nieznajomość prawa [Knowledge and ignorance of the law]*, "Państwo i Prawo" 1962, No. 4, pp. 580–582, idem, *Przepływ wiadomości o normach prawa [Message flow of legal norms]*, "Zeszyty Naukowe Uniwersytetu Jagiellońskiego. Prace Prawnicze" 1965, Vol. 22, pp. 69–72,

Ad 2. The next issue concerns the communication context in which legal and juridical terms are used. First of all, it should be noted that some legal or juridical terms revealed in the research material were first used by a non-professional participant in the proceedings,[498] and only later by the presiding judge. In addition, it should be noted that some of the terms included in Appendix 1 came directly from procedural documents formulated by participants in the proceedings. Some of the terms noted in the research material that were thus included in the text of the trial include *quoad usum division*, *maturity of the claim*, *reserved portion* or *principles of social coexistence*.[499] Sometimes this also happens with other intertextual acts of the presiding judge, such as when the presiding judge formulates a description of the participant's claims contained in the letter initiating the proceedings – **P:** *You request damages for unlawful termination of an employment contract without the notice period, in the amount of (...) and for overtime hours (...). You also requested correction of the certificate of employment.*[500]

In analyzing the issue of the presiding judge's use of legal and juridical terms in relation to the communication context, it was necessary to consider the impact of the use of this terminology on the course of the direct interaction taking place between the presiding judge and the non-professional participant at the trial. For this purpose, the results of the analysis carried out on the basis of research question 4ca on the metalinguistic acts of non-professional participants reporting that they do not understand a term or expressing a request for its clarification were used. During the analysis of the research material, very few (only 4) acts of this type were recorded. They concerned such terms as *claimant*, *defendant* (in criminal case), *legal status* and *bankruptcy*.[501] In the case of the first two terms, it was basically a question of who is the designator of the name, e.g. **Witness:** *Defendant, you mean Mr. X?* In the case of the third term, on the other hand, its use actually led to a communicative misunderstanding, with the term being used not by the presiding judge, but by a professional attorney:

M. Dudek, *Komunikowanie prawa w dobie pluralizmu kulturowego [Communicating law in the era of cultural pluralism]*, Kraków 2014, pp. 84–88.

498 See what terms were used by non-professional participants in Appendix 2.

499 In this case, it may happen that a non-professional participant of the proceedings will not be aware of these terms if the procedural document was formulated by a professional attorney, nevertheless, examples of this type illustrate a situation in which de facto it is not the presiding judge who decides on the appearance of the given terms in the text of the trial.

500 In this case, the presiding judge cited the contents of a non-professional claimant unrepresented by a professional attorney.

501 The last example is quite peculiar, as the participant reported that he did not understand the term, but the communication context indicated otherwise.

Attorney: *Ma'am, and what was the status of that apartment on X Street?*
Witness: *Status. Well for those days (...) it seemed, well, normal, the cooker was there, the big room....*
Attorney: *Legal status, please, I am not asking....*
Witness: *Legal? I do not understand the question.*
Attorney: *Who was the owner?*
P: *What was the right to this apartment? Do you know, or do you not know?*
Witness: *Well it was our apartment from the cooperative.*

It is worth noting in this context a peculiar example, as it is singular in the entire research material, of the communication act of a non-professional participant who asked for the opportunity to paraphrase a presiding judge's statement containing legal terms, although addressed to a professional attorney, to make sure he understood it correctly:

Participant (in non-contentious civil proceedings): *Can I in my own words say how I understood?*
P: *Of course.*
Participant: *This letter, my letter, right, arrived very late to another party and therefore there is a quarantine of fourteen days to respond to this letter.*
P: *You have understood very well.*

A clear example of a communicative misunderstanding over the terminology used was cited in the passage on the problem of one-way instructions (see Section 3.6.1) and concerned the instruction on the right to refuse to testify. Apart from the situations described above, there were no more cases of communicative misunderstanding related to the presiding judge's (or even other participants') use of legal or juridical terms **that would disrupt the natural course of interaction** involving a non-professional participant[502] in the research material.

Following the research procedure proposed in the study, it was necessary to pay attention to whether presiding judges explain the meaning of the legal and juridical terms they use when interacting with a non-professional participant. During the analysis of the research material, few communication acts of the presiding judge directly explaining the meaning of a term (possibly the essence of its designators) were recorded. Among the terms whose meaning was explained were: *appeal, Court and Economic Monitor, non-final judgment, copy of the ruling with a statement of finality, acceptance of inheritance with a benefit of inventory, oath, Supreme Court, court of inheritance, statement of finality, Constitutional Court, settlement, Social Security Law, formal motion, motion to justify the judgment,*

502 It should be emphasized that it is about the direct impact of the terminology used on the course of interaction, the influence of other factors, such as unfamiliarity or misunderstanding of one's own procedural role, will be discussed later.

motion under Article 387 of the Polish Code of Criminal Procedure, ancestor, court of first instance judgment, inheritance assurances, notice. These terms were explained in various ways – direct (by stating the content of the name), by indicating some designators or certain properties of the designator, or even by comparison, e.g. **P:** *(...) in the Court and Economic Monitor, such a periodical that collects, concentrates all court announcements, including this category* (...); **P:** *Do you file formal motions, for example, for adjournment of the trial?*; **P:** (...) the *essence of a settlement is that it should be voluntarily executed* (...); **P:** (...) *the legislator in the Social Insurance Law, which is such a constitution of social insurance.*

However, it should be recalled (this has already been pointed out in the discussion of instructions) that information on how to perform or the effects of a conventional act also constitutes, at least in part, an explanation of its name. Any instructions that were noted in the research material and that informed about these aspects of conventional acts, including procedural ones, were therefore examples of specific, more or less comprehensive definitions.

In this subsection, in accordance with the purpose indicated in its introduction, those communication phenomena are described in relation to selected aspects of the trial pattern, which undoubtedly reduce the potential risk of communicative misunderstanding associated with the use of legal and juridical terminology. However, this does not formulate the conclusion further that such a risk does not occur at all in the cases discussed. After all, communicative understanding, and consequently misunderstanding, is a mental phenomenon, perceptible to the observer insofar as external phenomena allow it to be inferred. Moreover, in the case of a misunderstanding, if it cannot be recognized on the basis of external phenomena, it will remain hidden to both the participants in the communication process and the observer. Nevertheless, the observations made here do not allow us to accept the assumption revealed in the introduction as an assertion of a general nature, that in every case the use of legal or juridical terms in the communication acts addressed to a non-professional participant at the trial impedes communicative understanding.

3.6.2.4. Presiding judge's communication acts which may reduce uncertainty and facilitate realization of procedural and interactional roles

From the point of view of a non-professional participant, a trial can be characterized by a significant degree of difficulty not only because of the use of particular linguistic means, but also because of the existence of a normative pattern of the trial. This pattern determines individual communication acts and occurrences (both in their structural and functional aspects), as well as procedural and interactional roles. Unfamiliarity with how the trial pattern is shaped in the structural aspect can promote a sense of confusion and uncertainty[503] – the participant does not know what acts will be performed and in what order. In turn, ignorance of the pattern in the functional aspect, procedural functions (which make up the procedural roles) and interactional roles can make it difficult for a non-professional participant to take certain acts in accordance with the normative pattern. This in turn can affect the efficiency of the implementation of the entire trial. Both situations described above are undesirable from the point of view of the non-professional participants.[504] The answers to research questions 2ad to 2ai (the content of these questions will be referred to in the individual passages of the text) are intended to give a picture of the presiding judge's activity in counteracting these undesirable phenomena.

3.6.2.4.1. Informing about procedural acts undertaken and the stage of the case investigation

Examination of the empirical material revealed that the presiding judge's activity in providing information on procedural acts undertaken or the stage of the case investigation (content of question 2ad) is significant. During the analysis, 449 cases of presiding judges providing information on acts taken, or not taken, and the stage of the case investigation were recorded. At the same time, it should be noted that the specified information was sometimes addressed to all persons present in the courtroom, and not only to non-professional participants.

In addition, the information provided to participants by the presiding judge varied in scope, i.e. some related to the specific session scheduled for the trial and the acts taken at it, while others related to acts taken as part of the entire trial, and others to the entire proceedings. Acts of the presiding judge which combined information of different scope, were also recorded.

As a consequence of what was stated above about the range of information provided, the different types of acts in question can be assigned slightly different functions. The realization of the leading-coordinating function of the presiding judge, as it has been characterized in the study, is primarily served by information activities that relate to the acts taken within the framework of a single session, possibly within the framework of the entire trial. This, in turn, allows the participant to create a so-called mental map,[505] corresponding to the information about the acts to be undertaken, and consequently reduces uncertainty in this regard.

---

503 See about the so-called cognitive uncertainty related to the need to explain, plan or obtain information , V. Greco, D. Roger, *Coping with Uncertainty: The Construction and Validation of a New Measure*, "Personality and Individual Differences" 2000, No. 4, pp. 519–534.

504 From the point of view of the efficiency of the implementation of the trial, too.

505 See about mental map as a linguistic tool to be used at the trial, *Handling Cases...*, op. cit., pp. 10–10.

First, the presiding judge's informative acts, which relate to the acts taken within the framework of a particular session, possibly within the framework of the entire trial will be characterized.

The analysis of the empirical material revealed informative acts, which could be called introductory due to the fact that the presiding judge performed them at the beginning of the court session, and they determined the pattern of acts taken within its framework, e.g. **P:** *Okay, then we will briefly examine you. We will admit evidence from the death certificate, marriage certificate and inheritance assurances*; **P:** *Today's date is set for examination of the opposition to the reported intervention*; **P:** *Ladies and gentlemen, we have scheduled the examination of two more witnesses today, we are ready to implement this* (...). This type of information is of particular importance, as it allows a non-professional participant to get an idea, at least in basic terms, of what acts will actually be undertaken during the session. Consequently, it allows to reduce uncertainty at the very beginning of the session. However, it should be noted that this type of introductory information was rare in the research material (only 5 examples).

In addition, the analysis revealed informative acts that related to acts taken within the framework of a specific stage of the trial carried out at a particular session, e.g. **P:** *Sir, the court orders evidentiary proceedings in the case, will examine witnesses* (...); **P:** *The court opens the judicial process and given that the prosecutor has not appeared, the court will read the accusations against you* (...).[506] The presiding judges also gave information relating to the entire trial, e.g. **P:** *The parties have already been questioned, only documentary evidence is still to come, and the trial at this session, by assumption, should end.*

Among the informative acts revealed in the research material, attention should be paid to those directed to non-professional participants immediately prior to the procedural act in which they participated. In the empirical material, the acts of the type in question concerned examination, so-called "informational examination" and submission of inheritance assurances (a total of 96). The highest frequency (82) was for information that concerned an examination, e.g. **P:** *You will be examined in the character of a witness today* (...); **P:** *I invite you to the railing, I instruct you that you will be examined in the character of a witness* (...); **P:** *You will be examined in the character of a party* (...); **P:** *I instruct you that you will be heard as a party* (...). Similar was the nature of the information regarding the so-called informational examination and inheritance assurances, but for obvious reasons they already occurred on a much smaller scale (14 in total), e.g. **P:** *I ask Mr. Claimant to railing,*

506 In the context of this example, it is worth noting that some of the presiding judge's statements informing about a certain procedural act, in addition, included an explanation as to why the act should be done, e.g. **P:** *Ladies and gentlemen, the situation is that the respondent has requested to adduce evidence from some documentary evidence on file* (...), *therefore the court will adjourn the trial* (...).

I will question you informatively; **P:** *We will accept inheritance assurances from you regarding who is included in the heirs of Mrs. XY.*

Presiding judges also informed about some elements of the complex procedural acts indicated in the previous paragraph, including the simpler acts co-creating them, e.g. **P:** *The court will take the personal data from you*; **P:** *The court will additionally take the oath from you, yes. I ask everyone to stand up and you to repeat after me*; **P:** *I will read to you what you said in the investigation*; **P:** *The questions now will be of the attorneys*; **P:** *I would now like to show you a number of documents* (...); **P:** *I will first read you the minutes of the examination before the authority and then we will supplement, if necessary, those explanations you have given.*

In the case of the information acts described in the previous two paragraphs, their coordinating function is clearly visible. This type of information is aimed directly at the entities involved in a given communication occurrence and allows them to direct their attention to a specific activity.

However, sometimes (6 cases) the informative acts on the above-mentioned complex procedural acts were of a negative nature, i.e. they informed that the given activity would not be carried out, e.g. **P:** *Well, Mr. Expert, I have to release you anyway, because today I cannot examine you, due to the fact that the party is not properly noticed about the date* (...); **P:** *Ladies and gentlemen, the court will certainly not examine all of you today, so I will release some of you here in a moment, yes, and you will receive a summons for the next examination.* Thus, they served a function quite different from the previously described informational acts. The presiding judge usually (4 cases) indicating that the participant would have to undertake a planned activity in the future.

Still other functions are informational acts, which concern individual procedural acts taken by the presiding judge (also acting as a court), that is, acts in which a non-professional participant does not actively participate, e.g. **P:** *Ladies and gentlemen, briefly. The court will explain the reasons for the decision* (...); **P:** *We will now play the recording of the son's examination, it is short* (...); **P:** (...) *the court will repeal of the fine for your failure to appear*; **P:** *The court will admit documentary evidence* (...), *these are also the documents that you submitted* (...). This type of information allows the participant, first of all, to set the perception of a certain content, such as why there was such a decision and not another.

Among such informational acts, those that convey information about the intention to close a trial (or judicial process as a part of the trial in some types of cases) are of particular importance, e.g. **P:** *Ladies and gentlemen, the court intends to close a trial* (...); **P:** *Ladies and gentlemen, the court is going to close the trial, before closing the trial, would any of you like to ask for something, to speak?* The particular importance of such information is related to the fact that the closing of a trial or judicial process ends the most important stage of the merits of the case. In this context, it is worth noting the second of the cited examples, in which the information about the intention to close a trial is combined with a question about the desire to undertake procedural activity.[507]

Among the informative acts on procedural acts of the presiding judge (or the court) were also recorded examples of acts informing about the acts, the performance of which results in the interruption of the court session, e.g. **P:** *After the examination of this witness, I will order a ten-minute break, yes*; **P:** *Ladies and gentlemen, today the court will adjourn the trial* (...), *because I still want to see the civil case file* (...); **P:** *Ladies and gentlemen, the court will adjourn the announcement of the judgment* (...).

Finally, it is still worth noting the presiding judge's communication acts, which informed about the acts taken throughout the proceedings, and the stage of the case investigation. Information of this type, admittedly, does not perform the function of directly coordinating the acts taken at a particular court session, but it allows the non-professional participant to create a mental map of those acts that have been taken or will be taken at all in the proceedings.

In the empirical material, there were recorded informational acts that related to the acts done in order to initiate the proceedings, e.g. **P:** *Ladies and gentlemen, the applicant has filed an application to our court to declare the acquisition of inheritance from* (...); **P:** *The subject matter of today's proceedings is the decision of the Social Insurance Institution* (...), *by which the authority denied you the right to a pre-retirement benefit* (...). *You have filed an appeal, in which you indicated that you request only the repeal or amendment of the decision, because this decision in your opinion is unjustified* (...). This scope also includes acts that were carried out by the court or other participants in between court sessions, e.g. **P:** (...) *the claimant's procedural document was received* (...); **P:** *The court requested the file indicated in the response to the lawsuit* (...); **P:** *Ladies and gentlemen, here was an expert opinion on immovable property valuation, you all received this opinion* (...).

In addition, the presiding judges took summary information acts. In doing so, they informed both of the acts that have been done in the case and those that are yet to be taken, e.g. **P:** *We have conducted almost all the evidence in the case, so once the proceedings are taken, we will only have a small section left to finish it* (...); **P:** (...) *and at the next session we could finish the case, you will submit these documents and the court will examine the parties*; **P:** *Valuation, examination of the parties and probably the end of the proceedings* (...).[508] In the context of the above

---

507 Most of the acts indicating the intention to close a trial (judicial process) revealed in the research material were accompanied by a question about the intention to engage in procedural activity (filing a motion or speaking).

508 It is worth noting here that the research material also recorded such examples of statements made by the presiding judge, which informed not only the procedural acts undertaken, but also their impact on the length of the proceedings, e.g. **P:** (...) *the proceedings will take quite a long time, if only because of the motions to adduce evidence submitted by you, and in particular the motion to adduce expert opinion evidence* (...). *At the moment, the waiting period for surveying opinions is roughly eight,*

examples, it is noteworthy that in each of the cited statements, the presiding judge, while informing about procedural acts, also indicated that their completion would result in the possibility of ending the proceedings. In this way, the presiding judge determined, more or less precisely (depending on the circumstances of the case), the moment when the proceedings would end. An act of this type allows a non-professional participant to create a mental map of the entire proceedings, which takes into account the moment of termination, which in turn can not only reduce the feeling of uncertainty in this regard, but also allow, for example, to plan further activity related to participation in the proceedings.

3.6.2.4.2. Explaining the meaning of procedural acts performed

The presiding judge's communication acts, which will be discussed below, unlike those described earlier, do not convey information that such an act has been or will be performed, but what the meaning of the act is – what it consists of or what effects it has. This type of act is of particular importance – not only can it lead to the elimination (or at least reduction) of the feeling of uncertainty associated with being a participant or observer of the procedural act being carried out, but it also conveys knowledge, and thus performs to some extent an educational function.[509]

In the analyzed research material, the presiding judge's communication acts, with the help of which he or she explained the meaning of each procedural act (the content of question 2ae), were recorded few (22 in total). Moreover, the presiding judge's questions to the non-professional participant as to whether he or she understood the meaning of the action being performed (the content of question 2ae) also were recorded (only 8). Actions of both types referred to different procedural acts.

Most often (7 cases), presiding judges explained the meaning of the act of giving an oath, e.g. **P:** *With the consent of the attorneys without an oath, which does not change this instruction, which does not change this obligation. Even without an oath, which only emphasizes the solemn nature of this act of giving a testimony as a witness, and you still have to follow this norm of preserving the principles of truthfulness, not to conceal any circumstances.*

The remaining fifteen acts explaining the meaning of the acts performed were mostly singular and concerned: (1) complex procedural acts (court settlement, informational examination), e.g. **P:** (…) *settlement consists in the parties entering into an agreement before the court, which has the force of a court judgment and*

---

twelve months (…). I feel obliged to warn you about this fact, we do not have the tools to discipline experts, for the reason that these geodetic opinions, as a rule, are quite extensive, they also require field work, and due to the fact that there are four surveyors for the entire area here in our province, when we try to press them, they send us back the file, indicating that they have forty opinions to do.

509 In this aspect, their function is similar to that of instruction, and sometimes identical to it.

ends the proceedings without conducting evidentiary proceedings, without hearing witnesses and without the need for deciding by the court of second instance (...): **P:** *This is an informational examination to illuminate the disputed circumstances, evidentiary Mr. Claimant will be questioned after the witnesses' testimony, then questions can be asked*; (2) procedural acts made by the parties or quasi-parties, e.g. **P:** (...) *I am already explaining to you what this is about* (...). *The lady has now stated that she is limiting it* [claim] *and wants from X* [date]. *For such a restriction I must have your consent. Do you give your consent? It is in your interest, it is from X, not from Y*; **P:** *What the Victim says about this, you stand up, I will explain. The defense counsel and the defendant have now filed a motion under Article 387 of the Polish Code of Criminal Procedure, consisting in the fact that they request that the punishment they propose here be imposed on the defendant, without any evidentiary proceedings, i.e. without the examination of witnesses* (...), *and in order for the court to grant such a request by the defendant and defense counsel, the victim must agree to it*; (3) procedural acts taken by the presiding judge (summons to trial, repeal of the ruling, motion to adduce documentary evidence, resolution of the judgment), e.g., **P:** *Taking advantage of the presence of the Ladies, the court summons you to this date for examination on pain of disregarding the evidence, i.e. an unexcused failure to appear will result in disregarding the evidence of the examination* (...); **P:** *The court repealed this fine, which it imposed on you by ruling of* (...); **P:** (...) *the second point, it only means that the court believes that in this proceeding you cannot* blame Social Insurance Institution *for issuing such a decision and not another (...) and this point, it only means that if this judgment is final, you will then receive this benefit with compensation, but without interest* (...); (4) other acts, e.g., **P:** *This announcement* [about the search for heirs] *is such a formal act, but it is also a warranty that no one in the future will be able to challenge this ruling of inheritance, yes, because if they want to do so in a year, in two, in three, then always such an act to change the ruling, to change the ruling regarding the confirmation of the inheritance acquisition, or an act for resumption of the proceedings, will be doomed to failure* (...).

On the other hand, of all the cases in which the presiding judge formulated a question about understanding the meaning of the procedural act performed, as many as half (4) referred to the accusation contained in the indictment or motion for punishment, e.g. **P:** *Did you understand the accusation against you?*; **P:** *Did you understand what you are accused for?* Other cases involved understanding the decision, the justification of the decision and the withdrawal of the appeal, e.g., **P:** *Did you understand the content of the decision?* Two points are worth noting: (1) in not a single case did the participants answer in the negative to the question posed by the presiding judge; (2) the presiding judge's questions (except for one on the withdrawal of the appeal) *de facto* concerned understanding the content of the procedural act in question, not its meaning, i.e. recognizing it as an act of a certain type.

3.6.2.4.3. Informing about the essence of court proceedings

Under the vague term "the essence of court proceedings" there are several phenomena of a slightly different nature. First, it is about the way in which court proceedings are shaped in their basic scope (the main procedural functions of the participants, the basic purpose of the proceedings). Second, about the way in which a particular stage of the proceedings (e.g., evidentiary proceedings) is shaped in its basic scope. Third, about the subject matter scope of a particular variety or sub-variety of court proceedings and the specific procedural goals or functions associated with that subject matter. Fourth, about the subject matter scope of a particular case and the specific procedural goals or functions associated with that subject matter. Analysis of the research material revealed 49 presiding judges' information acts relating to the essence of court proceedings (content of question 2af).

The smallest scope is created by informational acts on the basics of shaping court proceedings in general. Only two statements by the presiding judge were included in this category: **P:** *(...) the court, for its part, wishes you the best, but in a moment it will be applying the provisions, and there wishes have nothing, yes, to say (...) there have been times when the court has been very sorry to issue judgments unfavorable to the parties (...)*; **P:** *Mr. X, what effect this has is judged by the court. As a rule, it is the case that if someone does not submit evidence, he does not show his claims and they are dismissed, the demands. This is the rule that follows from legal provisions, but the court can never force you to submit documents, you want, you submit.* It is worth noting at this point that the above-mentioned information acts were taken under completely different circumstances. In the first case, they were part of the solicitation of a settlement, in the second they were a reaction to a statement by a non-professional participant outside the thematic frame of this acts. Consequently, these acts performed different functions, as they aimed at different goals. In contrast, the common feature of both of these informational acts was that their undoubted informational function was not the primary function.

Slightly more (3 cases) informative acts concerned the basic elements of shaping evidentiary proceedings, e.g., **P:** *(...) I cannot examine you as a party, because I have to examine the witnesses first, in order to be able to examine the parties, because the parties are examined when some circumstances have not been clarified, this is always auxiliary evidence (...)*; **P:** *(...) the court will conduct those evidences that you request (...).*

A more numerous class (9 cases) than the previous ones is formed by informational acts related to a variety or sub-variety of court proceedings. Presiding judges provided information related to inheritance, family and social security proceedings, e.g. **P:** *(...) in inheritance proceedings, the inheritance can be accepted or also rejected, if such a declaration is not made within six months of death, let's assume so, then this inheritance is acquired, it cannot be effectively rejected, and the court only states this in a ruling (...)*; **P:** *(...) the social security court examines the case within the limits of the contested decision, yes. That is, here the scope of the court's review is determined by the date of the disputed decision (...).* It is worth noting in this context that in the vast majority of cases (7), these acts were in some way provoked by a statement by a non-professional participant, for example, questioning the sense of conducting inheritance proceedings.

Undoubtedly, however, the most numerous class (35 cases) is formed by those presiding judge's informational acts that relate to a specific case. Within this class, two subclasses are clearly delineated, the first comprising 21 statements emphasizing the subject matter (and thus thematic) scope of a given case, and the second consisting of 14 informational acts emphasizing specific procedural functions or goals related to the subject matter of a given case.

Within the first subclass, information on the subject matter scope of a particular social security case is particularly numerous (10 cases), e.g. **P:** *We are hearing a case on the insured's appeal against two decisions, the decision of* (...) *on the coverage of social insurance for farmers for XY* (...) *and we are hearing an appeal against the decision of* (...) *on the termination of social insurance for farmers for XY* (...). Other examples of acts informing the scope of the subject matter of the case were also identified in the research material, e.g. **P:** *The case concerns the confirmation of the acquisition of inheritance from XY.* **P:** *This is a case from an application* (...) *to establish residency and issue custodial orders* (...). Among the types of acts discussed here, it is possible to identify acts that were performed at the very beginning of the court session. Their taking, therefore, was not a reaction to the participants' prior communication acts. However, there were also disclosed such statements informing about the subject matter of the case, which were a reaction to the acts of the participants, such as the extension of the evidence thesis – **P:** (...) *our case de facto does not concern those works that were carried out by your contractors, but actually concerns a different issue, that is, possibly existing basis for a motion to cut down a tree* (...).

As indicated above, the analysis of the research material revealed examples of statements made by the presiding judge that contained information about the specific procedural functions of the participants and the goals of the proceedings in a particular case. Acts of this type were in response to specific communication acts of the participants, such as going beyond the established thematic framework of the proceedings, e.g. **P:** (...) *the court is not concerned with your conflict that you have between each other on a daily basis and will not assess it globally* (...). *The court in this case is only concerned with examining whether* [date] *there was an infringement of personal rights of Mr. claimant or not.* Or they were a manifestation of the presiding judge's initiative, e.g., **P:** *The court's thing here is to determine how these contracts of mandate came about, what knowledge and who passed on to Mr. insured, that is, on the circumstances, with whom he drew up the contracts of mandate, what terms were agreed* (...).

Given the thematic diversity of the information acts described here, each of the information provided of a particular type allowed the non-professional participant of court proceedings to become oriented to a slightly different aspect of the pattern of court proceedings. As for the coordinating function of this information, on the other hand, it is particularly evident in cases in which the provision of information on the essence of the proceedings was a reaction to the prior communication acts of the participants.

3.6.2.4.4. Informing about procedural functions and interactional roles

Unfamiliarity with the normative pattern of the trial in terms of the procedural functions corresponding to the various procedural roles and interactional roles can not only create a sense of uncertainty in the non-professional participant, but also make it difficult to undertake certain procedural acts. The following will discuss those informational acts of the presiding judge that can significantly reduce the undesirable effects of ignorance of these elements of the normative pattern of the trial.

During the analysis of the research material, 35 cases of the presiding judge providing information on either procedural functions or interactional roles were recorded (content of question 2ag). In doing so, it should be noted that almost half (17 cases) of the communication acts of the type in question were the presiding judge's response to a non-professional participant's transgression of the normative pattern of the trial.

First of all, it is possible to point out the informational acts, which were related to particular procedural functions (26 cases) and were associated, respectively, with the procedural role of the: (1) witness, e.g. **P:** *Madam, let's make an agreement like this – you testify what you remember, if you do not remember, you say "I do not remember"* (...); (2) party (quasi-party), e.g. **P:** *You, according to Art. 6 of the Polish Civil Code, are obliged to present evidence to prove your point* (...), *if you say here that this statement is not completed by you and you did not have this awareness, then you must prove* (...);[510] (3) legal representative of the party, e.g. **P:** *Ma'am, there is a norm that indicates that this testimony, which is relevant in the case of a minor, the person who is the statutory representative of a minor gives as a party to the proceedings* (...), *as a mother you are testifying for the minor, not as a witness to the incident*; (4) court (presiding judge), e.g. **P:** *Ma'am, the court points out to you that you are not at a social gathering, but in the courtroom. In the courtroom, the court gives the floor, so please follow these requirements, otherwise the court may expel a person who does not meet these canons* (...).

Second, one can cite examples of acts that addressed the essence of particular interactional roles. It should be noted at this point that all of the acts considered interactional roles (9 in total) were related to the examination, e.g. **P:** (...) *there will be questions asked, please listen, now Ms. attorney is asking questions, and you answer to the court*; **P:** *Ms. Respondent, your attorney asks a question, your answer is*

510 It should be pointed out that analysis of the research material revealed examples of informational acts that were negative in nature, i.e., about what duties or competencies a party does not have, e.g., **P:** (...) *the credibility* [of the testimony] *is subject to the court's judgment, it is not subject to polemics by the party.*

directed to the court, please do not comment, do not speak at the same time, because it all interferes (...); **P:** *But you will be answering questions, I have a request that this should proceed in an orderly manner.* In this regard, it is worth noting that only in two cases the provision of information on the essence of the interactional role was not a consequence of exceeding the normative pattern in this regard.[511]

3.6.2.4.5. Informing about the thematic framework of particular communication occurrence

The ability to act within the thematic framework of a given proceeding or individual communication occurrences (complex procedural acts) is not just a matter of knowing the genre pattern of the trial. It is primarily the subject of cognition in a given case that determines the subject matter of the acts taken at the session scheduled for the trial. Particularly exposed to exceeding the pattern in this regard is the witness, who does not necessarily know exactly what part of the knowledge he or she is supposed to reproduce.

The analysis of the research material showed that the presiding judge's acts of information about the thematic scope of certain communication occurrences (content of question 2ah) primarily preceded the examination (both witnesses and party). However, only 29 acts in question were disclosed. In the analyzed cases, the presiding judges provided information about the thematic scope of the examination in three ways. The first was the most direct (16 cases), as it consisted of formulating a statement containing information about the scope of the examination's subject matter, e.g. **P:** *The court is interested in your report from the course of the incident* (...); **P:** *The court would like you to go over in your testimony to that moment when your parents required care and who actually provided it.* The second way (6 cases) was to use the evidence thesis contained in the evidence ruling, e.g. **P:** *Did you understand the content of the evidence thesis?* [Witness: *Yes*]; **P:** *Then please tell the court what you know about the circumstances covered by the evidence thesis in this case, and how you got this knowledge* [after reading the evidence ruling]; **P:** *Please tell the court what you know about these circumstances on which the court will examine you today* (...).The third way (7 cases), on the other hand, consisted in indicating the circumstances covered by the evidence thesis in the first question addressed to the examined person, e.g. **P:** (...) *what is known to you about the resolutions that the housing community adopted in connection with the meeting that took place in* (...)*, this is about the resolution* (...) *and the resolution* (...); **P:** *Please tell me if you remember the time of your husband's accident, what was your husband's*

511 The reason for the rather frequent transgression of the pattern of examination in its structural aspect can be attributed to the fact that this pattern provides for an unnatural way of communication, in which the answer is always directed to the court, regardless of the person of the questioner.

health condition after the accident, what was going on, what was the course of treatment, what were the ailments, what is it like today?[512]

Referring to the presiding judge's activity in informing about the thematic framework of the examination, two points should be noted. First of all, despite the absence of the presiding judge's activity in question, the examined person can get information about the thematic scope of the examination from the ruling of evidence. The prerequisite, of course, is that the evidentiary ruling designating this procedural act is presented at the trial.[513] Second, despite the fact that according to the normative pattern, the examination should begin with a free speech. However, the research material identified examples of examinations that began with more or less detailed questions. In contrast, in the case of examinations that began with free speech, the presiding judge relatively quickly moved on to asking detailed questions, or gave the floor to other participants authorized to ask questions.[514] Thus, it seems that the primary tool for setting or rather maintaining the thematic framework of the examination is posing relevant specific questions, rather than explicitly communicating the subject matter of the examination.

3.6.2.4.6. Questioning about willingness to perform procedural acts

Questions by the presiding judge about the willingness to perform procedural acts remain a constant element of the implementation of the trial.[515] This fact has already been taken into account at the stage of designing research questions (cf. assumptions for research question 2ai – Does the presiding judge ask non-professional participants if they want to perform a certain procedural act?). Therefore, during the analysis of the empirical material, the presiding judge's acts were taken into account, which were directly addressed to the non-professional participant of the proceedings (possibly participants), concerned a specific procedural act (possibly several acts), and, moreover, were in some sense unique.[516]

Analysis of the research material revealed 42 cases of communication acts in question.

Starting with examples of questions on procedural acts of lesser importance for the course of the proceedings and the procedural situation of the individual

---

512 Sometimes it was a few questions.

513 In the research material analyzed, witnesses were unlikely to be present in the courtroom in the course of issuing an evidentiary ruling setting the examination.

514 With two notable exceptions – the first being the testimony of a police officer in the character of a witness, and the second is the claimant's testimony as a party.

515 Such acts are usually taken either at the beginning of the examination or before the closing of a trial or judicial process.

516 E.g., a question about the willingness to perform a procedural act was directed to a non-professional participant, despite a previous question in this regard directed to all participants, or a question intended for a non-professional participant was more specific than questions directed to other participants.

participants (12 cases), we can point to those that concerned the request for confirmation of attendance at court and the repeal of the ruling imposing a fine on a witness, e.g. **P:** *Confirmation that you were in court you need for work?*; **P:** *Do you request the repeal of the fine that was imposed, because it was five hundred zlotys?*

The second class (10 cases) includes, in particular, questions concerning the supplementation of testimony by a witness or party, the submission of a specific procedural statement or the withdrawal of a motion to adduce evidence, e.g. **P:** *Is there anything else you would like to say that you think is relevant to the case, and that the court has not so far inquired into?* (...);[517] **P:** *As for the requests for examination of witnesses, the parties will say something from themselves, withdraw these requests so that the trial can be closed today* (...)*?* These type of questions may not only affect the entire court proceedings (e.g., the scope of the evidence gathered), but may also directly determine the course of the trial.

Questions about settlement and withdrawal of the appeal (in social security proceedings), (a total of 5), e.g. **P:** *Would you like to make a proposal for a settlement of some amount at this time?*; **P:** *Would you like to withdraw from the case?*, were also disclosed in the research material. Performing of these kind of procedural acts may lead to the termination of the proceedings.

Moreover, the analysis of the research material revealed fifteen examples of presiding judges' questions on the willingness to file motions to adduce evidence. First, questions concerning the desire to file motions to adduce evidence in general were revealed, e.g. **P:** *Please tell us, in view of the evidence that has been taken so far, the evidence from the examination of witnesses, what evidence do you still request, if any, should any more evidence be taken in the case, in your opinion?* Second – questions which concerned motions to adduce evidence relating to specific means of proof, e.g. **P:** *Do you think this evidence is necessary, would you like the court to conduct* (...) *that you are still examined by a doctor of occupational medicine?*; **P:** (...) *maybe we would still examine him?*; **P:** *And you want him to be a witness?*

Finally, an excerpt from the dialogue between the presiding judge and the defendant (in criminal case) initiated by a question about the desire to file a motion to adduce evidence will be recalled. The dialog illustrates the situation of a party's indecision in the matter of adducing evidence and the presiding judge's particular initiative in formulating a motion to adduce evidence:

P: *Would you like the court to examine any witnesses besides those listed?* (...) *Anyone else you would like to examine in this case who could clarify the issue of this gas?*

---

517 Sometimes the examination began with detailed questions, while at the end the presiding judge allowed the examined person to formulate a free speech, as in the cited example. This is the reverse order to that determined by the normative pattern of the trial.

Defendant: *I guess in terms of... to confirm my point, this is my partner, I could actually ask for....*

P: *Do you want to summons him as a witness?*

Defendant: *Actually, I am going to say that I am not sure, but I think I am going to have to....*

P: *Yes or no? We will immediately summons him to one date, maybe we can get all the witnesses examined and finish the case.*

Defendant: *We can give it a try.*

P: *And what would he say to the court?*

Defendant: *I mean I do not know, well can confirm the fact that I stayed with him (...).*

P: [for the minutes] *I request examination in the character of witness XY, resident of (...), on the circumstance of (...).*

3.6.2.5. Presiding judge's interference in the communication process between professional and non-professional participants

Research question 2b (Does the presiding judge interfere with how the interaction between a non-professional and professional participant is shaped?) was raised due to the fact that the interaction in the courtroom between the professional and non-professional participant is based on an unequal relationship. This is, of course, related to the different level of competence in the genre pattern of a trial. The possible interference of the presiding judge in an interaction of this type, in addition to the undoubted function of coordinating communication acts, performs in a certain sense a protective function against the non-professional participant in the proceedings. For this reason that it is of interest in this study.

During the analysis of the research material, 10 cases of interference by the presiding judge in the process of communication between a professional and non-professional participant were revealed. All cases involved interaction between a professional attorney and an examined person. However, the reasons for the intervention differed.

The most common (3 cases) reason for the presiding judge's intervention was suggestive questions. The presiding judge's response was to block the acts of either the attorney or the examined person, e.g. **P:** (...) *please do not try to force the witness to confirm what you say, yes;* **P:** *No, no, you do not have to answer. Generally, Mr. Attorney, suggesting the least.*

In other situations (2 cases) attorney's question was insufficiently understood, e.g., **P:** *Was this care, as I think that is what the attorney meant, covered by those funds that your mother possessed, or did you spend your own funds?*

In another situation, the presiding judge's intervention was caused by the content of a question that dealt with legal issues:

Attorney: *Please tell me, in what form according to the Polish Commercial Companies Code should the employment contract be concluded with you?*

P: *You are asking about legal provisions, Mr. Attorney, please ask for facts, okay.*

The reason for the presiding judge to intervene were also situations in which a non-professional participant did not know how to answer a question (2 cases), and did not understand the question posed (2 cases), such as:

Attorney: *And at the time there was an accident?*
Witness: *Well, but I do not understand the question now?*
Attorney: *The question is very simple!*
P: *Mr. Attorney, but maybe a little calmer, really, I have this suggestion that maybe these questions from the respondent should calm down a little bit.*
P: *Where at the time of the accident did the husband pay taxes, in what country, paid differently depending on what flag he was sailing under, I do not understand?*

In the context of the last example, it is worth noting that the subject of the intervention in this case was the manner in which the professional attorney asked the question.

At the end of these considerations, it should still be noted that the presiding judge's interference in the interaction between the professional and non-professional participant consisted of blocking communication acts, rephrasing the attorney's question, or took a mixed form.

3.6.2.6. Other acts of the presiding judge that may facilitate non-professional participants to communicate in the courtroom

The communication activities revealed during the analysis of the research material and described in the preceding sections do not, of course, exhaust the entire spectrum of means at the presiding judge's disposal that can facilitate the participation of a non-professional participant at the trial (or in court proceedings). The following will be discussed: (1) acts that create the so-called climate of interaction; (2) information of a technical nature and organizational facilities; (3) acts directly related to the performance of procedural acts. Acts of the above-mentioned types were revealed in the research material.

Re 1. Interactions between participants of the proceedings in Polish courts always occur in an institutionalized situation, serving clearly defined non-communication purposes. In particular, this has consequences in terms of a lack of equality among participants, a sense of distance, and a focus on the subject matter the case rather than on interpersonal relations. The analysis of the research material, however, revealed communication acts that somewhat alter the climate (atmosphere) of interaction in the courtroom. First, one can identify acts that reduce the distance[518] between the presiding judge and the non-professional participant, e.g.

518 An in-depth analysis of the issue of power distance in the courtroom in Polish courts was conducted by Michał Dudek and Mateusz Stępień. Their monograph deals with the problem of power distance between the judge and other participants of the trial and its manifestation in the communication process in the courtroom.

P: *We keep our fingers crossed! There are problems, but they can be solved without alcohol* (...), *good luck!* Second, such acts that make contact more friendly, e.g. **P:** *Please to the railing* (...) *lean on, it will be more comfortable, there is always such stability, that is what the railing is for, not for decoration, not to separate the court from the witness, but among other things also for this* (...), or such acts that could be called "off-topic speaking", e.g. **P:** *Tomorrow is your birthday, yes?* Third, such communication acts that are an expression of empathy, e.g. **P:** *Please do not get upset, yes, please, if you want, the court can order a pause. Can you speak?* [**Witness:** *Yes*]. *Maybe you want to sit down?* [**Witness:** *No, I will stand*]. *And if something were to happen, please tell me, yes.*

Re 2. Another class is formed by information that could be described as technical, as they concern, among other things, the arrangement of participants in the courtroom, the preparation of documents or the use of the microphone, e.g. **P:** *Ladies and gentlemen, please prepare your ID cards and come up to me with them as I ask*; **P:** (...) *the trial is recorded with an audio and video recording device* (...) *therefore I ask that you direct your statements to the microphone, yes.* This class is furthermore co-created by acts of organizational convenience, such as writing down to the participant the date of the next court session or the name of the motion, e.g. **P:** *You will get a piece of paper with the date, time and room, yes, because you will no longer receive a separate summons* (...), writing out a confirmation of attendance at court, handing out a model motion, telephoning the secretariat to prepare a form for the participant.

Ad 3. Within the third class, on the other hand, are communication acts of particular importance to the participants of the proceedings as they relate to the performance of particular procedural acts. The following will briefly discuss examples of communication acts revealed in the research material, which undoubtedly facilitate the performance of procedural acts by non-professional participants.

This class includes determining the meaning or content of an act done by a non-professional participant, e.g. **P:** *Before we proceed to the examination of witnesses, Ms. Claimant, the court has a question ... the court should treat your letter that you submitted to the file as a complaint?*, **Claimant:** *Well if you can* (...), **P:** *That is, as a complaint against the order on the motion for security, okay.*

The theoretical basis for the research conducted was Geert Hofstede's concept of power distance. However, this concept was further conceptualized by the authors, as a result of which they distinguished three levels of power distance: subjective, organizational and interactional. The primary research method used by the authors was structured passive observation of trials. Among other things, the authors concluded that judges tend to realize organizational power distance, which itself is high but inconsistent, and that if judges deviate from the baseline, organizational level of power distance, they mostly decrease the distance (increasing the distance is rare). See M. Dudek, M. Stępień, *Courtroom Power...*, op. cit.

Other acts of the presiding judge consisted in formulating the content of the act "for" the non-professional participant. A particularly clear example of such an act was the presiding judge's formulation of a declaration of acceptance or rejection of the inheritance.[519] Another example of this type of act was the formulation of an opening statement "for" a non-professional participant, in which case the presiding judge used the participant's prior statement contained in the letter initiating the proceedings, e.g. **P:** *You request compensation for unlawful termination of an employment contract without the notice period, in the amount of (...) and for overtime hours* (...). In this situation, the activity of the non-professional participant is limited to confirming the presiding judge's statement.

Participation at the trial is undoubtedly also facilitated for the non-professional participant by certain intertextual acts of the presiding judge, in particular, making inheritance assurances by confirming the assurances made by another participant (cf. examples on communication occurrences, Section 2.3.1) or initiating an intertextual reference by the presiding judge to the relevant procedural document, e.g. **P:** *Do you request as in the lawsuit?*; **P:** *Do you stand by your position expressed in objections?*

During the analysis of the research material, attention was also drawn to some of the questions posed by the presiding judge and some of the ways in which they were formulated that can facilitate a non-professional participant's procedural acts. Asking questions about certain legal acts (conventional acts in law) seems to be an activity that hinders, rather than facilitates, the non-professional participant's participation at the trial. However, taking inheritance proceedings as an example, a non-professional participant should demonstrate all those circumstances that will allow the court to issue a ruling regarding the confirmation of the inheritance acquisition in accordance with the applicant's request. Thus, the court must obtain information on, among other things, whether there were no already pending inheritance proceedings against the deceased, whether the participant has not obtained a certificate of inheritance, whether he or she has not made inheritance declarations, whether he or she has not renounced the inheritance of the deceased, and whether he or she has not been declared unworthy of inheritance. The analysis of the research material showed that the standard form of obtaining information on these issues is for the presiding judge to ask the relevant closed questions during the participant's inheritance assurances.[520] This results in the activity of the non-professional participant being reduced to answering either in the affirmative or negative. Compared to the necessity of independently formulating a statement

519 In all cases of willingness to make such a statement by a non-professional participant recorded in the research material, the content of the statement was formulated by the presiding judge.

520 As a result, inheritance assurances are actually more extensive than the normative pattern provides.

containing all the elements necessary to resolve a case of this type, this is a much simplified activity.[521]

However, answering these types of questions, while requiring only confirmation or denial, can be problematic. First of all, due to the fact that these questions necessarily contain elements of legal or juridical terminology (and the participant has not performed the acts referred to in the question[522]). Therefore, examples will be referred to here of ways of formulating questions that promote perception of their content and, consequently, facilitate answering them, e.g. (1) **P:** *Sir, have you ever been declared unworthy of inheritance by a court decision?*; (2) **P:** *Have you ever waived your inheritance from XY by signing any agreement with her about it?*; (3) **P:** *You did not waive your mother's inheritance through a notarized agreement with your mother?*; (4) **P:** *Before a notary did you not arrange for a certificate of inheritance? Did you go to a notary with any formalities after your father's death?*

In addition to the name of the legal acts, all of the above-mentioned questions contain brief information about some of the rules of its performance (in court, before a notary, by contract). It makes it easier for a non-professional participant to associate a given act with the circumstances that must have accompanied the act. In this context, it is worth noting the example in point 4. In this case, the participant's answer that he or she did not arrange any formalities with a notary after the death of the testator (which does not require knowledge of the institution of certificate of inheritance) is sufficient to conclude that the participant did not obtain such a certificate.[523]

Finally, it should be noted that the research material revealed other acts or communication behaviors of the presiding judge that can facilitate the non-professional participant's participation at the trial, but it is impossible to describe all of them here. It is known that factors facilitating participation in a given communication occurrence can be such diverse and sometimes difficult to perceive communication phenomena as tone of voice, speed of speech or acts that are a manifestation of linguistic politeness. In addition, the way they are perceived is often very subjective. It should also be noted that the indicated phenomena can equally well be a factor hindering communication. On the basis of the observation carried out for the purposes of this study, speaking too fast and too quietly could be considered a factor particularly unfavorable to communication.

---

521 Undoubtedly, the presiding judge's adoption of such a course of action also improves the conduct of the court session itself.

522 And this is most often the case, since inheritance proceedings have been initiated.

523 The presiding judge can derive such a conclusion by a simple but reliable inference: "If someone participated in the act of certifying the inheritance, then he or she participated in the act before the notary, so if he or she did not participate in the act before the notary, then he or she certainly did not participate in the act of certifying the inheritance".

Instead, it is worth noting that sometimes the presiding judge abandons the way of proceeding set by the normative pattern of the trial. Then, the communication process takes the form of a dialogue, which may concern not only what decision the court should make, but also how best to solve the problem giving rise to the request for this decision. Such cases were noted in the research material, but this was an exceptional way of proceeding, clearly related to the subject matter and mode of the proceedings.[524]

3.6.3. Implementation of the leading-order enforcing function

The leading-order enforcing function of the presiding judge is discussed last for a reason. The communication acts that will be characterized in this section are a kind of link between the description of the presiding judge's communication acts addressed to the non-professional participants and the description oriented towards the acts of the non-professional participants. This is because every reaction of the presiding judge that is an expression of the leading-order enforcing function and taken towards the non-professional participant is determined by the communication act or behavior of that participant.

The following will discuss situations in which the presiding judge reacted to the communication acts and behaviors of non-professional participants highlighted in research questions 3aa through 3ae, i.e., communicating with omission of the presiding judge or taking communication acts when the normative pattern of the trial does not provide for it, going outside the thematic frame of certain communication occurrences, and the vocabulary used. In addition, examples of other acts and behaviors of non-professional participants that triggered the presiding judge's response will be pointed out. Whereas, the issues addressed in question 3af (Does the presiding judge react to the communication acts of non-professional participants related to the creating of the participant's "face" in the proceedings?) will be discussed in the discussion devoted to this issue (see Section 3.7.2).

The quantitative date is presented on the Graph 2.

524 All such cases concerned family proceedings.

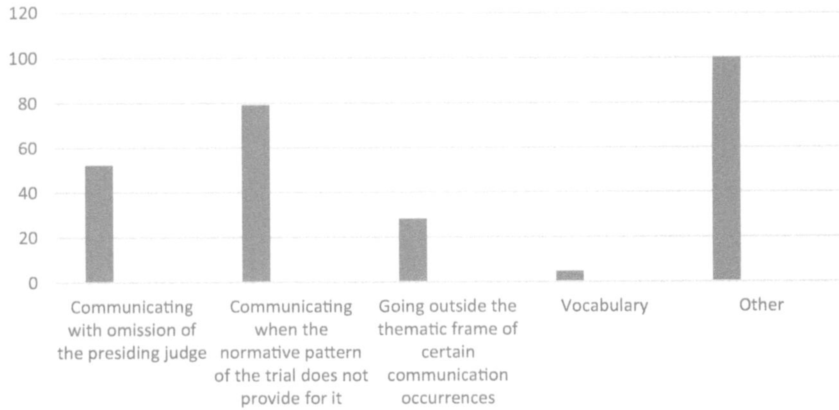

Graph 2. *Reasons for presiding judge's response in leading-order enforcing function*
Source: Own study.

With regard to the communication phenomena explicitly indicated in the research questions (i.e., excluding the "other" category), the most frequent reaction of the presiding judge was caused by communication acts of non-professional participants taken in situations where the pattern of the trial does not provide for this (79 cases). The most frequent (68 cases) transgression of the pattern in this regard occurred in connection with the examination and activities structurally similar to the examination (the so-called informational examination and submission of inheritance assurances). The communication acts of non-professional participants causing a response from the presiding judge primarily consisted of speaking while dictating into the minutes (33 cases), commenting or expressing a desire to refer to the statements of the examined person (16 cases), e.g. **Defendant (in misdemeanor proceedings):** *What are you coloring here!*, talking by participants, including during the examination of another participant (11 cases), attempting to supplement the statements of another participant, e.g. the examined person (6 cases), attempting by the examined person to consult with another participant (3 cases). Other acts that caused a response from the presiding judge included wanting to ask a question or make another statement during the statement of the reasons for the judgment (4 cases), speaking without giving the floor in situations other than examination (3 cases), interrupting the presiding judge (2 cases), and in one case commenting on the content of the judgment during its announcement.

Another class of acts that provoke a reaction from the presiding judge is formed by acts of communication with omission of the presiding judge (52 cases). As the analysis of the empirical material showed, in this case, the most frequent (49 times) transgression of the trial pattern occurred in connection with the examination and activities structurally similar to the examination. Acts that triggered the presiding judge's response consisted of the examined person answering the questioner rather than the presiding judge[525] (29 cases), communication between the parties (8 cases), e.g. **P:** *Okay, let's establish that I am the connection between you here, there is no possibility of conversation unless you are about settlement* (...), making a comment directly to the examined person (6 cases), attempting to consult the examined person with other participants[526] (5 cases), suggesting something to the examined person (4 cases). It is worth noting here that in one case the defendant's comment on the witness' testimony was considered by the presiding judge as a statement – **Defendant (in misdemeanor proceedings):** *The truth must be told, man, you are a Polish police officer, you must tell the truth, you know, I have the right to demand it as a citizen* (...).

On the other hand, as far as the non-professional participants' transgression of specific thematic frameworks is concerned, the acts of this type revealed in the research material (a total of 28 cases) involved both going beyond the thematic framework of specific procedural acts, e.g. **P:** *Okay, because we are going a little off topic, we are interested in your income*, their fragments, e.g. **P:** *Okay, but answer the question, where did this discount come from?*, as well as the entire proceedings, e.g. **P:** *No, no, listen a moment* (...), *formally speaking, the father of the minor XY is Mr. YX and these circumstances, even if you try to bring other circumstances, the court is not interested at all, yes.*

In contrast, the presiding judge rarely (6 cases) reacted to the use, or failure to use, specific vocabulary by non-professional participants. Of the total six cases, five involved the use of an inappropriate addressable phrase to refer to the court. In one case, the presiding judge's reaction was related to the use of a vulgar phrase by a witness in direct conversation with the presiding judge – **P:** *I inform you that I consider your behavior as violating the solemnity of the court* (...).

In addition, analysis of the research material revealed many other acts and behaviors of non-professional participants that contributed to the presiding judge's response. Of all the acts or behaviors included in the class "other", and there were equally a hundred of them, the most numerous subclass is formed by acts related to the asking of questions by non-professional participants during the

525 This type of act did not always elicit a response from the presiding judge. Based on observation, it can be assumed that usually the reaction was pragmatically justified, i.e. the presiding judge then reacted when directing the answer to the questioner actually impeded the flow of communication, especially dictating into the minutes. Maintaining eye contact with the examined person allows the presiding judge to control the flow of speech so that minutes can be taken. In cases where the examined person responds to the questioner, this can be made much more difficult. Instead, the natural reflex of a participant in face-to-face communication is to situate oneself facing another participant, that is, in the present case, the questioner.

526 Some acts of non-professional participants constitute a transgression of the pattern from the point of view of more than one aspect of its formation.

examination. This element of the examination has proven to be quite problematic for non-professional participants, and acts in this regard have repeatedly caused the presiding judge to react.[527] However, this issue will not be developed here, as the problems of non-professional participants related to asking questions during the examination will be discussed further. The remaining communication acts and behaviors of non-professional participants included in the class under discussion (31 in total) were primarily related to stepping outside the procedural role (13 cases), such as:

Authority of organizational entity:	*Your Honor, I would like to correct, because this is not related to the case! (...) I will demonstrate this ...*
P:	*Sir, I decide whether it is related to the case or not, if it is not, I waive the question.*
Authority...:	*Okay, sorry, sorry.*

In addition, this class is co-created by behaviors of a proxemic nature, involving either speaking to the court while seated or standing up from the seat without explicit permission from the presiding judge (a total of 12 cases). This class also included other communication behaviors: shouting (raised voice), laughing, and speaking too fast to prevent the minutes from being taken (a total of 4 cases), e.g. **P:** *Sir, the court has not yet issued of the judgment, you do not have to shout* (...), *sir, but calmly* (...); **P:** *Well, what are you laughing at and why?* [**Defendant (in misdemeanor proceedings):** *I am not laughing*] *Well how not, let's really behave in a serious manner.*

The unitary acts of answering the phone in the courtroom and attending the court session of the defendant (in misdemeanor proceedings) while intoxicated were also classified in the class in question. In the latter case, the consequence was a disciplinary sanction.

* * *

In accordance with the order of the issues discussed in Sections 3.6.1 through 3.6.3, the main conclusions derived from an analysis of the presiding judge's acts in carrying out the **leading-intermediary function** will be presented first.

Analysis of the research material in terms of giving instructions to non-professional participants showed that the activity of presiding judges (in Polish courts) in this regard is considerable (a total of 398 instructions were recorded in the research material). However, it should be noted that the most numerous class of all instructions were those explicitly specified in the normative pattern, which the presiding judge is obliged to give (273 instructions). The activity of presiding judges outside this class was also definitely noticeable. Indeed, presiding judges gave instructions developed through the practice (49), ad hoc instructions (47) and

527 In coding the data, it was recognized that there were 69 examples of presiding judges' reactions related to non-professional participants asking questions.

instructions of a mixed nature (29), thus adapting the activity associated with the implementation of the leading-intermediary function to the needs of a specific communication situation.

Due to the fact that instruction as a communication act can exhibit a considerable degree of difficulty (it conveys important and sometimes specialized information), during the analysis of the research material, special attention was paid to the ways of giving instructions, which, as it turned out, were characterized by considerable diversity in form. At the same time, examples of giving instructions that would consist of reading the legal provision or recalling its wording from memory were not revealed.

Thirty-six instructions given by the presiding judge after announcing the decision ending the proceedings were analyzed in depth. This analysis showed that presiding judges, when giving this type of instruction, used both linguistic means that increased and decreased the communicativeness of the statement. Among the former can be counted, e.g., the use of individual names instead of general names, giving instructions in a casuistic manner, the use of personal forms, the introduction to the instruction, or the order of information conveyed in the instruction reflecting the natural order in which acts are taken or occurrences occur. On the other hand, linguistic means that reduce the communicativeness of the instructions analyzed especially can include the use of legal and juridical terms.

Since, according to the normative pattern, the giving of instructions is an one-way communication act, there is a greater risk of a communicative misunderstanding between the sender and addressee of the instruction. Therefore, an effort was made to determine whether presiding judges take advantage of the fact of direct contact with the addressee of an instruction and transform the one-way act of giving an instruction into a communication occurrence. Analysis of the research material showed that presiding judges both ask the addressees of the instruction whether they have understood its content (75 examples), and use indirect forms, such as by ending the statement with a so-called "questioning yes", e.g. **P:** *I am instructing you on your obligation to tell the truth, yes (?).*

The communication phenomena analyzed from the point of view of the presiding judge's implementation of the **leading-coordinating function** were quite diverse and had a different impact on the communication process, of which non-professional participants of the proceedings are a part. During the analysis of the research material, attention was paid to the problem of the presiding judge's adaptation to the level of communication competence of the non-professional participant. First, examples of the presiding judge's explicit reference to the vocabulary used by the non-professional participant were analyzed. This analysis revealed a few (only 18) examples of this type of act, only some of them actually conducive to simplifying the process of communication between the presiding judge and the non-professional participant.

Moreover, during the analysis of the research material, examples were revealed of the use of those linguistic means that, in turn, may hinder the process of communication between the presiding judge and the non-professional participant. Legal and juridical terms are considered as such in this study. The analysis revealed examples of the presiding judge's use of both legal and juridical terms in communicating with non-professional participants. These terms were related to court proceedings, non-court proceedings and substantive law. Legal and juridical terms which could not be assigned to any of the above three classes were also noted. It should be recalled that all these terms are presented in an orderly manner in Appendix 1. However, despite the disclosure of many legal and juridical terms, it undoubtedly cannot be said that presiding judges' statements to non-professional participants in the proceedings are full of legal or juridical terms[528] (more on this in the Summary).

The examples of the presiding judge's use of legal and juridical terms in statements addressed to non-professional participants in the research material were also subjected to contextual analysis, i.e. taking into account elements of situational and communication context. At the outset of the analysis, it was assumed that the use of legal and juridical terms in statements addressed to non-professional participants impedes the communication process. Then, referring to the context of the use of these terms, examples were sought of communication acts and occurrences that falsify this assumption perceived as a general statement.

Contextual analysis conducted from the point of view of the situational context in particular showed that many of the legal or juridical terms used by presiding judges are closely related to the object of cognition in a given proceeding, and therefore to the main subject matter scope. Given that a court case is always "someone else's case", it seems reasonable to expect that, at the very least, the parties (quasi-parties) to the proceedings will be familiar with the basic terms related to the subject matter of the case. In addition, it may be that the legal and jurisprudential terminology related to the subject of cognition in the case will be familiar to non-professional participants in the proceedings due to the social, including occupational, roles they play. And finally, it may be that familiarity with certain legal or juridical terms will be related to the experience acquired during participation in court proceedings or in the proceedings preceding them (e.g., pre-trial investigations). All the situations indicated above were noted in the research material.

The contextual analysis, which considered the communication context of the use of legal and juridical terms in statements addressed to non-professional participants, revealed situations in which the presiding judge's use of specific terms was consequential. This included those incidents in which a term was first used by a non-professional participant or came from procedural documents, including those initiating the proceedings. In addition, the analysis of the research material looked for manifestations of the influence of the use of legal and juridical terms on the course of interactions involving non-professional participants. This analysis revealed only four metalinguistic acts by non-professional participants, in which they either indicated a misunderstanding of certain terms or expressed doubt in this regard, of which two cases involved referring the name of a procedural role to a specific participant (e.g., **Witness:** *Defendant, you mean Mr. X?*). One case of an

528 Such voices can sometimes be heard in discussions of courtroom communication.

obvious communication misunderstanding between the presiding judge and the witness was also revealed.[529]

The above observations lead to the conclusion that the use in the statements directed to non-professional participants of legal and juridical terms, in principle, did not lead to disruptions in the course of interaction in the analyzed cases. However, it should not be concluded from the above statement that it also did not or could not lead to a situation of communicative misunderstanding. After all, communicative misunderstanding is a mental phenomenon, insofar as it is noticeable to an observer (using such methods of observation as in this study), insofar as its existence can be inferred from observable phenomena.

Analysis of the empirical material also revealed a prevailing tendency for presiding judges to abandon the formulation of addressable phrases and names of participants of the proceedings using only the names of the relevant procedural roles.

It is worth noting further that the presiding judges' activity in explaining the meaning of certain legal or juridical terms did not turn out to be significant. Nineteen different terms were disclosed in the research material, the meaning of which the presiding judges explained, and they did so in various ways (by indicating the elements of the content of the name, the scope of the name, and even by comparison). However, it should be recalled that information on the rules of construction or rules of consequence of certain legal acts, including procedural acts, is at the same time a more or less exhaustive nominal definition of the name of such an act, as it indicates the elements of its content.

In further analyzing the communication activities of presiding judges related to the implementation of the leading-coordinating function, attention has been focused on activities that can facilitate the non-professional participants implementation of various procedural functions and interaction roles, and reduce the sense of uncertainty associated with participation in court proceedings (and at the trial).

The analysis conducted showed that the activity of presiding judges varied in intensity in the areas studied. Presiding judges appeared to be most active in terms of reporting on procedural acts taken, or not taken, and on the stage the case investigation (a total of 449 examples of this type of activity). The other types of acts already showed a lower frequency: (1) informing about the essence of the proceedings (49 examples); (2) asking about a non-professional participant's willingness to perform procedural acts (42); (3) informing about procedural functions or interactional roles (a total of 35); (4) explaining the meaning of procedural acts performed or expressing willingness to formulate such an explanation (a total of

529 It is worth recalling this example at this point, since it was discussed in the section on giving instructions rather than using legal and legal terminology – **P:** *You are the closest person to the defendant, therefore you have the right to refuse to testify. It is up to you whether you testify or not. Do you want to testify or not?*, **Witness:** *Well, **if I am sued**, I will testify, I have nothing to hide.*

30); (5) informing about the thematic frame of certain communication occurrences (29). In the context of the presiding judge's informational activities, it should be noted that some actions of this type were somehow provoked by non-professional participants of court proceedings, for example, by a revealed doubt about the advisability of the procedural act being undertaken or a participant's transgression of the trial pattern. Many times the intensity of the presiding judge's activity was closely related to the communication and situational context accompanying a particular interaction with a non-professional participant.

During the analysis of the research material, attention was also paid to the presiding judge's acts, which, in a certain sense, can perform a protective function against the non-professional participant. The analysis revealed ten cases of presiding judges intervening in the course of interactions between a non-professional and a professional participant of the proceedings. All of the cases of interference involved interactions between a professional attorney and an examined person.

Summarizing the communication acts taken by the presiding judge in carrying out the leading-coordinating function, it should be pointed out that in addition to the types of acts that were included in the research questions, the analysis of the research material revealed other acts that can facilitate the non-professional participant in carrying out procedural functions and interactional roles. These were divided into three classes: (1) acts that create a climate of interaction in the courtroom; (2) facilities of an organizational and technical nature; (3) acts that facilitate the non-professional participant's performing procedural acts. For the participation of the non-professional participants, the most important were, of course, those included in item 3, and consisted of determining the meaning or content of the procedural act performed by the non-professional participant, formulating the content of the procedural act "for" the non-professional participant, using various types of intertextual references, and formulating closed questions in order to determine the facts relevant to the proceedings.

As part of the summary on the presiding judge's acts as an implementation of the **leading-order enforcing function**, it is necessary to recall the most important conclusions formulated in this regard. Of the types of communication acts included in the research questions, the most frequent reaction of the presiding judge was provoked by the taking of communication acts by non-professional participants in situations where the pattern of the trial does not provide for this (79 reactions), communication between participants with the omission of the presiding judge (52 reactions). On the other hand, the presiding judge reacted least frequently (6 cases) to the vocabulary used by non-professional participants. Of the communication acts that were not included in the research questions on the presiding judge's implementation of the leading-order enforcing function, the presiding judge's reaction was most often triggered by acts related to the improper implementation of the questioner's interactional role. The results of the analysis of the research material in this regard revealed a significant problem related to the realization by non-professional participants of this element of the normative pattern of examination (more on this topic will be discussed in the Section 3.7.2.2).

3.7. Communication acts of non-professional participants

In the introduction it should be pointed out that the research material[530] takes into account the communication activity of 492 non-professional participants. This class consists of 237 non-professional participants who cannot be represented by a legal representative (e.g., witnesses), 120 non-professional participants who are not represented by a professional legal representative, and 135 non-professional participants represented by a professional legal representative (e.g. attorney).

3.7.1. Non-professional participants and a use of legal and juridical terms

3.7.1.1. Legal and juridical terms – empirical findings and contextual analysis

With regard to the statements of non-professional participants, it was also decided to extract all legal and juridical terms that occurred in these statements.[531] For clarity in the presentation of the results of the analysis, these terms are presented in Appendix 2. This allows a comparison of the results of the analysis of the research material in terms of the use of legal and juridical terms by presiding judges and by non-professional participants, especially since the same methods of categorizing the terms revealed in the research material were used. Different from the use of legal and juridical terms by presiding judges are the results of the analysis of terminology used by non-professional participants in the proceedings. The most numerous class is made up of terms that refer to substantive law and non-court proceedings – this is the case both for all the varieties of proceedings combined and each of them separately (see Appendix 2). This is followed by the class of terms related to court proceedings (see Appendix 2). On the other hand, the least numerous class is formed by terms that were not classified in the previous two classes, and in this case the results of the analysis in relation to non-professional participants and in relation to the presiding judge coincide (cf. Appendix 2 and the results of the analysis of the presiding judge's use of legal and juridical terms, Section 3.6.2.3.2).

530 Comprising 177 court sessions scheduled for the trial.

531 All the terminological, conceptual findings made in this monograph of legal and juridical terms for the analysis of the research material (cf. Section 3.6.2.3.1) and the method adopted therein for using the category of legal and juridical terms as an analytical category are also valid for this section. However, one should be aware that the degree of certainty that a non-professional participant uses a given term in the sense established in legal or juridical language is obviously less than in the case of a presiding judge. Then, however, when the use of terms is related to the participant's social, including occupational, role, the degree can be considered as high as in the case of the presiding judge.

Immediately apparent is the variation, sometimes considerable, in the number and variety of terms used by non-professional participants depending on the variety of proceedings in which they participate. The largest number of uses of legal and juridical terminology by non-professional participants was recorded in civil contentious proceedings, followed by labor law proceedings, social security proceedings and civil non-contentious proceedings (see Appendix 2 and the lists for the above-mentioned varieties of proceedings). Clearly fewer legal and juridical terms used by non-professional participants were recorded in family, misdemeanor, criminal and commercial proceedings (cf. Appendix 2 and the lists for the above indicated varieties of proceedings). Given such a clear differentiation between the above-mentioned varieties of proceedings, it is necessary to consider the reasons for this, and furthermore to contrast the above results with those obtained with regard to the presiding judge's communication acts.

First of all, it should be noted that for both the presiding judge's and non-professional participants' communication acts, the least number of terms relating to substantive law and non-court proceedings were revealed in misdemeanor, criminal and commercial proceedings.

Looking for reasons for this state of affairs, one can, of course, point out that commercial proceedings are the least in the research material. However, this can no longer be said with regard to criminal and misdemeanor proceedings. Moreover, it is probably not in the number of sessions analyzed within a given variety of proceedings that the reasons for the quantitative variation in the use of legal and juridical terminology should be found. It seems that the justification would have to be sought by taking into account the subject of cognition of these proceedings. Indeed, the subject of cognition was formed primarily by acts of a psychophysical nature, rather than conventional acts, including those related to the functioning of some entity of a conventional nature, which in turn was reflected in the lexical means used by the participants. This may seem *prima facie* rather surprising with regard to commercial proceedings. However, it should be borne in mind that many cases in commercial proceedings involve issues related to the non-performance or improper performance of various types of contracts (this is also the case in the research material analyzed). Thus, the names that appear in the participants' statements are used to describe psychophysical (especially technical) acts rather than conventional acts, including legal acts.

A separate analysis was made of the use of procedural role names by non-professional participants in addressable phrases and as names of participants in the proceedings. In the case of addressable phrases used by non-professional participants, the form containing the name of the procedural role was used most often (113 participants), with the usual form being an addressable phrase referring to the court, e.g. *Your Honor...*, *Please Your Honor.* This was followed by non-professional participants who used addressable phrases that did not contain the names of procedural roles (49 participants), and the least frequent was the combination of both forms – both within a given phrase and within the entire session scheduled for the trial (34 participants).

On the other hand, as for the names of the participants of the proceedings not appearing in the addressable phrases, the forms without the names of the procedural roles (263 participants) were by far the dominant ones in the research material, while being quite diverse and primarily referring to personal relationships between the participants in the proceedings, e.g. *sister, Mrs. X, husband, ex-husband, neighbor, colleague,* or *child.* Subsequently non-professional participants (47 participants) used mixed forms within a given court session – sometimes using the name of the participant's procedural role, and sometimes not. The rarest were cases in which non-professional participants within a given session used only the names of participants corresponding to their procedural roles (15 participants).

As part of the description of the results of the **contextual analysis**, it is first necessary to note the quantitative variation in the legal and juridical terms used depending on the variety of the proceedings. This fact (not the only one, by the way) testifies to the significant relationship between the lexical means, including terms, used within the trial and the elements of the situational meso-context, especially the subject of cognition in a given proceeding. Such terms derived from the research material include *dividend, bail mortgage, company board meeting, work permit, termination of employment contract, property separation, will, housing community, amendment notice changing the employment contract, repeal of co-ownership,* among others.

In the course of presenting the results of the contextual analysis of the presiding judge's use of legal and juridical terms (cf. Section 3.6.2.3.2), it was pointed out that some of them are related to the social, including occupational, role of non-professional participants, their life experience, including the experience of participating in court proceedings. Here it is worth looking at the above-mentioned elements of the situational micro-context from the point of view of legal and juridical terms used by non-professional participants.

The social role played by individual non-professional participants was primarily associated with terms relating to the functioning of housing communities, such as *costs of management of the shared part of the immovable property, board resolution, Premises Ownership Act, owner, co-owner, management of the immovable property, administrator established pursuant to Article 18 of the Premises Ownership Act.*

The legal and juridical terms related to the occupational roles of individual non-professional participants (both parties and witnesses) were clearly noticeable and diverse, such as: *contribution, member of the audit committee, member of a cooperative, capped mortgage established on the leased property, investor, construction manager, management contract, countersignature of the treasurer, municipal housing stock, preschool class, decision on the measure of placement in a youth sociotherapy center, right of tenants to acquire apartments without sale, proxy, recalculation of pension under Art. 55 in conjunction with Article 26 of the Law on Social Security Retirement Pensions, provisions of the Law on Public Procurement, auction, kindergarten point, social benefit fund regulations, representative of the bankrupt, agricultural production cooperative, resolution on the final distribution of the cooperative's property and payment of membership shares, resolution to put the cooperative in bankruptcy, resolution to place* [something] *in court deposits, contract (for author's supervision), building qualifications, sheltered workshop, ownership board established under Article 20.*

It is worth mentioning in this context some examples of statements in which non-professional participants used legal and juridical terms related to their occupational role, such as: **Respondent:** (...) *I proposed to the claimant to terminate the employment relationship by mutual agreement* (...); **Witness:** (...) *draft resolutions are... they contain when they are drafts, a written justification, and this was probably the case with this resolution or any amendment to the terms of privatization of public housing, where it was in colloquial language, and in any case less such strictly legal language to describe the intention and goal to which one wants to achieve* (...); **Witness:** (...) *when the law began to oblige, and rightly so, the creation of the so-called municipal housing stock, and then this stock had to be indicated* (...); **Authority of organizational entity:** (...) *they were not employee-owned companies, because employee-owned companies are created in a different form, it looks different, a cooperative is an indivisible economic entity, it is owned by the cooperators, not by the employees, the property belongs to the cooperators.*

All of the above examples testify not only to the relationship of the terminology used to a specific occupational role, but also to the high level of communication competence in the use of this terminology.

It is also important to note the legal and juridical terms used by non-professional participants, which are related to their life experience, but do not directly relate to some specific social, including occupational role, such as *credit, decision on inability to work, decision on divorce, income tax, loan, benefits drawn from tenancy contract, conversion of perpetual usufruct, repayment from division of [joint] property, property division case, divorce proceedings, discontinuation of the investigation, cessation of [marital] property contract, bill of exchange.* In order to more fully illustrate the described issue, it is worth citing a few statements by non-professional participants containing terms of the type in question, some of which demonstrate competence in the genre pattern of the trial, e.g. **Claimant:** *I maintain in full all the allegations made in the lawsuit and in the procedural document of* (...)*, at the same time I wanted to make a statement that* (...); **Respondent:** *Your Honor, since the file is on loan from the Attorney General's Office all the time, I wanted to say, for the record, that there are no proceedings pending against my person* (...) *I simply filed a complaint against the acts of prosecutors* (...); **Respondent:** *I, first of all, wanted to state that the court did not uphold the position of the cooperative on the issue of exclusion of me from membership, but simply I did not meet the limitation period for filing procedural document and the court ended the case without my participation* (...).

Considering the results of the contextual analysis presented above taking into account the reference to the situational context, it should be noted that knowledge of legal and juridical terminology can be associated with knowledge of legal norms of the minimum-role and *ad hoc* knowledge. It should be recalled that the same conclusion could be drawn with regard to legal and juridical terms used in presiding judge's statements addressed to non-professional participants.

Referring to the analysis taking into account the communication context of non-professional participants' use of legal and juridical terms, it should be noted that non-professional participants very rarely reported that they did not know how to express a given thought using adequate legal or juridical terms. Only three cases of such metalinguistic acts were recorded in the research material. The first act was related to the functioning of a housing community – **Witness:** (...) *so invoked, I do not know the legal language... from what I remember, there was a reference to an article from the statute of the community, I think, that a person who is insistently in arrears with fees and is a nuisance to the community, that here the community can pass such a resolution.* In the second case it was about maternity leave – **Applicant:** *At the moment she is on leave not maternity, only the short one like that, I do not know what it is called, maternity, I think, yes?* In the third, on the other hand – about the tenancy contract:

Witness: *It turned out that none of these tenants have these rooms listed in these such tenant leases, I do not know what the issue is....*
P: *For tenancy contracts....*
Witness: *Yes.*

3.7.1.2. Substituting legal and juridical terms for lexical means outside of this terminology and performing procedural acts in a "non-juridical" manner

Answering research question 4b (Do non-professional participants substitute legal and juridical terms for words and expressions outside of this terminology?) is not easy. The main difficulty is that it is not known to what extent a given legal or juridical term has been replaced by other lexical means in the utterance of a non-professional participant, and to what extent it has simply been omitted. This difficulty is further reinforced by the fact that the utterances of non-professional participants that do not contain legal or juridical terms are far more numerous than those that do. Due to the above difficulties, only examples of names taken from the utterances of non-professional participants that could be replaced by a legal or juridical term with the same subject reference will be cited here.

Many (58) of the names used by non-professional participants referred to various issues related to the employment relationship (including the establishment of the employment relationship, remuneration from the employment relationship, or termination of the employment relationship), e.g., *engagement, accept to work, boss, paycheck,* [salary] *on hand, get fired from work, earnings from work.*

In addition, there were recorded such examples (a total of 9) of names used by non-professional participants that were related to various issues of ownership, particularly its acquisition and loss, such as *the house was "saved" to the father, this bachelor apartment "was seen" on the parents, have* [something] *on ourselves, our apartment, write off from the land, give back the land.* As well as those that referred to various other legal acts, including procedural acts (a total of 17), such as *the court then did not give a divorce, damage was "pulled" from my insurance, judgment of visitation, break the contract.*

Names referring to criminal law can be arranged into a five-element class: *one year out of three, three out of five, conditional, application for self-punishment, ending of probation.* In addition, other terms that are difficult to assign to the above-distinguished classes should be mentioned: *commission for a group, on legal,* and *electronic court.*

It should be noted that in any case of substitution of legal or juridical terms, as understood here, the presiding judge did not block such linguistic act or formulate an admonition. In only one case did the presiding judge make sure he understood correctly:

Witness: *But it is about the judgment on visitation* (...)
P: *About contacts, yes, ruling on contacts?*

The last issue that will be discussed in this context concerns the performance of procedural acts by non-professional participants in a "non-juridical" manner – without the use of legal and juridical terms, deviating from the form that could be called typical for lawyers (cf. examples of that typical forms in the assumptions for research question 4ba in Section 3.5). It has already been pointed out in the literature that "self or 'lay' litigants bring the language, narrative modes, relevance criteria and argumentative strategies with which they are otherwise familiar into the courtroom".[532]

The analysis of the research material revealed 41 communication acts that were considered an example of performing a procedural act in a "non-juridical" manner. However, it should be noted that one case involved an act unknown to procedural law,[533] in three others the attempt to perform a procedural act was made by a participant not authorized to do so.[534]

---

532 See J. Yovel, *Language and Power...*, op. cit., pp. 27–53; see also P.M. Tiersma, L.M. Solan, *Cops and Robbers: Selective Literalism in American Criminal Law,* "Law and Society Review" 2004, Vol. 38, No. 2, p. 229 sqq.

533 In this case, a participant (in non-contentious civil proceedings) requested the court to exempt him from attending the court sessions scheduled for the trial, although he was not obliged to be present. This act was communicatively effective – the presiding judge explained that the participant's presence at court sessions was not mandatory, unless the participant was only noticed of them.

534 All three cases involved an attempt by witnesses to perform procedural acts. In the first – the witness requested for possibility to show documents and attach them to the case file, in response to this request the presiding judge asked the parties whether they were requesting that the documents be attached to the file. In the second – the witness requested that another witness be called, in response to this request the presiding judge instructed the witness that he had no authorization in this regard. In the third – the witness requested the repeal of the ruling regarding

The acts of non-professional participants performed in a "non-juridical" manner, primarily (31 cases in total) consisting of filing motions: (1) evidentiary (11), such as **Insured:** *Here I still wrote to this and got from the cooperative such a certificate and they still sent me (...), now I just got, because already my documents from this Social Insurance Institution to the court went through (...), once I drove up, they told me to hold until the trial, well I could not file, yes (...)*; **Participant:** *As I am on the floor, I would ask the court, this is my request, that the other side of the case, that is, Ms. XY, dutifully participate*, **P:** *Do you want the court to still summons the applicant?*, **Participant:** *Yes, for the reason that, well, you know, as with such cases, there are no documents, and you need to establish directly in court what happened and how it looked, because it is difficult to describe, right, like what the course of the case was*; (2) others (20 in total), and among them: (a) requests for the court to oblige the opposing party to perform a certain act, such as **Claimant:** *Is it possible to ask something? Maybe in this testimony, please, Your Honor, maybe you will order, Your Honor will order Mr. X to put what was the fee for (...) and whether my apartment was also included in this. Thank you*; (b) a motion to dismissal of the motion to adduce evidence of the opposing party, e.g. **Authority of organizational entity:** *Your Honor, well I would propose to dismiss this motion (...)*; (c) motions to confirm attendance in court, e.g. **Witness:** *Only today as if there could be some kind of confirmation that I was?*; (d) motions for reimbursement of the costs of proceedings, e.g. **Interested party in social security proceedings:** *Your Honor, we can apply for reimbursement of the costs too?*; (e) request for so-called voluntary submission to punishment, e.g. **Defendant:** *I request self-punishment (...) only I do not know how much it is specified there (...)*; (f) request for a copy of the minutes, e.g. **Participant:** *I would, as I always ask, I just want today's minutes as soon as possible, if there was such a possibility, even today*; (g) request to show a document in the case file, e.g. **Defendant (in misdemeanor proceedings):** *And is there a photo of the damage?*; (h) requests to speak for a procedural statement or additional testimony, e.g., **Witness:** *I wanted to clarify*.

The so-called dispositive acts (6 in total) were also noted: (1) withdrawal of the motion to adduce evidence, e.g. **Applicant:** *I think we have come to an agreement, then there is no meaning in questioning the witnesses*; (2) withdrawal of the appeal, e.g. **Insured:** *Well, I am already working, I found a job in Poland, then I work well, I withdraw*; (3) acceptance of the claim, e.g. **Respondent:** *Yes I agree (...) I am able to take it all on myself (...)*; (4) partial withdrawal of either the application or the claim, e.g.

P: *You report the house and home furnishings to be divided, yes?*
Applicant: *(...) I would like to just from immovable property.*
P: *So just immovable property, right?*

---

the defendant (in criminal case), in response to the request the presiding judge informed the witness that the ruling had already been repealed.

Applicant: *Yes.*
P: *Do you* [the participant] *agree to withdraw the motion for division of movable property and car and only deal with the house in the proceedings?*

Summarizing the results of the analysis of the research material in terms of non-professional participants performing acts in a "non-juridical" manner, two particularly important and closely related issues should be noted. First, non-professional participants, when performing procedural acts, used a variety of speech acts – from statements, i.e. acts of a descriptive nature, to acts with a suggestive function (requests, proposals and questions), and even acts of an optative nature. Secondly, all the acts recorded in the research material performed by non-professional participants in a "non-juridical" manner were communicatively effective. Such results of the analysis testify first of all to what was already recognized at the stage of reconstructing the genre pattern of a trial in Polish courts, that a procedural act can be at least communicatively effective regardless of the speech act that was used to formulate it and that was recognized at the stage of standard interpretation, unless such a speech act was chosen whose standard interpretation does not lead to recognition of a specific procedural act. Moreover, regardless of which speech act was used intentionally, and moreover, regardless of whether this intention consisted in intending to produce certain normative effects characteristic of a particular speech act or acting in accordance with the rules for performing such speech act, or in intentionally using a particular speech act, but with the knowledge that the normative effects that will arise will not be a consequence of performing an act at the level of a speech act, but at the level of a procedural act (such as a professional attorney's intentional use of a request as a form of courtesy). Against this background, it is easy to see the importance of the externalist rules for performing procedural acts.[535]

The analysis of the examples of the issue in question revealed in the research material also makes it possible to see how much the possibility of non-standard interpretation (i.e., other than that which leads to the recognition of the standard formulation of a given speech act) is affected by the fact that the communication process at the trial takes place in the form of face to face communication. It is not difficult to see that some of the examples cited above of the actual communication acts of non-professional participants diverge significantly from of the acts that could be called standard (typical) for the performance of particular procedural acts. Despite this, on the basis of the communication and situational context, these

535 The conditions for a successful speech act are internalistic when they concern the mental states of the participants in the communication, externalistic when they concern the non-mental elements of the situational context. Cf. R.M. Harnish, *Externalist...*, op. cit., p. 28. See an in-depth analysis of procedural acts performed in a non-juridical manner from the perspective of pragmalinguistics, particularly with regard to the phenomenon called "illocutionary agency externalism" (M. Witek, *Mechanisms of Illocutionary Games*, "Language and Communication" 2015, Vol. 42) in K. Gmerek, *Procedural Acts...*, op. cit.

acts were recognized by the presiding judge as aiming to perform a specific procedural act.

3.7.2. Implementation of procedural and interactional roles by non-professional participants

The analysis of the research material, the results of which will be presented below, was guided by research question 5 on how non-professional participants of court proceedings handle the implementation of procedural and interactional roles in certain aspects of the issue.

However, before the results of the analysis are presented, it is worth noting that a fragmentary picture of the implementation of specific procedural or interactional roles by non-professional participants is provided by the results of the study of the empirical material from the point of view of the presiding judge's communication acts. This is especially true of those communication acts and behaviors that gave rise to the presiding judge's response within the framework of his or her leading-order enforcing function, as they indicate ways of realizing specific procedural or interactional roles that go beyond the pattern of the trial (cf. the results of the analysis in this regard, Section 3.6.3).

3.7.2.1. Communication acts initiated by non-professional participants, including those related to the control of the course of the trial

Three types of acts that demonstrate the activity of non-professional participants at the trial and the ongoing analysis of its progress will be discussed below. These acts include: (1) initiating procedural acts; (2) controlling the written minutes; (3) formulating questions about legal issues and the course of the proceedings.

Re 1. The initiation of procedural acts in accordance with the normative pattern, with not so much the trial itself, but the court proceedings in general, is the domain of the parties or quasi-parties. It should be borne in mind that the realization of this aspect of the relevant procedural roles takes place primarily outside the trial and using written communication.

As a result of the analysis of the empirical material, 40 communication acts of non-professional participants in the proceedings were considered to be acts initiating specific procedural acts. This number is similar to the number of acts performed in a "non-juridical" manner, which were written above. However, the classes of acts revealed by these two analyses are not interchangeable, but intersect.

The common class includes those acts that were done in a "non-juridical" manner and initiated by a non-professional participant, and there were thirty of them in the research material. Outside the common class are those acts that were done in a "non-juridical" manner, but after being initiated by another participant, and these acts are not of interest in this discussion. Also not included in the common class are those acts that can be attributed to initiation, but contain relevant legal or juridical terms, the use of which, in terms of verbal form, at least approximates the typical form. Ten examples of such communication acts of non-professional participants were recorded in the research material. They consisted primarily (6 examples) of motions to adduce evidence. The remaining acts were individual and concerned motions (for a copy of the minutes, for adjournment of the trial, to show a document to a witness) and extension of the evidence thesis. It should be noted that none of these acts fully corresponded to the standard form, but only approached it due to the use of the relevant legal or juridical terms, such as: **Defendant (in misdemeanor case):** *Your Honor, because I still wanted to request an adjournment of the trial* (...); **Respondent:** *Your Honor, I, on this occasion, may file a motion, not to forget, for the claimant to submit evidence in the form of a resolution to put the cooperative in bankruptcy* (...); **Claimant:** *Your Honor, I would like to request that documentary evidence be attached to the case file* (...), *it may be relevant to the case.*

Re 2. The analysis of the empirical material in terms of control of the written minutes included the following types of acts: (1) requesting that a particular statement be recorded or that a portion of the minutes be read; (2) drawing the presiding judge's attention to the improper transposition of the participant's statements into the minutes; (3) supplementing and correcting statements while dictating them into the minutes.

With regard to the first issue, analysis of the research material revealed only three cases of non-professional participants requesting that a specific statement be recorded. In contrast, there was not a single case of a non-professional participant requesting the reading of an excerpt from the minutes. The reason for such low activity in the discussed area can be traced in particular to the way the written minutes are prepared. Basically, it involves the presiding judge dictating the participants' statements into the minutes (cf. Section 2.3.2.13), so that the participant can hear its contents. Non-professional participants were more active in controlling the dictation into the minutes. Nineteen cases of non-professional participants' acts of drawing the presiding judge's attention to the fact that he or she improperly transposed the participant's statement into the minutes were observed in the research material. The most common reason (16 cases) for the reaction were errors of a factual nature, that is, errors that changed the meaning of the participant's statement, such as:

1. P:	[for the minutes] (...) *took the number Y bus....*
Statutory representative of a minor:	*No, he did not take, he was supposed to take.*
2. P:	[for the minutes] (...) *he told me that he would not pay for it....*
Witness:	*Maybe it was not so precise that he said he would not pay, just that if we did not do what he wanted, he would not pay, he did not say he would not pay at all, no, well, to make it so precise.*
3. P:	[for the minutes] *This one was posted the day after the trial....*
Witness:	*No, the same day.*

Sometimes (3 cases) the cause of the reaction was linguistic errors involving incorrect repetition of a specific name, including the name given by the participant.

In conclusion, it should be pointed out that the research material revealed only six cases of non-professional participants supplementing and correcting their statements either during dictation or after dictation into the minutes. In five cases, the participant's act was simply to add a short statement. In contrast, in one case the claimant signaled a desire to make a correction – **Claimant:** *Your Honor, may I correct my statement?*

Re 3. The last of the three issues highlighted here relates to non-professional participants of court proceedings seeking information from the presiding judge on legal issues, including those related to court proceedings, and information related to the conduct of a particular proceeding.

With regard to information on legal issues, it should be pointed out that during the analysis of the research material, 47 statements by non-professional participants were recognized as communication acts of the type in question. Of those that referred to legal issues related to court proceedings (a total of 40), the most numerous were statements that concerned the release of witnesses from the obligation to remain at the court's disposal (16 cases), e.g. **Witness:** *Can I leave the court already?*; **Witness:** *Can I go back to work?* Some also referred to issues related to the substance or manner of certain procedural acts, including fees for their performance (15 in total), e.g. **Claimant:** *I still have a question (...) regarding this, regarding the attorney. Do I have to make a request within seven days, or what should it look like?*; **Insured:** *If I file an appeal, does that involve costs, yes?*; **Claimant:** *Do I have to write to the registrar's office for the judgment?*; **Applicant:** *Can we file this application today?* Still others concerned the entitlement to observe the trial (4 cases), such as: **Insured:** *Excuse me, can the wife attend?* and other procedural rights and obligations (5 in total), such as the entitlement to return the original documents at the end of the proceedings – **Applicant:** *Please Court, as I filed the documents, there is a deed of ownership, could I get it back?* or the obligation to be present at the trial – **Claimant:** *I will have to be?*

The remaining questions of non-professional participants on legal issues (7 in total) were not related to court proceedings and were individual in nature, and the issues the participants asked about were: (1) the transfer of ownership after acquisition of inheritance; (2) how to resolve disputes between the parents of a minor child; (3) liability for spouse's debts; (4) the possibility of recovering immovable property lost as a result of a crime; (5) entitlement to enter the property; (6) disturbance by a neighbor, and (7) the impact of collecting unemployment benefits on how to calculate the period of social insurance, e.g., **Applicant:** *Please, Your Honor, if we wanted to abolish this ownership in favor of mom?*; **Claimant:** (...) *only there will be the question of who will decide what school the child will go to, if my husband agrees that I should decide, how can this be resolved, does it have to be through the court?*

On the other hand, it should be pointed out that the analysis of the research material showed few cases (only 8) of non-professional participants formulating questions related to the course of the proceedings, most of which were singular and concerned: participants summoned to the next session scheduled for the trial (2 cases), such as: **Respondent:** *I have a question, are we also affected by this trial, or...?* and scheduled activities (1 case) – **Claimant:** *Excuse me Your Honor, may I ask, that is, on the next date there will simply be an examination of the parties, yes?*; the costs of proceedings that involve further court proceedings (1 case); the order of hearing cases after certain testators (1 case); sending a copy of the ruling (1 case) – **Applicant:** (...) [the ruling] *will come to me by mail, or in three weeks to report to the registry office?* or the return of the retained driver's license (2 cases). The reasons for the low activity of non-professional participants in the discussed area can be seen in particular in the considerable activity of presiding judges in informing about procedural acts undertaken in a given proceeding (cf. Section 3.6.2.4.1).

The issue of getting by non-professional participants information on legal issues was undertaken in this study in particular to get an answer to the question of whether non-professional participants take advantage of their presence at the court session and seek specific information on various legal issues. The answer turned out to be in the affirmative, although the number of revealed examples is not very large. However, underlying the formulation of this research question was also a desire to see how presiding judges respond to such questions posed by non-professional participants.

An analysis of the empirical material showed that in the case of questions on legal issues both related and unrelated to court proceedings, the presiding judge refused to answer the question in only two cases:

1. Witness: *Please Your Honor, as I am, I have two adult children, Mr. X is harassing me terribly, and what should I do, he goes, whistling after me....*

P: *Mrs. X, I am very sorry, but the court does not give legal advice.*

2. Respondent: *(...) if we are married, the wife takes credit (...), gets us into debt (...), do I still have it just, how is it legally, we in the marriage are responsible (...).*

P: *The court is not an advocate to advise you on how you should proceed. What we are dealing with here is what you say here and whether we can consider this claim (...).*

On the other hand, with regard to questions of non-professional participants related to the course of the proceedings in question, the presiding judge refused to answer the question only once. In this regard, it should be noted that the participant asked the question at a time when she was supposed to present possible motions to adduce evidence:

Applicant: *I mean I would just ask that at this time it be shown to us what court costs we will incur from this, because I will no longer support my brothers, they pay no taxes, no usufruct for five years....*

P: *But I am asking now about motions to adduce evidence, adjudication is another matter. Whether any evidence you want to report is important now (...).*

3.7.2.2. *Implementation of the elements of complex procedural acts that require special self-reliance – asking questions and formulating a free speech during examination*

A constant element of the normative pattern of the examination is to ask questions of examined persons. In addition, as part of the actual communication acts, it is the primary way of shaping the examination in terms of subject matter. If a participant in the proceedings, who is not represented by the attorney, wants to participate in shaping the examination, he or she not only has to use this tool, but also use it in a manner consistent with the normative pattern of the trial in Polish courts.

In the research material, both non-professional participants not represented by professional attorneys and those accompanied by attorneys participated in asking questions during the examination. Of a total of 88 communication occurrences in which non-professional participants asked questions (or at least performed communication acts that, according to the normative pattern of the trial, should be questions), only in fourteen cases was the question asked correctly. In 74 cases, various problems related to the discussed activity undertaken by non-professional participants were revealed. At the same time, it should be noted that some of these incidents exemplified a sequence of incorrectly asked questions or accumulated several different types of problems. Given the scale of the phenomenon in question, it is worth taking a particularly close look at it.

Analysis of the research material revealed that the mistake most often made by non-professional participants was to formulate a statement (i.e., act descriptive in nature) instead of a question (a total of 24 communication occurrences), such as:

Participant: *After mass, I immediately brought my father....*
P: *Sir, a question – not a statement, yes.*

Sometimes (7 cases) the statements took the form of an elaborate description of the situation, such as:

Respondent: *Okay, in that case, despite the proceedings conducted at the tax office you got summonses from me to produce invoices because a situation arose in the proceedings conducted at the tax office where you did not produce those invoices despite the summonses....*
P: *But do you want to ask a question?*

Other times (5 cases) it was a set of statements, descriptions of situations,[536] e.g.

536 It is worth noting from this example that sometimes non-professional participants are aware that they are making statements despite the fact that they should pose a question.

Defendant: *I was building (...) two bridges and I was a drunkard!*
P: *Is that a question?*
Defendant: *Well it was not, and now I will ask a question.*
Defendant: [to the witness] *My sister used to leave the house, right? She used to go out, I mean your sister, and my wife, but when there were small children, then she used to go out, and I do not know, because when I came back from work, because I at the construction site could not arrive on time, sometimes an hour, an hour and a half late, she would (...) stand in the hallway, she would have her things ready, she would create an argument with me and go out, I do not know if to her friend....*
P: *Is this a question or a story of some kind?*
Defendant: *Now I will ask a question.*
Defendant: [to the witness] *Do you know about the fact that she was ill with viral conjunctivitis and we were at the clinic, I saved her eyesight....*
P: [to the witness] *Do you know of a sister who has viral conjunctivitis?*

Another type of error (13 communication occurrences) consisted of a non-professional participant making – either instead of a question or within the assumption of a question – a comment, including: (1) to the testimony of a particular participant, e.g. **Participant:** *Also Mr. Witness emphasizes that the tree was healthy, repeatedly emphasizes that the tree was healthy, and here again interjects that because of its age. It is known that under ten years this tree will be healthy* (...), **P:** *But you are commenting again, and now is the time to ask possible questions, if you have no questions, then thank you very much to the Witness*; (2) to other acts of the examined person, such as: **Claimant:** *I will help you, because I am prepared as usual, as you were not prepared during the examination* (...), **P:** *Ma'am, no personal excursions please, just ask questions please*; (3) to the truthfulness of the examined person, e.g. **Claimant:** *I wanted to ask my sister why she came to court and is lying like this!*, **P:** *This is not a question about testimony.*

On a similar scale to the type of error discussed above, there were errors consisting of:

1. formulating suggestive questions (11 cases), such as:

1. Claimant: *Are all of the ones* [resolutions] *that are being challenged? I remind the witness that resolution number* (...) *is being challenged.*
P: *But I would ask you not to suggest an answer, yes, the witness said that these resolutions that are being challenged were on the notice, in this regard, please ask another question.*
2. Defendant (in misdemeanor proceedings): *Testifying, you say that you live in that, that area and you drive there. Is*

there a reason, for example, that there is some traffic jam there as a rule, or could the lights that are there be that cause? Could it be the lights being on (...).

P: *Sir, in a question there can be no suggested answer;*

2. going beyond the scope of the examination or proceedings in general (9 cases), such as:

1. Claimant: *In your opinion, does the board properly manage the immovable property in common, properly spend the community members' funds and properly account for them?*

P: *I will repeal of the question, of course, because it is not related to the case at hand.*

2. Claimant: *Did the witness (...) in my absence and the witness present here (...) accuse me of stealing documents?*

P: *I repeal this question, it is not related to the subject matter of this proceeding.*

In addition, non-professional participants formulated questions unsuited to the procedural functions of the individual participants examined, i.e., primarily those that dealt with certain regularities rather than individual facts ("as to an expert questions") and legal issues (a total of 6 cases), such as:

1. Claimant: *Do you know such a way to get a higher level of compaction of sand, there is compacted sand, how to get a higher level of compaction (...), do you know the method (...).*

P: *These are questions for the expert, whether Mr. X knows is irrelevant to the outcome of the case.*

2. Claimant: *(...) under what legal provision?*

P: *I will repeal this question.*

Subsequent errors already showed a lower frequency, and among them the most common was citing or discussing excerpts from the testimony of both the examined persons (4 cases), such as:

1. Defendant (in misdemeanor cases): *I am now referring to the testimony of driving behind the tram. You testify that you drove with Mr. X to write down the numbers, if I am not mistaken Mr. X (...).*

P: *Sir, please do not discuss the witness's testimony, just ask the question. Keep your mind focused on what you want, what you want to ask.*

2. Claimant: *Can Witness refer to testimony given earlier by previous witnesses that the contents of this resolution (...).*
P: *Ms. Claimant, the witness did not hear the testimony, please formulate the question.*

Further errors included duplicating questions, i.e., formulating the same questions as other participants or on those issues that the questioner had already talked about (3 cases), e.g.

Respondent: *Did you see that there is a garage at the end of the parking space?*
Respondent: *But I am asking something else, did you see?*
P: *But the witness already answered that he saw and parked so as not to block that garage entrance.*

Analysis of the research material also revealed two communication occurrences that accumulated different types of errors. In both cases, the non-professional participant made one comment on the examined person's testimony and two statements instead of a question.

Individual examples of errors related to the questioning of examined persons that are difficult to categorize into any of the above-mentioned classes have also been identified:

Defendant: *Since you are not my wife, you live with me, but since you are not my wife, that you do not live together with me. You yourself said "everyone lives on their own" in XXXX (...).*
P: *Maybe you should allow to answer. You asked and then you answer yourself, it does not make sense.*

The fact that the communication acts of non-professional participants described above triggered a response from the presiding judge (either blocking or admonishing) has already been written about in the section on the leading-order enforcing function of the presiding judge (cf. Section 3.6.3), here the issue will be developed further.

Analysis of the empirical material revealed that among the most common reactions of the presiding judge were acts of blocking the communication acts of a non-professional participant (a total of 68 cases).[537] These acts took various forms and consisted of:

537 It should be noted here that the total number of presiding judge's reactions discussed in this section is higher than the number of communication occurrences in which non-professional participants made mistakes related to asking questions during the examination. This is because some communication occurrences constituted a sequence of statements by non-professional participants that were incorrect from the point of view of the normative pattern of the trial, which triggered the presiding judge's reaction.

1. clarifying the question (13 cases), such as:

Claimant: *No, I only remember the moment when my mother was present in the kitchen, because she came (...).*
P: *Were you present in the kitchen at the time?*

2. admonition or suggestion that the participant's statement should be in the form of a question (35 cases), such as:

1. Respondent: *It was not like you said (...).*
P: *No, please ask a question, a question to the witness.*
2. P: *Is there anything you would like to ask the witness?*
Insured: *Well I said that (...).*
P: *A question, a question, you will tell, yes, but for now, do you know how to formulate a question so that Mr. X himself will answer?*

3. admonition and provide information on the mistake made or the essence of the procedural or interaction role played by the non-professional participant (12 cases), such as:

Authority of organizational entity: *Your Honor, Mr. X, do you remember that in the course of the examination, Mr. X wanted to interrupt, I said, I used a very rude word "We are going to the prosecutor's office, you cannot go like that", do you remember that (...).*
P: *Sir, I will not allow such an act, no, sir, you are imposing a certain vision of this activity and an account of it in a way that deviates from the two instructions already given to you, that we formulate our expectations here in the form of questions. It is the witness who is supposed to speak (...) [A]s you stand here in the* witness's *place, I will give you the floor, you will talk about the facts that you have accepted, that you want to reconstruct, now please ask questions;*

4. repeal of the question, or basically a part of it (4 cases), such as:

Respondent: *Are we laying pipes differently....*
P: *I repeal this question, this is a question for the* expert;

5. another act of blocking the communication act of a non-professional participant (4 cases), such as:

Defendant (in misdemeanor proceedings): *But about the 17:00, 18:00...?*
P: *But the witness do not remember.*

Another type of response by the presiding judge, while no longer related to blocking the communication act of a non-professional participant, was the repeal of the question:

1. without justification (5 cases), e.g..

Defendant (in misdemeanor proceedings): *Then what is the truth!*
P: *The court repealed the question;*

2. with an indication of the reason for repeal (5 cases), e.g..

Claimant: *And is the living room dirty?*
P: *I repeal this question, it is not related to the case.*

Yet another presiding judge's response, unconnected with blocking the speech of a non-professional participant, was to formulate a question "for" the participant (9 cases), such as:

Defendant: *I was an exemplary employee and was awarded the gold cross, silver cross (...) and I was a drunkard?!*
P: [to witness] *Was the defendant decorated with any orders?*

Analysis of the research material further revealed two individual examples of presiding judges' reactions unrelated to blocking a non-professional participant's statement. The first reaction involved blocking the witness's response, while the second involved dictating the non-professional participant's statement into the minutes as a procedural statement.

During the analysis of the research material, 25 situations were recorded, when the presiding judge provided non-professional participants not represented by a professional attorney (or defense counsel) with assistance in asking questions. This assistance consisted of showing the participant how to ask questions or formulating a question "for" the participant, such as:

Claimant: *One more question from me to the witness: in terms of the instrument that I was using, I mean the leveler, does the witness remember that if there were construction sites carried out on several sites by the company (...).*
P: *That is another way of asking: "Are you aware that there were more than one construction sites going on simultaneously, the company was doing more than one site at a time?". This question is suggestive, yes. First you have to establish one thing, then the other, yes.*

Summarizing the results of the analysis of the research material in terms of the questioning of non-professional participants of court proceedings during the examination, it should be stated with full confidence that the correct implementation of the normative pattern of the trial (in Polish courts) in this regard was a real problem for non-professional participants of court proceedings. However, the explanations (indication of the reasons) for the act of non-compliance with the normative pattern of the trial is no longer so clear. The errors described can, of course, be caused by ignorance of the norms determining the pattern of examination. However, it is possible, at least with regard to some cases revealed in the research material, to see a deliberate act, guided by the desire to use the moment to ask a question, to shape one's own position ("face") in the proceedings.[538] The communication phenomena indicated in the previous sentence are a **manifestation of the conflict between procedural and interactional roles**, which are associated with the implementation of different interactional strategies. The analysis of the research material showed that acts of this type are generally ineffective, as they are blocked by the presiding judge.

According to the normative pattern of the trial in Polish courts, the examination begins with the **free speech of the examined person**, in particular, with the answer to questions – What and from what source is known to the participant in the case? However, observation of the course of the examinations made it possible to make the observation that this stage of the examination is not always carried out. Therefore, not all the examples of examinations revealed in the empirical material were suitable for analysis from the point of view of problems with the realization of free speech. In those cases that were examined, in the vast majority of examples (106) free speech did not cause problems for non-professional participants. However, it should be noted that sometimes the statement was limited to a brief description of the subject matter of the proceedings or the nature of the witness's relationship with the parties.

The analysis of the research material revealed fifteen examples of examinations in which the realization of free speech caused non-professional participants various types of difficulties.[539] Most often (11 cases), the participants themselves revealed them: (1) by reporting that they did not know what to say, including where to start the statement, e.g. **Witness:** *I do not know, should I speak one by one, how was it?*, **Witness:** (...) *well I do not know how to define it now, to say* (...); or (2) by asking the presiding judge to ask questions, e.g. **Respondent:** *I would prefer the Court to ask me questions, because I do not know too much about* (...), **Witness:** *Please ask questions, because....*

538 Professional participants in the proceedings also try to use such methods, especially suggestive questions (cf. the presiding judge's interference in the process of communication between professional and non-professional participants, Section 3.6.2.5).

539 This did not take into account situations where the witness did not know what the case involved at all, because in these cases it was not the need to formulate a free speech that was the problem, but the unfamiliarity with the subject matter of the case.

However, other types of communication acts or behaviors were also identified as indicative of difficulties associated with the realization of free speech – silence (1 case), fatigue with long speech (1 case)[540] and referring to testimony given during the investigation (2 cases), e.g. **Witness:** *What I gave a testimony to the police, I stand by it all*; **Witness:** *In that testimony, I have already spoken.*

In most cases (8), the presiding judge's response was to ask a specific question, while in others it was to give the floor to a professional attorney to begin asking specific questions (2 cases), or to provide information about the normative pattern of the examination and the procedural roles (4 cases).

1. **Defendant (in misdemeanor proceedings):** *Can I ask for questions?*

P: *Sir, it is written in the Code that it is the defendant (also in misdemeanor case) who spontaneously gives explanations, and later the court, if necessary, asks questions.*

2. **Statutory representative of a minor:** *But what am I going to say now, that all about these lying down, how these stages were going through, or...?*

P: *You are testifying about what justifies the kind of benefit you are claiming on behalf of your son, the court will not tell you what to testify about, I gave you the floor to convince both the court and the opposing party here that this claim is legitimate, what you want to say, you will continue (...).*

3.7.2.3. Use of so-called "linguistic means of security" by non-professional participants

The decision to analyze the research material in terms of the title issue was influenced by the observation of trials in Polish courts. As a result of it, it became obvious that the linguistic means of security, as they are called in this study, are used by non-professional participants extremely often. This phenomenon is strongly related to the legal obligation to tell the truth and report the facts at the trial.[541] Due to the need to organize both the analysis itself and the argument presenting its results, the linguistic means of security have been divided into two classes – the first includes epistemic modalities (supposition and doubt), while the

540 An example of this type of difficulty was observed during the examination, the course of which was recorded by means of a video and audio recording device. The difficulty in realizing free speech was not related to the fact that the participant did not know what she was supposed to talk about, but to the fact that the speech was not interrupted either by the presiding judge's questions or by the need to produce written minutes.

541 Of course, with some exceptions primarily for the defendant (in criminal and misdemeanor proceedings).

second includes all other words and expressions that function as linguistic means of security.

3.7.2.3.1. Use of epistemic modalities – acts of supposition and doubt – by non-professional participants

It is emphasized that epistemic modalities can perform various functions in the communication process, including in the courtroom.[542] Instead, it is noted here that the non-professional participant's use of an act of supposition or doubt allows him or her to avoid making a statement that, as a descriptive speech act, could be subject to qualification from the point of view of truthfulness or falsity. By introducing the relevant modal judgment (epistemic modality) into the utterance, the non-professional participant signals that the state of affairs referred to in the propositional content is a state of affairs with varying degrees of probability. Since a modal judgment of this type introduces a subjective element into the utterance, it cannot be qualified from the point of view of logical value, and therefore it cannot be ruled on whether the participant was telling the truth.[543]

Analysis of the research material showed that non-professional participants in the proceedings very often use modal acts of the type in question (more than 330 cases[544]). The overwhelming majority were examples of the use of the act of supposition, acts of doubt were only slightly more than ten in the research material.

Acts of supposition were formulated by non-professional participants using initialization operators, e.g. ***I think***[545] *about* (...); ***I suppose*** (...); ***I suspect*** *from human error* (...); ***I think*** *it probably was.* The same operators were also placed in other parts of the utterances, such as: (...) *so* ***most likely*** *she consumed*; (...) *and no,* ***I think*** *he packed* (...); (...) *so there are* ***probably*** *some things lying there* (...); (...) ***I suspect*** *not everywhere* (...).

Non-professional participants also used the so-called autonomous operators, which are introduced into the utterance and allow to shape different meanings of the utterance, depending on where they are located,[546] e.g. (...) *and there the car* ***probably*** *will not enter at all*; *Also* ***rather*** *afternoon hours*; (...) ***rather*** *should not be*; (...) of *company X* ***probably*** (...); (...) *within* ***probably*** *Y days* (...).

---

542 See S. Sønderberg Mortensen, J. Mortensen, *Epistemic Stance...*, op. cit., p. 407.

543 For criminal liability, according to Polish law, in this regard, it is necessary that the testifier formulates a false statement and at the same time lies, that is, gives information contrary to his or her own conviction about the described state of affairs.

544 Due to the considerable number of examples. recognizing individual linguistic means sometimes consisting of one or a few words can be problematic. The number of examples given in this and the following section are only approximate.

545 See on different communicative functions of the expression "I think" in the context of trial discourse, M. Szczyrbak, *Verb patterns in trial discourse: The case of 'I think'*, "Discourse and Interaction" 2020, Vol. 13, No. 2.

546 A. Awdiejew, *Gramatyka interakcji...*, op. cit., p. 106.

In addition to the aforementioned modal operators, non-professional participants used other linguistic means to introduce the act of supposition, such as: (...) ***maybe*** *even deeper, I no longer remember the details* (...); *Well, I do not know,* ***maybe*** *some kind of* (...); (...) *I am just* ***guessing***.

In doing so, non-professional participants introduced acts of supposition expressing varying degrees of certainty – from strong supposition, e.g. ***Most likely****, because I would not "give my head" either* (...), to weak, e.g. *Jesus, I do not know, it* ***seems to me*** *that they have not returned.*

Analysis of the research material also revealed such cases in which non-professional participants justified the need for an act of supposition, such as *I said in my testimony that Mr. X had been drinking, probably, I am not sure, because I was driving, so from a distance I did not see.*

In contrast, acts of doubt were introduced by non-professional participants using the following modal operators, e.g. *Well,* ***not really*** (...); (...) ***I do not think*** *I directly called him* (...); (...) *which were* ***allegedly*** *damaged* (...); (...) ***I am not sure*** *it was as much as X weeks;* (...) *because I think,* ***I doubt that*** *she said* (...).

3.7.2.3.2. Use of other "linguistic means of security" by non-professional participants

The remaining linguistic means of security revealed in the research material form a class even more numerous than the one discussed above. In the course of analyzing the empirical material, it was possible to identify more than a thousand linguistic means of the type in question within the speech of non-professional participants. All of them can be divided into two subclasses – one, including linguistic means of security related to the obligation to inform about facts (prohibition of their concealment); the other, related to the obligation to tell the truth and prohibition of giving false testimony.

Starting with the first of these, it should be pointed out that the argument from lack of memory showed the highest frequency in the research material, as the communication acts of non-professional participants in which they indicated lack of memory were more than 470, e.g. ***I do not remember*** (...); (...) ***I do not remember exactly****, but it was the beginning of summer;* (...) ***I today cannot remember*** *when it was;* (...) ***I do not remember anymore****;* (...) ***at the moment I do not remember*** (...); *Well, precisely,* ***I do not really remember*** (...); *Your Honor,* ***I do not recall*** (...); ***I completely do not recall****;* (...) ***I still do not recall*** *it. In general,* ***I do not remember*** (...).

Sometimes the argument was combined in the utterance of a non-professional participant with justification, such as: ***I do not remember****, it was all under such stress that I* ***do not quite remember*** (...); (...) *I am nervous,* ***I do not remember*** (...).

Another argument about high attendance was from lack of knowledge. Communication acts in which non-professional participants indicated a lack of knowledge were recorded over 280, e.g. *No,* ***I do not know*** *that;* ***I have no idea*** (...); (...) ***I do not know exactly*** (...); (...) *the reasons* ***are not known to me*** (...).

As with the argument from lack of memory, analysis of the research material revealed examples of non-professional participants justifying their lack of knowledge, such as: (...) *I am not an expert,* ***I do not know*** (...); *I did not witness any incidents, so it is hard for me to say whether he said anything there or not* (...).

Another subclass within linguistic means of security is formed by linguistic means, which are related to the prohibition of giving false testimony. The highest frequency within this subclass was of linguistic means, the use of which makes it impossible, or at least difficult, to impute a lie to the participant of court proceedings. Through their use, the participant communicates that what he or she says is in accordance with his or her knowledge (conviction), or signals that he or she is giving a description of a given state of affairs in accordance with his or her knowledge, but stipulates that this knowledge may not be adequate to reality. In total, more than 120 linguistic means of this type were revealed in the empirical material, e.g. ***From what I remember, as I remember well*** (...); (...) *from what* ***is known to me*** (...); (...) ***to my knowledge*** *there is no claim to the community* (...); (...) *in the presence of,* ***if I am not mistaken*** (...); ***As far as I remember*** (...); (...) *if my* ***memory does not deceive*** *me* (...).

Another subclass is formed by linguistic means of indicating the source of knowledge (more than 70), e.g. *From what my* ***colleague told me****, it* (...); *It was the claimants who* ***told me*** *about it* (...); (...) *because* ***X told me****, this supposed* (...); *During supervision, this person was quite impulsive, aggressive and,* ***from information from the school****, unpredictable* (...); (...) *I did not see the incident directly,* ***I only know from stories***. In the case of the use of this type of linguistic means, if it turned out that the description of a given state of affairs in the participant's utterance was inconsistent with reality, responsibility could not be attributed to the participant due to this inconsistency, unless the lie is the mere information on the acquisition of certain knowledge from the person in question.

During the analysis of the research material, those linguistic means that introduced a subjective element into the utterances of non-professional participants, making it impossible to verify them from the point of view of logical value, e.g. *And according to* ***my assessment*** (...); (...) ***in my opinion****, it was an obvious manipulation of the case;* (...) *he worked the way he wanted,* ***that is*** *what* ***I believe*** (...); ***I believe*** *as a mother that it was not wrong; Your Honor,* ***in my opinion*** (...); ***In my opinion****, it was one big scam on the part of the employer;* ***I****, at least,* ***understood it this way*** (...). This type of linguistic means were used more than sixty times.

Other linguistic means of security were used by non-professional participants when the statement concerned detailed information. When a participant was unable or unwilling to provide precise data, he or she reached for means called for the purpose of the study "more or less", e.g. ***Around****, I am not able to* (...); ***Somewhere around*** (...); (...) ***three to four*** *weeks*. More than twenty such means were recorded in the research material.

To the last subclass, on the other hand, can be assigned those linguistic means used by non-professional participants that signal that a given claim of the participant is the result of an inference process, and as we know, this process can be unreliable, e.g. (...) *that* ***I can infer so***; (...) *well from the context* ***it could be inferred*** *that* (...). Analysis of the research material revealed few (less than 10) such linguistic means.

In addition, examples of communication acts combining means of different types were noted, such as *At the moment* ***I cannot remember****, but* ***I think*** *it was* ***more or less*** (...); (...) ***I do not know, I do not remember, I think*** (...).

It should also be noted that the use of linguistic means of security by non-professional participants was not the reason for the presiding judge's response under the leading-order enforcing function (cf. Section 3.6.3).

Based on an analysis of the empirical material in terms of the use of linguistic means of security by non-professional participants, it can be firmly established that the communication acts of non-professional litigants were very belaying. The use of various linguistic means of security testifies to awareness of this aspect of the procedural role, which involves the duty to tell the truth, including criminal liability for giving false testimony, of which the participants in the proceedings are instructed. In addition, it testifies to competence in the selection of linguistic means to avoid accusations of overstepping the norms applicable in this regard. The use of linguistic tools of security can also be a kind of testifying strategy – to say something in order not to say anything – using in particular arguments of lack of knowledge and lack of memory.[547]

To finalize, it is worth mentioning that the use of linguistic tools of security is part of a style of testimony described by some researchers as "powerless".[548] Some research findings suggest that the use of powerless style may affect witnesses' credibility assessment (reduce credibility), although the issue remains inconclusive.[549]

---

547 A similar testifying strategy is sometimes called "smoke screen strategy", see S. Sønderberg Mortensen, J. Mortensen, *Epistemic Stance...*, op. cit., p. 406.

548 "This style is characterized by the frequent use of words and expressions that convey a lack of forcefulness in speaking. Among the specific features of this style is the abundant use of hedges (prefatory remarks such as 'I think' and 'It seems like'; appended remarks like 'you know'; and modifiers such as 'kinda' and 'sort of'); hesitation forms (words and sounds that carry no substantive meaning but only fill possible speech pauses, such as 'uh,' 'um' and 'well'); polite forms (for example, the use of 'sir' and 'please'); and question-intonation (making a declarative statement with rising intonation so as to convey uncertainty). An additional feature of this style is the frequent use of intensifiers (for example, 'very,' 'definitely' and 'surely') – words that, though they normally increase the force of an assertion, may be so overused that they suggest that the speaker is not to be taken seriously in their absence. These features tended to occur together in the taped testimony, comprising a definite style in the delivery of testimony". See J.M. Conley, W.M. O'Barr, E.A. Lind, *The Power of Language: Presentational Style in the Courtroom*, "Duke Law Journal" 1979, Vol. 27, No. 6, p. 1380.

549 See J.M. Conley, W.M. O'Barr, E.A. Lind, *The Power of Language...*, op. cit.; cf. S. Sønderberg Mortensen, J. Mortensen, *Epistemic Stance...*, op. cit.; J.K. Thompson, *"Powerful/Powerless" Language in Court: A Critical Re-Evaluation of the Duke*

The research results presented in this book do not make it possible to resolve this issue. Indeed, the statements of witnesses would have to be confronted with their assessment by the court. However, there is a lack of adequate comparative material.

3.7.2.4. Ways of creating the "face" of non-professional participants

3.7.2.4.1. Shaping the perception of states of affairs

The function of shaping the perception of a certain state of affairs, which from the point of view of the subject matter of the proceedings or its participants is more or less relevant, can be performed by any utterance referring to this state of affairs. In the course of analyzing the research material, however, attention was paid to the linguistic means used by non-professional participants, which were clearly argumentative in nature and which, in accordance with the designed analytical categories, referred to specific rules drawn from attribution theory. At the same time, it should be noted that considering a given communication act of a non-professional participant to be explicitly argumentative is an interpretive act more prone to subjective judgments than other interpretive acts undertaken in the course of analyzing the research material for the purposes of this study.[550] Therefore, in principle, the quantitative data obtained in this regard[551] will not be exposed. However, in order to reflect the magnitude of the phenomenon in question, it can be pointed out that almost 350 communication acts of non-professional participants were considered as argumentative acts shaping the perception of certain states of affairs through the interpretation of empirical data.

3.7.2.4.2. The state of affairs as a reference point in the argumentative acts of non-professional participants

The state of affairs, which becomes the subject of the non-professional participants' argumentative acts, can be either favorable or unfavorable to them. The qualification in this regard can be made in relativity to the subject of the proceedings or, very generally speaking, the participant's life situation outside the proceedings.

It should also be recalled that according to the designed analytical categories, every state of affairs is beneficial to some *I* or *HE* (*SHE*, *THEY*).

Since the acts aimed at creating the "face" of a given participant are most consistent with the procedural functions of a party or quasi-party to the proceedings, the argumentative acts relating to *I* (party, quasi-party) that were revealed in the research material will be discussed first.

Language and Law Programme, "International Journal of Speech Language and the Law" 2002, Vol. 9, No. 2.

550 This applies not only to communication acts that help shape perceptions of states of affairs, but also to those that can shape perceptions of individuals.

551 If quantitative data is recalled, it will be given approximately.

Basic and at the same time the easiest to interpret is the argument that refers to the state of affairs favorable from the point of view of the subject matter of the proceedings for *I*, e.g. **Claimant:** (...) *on the contrary, it was me who at the board meetings raised several times the issues of more urgent things to be dealt with* (...), which in turn is from the point of view of the proceedings unfavorable to the opposing party. There is, of course, a similar construction of an argument that refers to a state of affairs unfavorable to *I* in relativization to the subject matter of the proceedings, e.g. **Insured:** *I, on the other hand, did not work fifteen years on the railroad, for various reasons I* (...), and which, consequently, is favorable to the opposing party.

A special type of situation, by the way, quite characteristic of court proceedings, is the one in which the state of affairs that is the reference point of the participant's argumentative acts is favorable to him or her because of the subject matter of the proceedings, but unfavorable from the point of view of his or her life situation outside the proceedings,[552] e.g. **Auxiliary prosecutor:** *It is not a month or two of* [harassment]*, it is almost three years, yes* [crying]; **Applicant:** *There was no help* (...) *from the husband.* In both of the examples cited above, non-professional participants presented a certain state of affairs as unfavorable. This state of affairs, however, is unfavorable only "in life", for given the subject matter of the proceedings, it is favorable to both the auxiliary prosecutor and the applicant, and therefore unfavorable from a procedural perspective to the defendant (in penal case) and the participant (in non-contentious civil proceedings), respectively.

Also noted in the research material were the argumentative acts of non-professional participants, which referred to a state of affairs presented as unfavorable to *I*, while irrelevant to the subject matter of the proceedings, e.g. **Participant:** [in the proceedings for the division of joint property] (...) *the applicant, Mr. X, simply did not let me into the apartment, and this is what caused the divorce* (...).

There are, of course, other configurations of states of affairs that are either favorable or unfavorable to individual participants in the proceedings, both in relativization to the subject matter of the proceedings and to the life situation of the participants outside the proceedings. It would be cognitively interesting to discuss the other argumentative acts of non-professional participants that refer to various such configurations, but will not be continued here.

Addressing the issue of the relationship between a certain state of affairs and the procedural or extra-procedural situation of a given participant serves in this study primarily to highlight how differently this relationship can be presented and interpreted. The fact that different states of affairs bear a different relationship to the situation of the participants is, of course, closely related to the contentiousness of court proceedings. At the same time, it should be noted that the analysis of the research material revealed that non-professional participants in the

552 Taking into account, of course, some intersubjective qualification criteria in this regard.

proceedings also refer in their argumentative acts to states of affairs that are irrelevant to the subject matter of the proceedings, but which, for some reason, they nevertheless want to talk about. This fact, on the other hand, makes it possible to note how different interests can stand behind the positions presented in a given court proceedings.

In addition, the analysis of the research material revealed that the relationship between a certain state of affairs and a given participant in the proceedings can be interpreted differently depending on the point of reference – either the subject of the proceedings or the participant's life situation. This is a peculiar feature of court proceedings, and consequently of the trial, and in general is already noticeable at the level of its pattern. Awareness of this fact will be important in further considerations.

3.7.2.4.3. Argumentative acts of non-professional participants – the rules of stability, selectivity, location and controllability

It is assumed in this studies that the possibility of attributing the utterance of a non-professional participant to any of the rules developed in attribution theory determines the argumentative nature of the utterance. Such an argumentative act at least lends itself to shaping the perception of a given state of affairs indicated in the propositional content of the utterance.

Analysis of the research material revealed that non-professional participants use communication acts that address all four rules developed in attribution theory.

Referring to the rule of stability, non-professional participants formulated statements both positively (*I/he/she/they always...*) and negatively (*I/he/she/they never...*), e.g. **Witness:** *I always scratched his hands to defend myself against him*; **Witness:** (...) *he was perpetually off somewhere* (...); **Witness:** *Well, of course he did, he used to come to our house all the time, and with my husband they drank* (...); **Defendant (in misdemeanor proceedings):** (...) *I come to the dogs for 10, 15 minutes, never by me the dog ran away, neither one nor the other*; **Witness:** (...) *no, we never paste the floor*; **Auxiliary prosecutor:** *He was not betrayed, I never betrayed him.*

Non-professional participants also reached for arguments related to the rule of selectivity, such as: **Respondent:** (...) *for XY years, as we have been running the school, this is the first time we have met a person who has entered into cooperation with us, in court, for the first time*; **Claimant:** *This was the first contract that I prepared for author's supervision, because I had no contact with something like this before.*

Argumentative acts relating to the rules of stability and selectivity were relatively easy to recognize and interpret, while searching for and interpreting the statements of non-professional participants based on the rules of location and controllability presented some difficulties, about which more below.

Referring to the rule of location, one can first point to the argumentative acts of non-professional participants, which characterized states of affairs as internal to specific entities. A given state of affairs is internal to a given entity was recognized in the course of analyzing the research material, in particular, on the basis of whether the non-professional participant characterized it as having been caused intentionally (purposely). Argumentative acts of this type included the following statements by non-professional participants, among others: **Witness:** (...) *this lady did not seem to follow the advances charged, that is, she set advances for herself according to her own criteria* (...); **Respondent:** *The justification was that she did not want to take care of her grandmother*; **Witness:** (...) *it was such a malicious act* (...); **Claimant:** (...) *with which she entered the lease in a malicious manner simply*; **Claimant:** *I tried to come out ahead, offered to help.*

It was helpful in recognizing whether a state of affairs was internal to an entity to point out by a non-professional participant that the state of affairs was related to the awareness of a particular entity or its characteristics, e.g. **Respondent:** *No, that is not true, Mr. X knew perfectly well what kind of apartment it was* (...); Witness: (...) *I reported corrections, defects in this foundation, which were due to the inability, in my opinion, of the contractor to perform* (...); **Witness:** *Well he had a cough because he smoked cigarettes.*

The research material also recorded argumentative acts that, for example, referred to both intentionality and consciousness, such as: **Respondent:** (...) *and Mr. XY knew it well, because he assured me of it all the time* (...).

On the other hand, the external causes of certain states of affairs can be organized into two basic classes: the first, which concentrates causes unrelated to the acts or behaviors of specific entities; the second, which is a set of causes related to the acts or behaviors of various entities.

The following statements can be given as examples of argumentative acts taken by non-professional participants and at the same time referring to the causes included in the first class – **Witness:** (...) *well Mr. X was blamed for the fact that the storm came* (...); **Witness:** (...) *I do not see the fault of this gentleman, because what influence did he have on the rainfall* (...) *it was a storm and it caused this damage.*

Among the reasons that make up the second of the above-mentioned classes, we can identify those that are related to the taking of some act by a specific entity: (1) a non-participant of the proceedings, e.g. **Insured:** (...) *and no one wants to accept me, because every manager says that I come under some protection and "you may get sick, you may not work, and we cannot fire you", and no one wants to accept me* (...); (2) being a participant of the proceedings, e.g. **Claimant:** (...) *the agency that miscalculated my benefit is to blame, well.* In addition, it is possible to distinguish such reasons, which are related to the lack of action expected by the participant of some entity, e.g. **Insured:** *I just resent that the municipality did not inform me* (...); **Insured:** *It did not communicate, that is why I have the most resentment against the municipality.*

The empirical material also revealed the argumentative acts of non-professional participants, in which they indicated that the achievement of a certain state of affairs depends on the decision of a certain entity, e.g. **Respondent:** *I am not even* *able to take on additional work to ensure this, because for any additional work I have to have approval* (...).

One can also cite examples of argumentative acts of non-professional participants that relate to causes from both distinguished classes, e.g., **Defendant:** *It was at such times when we drank alcohol together and when she started something to me, there was some kind of argument, but did I come and initiate on my own, there were no such situations.*

Reference should also be made to those acts of argumentation by non-professional participants in the proceedings, which can be interpreted by referring to the rule of controllability. According to this rule, states of affairs can be perceived as either controllable or uncontrollable by a given subject. Analysis of the research material revealed that non-professional participants describe various states of affairs as being controllable by some entity, e.g. **Claimant:** *I personally took care of my mommy with my husband*; **Claimant:** *In the meantime, I sent both reminders and requests* (...); or uncontrollable by some entity, e.g. **Defendant (in misdemeanor proceedings):** *At the last minute it pulled out in front of my car, I only managed to make a steering maneuver and hit this car*; **Defendant (in misdemeanor proceedings):** *I did not see him, that is one thing*. Taking into account two of the rules in question – location and controllability – one might suppose that a state of affairs that is apprehended as internal to some subject is at the same time perceived as controllable and, conversely, that which is described as external to the subject is at the same time uncontrollable by him or her. And indeed, many examples revealed in the research material confirm this regularity, but there are also examples that make us reject it as a general claim.

In the course of the analysis of the empirical material, examples of argumentative acts of non-professional participants that capture a given state of affairs as internal to a specific entity, but uncontrollable, or at least not fully controllable, were identified, e.g. **Witness:** (...) *they could not pay it because they did not know about it* (...); **Witness:** (...) *we were not aware that it could be so important, yes*; **Defendant:** *I did not know that I had an illegal connection made, but that is another issue* (...); **Witness:** *His health did not allow him to do that* [to look for work]; **Witness:** *The grandson is not working due to his health condition.*

At the end of the discussion of the results of the analysis of the argumentative acts of non-professional participants from the point of view of the rules developed in attribution theory, it is necessary to refer to some observations made by researchers regarding the tendency of people's perception of certain states of affairs. It has been noted that people apply the principles of attribution in a biased manner. Firstly, they tend to perceive negative states of affairs related to other people as caused by internal factors (related to a person's characteristics or caused intentionally), while they see the causes of positive states of affairs in external factors – this is the so-called fundamental attribution error.[553] Secondly,

---

553 V.M. McDermott, *Attribution Theory*, op. cit., p. 62; B. Gawronski, *Fundamental Attribution Error*, [in:] *Encyclopedia of Social Psychology*, eds. R.F. Baumeister, K.D. Vohs, Sage Publications 2007, Vol. 1, pp. 367–369.

they perceive positive and negative states of affairs differently in relation to themselves, that is, they are inclined to see the causes of positive states in their own qualities, acts (internal and controllable), while negative states are seen in external factors (external and uncontrollable). This second tendency is called defensive attribution or self-serving bias.[554] An analysis of the research material in terms of whether non-professional participants in the proceedings also manifest the tendencies described above would undoubtedly be cognitively valuable. However, the attempt to make such a comprehensive and systematic (and only such an analysis is methodologically justified in this case) analysis of the argumentative acts of non-professional participants faces significant difficulties.

The analysis of the statements of non-professional participants from the point of view of the tendencies indicated above in the way they perceive (or at least present) certain states of affairs is first made more difficult by the fact that a given state of affairs can be considered both in relation to the subject matter of the proceedings and to the life situation of a particular participant, and can be both favorable and unfavorable to him or her, depending on the relativization made. Further, the analysis is made more difficult by the fact that the argumentative acts of non-professional participants can sometimes be interpreted differently depending on which entity we make relevant to the interpretation. Therefore, with regard to each argumentative act revealed in the research material, such an analysis would require making specific decisions on the subject in question and, moreover, revealing them so that the research procedure is controllable. However, the framework of the study does not allow for such a systematic analysis, and ultimately for the best possible reasoned conclusion in this regard.

However, it is possible to point out some trends in the aspect under discussion. First, it is indeed noticeable that non-professional participants whose argumentative acts refer to *I* refer to defensive attribution.[555] Second, the characteristics of argumentative acts relating to *HE* (*SHE*, *THEY*) are more complicated than described by the so-called fundamental attribution error. This is particularly true for witnesses who (as has been pointed out several times before) may act in a situation of conflicting roles (procedural and social). For this reason, when witnesses testify "in favor" of a particular party, their statements are sometimes characteristic of defensive attribution.

---

554 V.M. McDermott, *Attribution Theory*, op. cit., p. 62; W.K. Campbell, E.A. Krusemark, *Self-Serving Bias*, [in:] *Encyclopedia...*, op. cit., Vol. 2, pp. 845–847.

555 Non-professional participants use a peculiar argument relating to the internal location of the causes of a given state of affairs, the occurrence of which, however, was uncontrollable. This is particularly true of the argument from ignorance.

3.7.2.4.4. *Other argumentative acts related to shaping perceptions of states of affairs*

As already emphasized in the section devoted to research categories related to the issue of creating "faces" of the participants of court proceedings, the four rules developed in attribution theory are treated in this study as convenient (for the researcher) analytical categories that allow identifying certain communication acts of non-professional participants as argumentative acts and characterizing them accordingly. In addition, they allow to indicate how the given argumentative acts are at least suitable for shaping perceptions of certain states of affairs and, consequently, of the participants themselves.

The fact that a certain communication act of a non-professional participant was not, using the rules developed in attribution theory, recognized during the analysis of the research material as an argumentative act, does not mean that it cannot perform such a function. The empirical material also revealed other linguistic means that are suitable for shaping the perception of certain states of affairs, although these acts – clearly argumentative – are of a different nature from those described above.[556]

Of all the communication acts of non-professional participants that were clearly argumentative and undoubtedly suitable for shaping perceptions of certain states of affairs, it is worth noting those that can be organized into classes of more than two elements.

First of all, it is necessary to pay attention to the linguistic means that were suitable for shaping the perception of a certain state of affairs by naming it in a certain way, e.g. **Claimant:** (...) *Mrs. X was disregarded and thrown out* (...); **Claimant:** (...) *after all, this is a mockery and a lie* (...); **Applicant:** *These are all slander and* (...); **Participant:** *My position has always been contrary to the position of these participants* (...), *I believe that this is a farce brought up by XY.* In commenting on the cited examples, it is necessary to point out that the linguistic means used are strongly emotionally charged (negatively). It is worth noting the last example, shaping the perception of the entire proceedings in which the participant takes part.

Another way of arguing used by non-professional participants was to play down the seriousness of some occurrence or, on the contrary, to exaggerate it, e.g. **Witness:** (...) *I do not know if it can be called a "collision", it was just an abrasion of the [car] mirrors*; **Defendant (in misdemeanor proceedings):** *Well, yes, I caused the accident, only here it is hard to say, it was a slight abrasion*; **Witness:** (...) *Mr. X made a huge mistake* (...).

---

556 Some of the linguistic means revealed in the research material may accompany those acts that are classified as argumentative from the point of view of the rules developed in attribution theory.

A type of argumentative act that can be called "objectivization" was also noted in the research material. This act consisted in the non-professional participant presenting information about a given state of affairs as inferred from sentences about other facts, or characterizing a given state of affairs as objectively impossible due to certain circumstances, e.g. **Defendant (in misdemeanor proceedings):** *The car was very damaged, certainly the force of the impact must have been very high*; **Witness:** *Looking at the damage to both cars, it must have been fast*; **Defendant (in misdemeanor proceedings):** *It is impossible for me to hit* (...).

3.7.2.4.5. Shaping the perception of persons

The scale of the phenomenon of non-professional participants shaping perception of persons is similar to that of shaping perception of states of affairs. In the course of the interpretive acts undertaken in the analysis of the research material, almost 320 communication acts of non-professional participants[557] were recognized as acts shaping perception of persons.

All communication acts categorized as acts in question can be divided into classes, taking into account the propositional content of a given utterance. Thus, one can distinguish statements relating to: (1) feelings and emotions; (2) characteristics of a person (knowledge, skills, experience, attitudes, character or value system); (3) someone's condition (health, willingness or awareness); (4) behavioral characteristics. It should be noted here that the statements of this type revealed in the research material referred to both *I* and *HE* (*SHE*, *THEY*).

Re 1. Referring to the communication acts of non-professional participants that appeal to feelings or emotions, it should first be noted that statements of this type do not have to go beyond the normative pattern of the trial in Polish courts. Utterances whose propositional content deals with feelings or emotions may have an expressive function, i.e. express feelings and emotions at the time of speaking, but not necessarily. They can also have a descriptive function, for example, when they report that some specific emotion accompanied the participant at a given moment. The utterances mentioned in the previous sentence, in the case of some varieties of court proceedings, are even necessary from the point of view of court cognition, for example, in some criminal cases or other cases in which issues of harm suffered as a result of some event are considered.[558]

---

557 The quantitative data indicated is given in approximate terms for the same reasons written about in relation to acts that allow to shape the perception of states of affairs.

558 In the course of analyzing the research material, both utterances that have an expressive function and those that can be categorized as descriptive utterances were taken into account (although, of course, resolution in this regard is sometimes difficult – albeit, from the point of view of the purposes of this study, irrelevant). This is because both types of utterances are suitable for shaping perception of persons in court proceedings.

First of all, it is worth looking at the communication acts of non-professional participants, in which they referred to the emotions and feelings of specific participants accompanying some event that is the subject of cognition in a given proceeding or they are the results of that events, e.g. **Witness:** (...) *she was upset, very broken down* (...) *the child was also closed, a little withdrawn* (...); **Claimant:** (...) *I was confused, I did not know what was going on* (...); **Witness:** *Well he was so depressed, so depressed*; **Witness:** *He was suffering and experiencing, because mom was not there*; **Witness:** (...) *she was shaken, it even happened that she cried* (...); **Claimant:** (...) *I was shocked, appalled by such behavior*; **Claimant:** (...) *and so I am still shaken to this day after that situation* (...); **Witness:** (...) *X is very tired of all this* (...).

The analysis of the research material also revealed a special type of utterance that serves a dual function. These are statements by witnesses who describe their feelings or emotions about some state of affairs caused by a particular participant in the proceedings. By taking this type of act, they shape the way they perceive their own person (through the prism of feelings and emotions) and, indirectly, the "face" of that participant in the proceedings who led to that state of affairs, e.g. **Witness:** (...) *well, and I felt somehow uncomfortable, as if* [the respondent] *was about to hit me* (...); **Witness:** *I do not remember anymore, I was more frightened by the screaming and behavior* [of the respondent] (...); **Witness:** *Well for me it was a shock at all, what people* [respondents] *are capable of, well, I cannot comprehend it, they left me with two sick people*; **Witness:** *I am also afraid of Mr. X* [the claimant] (...). In the second place, it is worth looking at those statements of non-professional participants that, while referring to feelings or emotions, give a picture of the relationship between the participants in the proceedings, e.g. **Authority of organizational entity:** (...) *I do not quite trust* [the other party] (...); **Claimant:** *Absolutely not, she did not communicate anything, because I was already enemy number one* [for the respondent] *at the time* (...); **Auxiliary prosecutor:** (...) *I feared for my life and the life of the child, yes*; **Witness:** (...) *and she was terribly afraid of him* [the claimant], *she* [the respondent] *was all bruised*; **Claimant:** *I have to say that I feel very cheated, because Mrs. X* [the respondent] *said that she wanted to buy this property* (...).

The examples cited above represent only a small sample of the non-professional participants' communication acts, which provide insight into the world of relations between the participants in a given proceeding. The possibility of learning about the relations linking the participants of the proceedings on the basis of the communication acts they undertake opens up a wide field of research, which, due to the framework of the study, cannot be exhaustively explored. Nevertheless, certain issues in this field should be highlighted.

All of the above-mentioned examples of statements refer to negative feelings and emotions.[559] Consequently, they reveal negative relationships between the

559 Other statements of the type in question that were revealed in the research material also mainly refer to negative feelings and emotions.

participants of the proceedings. This is, of course, not a surprising conclusion, given that interpersonal conflict is often at the root of court proceedings. Non-professional participants sometimes speak of feeling cheated by another participant in the proceedings, with this feeling accompanying the various states of affairs that are the subject of cognition in a variety of proceedings. The cited examples also indicate that attendance at the court session can sometimes be stressful for the participants precisely because of meeting that participant(s) with whom they have a conflictual relationship.

Analysis of the research material in terms of utterances by non-professional participants referring to emotions and feelings also revealed such utterances in which they referred to the emotions associated with attending a court session, e.g. **Authority of organizational entity:** *Well, I do not hide it, it is stressful, it is* [to be in court]; **Witness:** *Because I am nervous, sorry*; **Claimant:** (...) *I am nervous, I do not remember* (...); **Claimant:** (...) *at that time Mr. X* [witness] *was with me, now he is stressed, he cannot testify or something* (...). As a commentary on this type of communication acts, two recent examples are worth noting. The first is also an example of the participant's use of linguistic means of security, and the information about nervousness is a justification for lack of knowledge. The second, on the other hand, illustrates in a particularly clear way the situation when a party tries to shape the "face" of a witness whose testimony is inconsistent with the expectations.

The communication acts in which non-professional participants appeal to feelings and emotions are, of course, many more in the research material, but it is impossible to cite them all here.

Re 2. A separate class is also formed by the communication acts of non-professional participants revealed in the research material, in which they referred to the characteristics of the various persons. Within this class, one can particularly distinguish statements that refer to knowledge and skills or lack thereof, e.g. **Witness:** *She was a valued employee*; **Witness:** (...) *well he was simply an expert at his job* (...); **Witness:** (...) *in my opinion, I think I can say that, it was performed by people who were completely clueless about it* (...); **Witness:** (...) *I believe that he did not know* (...).

In addition, examples of communication acts that referred to a person's experience or lack thereof were revealed, such as: **Insured:** *I just wanted to add that my sister, when she hired me as an economist, made this decision because I had the right education, I graduated with a degree in economics, with a master's degree in engineering, I had many years of experience* (...), *I had experience in running my company* (...); **Claimant:** (...) *I did not have any experience with collisions, because this was my first collision in my life.*

Another subclass is formed by communication acts that refer to certain attitudes or value system, such as: **Respondent:** *I will say frankly, maybe I am so not quite of today, then if I made a decision and it was the result of my mistake, and I am responsible for that mistake, then I never shirk my responsibility and accept it* (...); **Claimant:** (...) *because I want to show that we approached the gas installation reviews honestly and professionally.*

The above types of utterances, of course, do not exhaust the entire diverse spectrum of communication acts of non-professional participants, which relate to the characteristics of specific entities. Within the framework of the subclass "other" can be specifically included statements, e.g. **Witness:** (...) *X is shy* (...) *he hides more behind his mother*; **Witness:** (...) *she is thorough, orderly, she had everything paid for, sorted* (...); **Insured:** (...) *the CEO was a mess, she abused alcohol* (...).

Re 3. Another of the distinguished classes is formed by the statements of non-professional participants relating to the state in which a particular person is. Within this class, three types of communication acts were distinguished. First are statements relating to the state of health of a specific person, e.g. **Witness:** *Well, as of today, he is actually a person dependent on third parties*; **Insured:** *Yes, just please speak louder, because I cannot hear, even with the hearing aid I can hear poorly.* Second are communication acts that refer to awareness of the existence of a certain state of affairs or the lack thereof, e.g. **Claimant:** (...) *and the truth is completely different and Mrs. X knows it very well, that it was a little different* (...); **Witness:** (...) *we were not aware that it could be so important, yes.* Whereas in the third – optative utterances, such as: **Claimant:** (...) *I would be very interested in regulating this issue today* (...).

Ad 4. The last class is formed by statements of non-professional participants, which contain characteristics of the behavior of a certain person or persons, e.g. **Witness:** (...) *it was all sick* (...), *he did harm to the child, I will never forgive him for that*; **Witness:** (...) *it was this gentleman who forbade me to park, but in a very aggressive, indecent way* (...); **Defendant (in misdemeanor proceedings):** (...) *moreover, she was very fanciful when she was testifying* (...).

To conclude the discussion of issues related to the formation of perception of persons, it can be added that some of the utterances of non-professional participants recorded in the research material were suitable for both the formation of perception of persons and states of affairs, such as: **Insured:** *I did not do it because I do not have the strength, I do not have the health* (...).

3.7.2.4.6. "Face" of the participants of court proceedings – further characterization of the phenomenon

The communication acts of non-professional participants of court proceedings, cited and discussed earlier, made it possible to show how the formation of "face" in court proceedings is implemented as part of the actual communication processes in the courtroom.

The phenomenon of shaping the "face" of (and by) the participants of court proceedings is considered in the study to be universal for court proceedings in general, and for trial in particular.

This study assumes, following Erving Goffman, that "face" is a certain type of self-image, while generally flattering. Taking into account the communication acts of non-professional participants revealed in the research material, it can be seen that not every image of the participant formed by it would be considered flattering from the point of view of certain intersubjective criteria, and perhaps even by the participant himself or herself.[560] This is closely related to the fact that a given state of affairs regarding a particular participant can be perceived as favorable and unfavorable at the same time, depending on whether the court proceedings or the participant's life situation is taken as a reference point. To put it another way – it is peculiar to communication in the context of court proceedings that participants sometimes expose those states of affairs (behaviors, characteristics, etc.) that are favorable to them from the point of view of the subject matter of the proceedings, and which they will not necessarily be willing to expose in other situations.

Another issue that should be noted concerns the violation of the "face" of the participants of the proceedings and its defense.

Starting with the issue of acts that violate the "face" of the participants of the proceedings, it should be pointed out that the analysis of the research material revealed many cases of such communication acts of non-professional participants. Among them, three basic types can be distinguished. The first type is formed by such utterances in which a non-professional participant refers only to another participant, and his or her communication act can be interpreted as violating "face", e.g. **Respondent:** (...) *wife* [the claimant] *tends not to pay* (...); **Witness:** (...) [the claimant] *is not very expert in these matters*; **Participant:** (...) *they took mom into their confidence, they* [the applicants] *just wanted mom to transfer her shares, nothing more.*

The second type is such utterances by non-professional participants, in which they both refer to other participants, violating their "face", and shape their own, such as: **Respondent:** (...) *Ms. X* [the claimant] *held my things, I suffered huge losses, I lost a lot of clients*; **Participant:** *We just do not agree, we built this house from the very beginning, together with my dad, they* [the applicants] *did not even take interest in the house* (...).

The third type, on the other hand, is formed by those acts that violate the "face", which are a reaction to a previous violation of the "face" of another participant, such as: **Respondent:** (...) *the witness swore here a moment ago that he would tell the truth, and now he is lying* (...), *but he is lying, clearly lying!*

In addition, it should be noted that the communication acts of non-professional participants, which were identified in the research material as violating the "face" of other participants, sometimes constitute typical examples of depreciating acts.[561]

560 This is especially true of those communication acts by non-professional participants in which they portray themselves as a victim of someone else's acts, usually another participant of the proceedings, such as: **Claimant:** *I believe that I have been cheated*; **Claimant:** *I have to say that I feel very cheated, because Ms. X* [respondent] *said that* (...).

561 On basic types of depreciating acts, M. Majewska, *Akty deprecjonujące siebie i innych. Studium pragmalingwistyczne [Acts of deprecation of self and others. A pragmalinguistic study]*, Kraków 2005. In the author's conception, "the property of deprecatory acts is that they always constitute an attack on the recipient's face"

The following utterance taken from the research material can be used as an exemplification of a typical act of vertical depreciation: **Witness:** (...) *because a normal person would not write such things* (...).[562] On the other hand, to illustrate the use of horizontal depreciation acts, the following utterance revealed in the empirical material can be cited: **Witness:** (...) *but with her earnings, I do not know what she* [the participant] *contributed.* Analysis of the research material revealed that non-professional participants also use defensive acts related to violations of their "face" such as: **Applicant:** *Your Honor, this is also to show my attitude towards the other person, because X* [the participant] *here portrays me as a lady's boxer, a man who at every step...broken ribs and everything the worst, well I would also like to build up myself in some way in the eyes of the High Court, hence here I mentioned the care also of this aunt, who is a stranger to me, Your Honor.*

It is worth highlighting in this context the fact that defensive acts related to violations of "face" are also performed by witnesses, and in relation to elements of their image that can be considered irrelevant to the court proceedings, e.g. **Witness:** (...) *and he says "I know who did it, I know who did it", he did not even apologize, and to talk such insults* (...). *As I do not feel guilty, I have never been punished, I have never done such things, please Your Honor*; **Witness:** *Your Honor, I, before I start to testify, I would like to clarify one thing, because I received a letter from my sister, in response to how she found out that I would be witnessing Mr. XY, she also accused me that I have an alcoholic husband, a drug addict son* (...), *so I asked my son to bring a certificate* (...) *and I do not have an alcoholic husband so much, because everyone drinks* (...).[563]

It has already been pointed out in these considerations that the communication acts of non-professional participants that shape the perception of states of affairs and persons, especially those that appeal to feelings and emotions, allow at least to some extent to look into the world of relations between the participants of the proceedings. In addition, there are such communication acts that signal a conflict of roles.

First of all, it should be pointed out that all communication acts of the parties and quasi-parties to the proceedings that can shape the perception of persons or states of affairs, which are formulated in the framework of testimony and are an

---

(M. Majewska, *Akty deprecjonujące...*, op. cit., p. 50), while deprecation can occur on two planes – vertical and horizontal. Vertical deprecation serves to place the recipient in a position of inferiority to the sender, while horizontal deprecation expresses the dismissal, the distancing of the sender from the recipient (M. Majewska, *Akty deprecjonujące...*, op. cit., pp. 59–61).

562 This, by the way, is an example of the type of deprecatory act that involves excluding a person from the class of "normal people" (M. Majewska, *Akty deprecjonujące...*, op. cit., p. 62 et seq.), in the cited example – the defendant (in penal case).

563 Such an act may suggest of a strong need to defend one's "face" even when a particular image does not serve some pragmatic purpose.

example of expressive, evaluative and sometimes optative utterances, are a manifestation of the conflict between the procedural and interactional roles. In addition, they are an example of resolving such a conflict (not necessarily fully consciously) in favor of the procedural role.[564]

In the second place, however, it is worth noting the examples of the communication acts of non-professional participants that the analysis of the research material revealed, which in turn signal a conflict of procedural and social roles. Two statements by witnesses will be cited to illustrate the issue: **Witness:** *No, please, Your Honor, I cannot refuse to testify, looking at the harm he* [the respondent] *suffered from the claimant* (...); **Witness:** *I thought that they would share this apartment or money, or in some way it would be, it turned out that when I read that the value of Mr. X's* [applicant's] *work is XY percent and my sister's* [participant's] is *YX percent* (...). *I am ashamed for my sister, for doing this, because they are due equally.*

In the first case, the witness had already revealed her attitude toward the claimant, undoubtedly going beyond both her designated procedural and interactional role even before she began testifying. In the second case, the witness already during her testimony expressed her attitude towards the participant and her attitude in the proceedings, as well as her approval of a certain way of settling the case, clearly going beyond the procedural role. In both cases, the conflict of roles was resolved in favor of the social role.

3.7.2.4.7. Use of systemic linguistic means of persuasion by non-professional participants

The last aspect of the phenomenon of creating the "face" of (and by) non-professional participants of the proceedings is special, as it concerns acts of a metalinguistic nature. The use of means of persuasion by the non-professional participants, which will be discussed below, serves to strengthen the effectiveness of their communication acts and, consequently, the proposed perception of certain states of affairs or persons.

The analysis of the empirical material based on the analytical categories developed for this purpose (see Section 3.5) revealed that non-professional participants most often used the following systemic means of persuasion:[565] (1) the observer effect (about 120 cases); (2) direct appeal to the sender's sincerity (97 cases); (3) the use of typical persuasive operators (96 cases).

---

564 Since many such examples have been cited in previous sections, they will not be cited again here.

565 All examples of the use of systemic means of persuasion were about 440 in the research material. This number is given as an approximation, due to the fact that the recognition of some means of persuasion was sometimes problematic, and this mainly concerned thematization and the observer effect.

Re 1. Considering the functional aspect of main complex procedural acts occurring at the trial, should not be surprising that non-professional participants most often used those means of persuasion, which are referred to as the "observer effect".[566] Of the various linguistic means that make up this means of persuasion, non-professional participants were most likely to use quotation. They cited both their own words and those of others, including other participants of the proceedings, and even excerpts from dialogues, such as: **Witness:** (...) *said: "What is going on, first you tell me to help you, and now I have some blockades put up"* (...); **Witness:** *And some lady in jumped out to us and shouted: "Girls, do you remember the registration* [number] *?". I say only XYZ, and she says: "Then write down further quickly", because she remembered* (...).

Examples of the use of linguistic means other than quotation related to the observer effect were also noted, such as: **Witness:** *Suddenly I was hit* (...); **Witness:** *Well it was a moment, I pulled out, well it was a moment* (...), *I pulled back* (...); **Witness:** (...) *people came suddenly, they jumped from behind the bushes somewhere*; **Witness:** (...) *we ran up to see what happened* (...) *and suddenly we started calling an ambulance.*

Re 2. The second most common means of persuasion used in the research material was direct reference to the sender's sincerity, e.g. **Witness:** *To tell you the truth, I found out at the last minute* (...); **Claimant:** *Please, Your Honor, maybe I will tell it like I know what the truth was* (...); **Witness:** *I do not hide the fact that at that time* (...); **Participant:** *I will say frankly that I never received a salary from him* (...). Using this type of persuasion, non-professional participants also often reinforced the linguistic means of security, such as: **Witness:** *I have no idea, I honestly do not know*; **Witness:** *I really do not remember, it was so long ago* (...); **Witness:** (...) *but I honestly do not remember well, I am not young* (...).

Re 3. In contrast, the third most common means of persuasion used by non-professional participants was the use of typical persuasive operators. The use of the operator "of course" was definitely predominant in the research material, e.g. **Claimant:** (...) *of course, it was two identical copies* (...); **Witness:** *Of course, they were very often not held* (...); **Defendant (in misdemeanor proceedings):** *Of course, I noticed* (...). Other utterances of this type were formulated using other persuasive operators, mainly the "after all", e.g. **Witness:** (...) *yes, after all, it is normal.*

The following means of persuasion were further used by non-professional participants: (1) reinforcing acts of certainty and exclusion (32 cases), e.g. **Insured:** (...) *I am one hundred percent convinced that* (...); **Witness:** *No, no, absolutely!*; **Claimant:** (...) *I am one hundred percent sure that he overheard* (...); **Witness:** *I have one hundred percent knowledge!*; (2) the use of operators that introduce the

566 The observer effect applies to statements describing specific events and, depending on the linguistic means chosen, involves appealing to the recipient's imagination or increasing the vividness of the message, implying that it is credible, A. Awdiejew, *Systemowe środki...*, op. cit., p. 75.

information in question as routine, repetitive (27 cases), e.g. **Witness:** *It was just like a regular meeting, the way we always met* (...); **Witness:** *Every time we met at the construction site* (...); **Witness:** *I was walking my dog as usual* (...); (3) the use of operators that introduce a piece of information as unique (22 cases), e.g. **Witness:** (...) *I saw a car driving strangely slowly* (...); **Witness:** *Which already at that time seemed suspicious to me, not very normal.*

Taking into account all the means of persuasion used by non-professional participants and revealed in the research material, the following were used least often: (1) thematization of a given piece of information, i.e. moving it to the level of assumed information (less than 20), e.g. **Claimant:** (...) *in my opinion, already the fact that they are spreading information that* is *lying, untrue* (...) *is a violation of the good opinion of me* (...); (2) operators suggesting verification of a given piece of information (17 cases), e.g. **Claimant:** (...) *in the course of all court cases, it came out that Mrs. X* (...); (3) operators referring to general knowledge or the recipient's knowledge (11 cases), e.g. **Witness:** (...) *everyone knew that this dog was from there, no secret*; **Claimant:** (...) *everyone already knew about it* (...); **Witness:** (...) *and we all know that the garage door is set back* (...).

The means of persuasion discussed, which serve to block verification of the truth of statements or the accuracy of assessments, do not have "causal power" in the meaning that they unavoidable lead to a blocking effect. This is an obvious statement and applies to the effectiveness of any means of persuasion. However, in the case of a communication process involving common conversation, in which the principles of cooperation are observed, a recipient who does not want to agree with the sender's proposed content should use communication metastrategy to justify its non-acceptance.[567] In the communication occurrences analyzed for the purpose of the study, in which a non-professional participant in the communication process with the court used such means of persuasion, metacommunication acts were not undertaken. This is, of course, related to the way in which the procedural role of the court and the basic communication occurrences carried out at the trial were formed. According to procedural norms, the statement of a participant of the proceedings that is part of the evidence will be subject to verification by the court anyway.

The systemic means of persuasion revealed in the research material and described here do not, of course, exhaust of all the means with a persuasive function that non-professional participants use. It is impossible to discuss them here. However, it is worth noting the persuasiveness of the message, which is related to its emotional character.[568] Indeed, it is not difficult to see that some of the examples of

---

567 For example, by stating: "I do not know anything about it", A. Awdiejew, *Gramatyka interakcji...*, op. cit., p. 143.

568 A. Awdiejew, *Systemowe środki...*, op. cit., p. 78, E. Laskowska, *Emotywizacja jako środek perswazji [Emotivation as a means of persuasion]*, [in:] *Manipulacja w języku...*, op. cit., p. 81 et seq.

non-professional participants' statements cited in this book are characterized by a significant degree of emotivization. This is primarily related to the use of emotionally charged vocabulary, which in the utterances of non-professional participants often appeared on the occasion of describing feelings and emotions accompanying certain states of affairs. In addition, attention should be paid to what goes beyond linguistic communication. In fact, observation of the course of the trial showed that the communication acts of non-professional participants are accompanied by symptoms of certain emotional states, such as crying and a specific intonation of the voice (most often a so-called raised voice).

3.7.2.4.8. Creating the "face" of the non-professional participants – reactions of the presiding judge

The last issue of creating the "face" of (and by) non-professional participants in the proceedings concerns the presiding judge's reaction to: (1) acts that shape perception of states of affairs; (2) acts that shape perception of persons; (3) use of persuasive means. With regard to the first point, it should be pointed out that only four cases of the presiding judge's reaction to acts of this type were recorded in the research material, such as:

Defendant (in misdemeanor proceedings): *I still wanted to say that I drive as a professional driver and I do maybe Y thousand, maybe a little more kilometers a year, and it has never yet happened in my life that I have been fined for a seatbelt, that is, that I had an unfastened seatbelt.*

P: *And what does that prove?*

In the case of the communication acts included in the second point, the analysis of the research material revealed five examples of presiding judge's reactions. Let the following dialogue serve as an exemplification:

Witness: *The police officer examined us in the presence of Ms. X and we did not even hear a word of apology (...), and I have such a grudge against Ms. X* [the defendant].

P: *Okay, but that is off the subject (...).*

On the other hand, with regard to the third point, it should be pointed out that the systemic means of persuasion used by non-professional participants revealed in the research material caused a response from the presiding judge only three times, e.g.:

Claimant: *I, Your Honor, if you do not mind, would like to submit, however, photocopies of those documents that were sent to me on e-mail by those persons deceived (...).* [act of thematization]

P: *No, this I will not accept, ma'am, no, this is not the process of other people defrauded, about the fact that you are promoting such a thesis, the court knows,*

> *this is the information presented, while whether there will be fraud here or not, it remains to be seen what will come out of all this.*

The fact that the examples revealed in the research material of the presiding judge's reaction to the acts of non-professional participants that shape the "face" are so few, shows that presiding judges give non-professional participants considerable freedom in this regard.

* * *

A trial in Polish courts is a communication occurrence of considerable difficulty for non-professional participants of court proceedings. First of all, due to unfamiliarity with the characteristic elements of its formation, and in connection with the importance that the participants in the proceedings attribute to the case being heard.

Taking into account the above two parameters, an attempt was made on the basis of the analysis of the research material to answer the question: How do non-professional participants of court proceedings find themselves in a court proceedings as a communication occurrence?

First, the issue of the use of legal and juridical terminology by non-professional participants was analyzed. All the legal and juridical terms used by non-professional participants revealed in the research material have been sorted out and included in Appendix 2. In this regard, it should be pointed out that the analysis of the research material revealed both examples of court sessions scheduled for the trial, during which non-professional participants did not use legal and juridical terms at all, and those where only one non-professional participant used more than twenty of them.

The use of legal and juridical terminology by non-professional participants, as in the case of the presiding judge, was subjected to a contextual analysis taking into account the situational and communication context. The analysis taking into account the situational context of the non-professional participant's use of legal and juridical terms showed that the terminological resource revealed was terms related to the subject of cognition in a given proceeding, the non-professional participant's social roles, including occupational roles, and life experience, including the experience of participating in court proceedings.

Moreover, it should be noted that non-professional participants very rarely (only 3 cases) reported that they did not know what legal term or juridical term would adequately express a given thought. Clear examples of non-professional participants in the proceedings replacing legal terms with lexical means outside this terminology were also revealed (58 cases). Notably, these expressions were communicatively effective (in one case, the presiding judge made sure he understood correctly). Moreover, no case of replacing an adequate term with a term of a non-terminological nature met with a presiding judge's response (either blocking further speech or admonition).

Undoubtedly, one of the most important conclusions that can be drawn from the analysis of the research material concerns the communicative effectiveness of procedural acts performed in a "non-juridical" manner. It should be recalled that all (a total of 41) disclosed procedural acts performed in a "non-juridical" manner (i.e., without adequate legal and juridical terms, without using typical forms) were communicatively effective.

Taking into account the results of the analysis of the research material on the substitution of legal and juridical terms by non-terminological vocabulary by non-professional participants and the performance of procedural acts in a "non-juridical" manner, as well as taking into account the features of the trial, it should be concluded that the use of legal and juridical terms by non-professional participants is not a prerequisite for effective communication in the courtroom. At the same time, it should be clearly emphasized that the above statement refers to the use of relevant legal and juridical terms, and it should not be concluded from it that the use of any linguistic means will provide non-professional participants of court proceedings with communicative effectiveness during the court proceedings. Firstly, the standard interpretation of a non-professional participant's utterance and the context of that utterance must lead to the recognition in it of a procedural act of a certain type. Secondly, the use of such linguistic means, which cause a loss of precision in the utterance, can lead to an inadequate reproduction of its content, and thus the content of a specific procedural act. Both of the above-mentioned situations can also lead to a disruption of the communication process at the trial when it is necessary to determine the meaning of a particular act or its content. It is worth recalling here that the analysis of the research material revealed that presiding judges give non-professional participants considerable freedom in the vocabulary they use (only in 6 cases it caused the presiding judge's reaction, cf. Section 3.6.3).

The analysis of the research material also took into account the activity of non-professional participants in initiating procedural acts, controlling the minutes and asking questions about legal issues (including those related to court proceedings) and the course of the proceedings.

With regard to the first issue, it should be noted that forty cases of non-professional participants initiating procedural acts were recorded in the research material, most of which (30) were done in a "non-juridical" manner. In the remaining ten cases, non-professional participants used verbal forms similar to the standard forms of individual procedural acts.

On the other hand, the activity of non-professional participants related to the control of the written minutes turned out to be low. Only three cases of requesting that a specific statement be recorded in the research material were disclosed. In contrast, there was not a single case of a non-professional participant requesting the reading of a specific section of the minutes. The reason for the lack of activity in the latter aspect can, of course, be attributed to the prevailing practice of dictating the participants' statements into the minutes, which at the same time allows them to read the minutes. The highest frequency (19 cases) was shown by the acts of non-professional participants related to the control of the written minutes, which consisted of correcting statements while dictating them into the minutes. The reasons for the reactions in these cases were factual and linguistic errors, as well as a lack of precision in reproducing the content of the non-professional participant's statements transposed into the minutes. All of the examples, although few in number, testify to the ongoing control of the activities of producing written minutes by non-professional participants at the trial.

Another issue that was analyzed in the research material was whether non-professional participants ask the presiding judge questions about legal issues and the conduct of the proceedings. In the case of questions on legal issues, including the legal situation of participants related to participation in the proceedings, analysis of the research material revealed 47 examples of such questions being posed. In contrast, the number of questions on the course of the proceedings was already much lower, as analysis of the research material revealed only eight questions of this type. The reasons for the low activity of non-professional participants in this aspect can be attributed in particular to the presiding judge's considerable activity in informing about the procedural acts undertaken (see the results of the analysis of the research material in this aspect, Section 3.6.2.4.1). In addition, it should be noted that in only two cases did the presiding judge refuse to answer a non-professional participant's question on a legal issue. In both cases the legal issue presented was not related to the subject matter of the case in question. In one case, the presiding judge refused to answer a question about the course of the proceedings, because it was posed at the time scheduled for a specific procedural act.

The empirical material was also analyzed from the point of view of the participation of non-professional participants in those parts of complex procedural acts that require special self-reliance. Asking questions of examined persons and formulating free speech during examination are considered such in the study.

The analysis of the research material in terms of how non-professional participants formulate questions during the examination revealed a real problem with the implementation of this element of the trial. Among the 88 communication occurrences analyzed in this regard, 74 were recorded with various mistakes made by non-professional participants. These consisted primarily of formulating a statement (an utterance descriptive in nature) or comment instead of a question, posing questions that were suggestive or beyond the scope of the subject matter of both the examination and the entire proceedings, failing to adapt questions to the procedural functions of the examined person, referring to and discussing the content of testimony, and duplicating questions. The reasons for this can be attributed to unfamiliarity with the way the pattern of the trial is shaped in this aspect, or the lack of sufficient communication competence of the non-professional participants in terms of the correct formulation of questions. However, at least in some of the cases revealed in the research material, one can see manifestations of a more or less conscious "procedural game" in the way non-professional participants act. Indeed, it cannot be ruled out that a given participant, in formulating a comment or description of a situation, tried to use the moment for asking questions to shape his or her own position in the proceedings. However, such acts were blocked by presiding judges, and if they were intended to be a manifestation of some kind of procedural strategy, then, at least in the research material, this strategy proved rather ineffective.

The errors that occurred in the implementation of the examination stage designed to ask questions had a significant impact on the interaction at the trial, forcing the presiding judge to implement a communication metastrategy aimed in particular at blocking the further act of the non-professional participant. Sometimes, they also significantly involved the presiding judge in helping to implement this element of the trial.

Free speech formulated during the examination also sometimes caused problems for non-professional participants (15 cases), although much more often they had no problem with its implementation[569] (106 cases). Most often (11 times) they informed the presiding judge of these problems themselves.

The next issues that were analyzed were closely related to the performance of procedural functions assigned to specific procedural roles. First of all, the communication acts of non-professional participants were analyzed in terms of the use of so-called "linguistic means of security", i.e. linguistic means, the use of which allows to avoid the accusation of speaking untruth, concealing the truth or the accusation of lying. Analysis of the research material showed that non-professional participants very often use the linguistic means of security. More than 330 cases of use of epistemic modalities (acts of supposition and doubt) and more than a thousand other linguistic means of security forming a rather diverse class were recorded. The use of such linguistic means by non-professional participants testifies, first of all, to their awareness of the validity of legal norms, which command the telling of the truth and prohibit its concealment; the participants in the proceedings are, moreover, instructed about these norms.

Secondly, the acts of non-professional participants that serve to create the "face" of participants of the proceedings were analyzed. The analysis of the research material revealed the linguistic acts of non-professional participants that can influence the perception of the participants in the proceedings (a total of about 670). These acts were attributed a distinctly argumentative character, with the shaping of the perception of specific participants taking place in two ways. First, by a specific way of presenting a given state of affairs, in relation to which the participant in the proceedings has some kind of relationship – this way could be called indirect. Second, by direct appeal to a given person (to his or her characteristics, value system or condition) – this way of acting could in turn be called direct.

The analysis of the argumentative acts of the two types indicated above made it possible to reveal various conflicts occurring against the background of the roles played by individual participants – both procedural and interactional roles.

569 However, it should be remembered that sometimes the free speech was reduced to a brief description of the subject matter of the proceedings or the nature of the relationship between the examined person and the parties or quasi-parties to the proceedings.

In addition, it made it possible to see certain interpersonal relationships, especially those of a conflictual nature. The research material recorded linguistic acts of non-professional participants that could be classified as violating the "face" of the participant.

Analysis of the empirical material also revealed about 440 examples of non-professional participants' use of systemic means of persuasion. Those means that non-professional participants reached for most often included the so-called observer effect, direct appeal to the sender's sincerity, and the use of typical persuasive operators (e.g., "after all").

The use of linguistic means related to the creation of "face" of (and by) non-professional participants in the proceedings shows that non-professional participants actively create their own position in the proceedings. They reached for argumentative and persuasive linguistic means adequate for this. Moreover, the analysis of the empirical material showed that non-professional participants had considerable freedom in the use of the means of the type in question. A total of only twelve cases were recorded of presiding judges' reactions to acts shaping perception of events, persons and persuasive acts. These reactions consisted of both blocking further acts of the non-professional participant (e.g., continuing to speak) and admonition (e.g., that the statement goes beyond the scope of the subject matter of the case).

Summary

The trial is an example of a normatively (legally) determined structure. It is the legislator who decides on the existence of a trial, determining its constitutive features, including the initiating moment. The legislator also decides on the formation of its structure, on the individual procedural acts undertaken within its framework, as well as on the competences and duties of the participants. Thus, on the basis of the legal norms, it is possible to reconstruct the normative pattern of the trial in Polish courts. Its characteristics in each case depend on the content of the legal norms that shape it at a given moment. Depending on the decision of the legislator, the normative pattern of the trial in diachronic terms can be characterized by considerable constancy or variability. It should be emphasized, however, that despite the changes in procedural acts, the basic elements of the formation of the trial, or what could be called the essence of the trial, remain relatively constant. Among the relatively constant elements of the trial in Polish courts and relevant to the communication process that takes place within it, we can primarily include: (1) the basic procedural functions of the various participants of the proceedings (this mainly refers to the court, the presiding judge, the parties and their representatives, and personal sources of evidence), sometimes emphasized in a symbolic way; (2) the arrangement of the interactional roles of the participants of court proceedings; (3) the presiding judge's leading function at the court session scheduled for the trial; (4) the blocking at the level of the normative pattern of the trial of direct two-way communication without the participation of the presiding judge; (5) the basic structure of dominance – the superior position of the court to other participants of proceedings and the equal position of the parties to each other; (6) the functional characteristics of the various communication occurrences.

However, the trial is not a closed structure, and not only in the sense that it is subject to change at the will of the legislator, but also in the sense that the pattern of the trial is shaped by the practice. In this regard, it should be noted that the implementation of the normative pattern, insofar as it determines the structure of individual acts and communication occurrences, is not sufficient to form a coherent interaction. The space between individual procedural acts or between the elements of these acts that are clearly defined at the level of the normative pattern must, in the course of realizing the actual process of communication, be filled with such communication acts that make this process coherent. Undertaking such acts is particularly within the limits of the presiding judge's leading function, while the choice of linguistic means and the way they are used is shaped by the practice.

The analysis of the research material also made it possible to detect other communication acts, which are determined by the practice and which no longer directly serve to make the communication process more coherent, but are driven by other goals. Above all, such acts include: (1) dictating the content of the minutes by the presiding judge; (2) supplementing the structure of the preliminary acts of making inheritance assurances with questions that go beyond the content of this evidentiary act; (3) using intertextual references – to the lawsuit at the preliminary stage of the civil trial and in the course of making inheritance assurances (to the assurances made earlier by another participant); (4) clearly structurally distinguishing the so-called "informational examination", in particular by using an initiating formula; (5) starting the examination of a party with the reading of the minutes made during the so-called informational examination.

The trial is not a closed structure also for the reason that certain features of the trial related to the way of formation of the normative pattern of the trial determine certain phenomena occurring in the communication process at the trial or features of its participants. The relationship that arises between a certain feature of the trial and the phenomenon or feature it determines can be either necessary, conditional or probabilistic. One feature of the trial that remains a strong determinant of the actual communication processes at the trial is the diversity of participants. The way in which a trial (as well as court proceedings in general) is shaped on the principle of diversity of participants determines, in particular, that the participants of proceedings have different communication competence, including different competence in the genre pattern of the trial.

The above statement became the starting point for the development of research questions and analytical categories. It was assumed that the lowest level of competence in the genre pattern of a trial is possessed by non-professional participants of court proceedings, while the highest level is possessed by the judge (in particular the presiding judge). Due to the above relationship, the implementation of the trial pattern may cause difficulties for non-professional participants. The presiding judge, at least to some extent, can counteract these difficulties.

In the discussion of communication in the courtroom, two scopes of difficulty in particular are highlighted – the use of legal and juridical terminology and the formalization of the communication process (see Introduction). And the following discussion will be limited to these two scopes.

Analysis of the research material in terms of the use of legal and juridical terminology in communication acts addressed to non-professional participants revealed many examples of such terms (see Appendix 1). Without a doubt, however, it cannot be said that the trial in Polish courts is full of legal and juridical terminology. This is evidenced by the fact that in the course of the multifaceted analysis of the research material, it was easily possible to note all communication acts addressed to non-professional participants that contain legal or juridical terms. In this regard, it should be noted that the primary activity of the common court at the trial is to perform cognitive acts aimed at learning facts. If the subject of cognition in a given proceeding is not legal acts or other subjects (in the broad sense) clearly defined by the law, communication about the subject of cognition can take place without using any legal or juridical terms. In this way, it was possible to explain the relatively small number of legal terms revealed in the analyzed court sessions set in commercial proceedings, in which the subject of cognition was primarily psychophysical acts, rather than conventional acts, including legal acts.

Therefore, it is worth considering whether it would be possible and reasonable to eliminate or at least reduce as much as possible the use of legal and juridical terms in communication involving non-professional participants – either by not using the relevant terms, or by replacing them with words and expressions taken from outside this terminology. The realization of the first postulate is impossible, since the use of relevant legal terms is sometimes a prerequisite for the implementation of procedural norms (for example, regarding the announcement of the judgment). The realization of the postulate of reducing the use of legal or juridical terminology as much as possible, on the other hand, is possible, the question is only – whether it is reasonable. In this context, it is important to note several significant issues. First of all, it should be remembered that certain legal terms are, in particular, the names of legal acts, including procedural acts, entities of a conventional nature or certain rights. These names, in addition to referring to clearly defined designators, connote the rules of construction of these actions (or entities), the rules of consequence for their performance, and, in the case of rights, the entitlements and powers that these rights create. Thus, when deciding to replace a given legal or juridical term with a term outside this terminology, the question must be answered whether achieving greater communicativeness of the utterance (at least in the assumption) will not come at the expense of its precision. This is because there is a risk that a non-professional participant will fail to relate the non-terminological name used to the object that is the designator of the relevant legal term. Consequently, this may expose him or her to the acquisition of information that is inadequate in terms of the legal norms.[570] The gravity of the lack of precision depends, of course, on what activity the information in question is provided (instructions, justification of the decision, etc.), and, moreover, which term (its replacement) it is about.[571]

On the other hand, seeking to limit as much as possible the use of legal and juridical terms in communication acts addressed to non-professional participants by eliminating these terms, rather than replacing them with non-terminological vocabulary, may in turn lead to a reduction in the presiding judge's informational acts, including instructions. Given that not all of the presiding judge's acts referred to in the previous sentence are subject to legal obligation, it is worth noting that an attempt to eliminate legal and juridical terms from communication acts to non-professional participants in a situation where the replacement of the

570 This issue is particularly relevant in the context of the modern tendency to simplify language. Striving to increase the communicativeness of communication acts should take into account the fact that in some cases preference should be given to precision, even if this involved the use of terms, that is, those lexical means whose knowledge *ex definitione* is subjectively limited.

571 Not every substitution of a legal or juridical term carries such a risk of communication misunderstanding as in the example in the footnote above, but it should always be taken into account.

relevant terms with other terms would result in a loss of precision could lead to the omission of a particular informational activity, which from the point of view of a non-professional participants would have to be considered unfavorable. In addition, it should be noted that the use of relevant legal or juridical terms has an educational function, as does the giving of instructions and taking other informative acts. Participation in court proceedings is always an element of socialization of members of a given society, and at the same time it is not excluded that the experience acquired on this occasion will not be used again (this is, moreover, indicated by the results of the analysis of the research material). It is also possible to imagine a situation that is undoubtedly unfavorable for a non-professional participant (causing a sense of uncertainty), in which, due to the fact that the presiding judge consistently avoided the use of legal or juridical terms at the trial, the participant becomes familiar with the relevant terms only in the written reasons for the final decision or at the appeal proceedings.

Given the above, it should be said that the most favorable situation from the point of view of a non-professional participant of court proceedings is when the presiding judge uses legal or juridical terms that are adequate in the given context, and furthermore explains their meaning. This is not to say that the explanation necessarily consists in pointing out the content of a given name. Analysis of the research material revealed examples of explaining certain terms by pointing out elements of the content of the name, the scope of the name, and even by comparison. It should be borne in mind that the rules of construction and rules of consequence of conventional acts, including legal acts, form the content of the name of such an act. Thus, informing (e.g., in an instruction) about how to perform a certain legal, including procedural act, and about the consequences of its performance, also constitutes a more or less comprehensive explanation of the name of such an act. Of course, this is not a sufficient condition for establishing communication with a non-professional participant, which leads to the highest possible level of communicative understanding. It is also necessary to take into account other linguistic and extra-linguistic means that increase the communicativeness of speech (e.g., developed as part of the plain language movement). So, since legal and juridical terminology is present in communication acts directed to non-professional participants (this is confirmed by the results of empirical studies), will be present (since legal norms in some circumstances prescribe the use of certain terms), and to some extent should be present, it is necessary to take the trouble to answer the question – To what extent does the use of legal and juridical terms at the trial constitute a significant communication barrier (language barrier) for a non-professional participants?

It is worth starting by recalling the results of the contextual analysis of the use of legal and juridical terms noted in the research material, which showed that the claim that in all cases the use of legal and juridical terms against non-professional participants in the proceedings is a factor that impedes communicative understanding cannot be accepted as true. The strongest support for rejecting such a claim (as general) is provided by the legal or juridical terms revealed in the research material, the familiarity of which by non-professional participants was evident. This familiarity was primarily related to knowledge of the subject matter of the proceedings (e.g., some of the terms used by the presiding judge came from procedural documents), life experience relating in particular to participation in court proceedings or pre-court proceedings, knowledge of legal norms related to the social, including occupational, role played by the non-professional participant.

In addition, the use of legal and juridical terms in communication acts addressed to non-professional participants did not, in principle, affect the continuity of the communication process taking place at the trial. The analysis of the research material revealed few (a total of 7) communication acts of non-professional participants of a metalinguistic nature, related to ignorance of certain legal or juridical terms. However, the explanation for the lack of significant activity in this area is not simple. There may be several reasons for this. First, it could have been that the non-professional participants whose communication acts were analyzed actually had no problem understanding certain terms, while a situation of communication misunderstanding cannot be excluded. Second, it could have been that the non-professional participants, despite their misunderstanding, did not signal it for other reasons beyond observation.

The problems described in the previous paragraph in explaining the lack of metalinguistic activity of non-professional participants related to possible misunderstanding of certain terms draw attention to a general problem concerning the study of language barriers. After all, the occurrence of language barriers is perceptible to the researcher (using standard methods of observation) insofar as they can be inferred from the communication acts and behavior of participants in the communication process. In other cases, the language barrier remains a purely mental phenomenon, and therefore unobservable to such a researcher. Thus, on the basis of the analysis of the research material, it is only possible to identify such situations in which the risk of a language barrier related to the use of legal and juridical terms was insignificant (such situations were revealed by the contextual analysis of the use of terms in communication acts addressed to non-professional participants), and those in which the barrier undoubtedly occurred (as in the case of metalinguistic acts of non-professional participants related to unfamiliarity with certain terms).

Concluding the discussion of issues related to the use of legal and juridical terms at the trial, it is still necessary to draw attention to the use of such terms by non-professional participants of court proceedings. In this context, undoubtedly, the most important conclusion reached by the analysis of the research material concerns the communicative effectiveness of procedural acts performed in a "non-juridical" manner. It should be recalled that all the disclosed procedural acts performed by non-professional participants in a "non-juridical" manner (41 in total) proved to be communicatively effective. Particularly important is the fact that such a result of the analysis is determined by the features of the trial in model terms. It has already been clearly indicated that the verbal form of communication act, as a rule, is not a constitutive feature of procedural acts, unless it is attempted using a speech act, the standard interpretation of which is incapable of leading to the recognition of a particular act as a procedural act of a given type. The consequence of this is that participants of court proceedings can effectively perform procedural acts that are relevant to them regardless of whether or not they use typical forms, including the relevant legal and juridical terms. Given that achieving the effect of performing a certain procedural act is the essence of the communication activity at the trial, it must be said that this observation is extremely important. Thus, in this aspect, it is not justified to say that unfamiliarity with legal and juridical terminology is a significant barrier to undertaking procedural acts at the trial, although it can undoubtedly sometimes hinder the communication process at the trial (e.g., when it becomes necessary to clarify the content of such an act). It is worth noting here that the resolution of possible doubts about the substance or content of procedural acts undertaken by non-professional participants is facilitated by the face-to-face contact at the trial, thanks to which such doubts can be removed on an ongoing basis.

It is now still necessary to address the formalization of the communication process at the trial in Polish courts and its possible impact on communication involving non-professional participants of court proceedings. Both the conventionalization and formalization of the acts and communication occurrences that take place at the trial are evident. Here, however, we are concerned with those elements of formalization of the relevant communication process that relate to its structure, including the arrangement of individual interactional roles, as well as the functional nature of specific communication occurrences.

It is necessary to begin with a reminder that the analysis of the research material revealed those moments, during the communication process in the courtroom, in which non-professional participants exceeded the pattern of the trial. Most often, the transgression of the normative pattern occurred in connection with the structural shaping of the communication process (taking communication acts at a moment when the pattern of the trial does not provide for it, and establishing communication with the omission of the presiding judge), as well as in connection with the implementation of that part of the examination that involves asking questions of the examined person. Undoubtedly, the formalization of the communication process at the trial causes certain difficulties when the participant in this process is a non-professional participant of court proceedings. Perhaps it would be reasonable to deformalize the process? Obviously not, and this position is supported by at least the following arguments.

First, the structure of the communication process at the trial was designed by the legislator to ensure the equality of participants in the proceedings at this stage of the court proceedings.[572] Second, the formation of a normative pattern

572 Dogmatics and case law emphasize the strong connection between the right to a hearing and the need to ensure equality (equality of arms) for the participants in the proceedings. "In particular, in court proceedings involving opposing parties,

of the structure of the communication process, including the interactional roles, improves the communication process at the trial, because its implementation does not involve the necessity of adjusting the communication pattern each time to the circumstances of a particular proceeding. In addition, it ensures the predictability of the communication process at the trial, especially when the normative pattern remains stable in this regard.[573] Third, the shaping of the structure of the communication process at the trial has an ordering character. The ordering character is manifested primarily in the function of the presiding judge (coordinating and ordering) or blocking of two-way communication between participants with the omission of presiding judge. Such a way of shaping the communication process at the trial reveals particular significance when communication between participants begins to manifest some of the features of communication in conflict, primarily those that carry a significant emotional charge. Fourth, the functional characteristics of particular communication acts or occurrences (e.g., the implementation of an information-verification strategy during the examination) are closely related to the implementation of non-communication goals, in particular, the learning of certain facts in the proceedings. Fifth, the pattern of the communication process at the trial is strongly rooted in culture. At the same time, it would be difficult to identify features of Polish society, including elements of the communication tradition, which would undoubtedly justify the need to deviate from the scheme of communication in the courtroom.[574]

To conclude the discussion on formalizing the communication process at the trial, it should be pointed out that a non-professional participant can easily play the interactional roles assigned to him or her in this process without knowing the structural design of the communication process in the courtroom. This is because it is the presiding judge who coordinates the activity at the trial and, especially importantly, gives the floor to the various participants in the communication process. On the other hand, if the presiding judge, for some reason (e.g., lack of dispute), finds the pattern of the communication process determined by the normative pattern of the trial inflexible, he or she has various means at disposal to make the process more flexible to a certain extent.[575]

---

their equal right to a hearing must be guaranteed", P. Grzegorczyk, K. Weitz, [in:] *Konstytucja RP...*, op. cit. At the level of the pattern of the trial, equality in this regard is ensured by appropriately shaping the communication process in structural terms.

573 Through the prism of stability and predictability, the importance of procedural formalism in general is seen, S. Cieślak, *Formalizm...*, op. cit., pp. 358–359.

574 As was done for indigenous Australians because of the extreme differences between their communication traditions and the demands placed on communication in the court of the common law system; see Section 2.3.2.3.

575 E.g., **P:** *Okay, let's establish that I am the connection between you here, there is no possibility of conversation unless you are about settlement* (...).

The analysis, made for the purpose of the study, of those communication acts of the presiding judge that could facilitate the participation of a non-professional participant at the trial, prompts an additional question – Is the level of activity of the presiding judge revealed in the research material sufficient in this regard? If one takes into account all the types of communication acts highlighted in the research questions that can facilitate a non-professional participant to participate at the trial or in court proceedings in general, one would have to answer in the negative. Indeed, the level of activity in which the presiding judge reaches for all of the types of activity highlighted in the study would be considered the most desirable, as long as their use proves appropriate to the circumstances. However, an important doubt arises – Whether such a state of affairs is possible? Addressing this doubt, it should be pointed out that taking acts that can facilitate a non-professional participant's participation at the trial or in the entire proceedings is, of course, within the framework of those presiding judges' functions, which in this study are referred to as leading-intermediary function and leading-coordinating function. This does not mean, however, that the presiding judge's activity in the scope in question is unlimited. The presiding judge must first take into account the boundary set by the principles of impartiality and act in such a way as not to expose himself or herself to accusation of failing to meet the so-called impartiality test. In addition, the presiding judge must take into account the limit set by norms that prohibit taking acts that could undermine confidence in his or her impartiality. The limit of the presiding judge's activity is also set by the role of the procedural authority, which the presiding judge has sometimes informed, e.g. **P:** *Mrs. X, I am very sorry, but the court does not give legal advice.*[576]

In addition to the limits of the presiding judge's activity set by the norms, including legal norms, it is still necessary to pay attention to limits of a pragmatic nature. Firstly, a given presiding judge's activity, although potentially facilitating a non-professional participant's participation at the trial or in the proceedings as a whole, is not always justified. This is at least to some extent dependent on the specific communication situation in which the communication process between the presiding judge and the non-professional participant takes place (in particular, on the characteristics of the non-professional participant, including his or her level of knowledge and communication competence). Secondly, to undertake all the types of activity that have been highlighted in the study, at all the moments that in some way justify this activity seems either impossible or at least very difficult in a single court session. It should be borne in mind that the presiding judge, during the court session, has a limited amount of time at his or her disposal, primarily intended for the implementation of certain procedural acts, those that aim to achieve the main purpose of the court proceedings, that is, the resolution of the case. Thus,

576 The statement was a response to the witness's question about legal issues that were neither related to the subject matter of the proceedings nor to the witness's procedural situation.

the activity of the presiding judge is conditioned, in the scope in question, both by the way the normative pattern of the trial, and by the circumstances of the specific court session at which this pattern is implemented. And both these aspects should be taken into account when estimating the level of activity of the presiding judge for the benefit of non-professional participants. At the same time, improving the communicativeness of communication acts addressed to non-professional participants does not require systemic changes – changes to the pattern of the trial itself. This is because the ability to use linguistic means that promote communicative understanding is part of the communication competence of the participants in a given interaction.

It is impossible to discuss or even recognize all the issues related to communication process at the trial in a single study. The importance of empirical study, in addition to its obvious cognitive value, manifests itself in the fact that it can bring important practical benefits. In the case of empirical study of those areas of sociocultural reality that are determined to some extent by the law, the dimension of practical benefits is special. This research allows for the diagnosis of a specific fragment of reality, which can then be modeled with appropriate legal instruments. Without a prior diagnosis, these instruments may prove inadequate.

The conclusions contained in this book – both those regarding the formation of the trial in Polish courts in model terms and those derived from the analysis of the research material – can be used for various purposes. First of all, they can be used to formulate, in terms of the formation of the normative pattern of the trial, possible *de lege ferenda* conclusions. In addition, they can be useful for formulating technical directives on, for example, ways to shape the course of interaction in the courtroom, including within the framework of projects related to the movement of plain language. Both of the above-mentioned goals set wide research fields. For this reason, they were either not addressed at all in this study, or only to a certain extent.

Attachments

Appendix 1. Legal and juridical terms in communication acts addressed to non-professional participants

I. Contentious civil proceedings

1. **Terms related to court proceedings:** indictment, case file, evidentiary act, admitting and conducting evidence of witness testimony, delivery, severe and direct property damage, evidence from personal sources of evidence, evidence from documents, expert opinion evidence, evidence from the institute's opinion, penalty of the deprivation of liberty, costs of court proceedings, legal representation costs, process material, (not) punished for giving false testimony, dismissal of the claim, dismissal of the motion, (dismissal of the) evidence, (copy, demand) of the lawsuit, criminal liability under Article 233 of the Polish Penal Code, criminal liability under Article 233 of the Polish Penal Code, response to the lawsuit, adjournment of announcement of judgment, adjournment of trial, appeal against the judgment, supplementary opinion, decision, deciding, opening of the trial, on pain of disregarding the evidence, (factual basis of the) claim, grounds under Article 207 Polish Code of Civil Procedure, sustaining the motion, consolidation of cases, closed court session, ruling on fining a witness, evidentiary proceedings, civil proceedings, criminal proceedings, instruction, right to refuse to testify, right to refuse to answer a question, finality, minutes, loss of case, under Article 304, examination (in the character of a witness, as a witness, witnesses, parties, as a party), (rote) oath, (examination of the) [court] case, examination of the opposition to the reported intervention, trial, giving false testimony, objection, pursuant to Article 157 § 1 Polish Code of Civil Procedure, procedural situation, appeal proceedings, professional secrecy, term (for publication, statutory), evidence thesis, (repeal of the) fine, (repeal of the) ruling, repeal of the question, empowerment, settlement, discontinuance of the proceedings, acceptance of the claim in full, summons, formal motion, motion to adduce evidence, (issuance, announcement of the) judgment, from the point of view of Article 207 Polish Code of Civil Procedure, being credited as evidence, closing a trial, ordering (a pause), allegation of failure to meet the term for, objections to the opinion [of expert], notice, suspension of the proceedings, complaint against the order on the motion for security, complaint, testimony, testifying, obligation [of the court], obligation to remove the lack of [a letter], release of [witness].
2. **Terms related to substantive law and non-court proceedings:** discharge [of the community board], discount, cooperative board member, housing community board member, lease rent, rent, promissory note declaration, debt, inheritance debts, discipline of public finance, economic activity, leaseholder, municipality, warranty, credit, dwelling, renter, expenditure on immovable

property, (infringement, protection of) personal rights, infringement of the right to use property, (non-existence, repeal of the) resolution, property, damages, announcement of liquidation of the cooperative, person authorized to represent the municipality, proxy, tax, quoad usum division, enforcement proceedings, deregistration proceedings, deduction, loan, statutory representative (of a child, minor), assumption of an obligation, appurtenance, regulations [of the community], representation of the [housing] community, disposal of housing community property, testator, cooperative tenant's [right to dwelling], company, employee-owned company, financial report [of the community board], sale, damage, will, insurance, resolution, resolution to give consent for the board of directors to file a lawsuit under Article 16 Law on Ownership of Premises, lease contract, [marital] property contract, tenancy contract, administration contract, loan contract, sales contract, contract of mandate, Immovable Property Management Act, (validity, invalidity of the) assignment contract, bill of exchange, claim, ownership, owner, joint property of spouses, housing community, disinheritance, maturity of the claim, reserved portion, advance on immovable property maintenance costs, advance, management of (common) immovable property, principles of social coexistence, (conclusion, performance, non-performance, termination, notice of the) contract, [civil-law] obligation.

3. **Other terms:** legislative act, norm, legal advice, normative basis, sanction, application of the provisions, law, according to the provision, legal compliance.

II. Non-contentious civil proceedings

1. **Terms related to court proceedings:** appeal, withdrawal (of proxy, motion for division of movable property), (admitting evidence of) expert opinion, admitting and conducting evidence of, delivery, evidence of (documents, witness testimony, visual inspection), fine, penalty of the deprivation of liberty, (punished for) giving false testimony, costs of proceedings, evidence, under Article 501, deliberations, dismissal of the motion, criminal liability, response to the motion, adjournment (announcement of the decision, trial), visual inspection, penalty, deciding the Supreme Court, inheritance declarations, declaration of (rejection of the inheritance, acceptance of the inheritance, acceptance of the inheritance directly, acceptance of the inheritance with the benefit of inventory), (sustaining) the motion, court session, ruling (evidentiary, regarding the confirmation of the inheritance acquisition, on the approval of waiver of the effects of failure to submit the inheritance declaration on time, final, not final, effective), evidentiary (proceedings, acts), proceedings (non-contentious, divorce, complaint proceedings), instruction, right to refuse to testify, final (adjudication, termination of proceedings), [court] minutes, code provision, provisions of the law on court costs, examination (of witnesses, expert, participant), informational (examination), oath, court's deposit account, claim, examination of the case, trial, extension of the motion, dissolution of marriage by court, divorce,

family court, inheritance, case (court, criminal, for acquisitive prescription), measure of evidence, content of the legal provision 520 § 1 of the Polish Code of Civil Procedure, title to court costs, repeal of the (fine, question), court settlement, validation, appointment of ex officio attorney, statutory term, (summons) to participate in the proceedings, motion (evidentiary, formal, to declare the acquisition of inheritance, justification of, for justification of the decision and delivery of the ruling with a statement of finality, for a copy of the ruling with a statement of finality, for acquisitive prescription of an easement), resumption of the proceedings, closing a trial, (order) search for heirs, principles of civil procedure, notice, suspension of proceedings in the case, complaint against the ruling, testimony, court fee stamps, obligation [by the court].

2. **Terms related to substantive law and non-court proceedings:** (marriage, succession, death) certificate, records (of civil status, from immovable properties registers), donation, administrative decision on permission to cut down [the tree], debt, inheritance debts, division of the inheritance, economic activity, adopted child, inheritance under the provisions of the Polish Civil Code, statutory inheritance, inheritance, farm, inheritance group, penalty of the deprivation of liberty, credit (mortgage), property (personal, inheritance, joint), minor, Court and Economic Monitor, under Article 33 Polish Family and Guardianship Code, acquisition of inheritance (by law, in whole, in part), renter, expenditures from joint property on personal property, expenditures from joint property, legal successor, immovable property, notary, copy of (land registers, complete birth certificate), severance payment (posthumous), limited parental authority, person entitled to inheritance, opening and announcement of will, opening of the inheritance, full parental authority, proxy, tax, possession, appointment (to the inheritance, heir), deprivation of parental authority, loan, employer, right (to the inheritance, perpetual usufruct of land), takeover of an immovable property, provisions of the Polish Civil Code, adoption, property separation, separation, Treasury, inheritance, heir (statutory), inheritance, testator, cooperative ownership of a dwelling, case (for division of the inheritance, for division of property separation, inheritance), witness to the making of the will, will (notarial, handwritten), share (in common property, inheritance), construction relief, contract (loan, marital property, for an indefinite period, for a definite period of time, lease of premises, division of the inheritance, waiver of inheritance, sale), entitlement to declaration of acceptance or rejection of the inheritance, cancellation of a will, unpaid leave, registry office, cessation of joint property, declaring (declared) unworthy of inheritance, creditor, ownership, owner, joint property of [spouses], co-owner, ascendants, release of the immovable property, remuneration [for work], rental of premises, inheritance assurances, marriage contract, report the acquisition of inherited property (estate) to the tax office, [civil-law] obligations, waiver of inheritance share, descendants, tax exemption.
3. **Other terms:** legal fiction, legal assistance, regulations, legal provisions, legal effects, legal status.

III. Commercial proceedings

1. **Terms related to court proceedings:** case file, admission of documentary evidence, admission of examination evidence, fine, penalty of arrest, penalty of the deprivation of liberty with a statutory penalty of up to three years, (punished for) giving false testimony, criminal liability (for giving false testimony), criminal liability under Article 233 of the Polish Penal Code, court session, proceedings, instruction, deprivation of liberty, right to refuse to answer a question, (final) decision, examination (in the character of...), examination in the character of a party, oath, publication of a ruling, trial, [court] case, repeal of the fine (for failure to appear), repeal of the ruling, repeal of the question, closing of the trial, order, testimony, testifying, according to Article 233 of the Polish Penal Code.
2. **Terms related to substantive law and non-court proceedings:** (liquidation) damage, lease, declaration of intent, subcontractor, transfer of claims, company, legal relationship, insurer, remuneration.
3. **Other terms:** legal provision, sanction.

IV. Labor law proceedings

1. **Terms related to court proceedings:** civil case file, (direct) severe property damage, (admission, taking) evidence, evidence (supplementary, of expert opinion, of examination), penalty of the deprivation of liberty, punished for giving false testimony, (consequences, significance) process material, evidence, (non-final) ruling, dismissal (of the claim, motion for ex officio attorney, motion for relief from court costs), criminal liability (for giving false testimony), adjournment of trial, announcement of judgment, facts, adjournment, pleading, sustaining the testimony, (evidentiary) proceedings, instruction on criminal liability for giving false testimony, lawsuit (for damages, for reinstatement), right to refuse to answer a question, right to refuse to testify, trial, trial for damages, examination (evidentiary, informational, as a party), oath, claim, court of second instance, labor court, [court] case, settlement, conciliation, summons, (request for) delivery of a copy of the order with reasons, court judgment, closing a trial, suspension of the proceedings, (adjudication of) damages, complaint, testimony, testimony.
2. **Terms related to substantive law and non-court proceedings:** annex to the contract, administrative decision on recalculation of retirement pension, disciplinary termination of the employment contract, leave equivalent, pension, general contractor, overtime hours, contractual penalty, management contract, countersignature, harm, guardianship, juvenile, validity (of work regulations, remuneration regulations), severance payment, damages for unlawful termination of an employment contract without the notice period, compensation for unlawful termination of [employment contract], full-time work, tax, agreement amending the employment contract, employer, employee, labor law, (president,

member of the) board [of the company], public procurement procedure, proxy (in company), labor code provisions, termination of the [employment] relationship by notice from the employer, termination of the employment contract without notice, (termination, notice) employment contract, legitimate interest of the employee, correction of the certificate of employment, association, non-material damage, occupational health and safety training, benefit (of a bonus nature, pension, due to an accident at work), certificate of employment, mode of termination of employment contract, insurance (property, accident), contract (for work, employment, (in)fixed-term, mandate), building qualifications, call for payment, (basic) remuneration, accident at work, notice changing the employment contract, causing damage, Social Insurance Institution, trade union.

3. **Other terms:** dogmatics, case law, legal effect, by operation of law.

V. Social security proceedings

1. **Terms related to court proceedings:** case file, appeal, (ineffectiveness, effectiveness) notice, withdrawal (of the appeal according to Article 203 of the Polish Code of Civil Procedure, combined with waiver of claim, lawsuit), admission of documentary evidence, delivery, evidence, (punished for, criminal liability for) giving false testimony, Polish Code of Civil Procedure, costs of proceedings, (material, motion for) evidence, (non-final) judgment, dismissal of the appeal, (copy) of judgment with justification, criminal liability, response to appeal, adjournment of the trial (date), adjournment of announcement of the judgment, appeal (against the decision), announcement of the judgment, adjudication, under penalty of omission of [party's] testimony, (sustaining) retirement pension application, joining cases for joint examination, separate adjudication, ruling (discontinuance of the proceedings), proceedings (before the court), evidentiary proceedings, (appointment, admission) of expert opinion evidence, right (to refuse to testify, appeal, motion for reimbursement of the costs of proceedings), final decision, trial, loss of the [court] case, examination, oath, examination (of the appeal against the decision, case), examination, court (appellate, regional, of first instance, social security, higher instance), Supreme Court, factual status, legal status, property damage, appeals, validation (of the judgment), evidentiary determination, (supplementary) heard as a party, (according to, premises of) Article 203 and Article 469 Polish Code of Civil Procedure, summons [witnesses] ex officio, application for (appointment of ex officio attorney, reasons for order, reasons for judgment), issuance of the judgment, informative explanations, implementation of a judgment, exclusion of the case for separate examination, judgment, closing a trial, ordering (a break), adjudication, objections to the expert's opinion, complaint, testimony, consent to withdrawal of the [appeal], change the contested administrative decision, obligation [by the court].

2. **Terms related to substantive law and non-court proceedings:** member of (supervisory board, agricultural production cooperative, board), [administrative] decision, economic activity, (railroad) retirement pension, conversion hectare, Agricultural Social Insurance Fund, Constitution, liquidation, under Article 27, legal successor of agricultural cooperatives, coverage of social insurance for farmers, calculation of retirement pension under Article 26 in connection with Article 55 under the Law of December 17, 1998 on pensions from the Social Insurance Fund, liability of the pension authority, declaration of bankruptcy (of the company), period of social insurance coverage, authority, disability certificate, cooperating person, payer (of contributions), subject to compulsory insurance: pension, disability, sickness and accident insurance due to employment under an employment contract, being subject by law to social insurance of farmers, (basis of) the contribution assessment, non-agricultural economic activity, work under special conditions, employer, employee, right to (pension, reduced-age retirement pension, retirement pension in special conditions, early retirement pension, pension, disability pension for incapacity for work, pre-retirement benefit), chairman of the board of directors, minutes of the examination before the authority, chairman of the supervisory board, reasons indicated in Article 2(1) of the Law on pre-retirement benefits, award of retirement pension under Article 26 in connection with Article 53 of the Pension Law, granting the right to a disability pension for partial incapacity for work, pension, resignation from the board of a bankrupt company, farmer, termination of employment contract by mutual agreement, social security contributions, company, starost, length of employment (under special conditions), contributory and non-contributory insurance period, employment relationship, receiver, social security system, Constitutional Tribunal, insurance (pension, social), repeal of the administrative decision, contract (civil law, for work, of mandate), bankruptcy, determination of social security obligation, social security law, agricultural land, retirement age, (owner of) farm, motion for a pension, entry in the Central Register [of Economic Activities], (exclusion from, cessation) of social insurance of farmers, remuneration under contract of mandate, Social Insurance Institution, principle of acquired rights, principles of social coexistence, certificate of non default in payment of social security contributions, health and labor fund, according to (Article 3(1) and (2) of the Act of December 20, 1990 on social insurance for farmers, Articles 5 and 7 of the cited Act, Article 6 of the Polish Civil Code) .
3. **Other terms:** advocate, legal fiction, interpretation of legal provisions, legal language, (valid) legal provisions, juridical language, law, legal counsel, content of the provision, law, legislator, elimination of the provision from the legal system, ministerial order, in accordance with the provision.

VI. Proceedings before the family court

1. **Terms related to court proceedings:** case file, appeal, withdrawal of the (claim, [evidentiary] motion), (admission, taking) evidence, service, evidence (of examination), punished for giving false testimony, costs of proceedings, guardian for a person unknown from the place of residence, evidence, guardianship, deliberation on the decision, juvenile, (non-final) court decision, proclamation, copy of judgment, adjournment of announcement of judgment, announcement of the order, [expert] opinion, decision ending the proceedings in the case, deciding, procedural document, pleading, under criminal liability, sustain (lawsuit, motion), ruling (on the establishment of a legal guardianship, with the validity stated), criminal proceedings, action, lawsuit for alimony judgment, right (to defense, to refuse to answer a question, to refuse to explain, to appeal, to appoint defense counsel, to refuse to testify), (right to file) objection, examination (in the character of a..., participant, supplementary), publication of decision, claim, (rote of the) oath, (examination, settlement) of [court] case, divorce, rigor of immediate enforceability, court (district, regional), case of (alimony, property division, divorce), pedagogical measure, (for) costs of unpaid legal aid provided ex officio, granting of security, settlement, discontinuance [of the proceedings], admonition [pedagogical measure], (validation) of the decision, justification of the decision, summons, request for (justification of the decision, issuance of a copy of the decision with finality), procedural motions, (initiation of) proceedings before the court, explanations of the juvenile, enforceability [of the judgment], (divorce, default) judgment, hearing, interview [of guardian], closing a trial, order, custodial orders, alimony judgment, contesting [the court decision], notice, suspension [of the proceedings], testimony, testifying, (permission to perform) an act that exceeds the ordinary management of the minor's property, filing a lawsuit, court fee stamps, (exemption from) court costs.
2. **Terms related to substantive law and non-court proceedings:** criminal deed, rent, debt, eviction, bailiff, credit, community property, minor, domicile, acquisition of property, notary, bonds, maintenance obligation, legal guardian, (declaration of) rejection of the inheritance, full legal capacity, attorney, family emergency, possession, right of contact with a child, demoralization process, entrepreneur, taxpayer's income from rental and lease contract, taxpayer's income from employment, adoption, foster family, separation, company, custody of a minor, custody report, will, shares of [company's] revenue, employment contract, tax office, (establishment of) property separation, contribution [to the company], (deprivation, limitation of) parental authority, ownership, exercise of parental authority, renting (of an apartment), from renting, penitentiary, permanent residence permit.
3. **Other terms:** legal provision.

VI. Criminal and penal fiscal proceedings

1. **Terms related to court proceedings:** indictment, delivery, proof, (penalty of) deprivation of liberty, punished for giving false testimony, under Article 183 of the Polish Code of Criminal Procedure, under Article 387 of the Polish Code of Criminal Procedure, dismissal of the civil action, (copy of the) indictment, announcement of the judgment, probationary period, decision, prosecution, closest person, (sustain) testimony, victim, evidentiary proceedings, criminal proceedings, simplified proceedings, instruction, adhesion suit, right to refuse to answer the question, (right to file) appeal, (right to request) reasons for judgment, (right to) refuse to testify, (right to) make explanations, individual prevention, general prevention, process, minutes (of interrogation), examination (of witnesses), court case, oath, examination of the case, trial, labor court, civil case, [court] case, contents of Article 175 Polish Penal Code, content of Article 182 Polish Code of Criminal Procedure, reasons [of judgment], recognition of documents as disclosed without reading, sentencing conditions, summons, guilty (of the committed act), motion to adduce evidence, motion under Article 387 Polish Code of Criminal Procedure, explanations, (non-final) judgment, judgment with reasons, closing of the judicial process, ordering the execution of the punishment, ordering, charge, (adjudication) costs of (court) proceedings, notice, suspension of execution of the punishment, complaint, testimony.
2. Terms related to substantive law and non-court proceedings:

(an act under Article..., at the conjunction with Article...) of the Polish Penal Code, an act under Article 190a(1) of the Polish Penal Code, fine, penalty of the deprivation of liberty, Polish Penal Code, confrontation, financial benefit, reparation of damage, no criminal record, liability for crime, suspect, Police, pre-trial investigation, criminal legislation, crime, crime of document forgery, crime of fraud, similar crime, crime of stalking, intentional crime, divorce, company, perpetrator [of a crime], labor certificate, (telecommunication) contract, compensation.

3. **Other terms:** not present.

VII. Misdemeanor proceedings

1. **Terms related to court proceedings:** case file, appeal, delivery, evidence, punished (by order of arrest, deprivation of liberty), punished (by court, for giving false testimony), Polish Code of Procedure for Misdemeanor Cases, evidence, under Article 49(1) of the Law on the Common Court System, (non-final, challenged) judgment, defendant in misdemeanor case (accused of....), copy (of a motion for punishment, judgment with justification), adjournment of the trial, (opening, closing) of the trial, sustain (explanations, testimony), Police, committing the (alleged) act, ruling, evidentiary proceedings, instruction, right to (refuse) to testify in a case, right to (refuse) to answer a question, right (to refuse to testify, give evidence), finality (ruling), general prevention,

specific prevention, examination (in the character of...), oath, examination of the case, deciding the case, trial, judge adjudicating the case, case [court], degree (of social harmfulness, culpability), repeal of a question, acquittal, procedural rights, validation, being found (not)guilty, summons, motion to adduce evidence, evidence (for delivery of a copy of the judgment with reasons), formal motions, judgment, order, (alleged) act, charge(s), adjudication, notice, complaint, testimony, testifying.
2. **Terms related to substantive law and non-court proceedings:** Article 92(1) of the Polish Misdemeanor Code, Article 97 of the Polish Misdemeanor Code, act under Article 86(1), decision (on retention of driving license), administrative (starost's) decision, report of a crime, administrative authority, Police, prosecutor's office, Border Guards, Municipal Guards, entitlement to drive, ownership, offense under Article 86(1), misdemeanor, retention of driving license, conclusion of contract (civil law, employment).
3. **Other terms:** not present.

Appendix 2. Legal and juridical terms used by non-professional participants

I. Contentious civil proceedings

1. **Terms related to court proceedings:** criminal case file, order for payment, dismissal, [expert] opinion, oath, (court) session, [court] ruling, ruling regarding the confirmation of the acquisition of inheritance, criminal proceedings, bankruptcy proceedings, deposit proceedings, instruction, lawsuit for termination of the contract, lawsuit, sue, criminal trial, examination, main trial, trial (court), court of appeal, civil court, labor court, conviction by final judgment, [court] case for damages, divorce case, court case, objection, facts, limitation period for filing procedural document, Constitutional Tribunal, [court] settlement, discontinuance [of proceedings], acquittal, summons, applying to the court for revocation of the resolution, testimony.
2. **Terms related to substantive law and non-court proceedings:** alimony, notarial deed, annex to the contract, contribution, audit committee member, cooperative member, rent, [administrative] decision, building permit decision, debt, dividend, economic activity, lease, tenant, eviction, retirement pension, (main) tenant, municipality, warranty, capped mortgage established on the leased property, prenup, investor, construction manager, confrontation, costs of management of the shared part of the immovable property, land registers, (liquidation) damage, inheritance mass, municipal housing stock, investor supervision, renter, property, Polish [construction] norms, compulsory education, protection of personal rights, damages, [administration] authority, [cooperative] authority, proxy, VAT payer, (income) tax, VAT, suspected crime, business entity, core curriculum, division of common property, Police, insurance policy,

putting the cooperative into liquidation, proceedings conducted at the tax office, deduction, appointment as president of the cooperative, building permit, loan, benefits, construction law, right of tenants to acquire apartments without sale, Attorney General's Office, prosecutor's office, proxy, company, examination, fiscal crime, supervisory board [of the cooperative], benefit fund regulations, complaint, pension, representative of the bankrupt, warranty [for defects], claim, termination [of contract] by mutual agreement, termination [of contract] with three months' notice, divorce, inheritance, heir, (housing) cooperative, (employee-owned) company, limited liability company, sale (of immovable property), cooperative statute, [housing] community statute, educational subvention, will, personal accident insurance, liability insurance, resolution on the final distribution of the cooperative's property and payment of membership shares, resolution to put the cooperative in bankruptcy, resolution to place [something] in court deposits, resolution of the [housing community] board, civil law contract, lease contract, management contract, loan contract, preliminary (sale) contract, contract of mandate, building qualifications, Premises Ownership Act, Cooperative Law, significant defects, insignificant defects, general meeting of the cooperative, bill of exchange, call for payment, claim, owner [of premises], co-owner [in a company], co-owner, contractor, accident at work, secured by a capped mortgage, deposit, compensation, advance payment of income tax, [housing community] management, (common) immovable property management, owner management appointed under Article 20, administrator established pursuant to Article 18 of the Premises Ownership Act, [housing] community administrator, (conclusion, signing, termination) of contract, pursuant to construction law, contractor, repeal of co-ownership, [civil-law] obligation, return of the discount for the purchase of a municipal apartment.

3. **Other terms:** Law Journal, legal language, have the right, invalidity by the law, amendment, legal trade, civil liability, legal opinion, legal solution, law, draft resolution [local law act], legal provision, regulations, ordinance, legal status, lawful status, Act, authorization, entry into force of the law's provisions.

II. Non-contentious civil proceedings

1. **Terms related to court proceedings:** appeal, penalty of the deprivation of liberty, court costs, order for payment, court session, petition, trial, case before the court, divorce proceedings, [court] settlement, motion for acquisitive prescription, judgment, testimony.
2. **Terms related to substantive law and non-court proceedings:** notarial deed, alimony, donation, [administrative] decision, lease, retirement pension, prenup, investor, bailiff, loan, lease, immovable property, contrary to the construction law, rejection of inheritance, declaration of intent, proxy, attorney, tax, Police, deduction, building permit, loan, lease contract benefits, employee,

bonus (regulatory), conversion of perpetual usufruct, pension, survivor's pension, divorce, inheritance, repayment from division of property, cooperative, oral will, insurance, discontinuation of the investigation, (sale) contract, tenancy contract, [property] separation contract, preliminary contract, maternity leave, cessation of joint property [of spouses], usufruct, bill of exchange, ownership, owner, co-owner, rent, detention, suspension of the proceedings [enforcement proceedings], permission, [civil-law] obligation.
3. **Other terms:** have the right, validity, law.

III. Commercial proceedings

1. **Terms related to court proceedings:** oath, objections to the [expert's] opinion.
2. **Terms related to substantive law and non-court proceedings:** annex [to the contract], business, VAT, business entity, deduction, (written) contract, co-owner, suspension of the [business] activity.
3. **Other terms:** legal provisions.

IV. Labor law proceedings

1. **Terms related to court proceedings:** pursuit of claims under civil law, guardianship, decision on the measure of placement in a youth sociotherapy center, [court] proceedings, trial, extension of suit, [court] case, pedagogical measure, summons, court order, testimony.
2. **Terms related to substantive law and non-court proceedings:** annex (to the contract), Article 43 which allows…, working time, dividend, economic activity, general contractor, warranty, investor, management contract, countersignature of the treasurer, cost of revenue, [professional] guardian, prize, contrary to the law of [collective labor] agreement, preschool class, damages, attorney, income tax, insurance policy, employer, bonus, president of the [company's board], provisions of the Public Procurement Law, auction, kindergarten point, [company's] board of directors, regulations, pension, claim, termination of employment contract by mutual agreement, termination of employment contract, company (State Treasury), limited liability company, installment sale, damage, resolution of [company] board, shares [in company capital], contract (for author's supervision), non-competition agreement, contract of mandate, building qualifications, termination of employment contract by termination by notice given by employer, under Article 52, general shareholders' meeting, owner, partners of a company, rent, termination of a collective [labor] agreement, amendment notice, public procurement, board of directors, order of a president of a city, detention, ordinary shareholders' meeting, exemption from the obligation to work.
3. **Other terms:** by virtue of acquired rights, in accordance with applicable law.

V. Social security proceedings

1. **Terms related to court proceedings:** dismissal of the appeal, court of appeal, Supreme Court resolution, judgment, objections to the expert's opinion.
2. **Terms related to substantive law and non-court proceedings:** mayor, [administrative] decision, lease, Polish Code of Criminal Procedure, acquisition of the right to a retirement pension at the general age, criminal liability, payer [of contributions], income tax, (signing) contract, enforcement proceedings, employee, enterprise, assumption of obligations, recalculation of pension under Article 55 in connection with Article 26 of the Law on Social Security Pensions, agricultural production cooperative, municipal corporation, sale, labor certificate, agricultural insurance, resolution, [employment] contract for an indefinite period, contract of mandate, early retirement pension, Social Security Law, issuance of [administrative] decision, sheltered workshop, Social Insurance Institution, certificate of no arrears [with social security contributions], concluding an installment agreement, according to the Polish Civil Code, according to the Polish Labor Code, principal, [administrative-legal] obligation.
3. **Other terms:** interpretation of legal provisions, acquire right to, validity of norm, provision, law, legislator.

VI. Proceedings before the family court

1. **Terms related to court proceedings:** divorce decree, petition, witness examination, trial, court of first instance, property division case, divorce case, court decision, testimony.
2. **Terms related to substantive law and non-court proceedings:** alimony, occupational disease, rent, debt, economic activity, retirement pension, credit, lease, immovable property, decision on inability to work, tax, (signing, termination) contract, division of [joint] property, loan, assumption of an [civil-law] obligation, restoration of possession, claim, property separation, divorce, partnership, insurance, loan contract, contract of mandate, ownership, rent.
3. **Other terms:** legislator.

VII. Criminal and penal fiscal proceedings

1. **Terms related to court proceedings:** court costs, restraining order, examination, summons, testimony.
2. **Terms related to substantive law and non-court proceedings:** Police, prosecutor's office, company, labor certificate, (employment) contract, owner, compensation, detention of the offender.
3. **Other terms:** according to the legal provisions that are in force.

VIII. Misdemeanor proceedings

1. **Terms related to court proceedings:** court file (in misdemeanor case), accused of..., adjournment of the trial, conduct of [court] proceedings, examination, trial, deposition, testimony.
2. **Terms related to substantive law and non-court proceedings:** economic activity, refusal to accept the [criminal] fine, appeal against an [administrative] decision, attorney, insurance policy, work permit, prosecutor's office, examination, property separation, giving false testimony to the Police, owner, explanations, Order of the Chief of Police number 17 dated July 5, 2007 § 4(7), driver's license detention, [road] sign B-35.
3. **Other terms:** not present.

Figures

Graphs

Tables

References

Adler R.B., Rodman G., du Pré A., *Understanding Human Communication*, 12th edition, New York 2014.

Adler R.B., Rosenfeld L.B., Proctor II R.F., *Interplay: The Process of Interpersonal Communication*, 14th edition, New York 2018.

Ajdukiewicz K., *Język i poznanie [Language and Cognition]*, Vol. 1, Warszawa 1960.

Archer D., *Cross-examining lawyers, facework and the adversarial courtroom*, "Journal of Pragmatics" 2011, Vol. 43.

Aristotle, *Poetics*, [in:] *The Complete Works of Aristotle*, ed. J. Barnes, Vol. 2, Princeton 1984.

Austin J.L., *How to Do Things with Words*, Oxford 1962.

Awdiejew A., *Gramatyka interakcji werbalnej [Grammar of Verbal Interaction]*, Kraków 2004.

Awdiejew A., *Systemowe środki perswazji [Systemic Means of Persuasion]*, [in:] *Manipulacja w języku [Manipulation in Language]*, eds. P. Krzyżanowski, P. Nowak, Lublin 2004.

Awdiejew A., Habrajska G., *Wprowadzenie do gramatyki komunikacyjnej [Introduction to Communication Grammar]*, t. 2, Łask 2006.

Awdiejew A., Habrajska G., *Komponowanie sensu w procesie odbioru komunikatów [Composing Sense in the Process of Receiving Messages]*, Łódź 2010.

Bakhtin M., *The Problem of Speech Genres*, [in:] *Modern Genre Theory*, ed. D. Duff, New York 2014.

Banaszak G., Kmita J., *Społeczno-regulacyjna koncepcja kultury [Socio-Regulatory Concept of Culture]*, Warszawa 1991.

Bartmiński J., *Styl potoczny jako centrum systemu stylowego [The Colloquial Style as the Center of the Style System]*, [in:] *Synteza w stylistyce słowiańskiej [Synthesis in Slavic style]*, ed. S. Gajda, Opole 1991.

Bateson G., *Mind and Nature: A Necessary Unity*, Hampton Press 2002.

Beach W.A., *Temporal Density in Courtroom Interaction: Constraints on the Recovery of Past Events at Past Events in Legal Discourse*, "Communication Monographs" 1985, Vol. 52, No. 1.

Bednarek G.A., *Polish vs. American Courtroom Discourse: Inquisitorial and Adversarial Procedures of Witness Examination in Criminal Trials*, Palgrave Macmillan 2014.

Berger C.R., Roloff M.E., Roskos-Ewoldsen D.R., *What Is Communication Science*, [in:] *The Handbook of Communication Science*, eds. C.R. Berger, M.E. Roloff, D.R. Roskos-Ewoldsen, 2nd edition, Sage Publications 2010.

Bielecka-Prus J., *Problem kontekstu w teoriach komunikacji społecznej [The Problem of Context in Theories of Social Communication]*, "Studia Socjologiczne" 2012, Vol. 204, No. 1.

Bielecka-Prus J., Horolets A., *Rekonstrukcja praktyk analizy dyskursu na podstawie wybranych anglojęzycznych czasopism dyskursywnych [Reconstruction of Discourse Analysis Practices Based on Selected English-Language Discourse Journals]*, "Przegląd Socjologii Jakościowej" 2013, Vol. 9, No. 1.

Blanck P.D., *Off the Record: Nonverbal Communication in the Courtroom*, "Stanford Lawyer" 1987, Vol. 21, No. 2.

Blanck P.D., Rosenthal R., Hart A.J., Bernieri F., *The Measure of the Judge: On Empirically-Based Framework for Exploring Trial Judges' Behavior*, "Iowa Law Review" 1990, Vol. 75, No. 3.

Bloom J., Powdermaker K., *The Jury Likes Me, the Jury Likes Me Not: Building Rapport in the Courtroom*, "Texas Bar Journal" 2006, Vol. 69, No. 6.

Bogucki O., *Przeprowadzanie dowodów w postępowaniu cywilnym z perspektywy koncepcji czynności konwencjonalnych [Taking Evidence in Civil Proceedings from the Perspective of the Concept of Conventional Acts]*, [in:] *Konwencjonalne i formalne aspekty prawa [Conventional and Formal Aspects of Law]*, ed. S. Czepita, Szczecin 2006.

Bogucki O., *The Derivational Theory of Legal Interpretation in Polish Legal Theory*, "International Journal for the Semiotics of Law" 2020, No. 33.

Bogucki O., Zieliński M., *Zasada bezstronności – art. 4 k.p.k. a podstawy środka odwoławczego [The Principle of Impartiality – Article 4 of the Polish Code of Criminal Procedure and the Grounds of Appeal]*, "Palestra" 2009, No. 11–12.

Bogucki O., Zieliński M., *Rozdział 1. Zasady prawa z perspektywy ogólnej teorii prawa [Chapter 1. Principles of Law from the Perspective of General Legal Theory]*, [in:] *System prawa karnego procesowego [System of Criminal Procedural Law]*, Vol. 3: *Zasady procesu karnego [Principles of the Criminal Process]*, ed. P. Wiliński, Warszawa 2014.

Borucka-Arctowa M., *Komunikacja między sądami a społeczeństwem [Communication between the Courts and Society]*, [in:] *Sądy w opinii społeczeństwa polskiego [Courts in the Opinion of the Polish Society]*, eds. M. Borucka-Arctowa, K. Pałecki, Kraków 2003.

Borucki M., *Temida staropolska. Szkice z dziejów sądownictwa Polski szlacheckiej [Old Polish Temida. Sketches from the History of Judiciary of the Polish Nobility]*, Warszawa 1979.

Bugajski M., *Język w komunikowaniu [Language in Communication]*, Warszawa 2007.

Bühler K., *Theory of Language: The Representational Function of Language*, John Benjamins 2011.

Burdziej S., *Sprawiedliwość i prawomocność. O społecznej legitymizacji władzy sądowniczej [Justice and Finality. On the Social Legitimacy of Judicial Power]*, Toruń 2017.

Burdziej S., Guzik K., Pilitowski B., *Fairness at Trial: The Impact of Procedural Justice and Other Experiential Factors on Criminal Defendants' Perceptions of Court Legitimacy in Poland*, "Law and Social Inquiry" 2019, Vol. 44, No. 2

Burnett A., Badzinski D.M., *Judge Nonverbal Communication on Trial: Do Mock Trial Jurors Notice?*, "Journal of Communication" 2005, Vol. 55, No. 2.

Campbell W.K., Krusemark E.A., *Self-Serving Bias*, [in:] *Encyclopedia of Social Psychology*, Vol. 2, eds. R.F. Baumeister, K.D. Vohs, Sage Publications 2007.

Charnock R., *Overruling as a Speech Act: Performativity and Normative Discourse*, "Journal of Pragmatics" 2009, Vol. 41, No. 3.

Choduń A., *Norma językowa a dyrektywy redagowania tekstów aktów prawnych [Linguistic Norm and Directives for Drafting Legal Texts]*, [in:] *Konwencjonalne i formalne aspekty prawa [Conventional and Formal Aspects of Law]*, ed. S. Czepita, Szczecin 2006.

Choduń A., *Słownictwo tekstów aktów prawnych w zasobie leksykalnym współczesnej polszczyzny [Vocabulary of Texts of Legal Acts in the Lexical Resource of Modern Polish Language]*, Warszawa 2007.

Choduń A., *Założenia dotyczące zasad techniki prawodawczej i wprowadzania ich zmian (język, teksty i konteksty) [Assumptions about the Principles of Legislative Technique and Their Amendments (Language, Texts and Contexts)]*, [in:] *Zasady techniki prawodawczej – perspektywa zmian. Materiały pokonferencyjne [Principles of Legislative Technique – a Perspective of Change. Post-Conference Materials]*, Warszawa 2014.

Choduń A., Czepita S., *Profesor Maciej Zieliński. Uczony, Nauczyciel, Wychowawca [Professor Maciej Zieliński. Scientist, Teacher, Educator]*, [in:] *W poszukiwaniu dobra wspólnego. Księga jubileuszowa Profesora Macieja Zielińskiego [In Search of the Common Good. A Jubilee Book by Professor Maciej Zieliński]*, eds. A. Choduń, S. Czepita, Szczecin 2010.

Choduń A., Zieliński M., *Jak sądy i trybunały komunikują się z obywatelami [How courts and tribunals communicate with citizens]*, [in:] *Kultura zachowań językowych Polaków. Materiały z VIII Forum Kultury Słowa. Rzeszów 20–22 października 2011 [The Culture of Linguistic Behavior of Poles. Materials from the VIII Forum on the Culture of Words. Rzeszów 20–22 October 2011]*, ed. M. Krauz, K. Ożóg, 2013.

Chomsky N., *Aspects of the Theory of Syntax*, Cambridge 1964.

Cieślak S., *Formalizm postępowania cywilnego [Formalism of Civil Proceedings]*, Warszawa 2008.

Clark H.H., *Using Language*, Cambridge 1996.

Conley J.M., O'Barr W.M., *Rules versus Relationships: The Ethnography of Legal Discourse*, Chicago 1990.

Conley J.M., O'Barr W.M., Allan Lind E., *The Power of Language: Presentational Style in the Courtroom*, „Duke Law Journal" 1979, Vol. 27, No. 6.

Cudak R., *Genologiczne pogranicza i ekwiwalencje [Genological Borderlands and Equivalences]*, [in:] *Gatunki mowy i ich ewolucja [Speech Genres and Their Evolution]*, Vol. 4: *Gatunek a komunikacja społeczna Genre and social communication*, ed. D. Ostaszewska, Katowice 2011.

Cummings L., *Pragmatic Disorders in Forensic Settings*, [in:] *Pragmatics and Law: Practical and Theoretical Perspectives*, eds. F. Poggi, A. Capone, Cham 2017.

Czapska J., *Konflikty związane z pełnieniem roli prawnika-uczestnika wymiaru sprawiedliwości*, [in:] G. Skąpska, J. Czapska, M. Kozłowska, *Społeczne role prawników (sędziów, prokuratorów, adwokatów) [Social roles of Lawyers (Judges, Prosecutors, Advocates)]*, Wrocław 1989.

Czepita S., *Reguły konstytutywne a zagadnienia prawoznawstwa [Constitutive Rules and Issues of Jurisprudence]*, Szczecin 1996.

Czepita S., *Formalizacja a konwencjonalizacja działań w prawie [Formalization vs. Conventionalization of Actions in Law]*, [in:] *Konwencjonalne i formalne aspekty prawa [Conventional and Formal Aspects of Law]*, ed. S. Czepita, Szczecin 2006.

Czepita S., *Formalizacja i konwencjonalizacja w systemie prawnym [Formalization and Conventionalization in the Legal System]*, [in:] *System prawny a porządek prawny*, eds. O. Bogucki, S. Czepita, Szczecin 2008.

Czepita S., *O koncepcji czynności konwencjonalnych w prawie [On the concept of conventional acts in law]*, [in:] *Wykładnia Konstytucji. Aktualne problemy i tendencje [Interpreting the Constitution. Current Problems and Trends]*, ed. M. Smolak, Warszawa 2016.

Czepita S., *On the Concept of Conventional Act in Law and its Types*, "Ruch Prawniczy, Ekonomiczny i Socjologiczny" 2017, No. 1.

Damaška M.R., *Evidence Law Adrift*, Yale 1997.

de Beaugrande R., Dressler W., *Introduction to Text Linguistics*, Longman 1981.

Di Conza A., Abbamonte L., Scognamiglio L., Gnisci A., *Accommodation Strategies in Italian Courtroom Examinations: A Cross-Disciplinary Analysis of the Reciprocal Effects of Question-Answering*, "US-China Law Review" 2012, Vol. 9.

Dobek-Ostrowska B., *Podstawy komunikowania społecznego [Basics of Social Communication]*, Wrocław 1999.

Dolecki H., *Postępowanie cywilne. Zarys wykładu [Civil Procedure. Outline of a Lecture]*, 6th edition, Warszawa 2015.

Domachowski W., *Funkcjonowanie sali sądowej [Functioning of the Courtroom]*, [in:] *Psychologia i prawo. Między teorią a praktyką [Psychology and the Law. Between Theory and Practice]*, eds. E. Habzda-Siwek, J. Kabzińska, Sopot 2014.

Dudek M., *Komunikowanie prawa w dobie pluralizmu kulturowego [Communicating Law in the Era of Cultural Pluralism]*, Kraków 2014.

Dudek M., Stępień M., *Courtroom Power Distance Dynamics*, Cham 2021.

Dudek M., Stępień M., *On the Need to Study Processes of Taking Minutes from Case Hearings: Contribution to and Call for Future Research*, "International Journal for the Semiotics of Law" 2021, Vol. 34.

Dumas B.K., *Language of Jury Instructions*, [in:] *The Encyclopedia of Applied Linguistics*, ed. C.A. Chapelle, Blackwell Publishing 2013.

Dunaj B., *Kategoria oficjalności [Category of Officiality]*, [in:] *Współczesna polszczyzna mówiona w odmianie opracowanej (oficjalnej) [Modern Spoken Polish in the Elaborated (Official) Variety]*, eds. Z. Kurzowa, W. Śliwiński, Kraków 1994.

Duszak A., *Tekst, dyskurs, komunikacja międzykulturowa [Text, Discourse, Intercultural Communication]*, Warszawa 1998.

Eades D., *"Evidence Given in Unequivocal Terms": Gaining Consent of Aboriginal Young People in Court*, [in:] *Language in the Legal Process*, ed. J. Cotterill, Palgrave Macmillan 2002.

Fiske J., *Introduction to Communication Studies*, 2nd edition, London-New York 1990.

Försterling F., *Attribution: An Introduction to Theories, Research and Applications*, Hove 2001.

Gajda S., *Gatunkowe wzorce wypowiedzi [Genre Speech Patterns]*, [in:] *Współczesny język polski [Contemporary Polish Language]*, ed. J. Bartmiński, Lublin 2001.

Gajda S., *Styl naukowy*, [in:] *Współczesny język polski [Contemporary Polish Language]*, ed. J. Bartmiński, Lublin 2001.

Gawronski B., *Fundamental Attribution Error*, [in:] *Encyclopedia of Social Psychology*, Vol. 1, eds. R.F. Baumeister, K.D. Vohs, Sage Publications 2007.

Gizbert-Studnicki T., *Postępowanie sądowe jako złożony dyskurs – zagadnienia pragmatyki języka sali sądowej [Court proceedings as a complex discourse – issues of pragmatics of the language of the courtroom]*, paper presented on Polish Language Congress in Katowice, 4–6 of May 2011, www.rjp.pan.pl/index.php?option=com_content&view=article&id=1376&Itemid=50, access 20.12.2022.

Gizbert-Studnicki T., K. Płeszka, J. Woleński, *20th-Century Legal Theory and Philosophy in Poland*, [in:] *Legal Philosophy in the Twentieth Century: The Civil Law World*, eds. E. Pattaro, C. Roversi, Springer Netherlands 2016.

Gmerek K., *Rozprawa sądowa jako zdarzenie komunikacji społecznej [Trial as a Social Communication Occurrence]*, Szczecin 2019.

Gmerek K., *Procedural Acts as Double-Conventionalized Acts: Considerations on Conventional Acts Performed in a Courtroom Discourse*, "International Journal for the Semiotics of Law" 2021, Vol. 34, No. 1.

Goban-Klas T., *Media i komunikowanie masowe. Teorie i analizy prasy, radia, telewizji i Internetu [Media and Mass Communication. Theories and Analysis of Press, Radio, Television and the Internet]*, Warszawa 2005.

Goffman E., *The Presentation of Self in Everyday Life*, New York 1986.

Goffman E., *Interaction Ritual: Essays in Face-to-Face Behavior*, New Jersey 2005.

Grabias S., *Interakcja językowa i jej uwarunkowania. Perspektywa lingwistyczna [Linguistic Interaction and Its Determinants. A Linguistic Perspective]*, [in:] *Bariery i pomosty w komunikacji językowej Polaków*, eds. J. Bartmiński, U. Majer-Baranowska, Lublin 2005.

Grabias S., *Język w zachowaniach społecznych [Language in Social Behavior]*, Lublin 1994.

Grice P., *Studies in the Way of Words*, Cambridge 1989.

Griffin E., *A First Look at Communication Theory*, 8th edition, New York 2011.

Greco V., Roger D., *Coping with uncertainty: The construction and validation of a new measure*, "Personality and Individual Differences" 2000, No. 4.

Grochala B., *Kompetencja komunikacyjna a gatunek – o relacji internetowej na żywo [Communication Competence and Genre – about Live Internet Reporting]*, "Acta Universitatis Lodziensis. Kształcenie Polonistyczne Cudzoziemców" 2013, Vol. 20.

Grochowski G., *Czy istnieje tekst poza gatunkiem? [Is there a text beyond genre?]*, [in:] *Gatunki mowy i ich ewolucja [Speech genres and their evolution]*, Vol. 2: *Tekst a gatunek [Text vs. genre]*, ed. D. Ostaszewska, Katowice 2004.

Gross S., *(Descriptive) Externalism in semantics* [in:] *The Routledge Handbook of Semantics*, ed. N. Riemer, Routledge 2015.

Grzegorczyk P., Weitz K., [in:] *Konstytucja RP [Constitution of the RP]*, Vol. 1: *Komentarz do art. 1–86 [Commentary on Articles 1–86]*, eds. M. Safjan, L. Bosek, 1st edition, Warszawa 2016, Legalis 2017.

Grzegorczykowa R., *Wstęp do językoznawstwa [Introduction to Linguistics]*, Warszawa 2007.

Habermas J., *The Theory of Communicative Action*, Vol. 1: *Reason and the Rationalization of Society*, Boston 1984.

Habrajska G., *Kompetencja stylistyczna w interakcji [Stylistic Competence in Interaction]*, [in:] *Stylistyka a pragmatyka [Stylistics vs. Pragmatics]*, ed. B. Witosz, Katowice 2001.

Handling Cases Involving Self-Represented Litigants. A Benchguide for Judicial Officers, Judicial Council of California 2019.

Harnish R.M., *Externalism and Internalism in Speech Act Theory*, "Lodz Papers in Pragmatics" 2009, Vol. 5, No. 1.

Heffer Ch., *The Language of Jury Trial: A Corpus-Aided Analysis of Legal-Lay Discourse*, Palgrave Macmillan 2005.

Heffer Ch., *Jury Trial Discourse*, [in:] *The International Encyclopedia of Language and Social Interaction*, associate eds. K. Tracy, general ed., C. Ilie, T. Sandel, John Wiley and Sons 2015.

Heffer Ch., *Narrative Practices and Voice in Court*, [in:] *Handbook of Communication in the Legal Sphere*, ed. Jacqueline Visconti, Berlin-Boston 2018.

Hofmański P., Zabłocki S., *Elementy metodyki pracy sędziego w sprawach karnych [Elements of the Methodology of the Judge's Work in Criminal Cases]*, 2nd edition, Warszawa 2011.

Huutoniemi K., Klein J.T., Bruunc H., Hukkinen J., *Analyzing Interdisciplinarity: Typology and Indicators*, "Research Policy" 2010, Vol. 39, No. 1.

Hymes D., *Fundations in Sociolinguistics: An Ethnographic Approach*, University of Pensylvania Press 1974.

Hymes D., *Vers la compétence de communication*, Paris 1991.

Jacko J.F., *Ontologie sytuacji komunikacyjnej w empirycznych naukach humanistycznych [Ontologies of the Communication Situation in the empirical humanities]*, [in:] *Sytuacja komunikacyjna i jej parametry [Communication Situation and Its Parameters]*, ed. G. Sawicka, Bydgoszcz 2010.

Jadacka H., Markowski A., Zdunkiewicz-Jedynak D., *Poprawna polszczyzna. Hasła problemowe [Correct Polish. Problem Entries]*, Warszawa 2008.

Jakobson R., *W poszukiwaniu istoty języka 2 [In Search for the Essence of Language 2]*, Warszawa 1989.

Janusz-Pohl B., *Formalizacja i konwencjonalizacja jako instrumenty analizy czynności karnoprocesowych w prawie polskim [Formalization and Conventionalization as Instruments of Analysis of Acts in Criminal Proceedings in Polish Law]*, Poznań 2017.

Janusz-Pohl B., *Definitions and Typologies of Acts in Criminal Proceedings. Perspective of Conventionalisation and Formalisation*, Poznań 2017.

Kiełkowski T., *Nabycie prawa na mocy decyzji administracyjnej [Acquisition of a Right by Administrative Decision]*, Warszawa 2012.

Kmita J., *O kulturze symbolicznej [On Symbolic Culture]*, Warszawa 1982.

Kmita J., Nowak L., *Studia nad teoretycznymi podstawami humanistyki [Studies on the Theoretical Foundations of the Humanities]*, Poznań 1968.

Kołodziejek E., Choduń A., eds., *Mówi się, czyli o wymowie i wymowności Polaków. Materiały IX Forum Kultury Słowa. Szczecin 9–11 października 2013 [Speech, on the articulation and eloquence of Poles. Materials of the IX Forum on the Culture of Words. Szczecin 9–11 October 2013]*, Szczecin 2016

Koper R., *Jawność rozprawy głównej a ochrona prawa do prywatności w procesie karnym [Publicity of the Main Trial and the Protection of the Right to Privacy in the Criminal Process]*, Warszawa 2010.

Kuhn T., *The Structure of Scientific Revolutions*, Chicago 1960.

Kulczycki E., *Dwa aspekty komunikacji. Założenia komunikologii historycznej [Two Aspects of Communication. Assumptions of Historical Communicology]*, Poznań 2015.

Kulczycki E., *Kulturowo-obiektywne istnienie procesu komunikacji [The Cultural-Objective Existence of the Communication Process]*, "Kultura i Historia", http://www.kulturaihistoria.umcs.lublin.pl/archives/2997, access 20.12.2022.

Kulczycki E., *Teoretyzowanie komunikacji [Theorizing Communication]*, Poznań 2012.

Kurcz I., *Psychologia języka i komunikacji [Psychology of Language and Communication]*, Warszawa 2005.

Kurzon D., *It Is Hereby Performed...: Explorations in Legal Speech Acts.* Amsterdam-Philadelphia 1986.

Labocha J., *Odbiorca w tekście i wypowiedzi [Recipient in Text and Speech]*, [in:] *Styl a tekst. Materiały międzynarodowej konferencji naukowej. Opole 26–28.09.1995 [Style and Text. Materials of the International Scientific Conference. Opole 26–28.09.1995]*, eds. S. Gajda, M. Balowski, Opole 1996.

Laskowska E., *Emotywizacja jako środek perswazji [Emotivation as a Means of Persuasion]*, [in:] *Manipulacja w języku [Manipulation in Language]*, eds. P. Krzyżanowski, P. Nowak, Lublin 2004.

Lee Hoffman J., Weiner A., *The Juror as Audience: The Impact of Non-Verbal Communication at Trial*, "Litigation Journal" 2013, Vol. 32, No. 3.

Levi J.N., *The Study of Language in Judicial Process*, [in:] *Language in the Judicial Process*, eds. J.N. Levi, A. Graffam Walker, Springer Science Business Media 1990.

Levinson S.C., *Pragmatics*, Cambridge 1983.

Loewe I., *Polska genologia lingwistyczna. Rekonesans [Polish Linguistic Genology. Reconnaissance]*, "Tekst i Dyskurs" 2008, No. 1.

Lora J., *Komunikacja sądów z obywatelami – badania empiryczne, wnioski, rekomendacje zmian [Communication of Courts with Citizens – Empirical Research, Conclusions, Recommendations for Change]*, Warszawa 2009.

Łazarska A., *Rzetelny proces cywilny [A Fair Civil Trial]*, Warszawa 2002.

Łojko E., *Działalność zawodowa prawników a wykluczenie prawne [Professional Activities of Lawyers and Legal Exclusion]*, [in:] *Prawo i wykluczenie. Studium empiryczne [Law and exclusion. An Empirical Study]*, ed. A. Turska, Warszawa 2010.

Maisel W., *Archeologia prawna Polski [Legal Archaeology of Poland]*, Warszawa–Poznań 1982.

Majewska M., *Akty deprecjonujące siebie i innych. Studium pragmalingwistyczne [Acts of Deprecation of Self and Others. A Pragmalinguistic Study]*, Kraków 2005.

Malliday M.A.K., *Explorations in the Functions of Language*, London 1973.

Markiewicz K., *Zasady orzekania w postępowaniu nieprocesowym [Rules of Adjudication in Non-Adversarial Proceedings]*, Warszawa 2013.

Markowski A., *Kultura języka polskiego. Teoria. Zagadnienia leksykalne [Culture of the Polish Language. Theory. Lexical Issues]*, Warszawa 2005.

Matczak M., *Does Legal Interpretation Need Paul Grice? Reflections on Lepore and Stone's Imagination and Convention*, "Polish Journal of Philosophy" 2016, Vol. 10, No. 1.

Mattelart A., Mattelart M., *Theories of Communication: A Short Introduction*, London 1998.

Mayenowa M.R., *Poetyka teoretyczna. Zagadnienia języka [Theoretical Poetics. Issues of Language]*, Wrocław 2000.

Mazzarella D., Negro A., Penco C., *Contexts: Everything You Always Wanted to Know about Context (But Were Afraid to Ask)*, "Argumenta" 2022, Vol. 8, No. 1.

McDermott V.M., *Attribution Theory*, [in:] *Encyclopedia of Communication Theory*, eds. S.W. Littlejohn, K.A. Foss, Sage Publications 2009.

McQuail D., *MaQuail's Mass Communication Theory*, 6th edition, London 2010.

Meibauer J., *What Is a Context*, [in:] *What Is a Context: Linguistic Approaches and Challenges*, eds. R. Finkbeiner, J. Meibauer, P.B. Schumacher, Amsterdam-Philadelphia 2012.

Mich W., *Prolegomena do historii komunikacji [Prolegomena to the History of Communication]*, Vol. 1: *O komunikacji [About Communication]*, Lublin 2014.

Miles M.B., Huberman A.M., *Qualitative Data Analysis*, 2nd edition, Thousand Oaks 1994.

Morreale S., Spitzberg B., Barge J., *Human Communication: Motivation, Knowledge and Skills*, 2nd edition, Thomson Wadsworth 2007.

Myers D.G., *Social Psychology*, 10th edition, New York 2010.

Najda M., A. Rutkowska, D. Rutkowski, *Psychologia sali sadowej. Jak komunikacja i emocje wpływają na postrzeganie sprawiedliwości [Courtroom Psychology. How Communication and Emotions Affect Perceptions of Justice]*, Bielsko-Biała 2021.

Najstarszy Zwód Prawa Polskiego [The Oldest Law of Poland], compiled by J. Matuszewski, J. Matuszewski, Łódź 1995.

Navarro-Reyes J., *Speech Acts, Criteria and Intentions*, "Lodz Papers in Pragmatics" 2010, Vol. 6, No. 1.

Nęcki Z., *Komunikacja międzyludzka [Interpersonal Communication]*, Kraków 1996.

Nowak L., *A Concept of Rational Legislator*, [in:] *Polish Contributions to the Theory and Philosophy of Law*, ed. Z. Ziembiński, Amsterdam 1987.

Nowak L., Wronkowska S., Zieliński M., Ziembiński Z., *Czynności konwencjonalne w prawie [Conventional Acts in Law]*, "Studia Prawnicze" 1972, Vol. 33.

Nowak L., Wronkowska S., Zieliński M., Ziembiński Z., *Conventional Acts in Law*, [in:] *Polish Contributions to the Theory and Philosophy of Law*, ed. Z. Ziembiński, Amsterdam 1987.

Nowak S., *Metodologia nauk społecznych [Methodology of the Social Sciences]*, Warszawa 2011.

Ollivier B., *Les sciences de la communication. Théories et acquis*, Armand Colin 2007.

Olson S.R., *Teoria komunikowania: ponowne rozpatrzenie kwestii [Communication Theory: Reconsidering the Question]*, [in:] *Współczesne systemy komunikowania [Contemporary Communication Systems]*, ed. B. Dobek-Ostrowska, Wrocław 1998.

Ożóg K., *Ustna odmiana języka ogólnego [Oral variety of the common language]*, [in:] *Współczesny język polski [Contemporary Polish Language]*, ed. J. Bartmiński, Lublin 2001.

Paprzycka K., *Normative Expectations, Intentions and Beliefs*, "The Southern Journal of Philosophy" 1999, Vol. 37.

Penco C., *Contexts in Philosophy: Pragmatic Competence as Filter*, https://www.openscience.fr/Contexts-in-philosophy-pragmatic-competence-as-filter, access 2.06.2023.

Peno M., Bogucki O., *Principles of Criminal Liability from the Semiotic Point of View*, "International Journal for the Semiotics of Law" 2021, Vol. 34.

Piekot T., Moroń E., Zarzeczny G., *Prosto po polsku – przyjazne upomnienia [Simple in Polish – Friendly Admonitions]*, https://biznes.newseria.pl/files/1097841585/raport_prosto_po_polsku_-_przyjazne_upomnienia.pdf, access 22.12.2022.

Pietruszczak A., *Podstawy teorii części [Fundamentals of Parts Theory]*, Toruń 2013.

Pilitowski B., Burdziej S. eds., *Court Monitoring Methodology*, Toruń 2013

Pisarek W., *Wstęp do nauki o komunikowaniu [Introduction to Communication Science]*, Warszawa 2008.

Poggi F., *Law and Conversational Implicatures*, "International Journal for the Semiotics of Law" 2011, Vol. 24.

Poggi F., *Conversational Implicatures of Normative Discourse*, [in:] *Further Advances in Pragmatics and Philosophy: Part 2 Theories and Applications*, eds. A. Capone, M. Carapezza, F. Lo Piparo, Cham 2019.

Poggi F., *Against the Conversational Model of Legal Interpretation: On the Difference between Legislative Intent and Speaker's Intention*, "Revus" 2020, Vol. 40.

Recanati F., *Meaning and Force. The Pragmatics of Performative Utterances*, Cambridge 1987.

Recanati F., *Contextualism: Some Varieties*, [in:] *The Cambridge Handbook of Pragmatics*, eds. K. Allan, K. Jaszczolt, Cambridge 2012.

Repko A.F., Szostak R., *Interdisciplinary Research: Process and Theory*, 4th edition, Los Angeles 2021.

Riemer N., *Internalist Semantics: Meaning, Conceptualization and Expression*, [in:] *The Routledge Handbook of Semantics*, ed. N. Riemer, Routledge 2015.

Rossner M., Tait D., McKimmie B., Sarre R., *The Dock on Trial: Courtroom Design and the Presumption of Innocence*, "Journal of Law and Society" 2017, Vol. 44, No. 3.

Rubacha K., *Metodologia badań nad edukacją [Methodology of Education Research]*, Warszawa 2008.

Rutkowska-Ząbczyk E., [in:] *Kodeks postępowania cywilnego. Komentarz [Polish Code of Civil Procedure. Commentary]*, ed. A. Marszałkowska-Krześ, Legalis 2017.

Rymaszewski Z., *Z badań nad funkcjonowaniem sądów prawa polskiego w średniowieczu. Czynności woźnego sądowego [From Research on the Functioning of Polish Law Courts in the Middle Ages. Activities of a Court Usher]*, Warszawa 2010.

Rzeszutko M., *Rozprawa sądowa w świetle lingwistyki tekstu [Trial in the Light of Text Linguistics]*, Lublin 2003.

Samborski E., *Zarys metodyki pracy sędziego w sprawach karnych [Outline of the Methodology of the Judge's Work in Criminal Cases]*, 6th edition, Warszawa 2013.

Sawicka G., *Konwencja a kompetencja komunikacyjna [Convention and Communication Competence]*, [in:] *Język w komunikacji [Language in Communication]*, Vol. 1, ed. G. Habrajska, Łódź 2001.

Schwarz N., *Cognition and Communication: Judgmental Biases, Research Methods and the Logic of Conversation*, Erlbaum 1996.

Searle J.R., *Speech Acts. An Essay in the Philosophy of Language*, Cambridge 1969.

Sikorski Cz., *Język konfliktu. Kultura komunikacji społecznej w organizacji [The Language of Conflict. The Culture of Social Communication in an Organization]*, Warszawa 2005.

Silars A.L., *Interpersonal Conflict*, [in:] *The Handbook of Communication Science*, eds. C.R. Berger, M.E. Roloff, D.R. Roskos-Ewoldsen, 2nd edition, Sage Publications 2010.

Skąpska G., *Dramaturgia procesu sądowego [Dramaturgy of the Judicial Process]*, [in:] G. Skąpska, J. Czapska, M. Kozłowska, *Społeczne role prawników (sędziów, prokuratorów, adwokatów) [Social Roles of Lawyers (Judges, Prosecutors, Advocates)]*, Wrocław 1989.

Skibiński A., *Gregory Bateson i kontekstowa teoria komunikacji. Różnica, która czyni różnicę i wzorzec, który łączy [Gregory Bateson and Contextual Communication Theory. The Difference that Makes the Difference and the Pattern that Connects]*, [in:] *Komunikologia. Teoria i praktyka komunikacji [Communicology. Theory and Practice of Communication]*, eds. E. Kulczycki, M. Wendland, Poznań 2012.

Skoczeń I., *Implicatures within Legal Language*, Cham 2019.

Sobkowiak B., *Procesy komunikowania się w organizacji [Communication processes in the organization]*, [in:] *Współczesne systemy komunikowania [Contemporary Communication Systems]*, ed. B. Dobek-Ostrowska, Wrocław 1998.

Sønderberg Mortensen S., Mortensen J., *Epistemic Stance in Courtroom Interaction*, [in:] *Pragmatics and Law: Practical and Theoretical Perspectives*, eds. F. Poggi, A. Capone, Cham 2017.

Sperber D., Wilson D., *Relevance: Communication and Cognition*, 2nd ed., Oxford 1995.

Stalnaker R., *Common Ground*, "Linguistics and Philosophy" 2002, No. 25.

Stewart J., *Interpersonal Communication: Contact between Persons*, [in:] *Bridges Not Walls: A Book About Interpersonal Communication*, ed. J. Stewart, 5th edition, New York 1990.

Stephens Ch., Pringle J., *Identify Your Audience*, [in:] *Plain Language in Plain English*, ed. Ch. Stephens, Vancouver 2010.

Stępień M., Dudek M, *The Courtroom as a Built Environment: On the Usefulness of Amos Rapoport's Theoretical Framework*, "Oñati Socio-Legal Series" 2021, Vol. 11, No. 6(S).

Strawson P.F., *Intention and Convention in Speech Acts*, "The Philosophical Review" 1964, Vol. 73, No. 4.

Strączyński M., *Język prawniczy – przyczyny i charakterystyka błędów i niezrozumiałości sformułowań [Juridical language – causes and characteristics of errors and incomprehensibility of expressions]*, paper presented on Polish Language Congress in Katowice, 4–6 of May 2011, www.rjp.pan.pl/index.php?option=com_content&view=article&id=1378, access 20.12.2022.

Stroud N., *Non-Adversarial Justice: The Changing Role of Courtroom Participants in an Indigenous Sentencing Court*, [in:] *Proceedings of the International Association of Forensic Linguists' Tenth Biennial Conference, Centre for Forensic Linguistics*, Birmingham 2012.

Studnicki F., *Przepływ wiadomości o normach prawa [Message flow of legal norms]*, "Zeszyty Naukowe Uniwersytetu Jagiellońskiego. Prace Prawnicze" 1965, Vol. 22.

Studnicki F., *Znajomość i nieznajomość prawa [Knowledge and ignorance of the law]*, "Państwo i Prawo" 1962, No. 4.

Szacoń G., *Proces cywilny na tle koncepcji czynności konwencjonalnych – formalizacja czynności faktycznych i konwencjonalnych [Civil Process against the Background of the Concept of Conventional Acts – Formalization of Factual and Conventional Acts]*, [in:] *Konwencjonalne i formalne aspekty prawa [Conventional and Formal Aspects of Law]*, ed. S. Czepita, Szczecin 2006.

Szczepankowska J., *Semantyka i pragmatyka językowa. Słownik podstawowych pojęć z zadaniami i literaturą przedmiotu [Linguistic Semantics and Pragmatics. Dictionary of Basic Concepts with Tasks and Literature on the Subject]*, Białystok 2011.

Szczyrbak M., *Verb Patterns in Trial Discourse: The Case of 'I think'*, "Discourse and Interaction" 2020, Vol. 13, No. 2.

Szczyrbak M., *Closing Argument as Multimodal Oratory: Insights from the Chauvin Trial*, "International Journal for the Semiotics of Law" 2023, Vol. 36.

Szymków-Gac M., *Przesłuchanie w polskiej rozprawie karnej. Studium pragmalingwistyczne [Examination in the Polish Criminal Trial. A Pragmalinguistic Study]*, Warszawa 2019.

Temple N., Simon J. eds., *Architecture and Justice: Judicial Meanings in the Public Realm*, London 2013.

Thompson J.K., *"Powerful/Powerless" Language in Court: A Critical Re-evaluation of the Duke Language and Law Programme*, "International Journal of Speech Language and the Law" 2002, Vol. 9, No. 2.

Tiersma P.M., Solan L.M., *Cops and Robbers: Selective Literalism in American Criminal Law*, "Law and Society Review" 2004, Vol. 38, No. 2.

Tkaczuk M., *Średniowieczny proces w zwyczajowym prawie polskim [Medieval Trial in Customary Polish Law]*, „In Gremio" 2005, No. 12.

Tokarczyk R., *Proksemika ogólna jako podstawa proksemiki sądowej i proksemiki prawniczej [General Proxemics as the Basis of Forensic Proxemics and Legal Proxemics]*, "Annales Universitas Mariae Curie-Skłodowska. Sectio G, Ius" 2009/2010, Vol. 56/57.

Trosborg A., *Statutes and Contracts: An Analysis of Legal Speech Acts in the English Language of the Law*, "Journal of Pragmatics" 1995, Vol. 23, No. 1.

Trzeciakowska A., *Obserwacja jako metoda stosowana w badaniach nad procesem komunikacji [Observation as a Method Used in the Study of the Communication Process]*, [in:] *Komunikowanie się w sytuacjach społecznych. Analizy psychologiczne [Communicating in Social Situations. Psychological Analysis]*, ed. T. Rzepa, Szczecin 2002.

Waltoś S., Hofmański P., *Proces karny. Zarys systemu [The Criminal Process. Outline of the System]*, wyd. 11, Warszawa 2013.

Watzlawick P., Bavelas J.B., Jackson D.D., *Pragmatics of Human Communication: A Study of Interactional Patterns, Pathologies and Paradoxes*, W.W. Norton and Company 2011.

Weber M., *Gospodarka i społeczeństwo. Zarys socjologii rozumiejącej [Economy and Society. An Outline of Interpretive Sociology]*, Warszawa 2002.

Wendland M., *Czy optymistyczna ocena kondycji nauki o komunikacji w Polsce jest zasadna? [Is the Optimistic Assessment of the Condition of Communication Science in Poland Justified?]*, "Lingua ac Communitas" 2010, Vol.

Wendland M., *Konstruktywizm komunikacyjny [Communication Constructivism]*, Poznań 2011.

Wendland M., *Działanie komunikacyjne a przekazywanie informacji [Communication Action vs. Information Transfer]*, [in:] *Komunikologia. Teoria i praktyka komunikacji [Communicology. Theory and Practice of Communication]*, eds. E. Kulczycki, M. Wendland, Poznań 2012.

Wendland M., *Pojęcie komunikacji w poznańskiej szkole metodologicznej [The Concept of Communication in the Poznan School of Methodology]*, "Filo-Sofija" 2012, Vol. 12, No. 18.

Wendland M., *Filozoficzne i metodologiczne podstawy historii komunikacji [Philosophical and Methodological Foundations of Communication History]*, Poznań 2014.

Wieczorkiewicz-Kita J., *Zagadnienie wyrokowania w procesie karnym w świetle koncepcji czynności konwencjonalnych [The Issue of Sentencing in the Criminal Process in the Light of the Concept of Conventional Acts]*, [in:] *Konwencjonalne i formalne aspekty prawa [Conventional and Formal Aspects of Law]*, ed. S. Czepita, Szczecin 2006.

Wierzbicka A., *A Semantic Metalanguage for a Crosscultural Comparison of Speech Acts and Speech Genres*, "Language in Society" 1985, Vol. 14, No. 4, pp. 491–492.

Wilkoń A., *Typologia odmian językowych współczesnej polszczyzny [Typology of Linguistic Varieties of Contemporary Polish Language]*, Katowice 2000.

Wilmot W.W., Hocker J.L., *Interpersonal Conflict*, 10th edition, New York 2018.

Winczorek J., Maranowski P., *Komunikacja w sądach po reformie kpc. Raport z badan [Communication in the Courts after the Reform of the Polish Code of Civil Procedure. Research Report]*, Warszawa 2014.

Witczak-Plisiecka I., *Legal Speech Acts in a Cognitive Linguistic Perspective: Focus on Modality*, "Comparative Legilinguistics. International Journal for Legal Communication" 2009, No. 1.

Witek, *How to Establish Authority with Words: Imperative Utterances and Presupposition Accommodation*, [in:] *Theory of Imperatives from Different Points of View (2)*, eds. A. Brożek, J. Jadacki, B. Žarnić, Warszawa 2013.

Witek M., *Three Approaches to the Study of Speech Acts*, "Dialogue and Universalism" 2013, No. 1.

Witek M., *Mechanisms of Illocutionary Games*, "Language and Communication" 2015, Vol. 42.

Witosz B., *Genologia lingwistyczna. Zarys problematyki [Linguistic Genology. Outline of the Problematic]*, Katowice 2005.

Witosz B., *Tekst i/a gatunek. Jeden czy dwa modele? [Text and/or Genre. One or Two Models?]*, [in:] *Gatunki mowy i ich ewolucja [Speech Genres and Their Evolution]*, Vol. 2: *Tekst a gatunek [Text vs. Genre]*, ed. D. Ostaszewska, Katowice 2004.

Witosz B., *Tekstowe i kontekstowe wyznaczniki stylu – próba systematyzacji (?) i problematyzacji [Textual and Contextual Determinants of Style – An Attempt at Systematization(?) and Problematization]*, [in:] *Współczesne analizy dyskursu. Kognitywna analiza dyskursu a inne metody badawcze [Contemporary Discourse Analysis. Cognitive Discourse Analysis vs. Other Research Methods]*, eds. M. Krauz, S. Gajda, Rzeszów 2005.

Witosz B., *Interakcyjny model relacji gatunku i dyskursu w przestrzeni komunikacyjnej [An Interactive Model of the Relationship between Genre and Discourse in the Communication Space]*, [in:] *Gatunki mowy i ich ewolucja [Speech Genres and Their Evolution]*, Vol. 4: *Gatunek a komunikacja społeczna Genre and social communication*, ed. D. Ostaszewska, Katowice 2011.

Wojtak M., *Gatunki prasowe [Press Genres]*, Lublin 2004.

Wojtak M., *Genologia tekstów użytkowych [Genology of Applied Texts]*, [in:] *Polska genologia lingwistyczna [Polish Linguistic Genology]*, eds. D. Ostaszewska, R. Cudak, Warszawa 2008.

Wojtak M., *Pragmatyczne aspekty analiz stylistycznych tekstów użytkowych [Pragmatic Aspects of Stylistic Analyses of Applied Texts]*, [in:] *Stylistyka a pragmatyka [Stylistics vs. Pragmatics]*, ed. B. Witosz, Katowice 2001.

Wojtak M., *Osobliwe byty gatunkowe i tekstowe w ich uwikłaniach komunikacyjnych [Peculiar Genre and Textual Beings in Their Communication Entanglements]*, [in:] *Gatunki mowy i ich ewolucja [Speech Genres and Their Evolution]*, Vol. 4: *Gatunek a komunikacja społeczna [Genre and Social Communication]*, ed. D. Ostaszewska, Katowice 2011.

Wojtak M., *Wzorce gatunkowe wypowiedzi a realizacje tekstowe [Genre Patterns of Speech vs. Textual Realizations]*, [in:] *Gatunki mowy i ich ewolucja [Speech Genres and Their Evolution]*, Vol. 2: *Tekst a gatunek [Text vs. Genre]*, ed. D. Ostaszewska, Katowice 2004.

Wojtak M., Siwiec A., *Świadomość stylistyczna na tle wybranych składników jej kontekstu pojęciowego [Stylistic Awareness against the Background of Selected Components of Its Conceptual Context]*, [in:] *Mowa rozświetlona myślą. Świadomość normatywno-stylistyczna współczesnych Polaków [Speech Enlightened by Thought. The Normative-Stylistic Awareness of Contemporary Poles]*, ed. J. Miodek, Wrocław 1999.

Wronkowska S., Zieliński M., Ziembiński Z., *Zasady prawa. Zagadnienia podstawowe [Principles of Law. Basic Issues]*, Warszawa 1974.

Wróblewski B., *Język prawny i prawniczy [Legal and Juridical Language]*, Kraków 1948.

Wyrwas K., *Skarga czy podanie? Kontaminacja wzorców tekstowych w strukturze adaptacyjnej gatunku mowy [Complaint or Application? Contamination of Textual Patterns in the Adaptive Structure of the Speech Genre]*, [in:] *Stylistyka a pragmatyka [Stylistics vs. Pragmatics]*, ed. B. Witosz, Katowice 2001.

van Dijk T., *The Study of Discourse*, [in:] *Discourse as Structure and Process*, ed. T. van Dijk, London 1997.

Yovel J., *Language and Power in a Place of Contingencies: Law and the Polyphony of Self-Representation*, "Studies in Language and Society" 2013, No. 5.

Zabierowska K., *O „wielogłosowości" tekstów oficjalnych [On the "polyphony" of Official Texts]*, [in:] *Współczesna polszczyzna mówiona w odmianie opracowanej (oficjalnej) [Modern Spoken Polish in the Elaborated (Official) Variety]*, eds. Z. Kurzowa, W. Śliwiński, Kraków 1994.

Zeidler K., *Aesthetics of Law*, Gdańsk-Warszawa 2020.

Zieliński M., *Poznanie sądowe a poznanie naukowe [Judicial Cognition vs. Scientific Cognition]*, Poznań 1979.

Zieliński M., *Języki prawne i prawnicze [Legal and Juridical Languages]*, [in:] *Polszczyzna 2000. Orędzie o stanie języka na przełomie tysiącleci [Polish Language 2000: An Announcement on the State of Language at the Turn of the Millennium]*, ed. W. Pisarek, Kraków 1999.

Zieliński M., *Wykładnia prawa. Zasady, reguły, wskazówki [Legal Interpretation. Principles, Rules, Hints]*, 7th edition, Warszawa 2017.

Zieliński M., Ziembiński Z., *Uzasadnianie twierdzeń, ocen i norm w prawoznawstwie [Justifying Claims, Judgments and Norms in Jurisprudence]*, Warszawa 1988.

Ziembiński Z., *Logika praktyczna [Practical Logic]*, 26th edition, Warszawa 2011.

Ziembiński Z., *Competences and Competence Norms*, [in:] *Poznań School of Legal Theory*, eds. M. Smolak, P. Kwiatkowski, Leiden 2021.

Ziembiński Z., *Norms of Conduct*, [in:] *Poznań School of Legal Theory*, eds. M. Smolak, P. Kwiatkowski, Leiden 2021.

Ziembiński Z., Wronkowska S., *Zarys teorii prawa [Outline of Legal Theory]*, Poznań 2001.

Ius, Lex et Res Publica
Studies in Law, Philosophy and Political Cultures

Edited by
Anna Jaron

Vol. 1 Anna Jaron: Socio-Economic Constitutional Rights in Democratisation Processes. An Account of the Constitutional Dialogue Theory. 2012.

Vol. 2 Stanisław Filipowicz: Democracy – The Power of Illusion. 2013.

Vol. 3 Teresa Dukiet-Nagórska (ed.): The Postulates of Restorative Justice and the Continental Model of Criminal Law. As Illustrated by Polish Criminal Law 2014.

Vol. 4 Agnieszka Kupzok: Enforcement of Patents on Geographically Divisible Inventions. An Inquiry into the Standard of Substantive Patent Law Infringement in Cross-Border Constellations. 2015.

Vol. 5 Alicja Jagielska-Burduk / Wojciech Szafrański: Legal Issues in Cultural Heritage Management. A Polish Perspective. 2016.

Vol. 6 Maciej Mataczyński (ed.): The Takeover of Public Companies as a Mode of Exercising EU Treaty Freedoms. 2017.

Vol. 7 Maciej Barczewski (ed.): Value of Information. Intellectual Property, Privacy and Big Data. 2018.

Vol. 8 Pawel Smoleń, Marcin Burzec: Introduction to Polish Tax Law. 2018.

Vol. 9 Łukasz Pohl, Konrad Burdziak: Judicial Interpretation of the 1997 Criminal Code Provisions on Self-Defence. 2019.

Vol. 10 Adam Szot: Judicial Review of Administrative Discretion. The Influence of Court Decisions on Administrative Actions. 2019.

Vol. 11 Michał Peno / Konrad Burdziak (eds.): The Concept of Modern Law. Polish and Central European Tradition. 2019.

Vol. 12 Leszek Leszczyński / Bartosz Liżewski / Adam Szot (eds.): Potential of Precedent in the Statutory Legal Order. 2019.

Vol. 13 Łukasz Bolesta: In Search of a Model for the Legal Protection of a Whistleblower in the Workplace in Poland. A legal and comparative study. 2020.

Vol. 14 Paweł Chmielnicki / Adam Sulikowski (eds.): New Perspectives on Legislation. A Comparative Approach. 2020.

Vol. 15 Marcin Burzec / Beata Kucia-Guściora / Paweł Smoleń: Agricultural Activity in Poland: A Fiscal and Legal Study. 2020.

Vol. 16 Magdalena Półtorak / Ilona Topa (eds.): Women, Children and (Other) Vulnerable Groups. Standards of Protection and Challenges for International Law. 2021.

Vol. 17 Josef Albert Fox: Die polnische Verfassung vom 3. Mai 1791. Hintergründe der Entstehung und der Außerkraftsetzung. Stellung Polens im Zeitalter der Aufklärung. 2021.

Vol. 18 Barbara Janusz-Pohl (ed.): Juvenile Justice Systems: Poland-Brazil-Portugal. 2021.

Vol. 19 Leszek Leszczyński: General Reference Clauses in the Judicial Process. Context of Legislative Intentions Interpretative Discretion. 2021.

Vol. 20 Francisco J. Campos Zamora: Das Problem der Begründung richterlicher Entscheidungen. Eine Analyse auf der Grundlage der Theorie der juristischen Argumentation. 2021.

Vol. 21 Aneta Skorupa-Wulczyńska: Language Rights of the Citizen of the European Union. 2022.

Vol. 22 Mateusz Osiecki: International Legal Aspects of Aerial Terrorism. Methods of Law Enforcement in Avia-tion. 2022.

Vol. 23 Vladimír Sharp / Gabriela Blahoudková / Jakub Handrlica (eds.): Law, Pandemics and Ownership Restrictions. 2022.

Vol. 24 Piotr Kasprzyk / Anna Konert: Drones – Future of Aviation Law? Interference of Public Law in Private Law. 2023.

Vol. 25 Szymon Pawelec (ed.): Consensual Procedures in Criminal Law – Comparative Perspective. 2023.

Vol. 26 Dorota Pudzianowska: The Statelessness in Public Law. 2023.

Vol. 27 Bogusław Przywora / Aleksander Wróbel: Formalised Access to Pre-jurisdictional Free Legal Aid. Analysis based on Example of Ukraine, Poland, Great Britain and Sweden. 2023.

Vol. 28 Ewa Dawidziuk / Patricia Panero / Anna Tarwacka (eds.): Family, Law, and Society: from Roman Law to the Present Day. 2023.

Vol. 29 Marian Grzybowski / Bogusław Przywora / Aleksandra Syryt (eds.): Free Legal Aid, Theory, Legal Basis and Practice. European Standards. 2023.

Vol. 30 Karolina Gmerek: Trial as a Social Communication Occurrence. Interactions Between Professional and Non-professional Participants of a Trial. 2023.

www.peterlang.com

www.ingramcontent.com/pod-product-compliance
Ingram Content Group UK Ltd.
Pitfield, Milton Keynes, MK11 3LW, UK
UKHW041825100926
8556IPUK00002B/31

9 783631 902653